W9-BLF-504

Languages of the World

What do all human languages have in common and in what ways are they different? How can language be used to trace different peoples and their past? Are certain languages similar because of common descent or language contact? Assuming no prior knowledge of linguistics, this textbook introduces readers to the rich diversity of human languages, familiarizing students with the variety and typology of languages around the world. Linguistic terms and concepts are explained, in the text and in the glossary, and illustrated with simple, accessible examples. Eighteen language maps and numerous language family charts enable students to place a language geographically or genealogically. A supporting website includes additional language maps and sound recordings that can be used to illustrate the peculiarities of the sound systems of various languages. "Test yourself" questions throughout the book make it easier for students to analyze data from unfamiliar languages. This book includes fascinating demographic, social, historical, and geographical information about languages and the people who speak them.

ASYA PERELTSVAIG is a lecturer in the Department of Linguistics at Stanford University.

Languages of the World
An Introduction

ASYA PERELTSVAIG

CAMBRIDGE UNIVERSITY PRESS
Cambridge, New York, Melbourne, Madrid, Cape Town,
Singapore, São Paulo, Delhi, Tokyo, Mexico City

Cambridge University Press
The Edinburgh Building, Cambridge CB2 8RU, UK

Published in the United States of America by Cambridge University Press, New York

www.cambridge.org
Information on this title: www.cambridge.org/9780521175777

© Asya Pereltsvaig 2012

This publication is in copyright. Subject to statutory exception
and to the provisions of relevant collective licensing agreements,
no reproduction of any part may take place without the written
permission of Cambridge University Press.

First published 2012

Printed in the United Kingdom at the University Press, Cambridge

A catalogue record for this publication is available from the British Library

Library of Congress Cataloguing in Publication data
Pereltsvaig, Asya, 1972–
Languages of the world : an introduction / Asya Pereltsvaig.
    p.   cm.
Includes bibliographical references and index.
ISBN 978-1-107-00278-4 (hardback)
1. Language and languages – Study and teaching.   2. Multilingualism.   I. Title.
P53.P4443   2012
417′.7 – dc23   2011041738

ISBN 978-1-107-00278-4 Hardback
ISBN 978-0-521-17577-7 Paperback

Additional resources for this publication at www.cambridge.org/pereltsvaig

Cambridge University Press has no responsibility for the persistence or
accuracy of URLs for external or third-party internet websites referred to
in this publication, and does not guarantee that any content on such
websites is, or will remain, accurate or appropriate.

To my mother, Freyda Pereltsvayg, ז״ל

Contents

Figures

Maps

Tables

Words, words, words …

Words are often the first thing that fascinate us about a language, whether our own or a more exotic one. The words on the cover of this book are those that at some point have captivated me. Some of these words have exquisite, intriguing or plain weird meanings; others mesmerize by their beautiful or otherwise unusual sound or attract by the look of their orthography.

Among the words with beautiful meanings are the Brazilian Portuguese *cafuné* meaning 'to soothe someone by tenderly running one's fingers through their hair'; my mother used to do that and this book is dedicated to her memory. Similarly delicate is the Japanese word (儚い) (pronounced [hakanai]) which refers to 'something that, in its ephemeral nature, reminds you of how short and beautiful life is, for example, cherry blossoms' (more on Japanese in Chapter 11).

Two words with heart-warming meanings made my list: the Dutch *gezelligheid* 'time spent with loved ones in a cozy atmosphere of togetherness' and the Yiddish מאַמעלאָשען (pronounced [mame′loshen]) meaning literally 'mother tongue' but referring most often specifically to Yiddish itself. In addition to being the speakers' native tongue, Yiddish was literally the language of mothers, while fathers prayed and traded in Hebrew (more on Yiddish in Chapter 12).

And some words have a meaning I wish we could express in English but a good translation is sorely lacking: one example of this is the Scots word *kilfuddoch* meaning roughly 'a meeting and discussion' but then also so much more (Scots is discussed in Chapter 2).

Other words fascinate me not so much by their meaning but by the way the meaning derives from the parts of the word. Take, for example, the Tok Pisin word *manmeri* 'people': it is composed from two parts, *man* (from the similar-sounding English word) plus *meri* from the English *Mary*, extended in Tok Pisin to mean all women, regardless of their name (I discuss Tok Pisin in Chapter 12). Or consider the Russian word *лоботряс* (pronounced [laba′trjas]), which comes from the words *lob* 'forehead' and *trjasti* 'shake' and means 'a lazy person, a do-nothing' – I hope you are not such a person and will read this book!

There are also words with beautiful or peculiar sound to them. One of my favorite examples is the Hebrew word בקבוק meaning 'bottle'. It is pronounced [baq′buq]; say it over and over again and it sounds like wine being poured from a bottle, doesn't it? (Turn to Chapter 5 for a further discussion of Hebrew.)

But perhaps the most strange sounds that have captivated the popular imagination in recent years are the click sounds, found in languages of southern Africa.

To illustrate, here is a Xhosa word *ukúk!^{h}ola* meaning 'perfume': the sound represented here as k!^{h} is a voiceless aspirated alveopalatal click (now, that's a mouthful!). How exactly click sounds like this are pronounced is explained in Chapter 6 of this book.

Among words with unusual (for us, English speakers) sound are the Tagalog *ngilo* meaning 'to have tooth-edge pain', but also 'the physical sensation of nails scratching the chalkboard' and the Warlpiri *ngarrka* 'man'; both of these words start with the [ŋ] sound that in English is found only at the end of words (e.g. si*ng*) and in the middle of words (e.g. si*ng*ing). Tagalog is discussed in Chapter 8 and Warlpiri – in Chapter 9.

Speaking of word-initial consonants, some languages allow us to pile them up in a way that exceeds our English-based expectations. Two examples of that are the Polish word *chrząszcz* 'beetle' and the Georgian word გვფრცქვნი 'he peeled us' pronounced [gvprskvni], with eight consonants in the beginning! (Georgian is one of the languages discussed in Chapter 4.)

Notice also that this Georgian word expresses a meaning that we would render with a three-word sentence. It is not unusual in the world's languages to have words with sentence-like meaning; an additional example comes from Cherokee, where the word ᏌᎣᏏ (pronounced [hinvsi]) means 'hand him something flexible (like clothes, rope, etc.)'. Native American languages such as Cherokee are discussed in Chapter 10.

The last group of words here are interesting for the way they are written. For example, the French word *août* 'August' uses four letters to represent just one sound [u] (and you thought English spelling was the champion of perverseness?!). In contrast, the spelling of the Danish word *ø* 'island' is so minimal, it looks like the mathematical symbol for an empty set.

Finally, I included a few words to represent several more exotic writing systems: the Greek αλφάβητο 'alphabet' (after all, it was the Greeks who came up with the concept!), the Sanskrit ऋतु 'season' (pronounced [r̥tu], with the initial vowel sound), the Arabic كتب 'book', pronounced [kitab] and representing the best-known tri-consonant Semitic root K-T-B (this vowel-less nature of Semitic roots is explained further in Chapter 5).

Last but not least is the Udmurt expression гажаса ӧтиськом 'welcome', pronounced [gažasa ötis'kom]; Udmurt is a Finno-Ugric language (see Chapter 3), but like many other languages in the former Soviet Union it uses the Cyrillic alphabet, even though it is not related to Slavic languages for which this alphabet was originally invented.

Acknowledgements

This book has required a great deal of work collecting information and figuring out the best way to present it. It is my pleasure to express my gratitude to all those who have helped to make this book a reality.

First, the three *sine qua non*:

- Helen Barton, my editor at Cambridge University Press, who first suggested that I write a textbook to go with the course that I was teaching at Stanford University at the time: her continuing support, encouragement and guidance through the publication process made this book possible;
- Martin Lewis, a geographer extraordinaire: our frequent discussions of history, geography and languages shed new light on many issues discussed throughout this book and his help with the matters of cartography was invaluable;
- Karen Sherwood Sotelino, who has read different versions of the manuscript and suggested many improvements to the content, presentation and style: without her, this book would have been full of unexplained terminology, clumsy sentences and missed opportunities to use this or that English article.

I am also very grateful to all those who read parts of the manuscript, asked challenging questions, caught factual and stylistic errors, mentioned tidbits of interesting information about various languages and provided references to useful sources which I would not have found otherwise (in alphabetical order): Doug Ball, Renee A. Berger, David Erschler, Stephane Goyette, Joel Hoffman, Pavel Iosad, Olga Kagan, Ekaterina Lutikova, Johanna Nichols, Sergei Tatevosov and Rory van Tuyl. I am also indebted to the anonymous reviewer for Cambridge University Press, who provided suggestions for significant improvements.

In addition, I'd like to thank my students of the various instantiations of the "Languages of the World" course at Stanford University's Linguistics Department, Stanford Continuing Studies Program, Santa Clara University OLLI, San Francisco State University OLLI and the Forum at Rancho San Antonio, as well as the readers of my Languages of the World blog who took the time to share their comments.

Finally, I wish to express thanks to Byron Ahn, Venelina Dimitrova, Rebecca Greene, Patrycja Jablonska, Kasia Miechowicz-Mathiasen, Stephanie Shih and Vitaliy Rayz for suggesting some great words for the cover of this book.

Abbreviations used in the glosses

1	first person
2	second person
3	third person
A	agent-like argument of a canonical transitive verb
ABL	ablative
ABS	absolutive
ACC	accusative
ADESS	adessive
ANTIP	antipassive
AOR	aorist
APPL	applicative
ART	article
ASP	aspect
AT	actor topic
AUX	auxiliary
CLF	classifier
COMP	complementizer
CONT	continuative
CT	circumstantial topic
DAT	dative
DEF	definite
DU	dual
DUR	durative
ERG	ergative
EVID	evidential
F	feminine
FACT	factitive
FORM	formal
FUT	future
GEN	genitive
HAB	habitual
HON	honorific
INS	instrumental
INTNS	intensifier
IPFV	imperfective

LOC	locative
M	masculine
NEG	negation
NFUT	non-future
NMLZ	nominalizer/nominalization
NOM	nominative
OBJ	object
OBL	oblique
P	patient-like argument of a canonical transitive verb
PART	particle
PASS	passive
PFV	perfective
PL	plural
POSS	possessive
POTENT	potential
PROG	progressive
PRS	present
PRTV	partitive
PST	past
PUNC	punctual
Q	question particle/marker
REFL	reflexive
REL	relative
SBJ	subject
SG	singular
SGL	singulative
TMA	tense-mood-aspect
TR	transitive
TT	theme topic

1   Introduction

April 26, 1607. After a long 144 day voyage, three ships belonging to the Virginia Company of London and led by Captain John Smith make landfall at the southern edge of the mouth of the Chesapeake Bay, which they name Cape Henry. Shortly thereafter, they are forced to move their camp along the estuary, to a new location eventually known as "James Towne" or Jamestown, Virginia. Almost immediately, they encounter a group of "American Indians" who communicate with each other in what surely sounds like language, only it is quite different from the English of the Virginia Company settlers. Sure enough, there are words in this language and just like back home, people from different places pronounce the same words somewhat differently. But to an English ear, these words are unrecognizable: not only are there words for things unfamiliar to the English settlers (some of which will later be taken into the English language, like *raccoon*, *moccasin*, *opossum* and others), but even words for familiar objects and concepts sound different: for example, the word for 'sun' is either *nepass* or *keshowghes* and the word for 'copper' is either *matassen* or *osawas*. And it is not just the words that are different, but so is the way the words are put together: for example, grammatical objects in this language typically precede rather than follow the verb. This pattern would not have surprised the settlers, had they come from the Basque country or Turkey or Japan, or even had they arrived 700 years earlier, but for the Virginia Company men it must have been a striking pattern. The differences between the language of these "American Indians" and English are so ear-grating that the English settlers start compiling lists of "American Indian" words: Captain John Smith himself compiles a list of about fifty words and William Strachey publishes a "dictionary" of the language containing about 1,000 words. Today, most of what we know about this language – called Powhatan and attributed to the Eastern Algonquian branch of the Algonquian language family (see Chapter 10) – derives from the descriptions of seventeenth- and eighteenth-century writers, as the language died in the 1790s when its speakers switched to English.

At about the same time as the English are colonizing the eastern seaboard of what will become the United States, the Russians are pushing into Siberia. Twenty-five years after the first encounter between the Virginia Company men and the Powhatan Indians, a Russian company of twenty or so men led by Pyotr Beketov land on the shores of the Lena River and, on September 25, 1632, found the fortified town of Yakutsk. As they settle the frozen expanse of Northeastern Siberia, the Russians too come into contact with people who speak a language quite distinct from their own.[1] These people call themselves *Sakha* (with the stress on the last syllable) and the language – *Sakha Tyla*, but today the better known name for this group and their language is Yakut. As with Powhatan and English, Yakut is quite novel for the Russian speakers: it has some sounds that are unfamiliar to the Russian ear (such as the front rounded vowels [y] and [ø], as in the French words *chute* 'fall' and *peu* 'few', respectively); words are completely unrecognizable and can often be quite long; and sentences have the Subject-Object-Verb (SOV) order that would not surprise Powhatan speakers, but is peculiar for the Russians. So like the English settlers in North America, the Russians start compiling word lists and recording texts in Yakut. Yet, curiously, the first printed text in Yakut was not in a Russian book, but in a treatise titled *Noord en Oost Tartarye* ("North and East Tatars"), published by the Dutch cartographer Nicolaes Witsen in 1692 in Amsterdam. Today, Yakut fares much better than Powhatan: it is spoken by approximately 350,000–450,000 speakers.[2]

A decade after the Russians founded Yakutsk, another Dutchman, Abel Tasman – a seafarer, explorer and merchant in the services of the Dutch East India Company (*VOC* in Dutch) – sails to New Zealand, Tonga and Fiji. There, he and his men encounter people who speak languages quite distinct from Dutch but similar to each other: Maori, Tongan and Fijian. Once again, the words in these languages strike the Dutch explorers as different, and so do the grammatical patterns; for example, sentences in these languages typically start not with the grammatical subject, as do sentences in Dutch, as well as English, Russian, Yakut and Powhatan, but with the verb. And like the English settlers and the Russians, the Dutch are so staggered by the dissimilarities between their own language and the newly discovered ones that they start compiling word lists and grammars, which laid foundation for the later realization that all of these languages – and numerous others – belong to the same language family, the Austronesian family (discussed in more detail in Chapter 8). Today, Maori is spoken by 60,000 people in New Zealand, Tongan – by 96,300 people in Tonga, and Fijian by 360,000 people in Fiji.

Nor were these encounters between the English and the Powhatan Indians, the Russians and the Yakut, the Dutch and the Austronesians isolated phenomena. In fact, such encounters between speakers of very different languages happened over and over again in the course of human history, whenever one group moved to a new territory and encountered another group; after all, no reports have ever been made of any human group that did not have language. Whether these encounters between different linguistic groups were peaceful or otherwise, they naturally led

---

[1] Unlike the English, who had never encountered anything like the Powhatan language, Russians had had some exposure to languages related to Yakut (that is, Turkic languages; see Section 5.1). However, their exposure was limited enough and the Turkic languages they had been exposed to were different enough to Yakut for it to sound quite exotic to the Russian ear.

[2] The numbers for speakers of various languages cited throughout this book are based on the figures given in the *Ethnologue*, as discussed below in Section 1.3.

to linguistic curiosity on both sides, linguistic interaction and, ultimately, changes in the languages of both groups. This book is about diverse human languages and the peoples who speak them, how these languages came to be spoken where they are now spoken, how they interacted and changed each other.

While people are typically first struck by the differences between their own language and another language they encounter, as were the English, the Russians and the Dutch in the encounters described above, it is also the similarities between languages that are interesting. Although it is tempting to focus on the differences between languages, their peculiarities and the "exotic" elements found in some languages but not in most, in this book we will also examine patterns of commonality across languages. After all, the "exotic" can only be understood in contrast to the "mundane".

An investigation of the world's languages can also shed new light on the question of the relatedness of peoples who speak these languages. As we will see throughout this book, linguistic studies have been instrumental in figuring out the past of Native Americans, the Yakut, the inhabitants of the South Sea Islands, as well as the Hungarians, the Lapps and the Gypsies. In recent years, the toolkit of a historian of human populations – which already contained tools from archeology and linguistics – has been enriched by the addition of new genetic methodologies. Sometimes, the new evidence from genetic studies provides additional support for the conclusions of linguists, and in other cases genetic studies contradict linguistic ones – in this book, we will review examples of both. Thus, one of the goals of this book is to show that a study of human languages, enhanced by evidence from other disciplines, such as anthropology, archeology, history and genetics, leads us to a better understanding of the human condition.

Most of this book (Chapters 2–10) is organized around different parts of the world, defined not by the familiar division into continents like Eurasia or even geopolitical regions like Europe, but based on geolinguistic factors.[3] Thus, Europe, parts of the Middle East and India are considered in the same chapters (Chapters 2–3) which concern the Indo-European languages (Chapter 2) and the non-Indo-European languages of this region (Chapter 3). Conversely, languages of Africa become the subject of two different chapters: languages of North Africa are introduced in Chapter 5 together with languages of the Middle East and Central Asia, while languages of sub-Saharan Africa are the topic of Chapter 6. The remaining two chapters are dedicated to other issues, such as macro families (Chapter 11) and mixed languages (Chapter 12). Chapters 2 through 10 also contain "focus on" sections concerned with either general issues, such as field linguistics or language change, or controversies surrounding specific languages (e.g. Dyirbal or Pirahã). But before we can examine languages in various parts of the world, a more general question of what language is and how many languages exist must be addressed.

---

[3] For a critique of geographical division of the world into continents; see, for instance, Lewis and Wigen (1997).

1.1   Languages, dialects and accents

Ferdinand de Saussure (1916), a Swiss linguist considered to be one of the fathers of twentieth-century linguistics, in his *Cours de Linguistique Générale* (*Course in General Linguistics*) defines language as "a product of the collective mind of linguistic groups". But this does not help much in drawing the boundary between one language and another: after all, it is not clear who is or is not to be included in any given "linguistic group". Take any two people, even close relatives, and they are sure to speak at least slightly differently. Yet, it is not insightful to say that there are as many languages in the world as there are individual people!

Another way of defining languages is in geopolitical terms, as in the popular aphorism commonly attributed to the Yiddish linguist Max Weinreich (although there is some debate as to whether he actually coined it or just published it): "A language is a dialect with an army and navy". Indeed, it is often the case that we consider two linguistic varieties as distinct languages (rather than dialects of the same language) when they are associated with distinct flags and other trappings of a national state. For example, a language that was known up to the beginning of 1990s as Serbo-Croatian has recently "broken" into not just two but four languages, each claiming distinctness from the others and attempting as hard as they can to purge each other's influences: Serbian, Croatian, Bosnian and Montenegrin. Similarly, the differentiation between Danish, Norwegian and Swedish as three separate languages might not have existed were it not for the fact that these are spoken in three different countries.

Conversely, many countries are multilingual. For example, Belgium has three distinct linguistic zones: the Flemish (Dutch) zone in the north, the Walloon (French) zone in the south and the German-speaking zone in the east. Brussels, the seat of the European Parliament, is a bilingual city in its own right and can be considered a fourth linguistic zone of Belgium. Likewise, Switzerland has four linguistic zones: French-speaking in the west, German-speaking in the north and center, Italian-speaking in the southeast and Romansch-speaking in the east.

Because of these discrepancies between linguistic varieties and geopolitical divisions, linguists prefer the definition of language in terms of "mutual intelligibility": if two linguistic varieties are mutually intelligible, they are considered dialects of the same language, and if they are not, they constitute distinct languages. However, even this definition of language vs. dialect is not without problems. Most obviously, mutual intelligibility is a matter of degree and is relative to a text or situation: the same two speakers may have an easier or harder time understanding each other depending on the topic of conversation and even on how they phrase what they are saying. Furthermore, the degree of mutual intelligibility or similarity between languages depends on who assesses it: a person who does not speak either of the languages is more likely to perceive similarities than differences between them, while a person speaking one of the languages would focus more on the differences and would, as a result, assess the languages as more different than a non-speaker would.

But the problem actually runs deeper: when gauging the degree of mutual intelligibility, what we are comparing is (snippets of) texts, rather than languages, which are cognitive systems of rules in the minds of the speakers that allow them to produce such texts. To illustrate what I mean by this, let's consider the following sentences in English and Norwegian:

(1.1)   English: *We shall sing tomorrow.*
               Norwegian: *Vi skal synge i morgen.*

Word for word, these two sentences are very much parallel: *we/vi, shall/skal, sing/singe, tomorrow/i morgen.* Note also that the word order is the same in both English and Norwegian. But now let's rephrase those sentences to start with 'tomorrow':

(1.2)   English: *Tomorrow we shall sing.*
               Norwegian: *I morgen skal vi synge.*

The words, of course, remain the same, but the order of the words now differs: in English, *tomorrow* is followed by the grammatical subject *we*, which is in turn followed by the auxiliary verb *shall*, while in Norwegian *i morgen* 'tomorrow' is followed by the auxiliary verb *skal* 'shall', which is in turn followed by the subject *vi* 'we'. In fact, in the absence of intonation (in speech) or punctuation marks (in writing), the Norwegian sentence in (1.2) may be taken by an English speaker to be a question: 'Tomorrow, shall we sing?'

What we see in these examples is that the degree of mutual intelligibility (or similarity) may be dependent on the actual phrasing: the sentences in (1.1) are much more similar than those in (1.2). Why such a discrepancy? To understand it, we need to examine not sentences, but grammatical rules that underlie them. And such rules differ from English to Norwegian in a consistent way: the English word order in both (1.1) and (1.2) is achieved by placing the auxiliary verb after the subject, while the Norwegian word order in both sentences is achieved by placing the auxiliary verb in the second position, regardless of whether the first position is occupied by the subject (*vi* 'we') or an adverb (*i morgen* 'tomorrow'). Linguists refer to this rule in Norwegian as *Verb-Second*, or V2 for short. Two different rules may, on occasion, produce very similar outputs, as in (1.1), creating an impression of a greater similarity between two languages than really exists. Conversely, an impression of a greater dissimilarity may be created by heavily using dialectal words or dialectal pronunciation features.

The task of drawing boundaries between dialects and languages is even more difficult because of the phenomenon of DIALECT CONTINUUM, when a range of dialects is spoken across some geographical area, with the dialects of neighboring areas differing from each other only slightly, and the dialects from the opposite ends of the continuum being much less similar to each other and possibly not mutually intelligible at all. Think of it as a "game of telephone" when one player whispers a word to the next person in the chain, who in turn whispers it to the next person and so on: what each person whispers to the next is quite similar to what was whispered to them, but what the last person in the chain hears may be quite different from what the first person said. One example of a dialect continuum is the so-called Continental West Germanic dialect continuum, including all varieties of High German (spoken in the German-speaking parts of Switzerland, Austria and in southern parts of Germany, around Munich and Nuremberg), Middle German (spoken around Frankfurt-am-Main, Cologne and Dresden) and Low German (spoken in the northern parts of Germany, around Bremen, Hamburg and Kiel), as well as Dutch and Flemish. If one travels, for example, from Bern through Munich, Frankfurt, Hamburg and into Antwerp or Bruges, one will encounter many local linguistic varieties, each of which is quite similar to the previous one, but a person from Bern and a person from Antwerp will not be able to understand each other – if each of them speaks in their local variety. And just a few generations ago, the same was true even for two German speakers – one from Munich and one from Hamburg; the only way they were able to converse was to revert to the Standard German, the variety used in education, the media and administration (today, Hamburg is mostly High German speaking).

Note also that the boundary between what is called German and what is called Dutch is rather arbitrary and based to a large degree on the geopolitical divisions rather than on linguistic factors. Thus, Low German dialects in northern Germany are in some ways more similar to Dutch varieties across the border than to High German dialects in southern Germany. For instance, where both Low German and Dutch have STOP CONSONANTS such as [k, t, p], as in *maken* 'to make', *dat* 'that' and *dorp* 'village', High and Middle German have FRICATIVE CONSONANTS such as [x, s, f], as in *machen* 'to make', *das* 'that' and *dorf* 'village' (compare also the German/Dutch *dorp/dorf* with the English *thorp*).[4] The imaginary line between the Low German/Dutch varieties with [k], on the one hand, and High and Middle German varieties with [x], on the other hand, is known as the Benrath line (or, more informally, *machen–maken* line). Similarly, the [t]/[s] and [p]/[f] lines run through Middle German dialects but they do not coincide precisely with the [k]/[x] (Benrath) line.

Generally, such geographical boundaries of a certain linguistic feature – be it a pronunciation of a consonant or a vowel, a certain lexical choice or the use of some syntactic construction – are known as ISOGLOSSES. Typically, major dialects or even groups of dialects are demarcated by a bundle of such isoglosses. Note that dialectal divisions as defined by isoglosses need not coincide with language boundaries based on geopolitical realities: for example, Galician, spoken in the northwestern corner of Spain and considered by some to be a dialect of Spanish, is on the same side of many isoglosses as Portuguese varieties and not as other Spanish dialects. Moreover, if one travels from northern Portugal through northern

---

[4] The fricative consonant [x] is not commonly found in English. It is the final sound in the German pronunciation of *Bach*.

Spain, (southern) France and into Italy, one encounters a series of dialects each of which is similar to the neighboring ones but quite distinct from the ones further away. Hence, this area is known as the Western Romance dialect continuum.

Dialect continua are found not only in Western Europe, but in many other parts of the world. Elsewhere in Europe we find dialectal continua among varieties of East Slavic languages (Russian, Byelorussian, Rusyn and Ukrainian) and among varieties of South Slavic languages (Slovene, Croatian, Bosnian, Serbian, Macedonian and Bulgarian), and outside of Europe dialect continua have been described in the Turkic-speaking world (see Chapter 5), the Arabic-speaking parts of North Africa and the Middle East (see Chapter 5), the Persian-speaking area (see Chapter 2), as well as among varieties of Algonquian languages in Northeastern US and Canada, and among varieties of Eskimo-Aleut languages in Alaska and Northern Canada (see Chapter 10), to mention just a few.

While the distinction between dialects and languages is drawn based on mutual intelligibility, a finer distinction is sometimes drawn between dialects and accents (note that this distinction is commonly used in Britain, but not as commonly in the US). Dialects can differ from each other in many ways, including pronunciation, word meaning and use, and grammatical features, while the term "accent" is reserved for varieties solely with distinct pronunciation patterns. Accents are typically very local and may be limited to a single city or a small rural area. One example of a local accent is the Liverpool accent: some of its characteristic features include using a fricative consonant in place of a stop (e.g. [bajx] instead of [bajk] for 'bike'), as well as using the same vowel as in words *full* and *put* for words like *love* and *blood*.[5] In contrast, the local variety of English found in Newcastle is not just an accent but is a full-blown dialect (known as the Geordie dialect), with characteristic pronunciation patterns such as using the aforementioned vowel of *full* in words like *love*, as well as with characteristic grammatical features such as allowing two modals in a row (as in *She might could come tomorrow*) and using past tense forms of the so-called irregular verbs instead of participial forms (as in *I've took it* or *You done it, did you?*; see Trudgill 1999: 13).[6]

1.2   Language families

We have seen in the previous section that several mutually intelligible dialects (or even local accents) can be viewed as constituting one bigger linguistic

---

[5] The latter feature, namely the non-distinct pronunciation of the vowels in *full* and *love* and similar words, is typical for many northern English dialects and accents.

[6] The lack of distinction between past tense and participial forms of irregular verbs is not as strange as it might sound: think about the so-called regular verbs – in Modern English they do not distinguish past tense and participial forms (unlike in other Germanic languages and earlier forms of English; see Eide 2009).

variety, often referred to as a language. For example, Swiss German, Bavarian German and Plattdeutsch (Low German) can be grouped under the heading of the German language. Similarly, dialects (or possibly even dialect groups) like Canadian English, Scottish English and Australian English, and even more local dialects/accents like New York City English, Liverpool English and Geordie (Newcastle English) can be bunched together under the heading of the English language.

In a similar fashion, several related languages may be seen as constituting a language family. For example, German, Dutch, Frisian and English are all members of the West Germanic language family. As with human biological families, a language family is a phylogenetic unit: a classification of languages into a language family implies that they descend from a common parent language, known as a proto-language. Thus, German, Dutch, Frisian, English and other members of the West Germanic family all descended from a common parent language, known as Proto-West-Germanic (it is quite common to name this parent language "proto-X", with X being the name of the language family, although as we will see below, this is not always the case).

Just as with human biological families, a given language family can be viewed as part of a larger, more extended family (for example, your nuclear family is part of a larger family including grandparents, aunts, uncles and cousins). For example, the West Germanic family is part of a larger Germanic family. The common parent language of the Germanic family is – you guessed it! – Proto-Germanic. The Germanic family includes other branches or subfamilies, namely North Germanic and East Germanic families/branches (unfortunately, the term "language family" is not reserved for a particular level in the family tree, which can lead to some degree of confusion).[7] The Germanic family, in turn, is part of an even larger language family called the Indo-European family. And yes, its common parent language is known as the Proto-Indo-European, or PIE for short (we will discuss the Indo-European language family in more detail in Chapter 2). This family relationship is schematized by the family tree in Figure 1.1.

And just as members of human biological families typically share observable characteristics, such as facial features, skin color, predisposition to certain medical conditions and so on, so languages in a given language family share certain observable linguistic characteristics, such as words, sounds and grammatical patterns. For example, almost all languages in the Germanic family share the common Verb-Second pattern, mentioned in the previous section. Whether the sentence starts with a subject or an adverb such as 'yesterday' (or even a grammatical object), the verb must come immediately after, in the second position in

---

[7] The common parent language of the North Germanic language family is not referred to as "Proto-North-Germanic" (although it could be called that) because it is more commonly known from historical records as Old Norse.

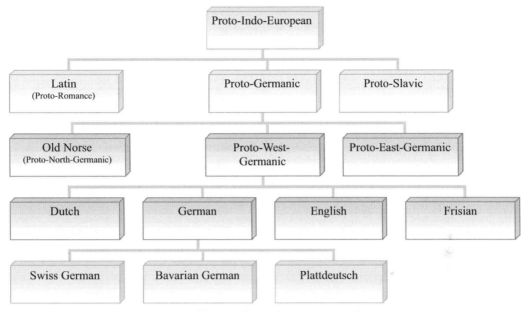

Figure 1.1. *Partial tree of family relationships amongst Indo-European languages.*

the sentence. This pattern is found, for example, in Dutch, German and Swedish (see an additional example of the Verb-Second pattern in Norwegian in (1.2) above).

(1.3) a.   Dutch: *Gisteren* **las** *ik   dit   boek.*
                     yesterday read I   the   book

     b.   German: *Gestern* **las** *ich dieses Buch.*
                     yesterday read I   the   book

     c.   Swedish: *Igår*   **läste** *jag denna bok.*
                     yesterday read   I   the   book

In fact, English is just about the only Germanic language that does not rely on the Verb-Second pattern: in English if the sentence starts with anything but the grammatical subject, the verb must follow the subject, thus coming in the third rather than second position in the sentence:

(1.4)   English: Yesterday I **read** the book.

This makes English somewhat of an oddity among Germanic languages (and there are several other properties that make English equally unlike its Germanic brethren). Still, English shares many other linguistic features with the rest of the Germanic family to support its classification as a Germanic language. For example, it has a basic two-way tense system, the present and past, with the past tense being formed in one of two basic ways: by adding the suffix -ed, as with *play–played*, or by changing the vowel in the root, as in *sing–sang*. English also has the basic word-initial stress system characteristic of Germanic languages, although many non-Germanic LOANWORDS exhibit non-initial stress. These Germanic traits of English are inherited from the Proto-Germanic, while the non-Germanic-like traits have been acquired through contact with non-Germanic languages, such as the Celtic languages that were spoken in the British Isles prior to the Germanic invasions of the fifth century CE and Norman French, which was brought to England by William the Conqueror and his men (and women!).

Note that if one considers the Verb-Second pattern more closely, one can still see traces of it in Modern English: if a sentence starts with a negative adverb such as *never* or phrases containing *only*, the verb must come in the second position (this is particularly clear if the verb in question is an auxiliary or a modal rather than a main verb):

(1.5)   *Never* **have** I seen such a creature!
         Only under certain circumstances **would** a verb precede a subject in English.

There are many language families around the world and most known languages have been classified as belonging to one family or another. Some of these classifications are pretty well established, while others are less well understood, more tentative or even hotly debated. In general, the better known the history of a certain linguistic group, the more established the family classifications; conversely, the further up the family tree one goes, the more tentative the proposals are. As we proceed throughout our world linguistic tour in the course of this book, we will discuss these family classifications – both well established and more tentative ones – in greater detail.

Not only are some linguistic classifications tentative, but some languages resist classification into any known language family; they are like orphans not having any living relatives amongst the world's languages. Such languages with no family connection to other languages are known as ISOLATES. As with the term "language family", the term "isolate" is not restricted to any given level of the family classification. Thus, a language might be an isolate within a large family, meaning that it shows no close family relationship with any other language in that family. An example of such an isolate is Modern Greek: it is a member of the Indo-European language family, but within that family it is not more closely related to any particular language than to any other language. It is now widely assumed that this situation arose because other languages in the once larger Hellenic branch of the Indo-European family have died out, leaving Modern Greek as the only representative of that branch. There are also perfect isolates; that is, languages that are not known to be related to any other human language. Two examples of such perfect isolates are Basque (spoken by approximately 650,000 people in the Basque country of Spain and France) and Burushaski (spoken by approximately 87,000 people in Pakistan).

1.3   Linguistic diversity

It is impossible to discuss the world's languages without addressing the question of how many languages there are. It is a difficult question, though, and answers vary from source to source. There are at least two good reasons why linguists cannot say outright "There are X-many languages in the world": one is a lack of clear criteria for defining a language versus a dialect, as discussed above, and the other has to do with language extinction. Thus, whether one counts Serbo-Croatian as one language or as four (Bosnian, Croatian, Montenegrin and Serbian), or whether Hindi and Urdu are considered two separate languages or just one (sometimes referred to as Hindustani), or whether Arabic is considered a single language or a family of about 40 languages – all of these decisions affect the total number of languages. To further compound the matter, the number of languages is not stable, with old dialects gradually emerging as distinct languages and also with existing languages dying out. Thus, the number of languages spoken in the world at the time I write this book may not be accurate by the time you read it. So the number of the world's languages that I am going to give you now should be taken with a grain of salt; nonetheless, a good estimate is in the environs of 6,500–7,000 languages.

Just as it is difficult to give an exact number of the world's languages, it is difficult to give a precise and accurate number of speakers for each language. Of course, part of the reason is that people are born and die, and children can be considered as speakers of a given language at a certain age, depending on their rate of development. But there are even more serious problems in figuring out just how many people speak any given language. One difficulty, which has already been mentioned before, is knowing just who belongs (or does not belong) to a linguistic group associated with a language in question. Another issue is whether to include only native speakers or also people who speak a given language as a second (or third, etc.) language. This is particularly problematic for languages that serve as a LINGUA FRANCA in various parts of the world, including English, Spanish, Swahili and many others. Finally, not for all languages is such demographic information readily available or reliable. This is true even for countries with a developed census system, such as the US, where the population census includes a question about the language spoken by the respondent, but one can supply any label one chooses, so that the results list both "Mandarin" and "Chinese" as distinct languages, even though the latter is an umbrella term for several languages, including Mandarin (see Chapter 6).

A reasonably good source of thorough and reliable geographical and demographic information about the world's languages is the *Ethnologue*, a web and print publication of SIL International, a Christian organization studying lesser known languages and originally aimed at providing the speakers of all the world's languages with Bible translations into their native tongues. This resource can be purchased in print format or browsed online (www.ethnologue.com). Most numbers of speakers for various languages cited in this book are from the *Ethnologue*.

But whatever the precise numbers of speakers for the various languages are, it is quite clear that there is a great deal of unevenness amongst the world's languages: some languages are "small", spoken by just a few hundred or even just a few speakers, while other languages are "giants" with millions of speakers. Thus, about 14% of the world's population speak the world's largest language, Mandarin Chinese, while at the other end of the spectrum, about 14% of the world's population speak one of 3,346 "small" languages. In fact, the median size for a language today is just 6,000 speakers; in other words, half the languages in the world are spoken by 6,000 or more people, and half are spoken by 6,000 or fewer people.

When it comes to language families, the biggest families – by the number of individual languages – are the Niger-Congo family with over 1,500 languages spoken in much of sub-Saharan Africa (see Chapter 6), the Austronesian language family with over 1,200 languages spoken in Southeast Asia, Oceania and on Madagascar (see Chapter 8), and the Trans-New-Guinea language family with over 500 languages (see Chapter 9). The Indo-European language family only comes at number four with 449 languages. Still, it is the world's largest language family by the number of speakers, with approximately 45% of the world's population speaking an Indo-European language such as Spanish, English, Hindi, Portuguese, Bengali, Russian or French. The Indo-European language family also happens to be one of the best-studied language families, whose history, as well as the histories of its individual languages, is quite well known. This is the family we will consider in detail in the next chapter.

2   Indo-European languages

In Chapter 1, we saw that the world's languages can be classified into language families, with the implication that all languages in a given family descend from a common ancestral language, or proto-language. In this chapter we turn to the most populous and one of the best-studied language families, namely the Indo-European language family.

Luckily for the study of Indo-European comparative linguistics, many of these languages have extremely old surviving written records: for example, the earliest records of Hittite go back to around 1,800 BCE; the earliest inscriptions in Mycenaean Greek date from 1,300 BCE; the oldest part of the Rigveda (written in an archaic dialect of Old Indic) probably goes back as far as 1,200 BCE; most ancient scriptures in Avestan, the liturgical language of Zoroastrianism, date from about 600 BCE; the Achaemenid Records in Old Persian are from about 500 to 400 BCE; and the oldest Latin inscriptions date from the sixth century BCE.

2.1   Discovery of the Indo-European family and comparative reconstruction

Prior to the eighteeth century, scholars of history based their work on tenuous accounts by ancient historians coupled with literal interpretations of the Bible, sprinkled with pious and often politically motivated fabrications of medieval monks. It was James Parsons, an English physician, antiquary and author, who recognized the importance of another source of hitherto untapped evidence bearing on the most ancient peoples of Europe and Asia – their languages.

The idea that European languages exhibit close affinity had been remarked on even earlier, when Joseph Scaliger, a French religious leader and scholar, attempted to divide the languages of Europe into four groups based on their word for 'god'.[1] He classified what we now call Germanic languages as the *gott* group (think about English *god*, Dutch *god*, Swedish *gud*, German *gott* and so on), contrasted with what we now call Romance languages (Scaliger's *deus* group,

---

[1] Joseph Scaliger was also a strong believer in the power of grammar. He wrote: "I wish to be a good grammarian. Religious discord depends on nothing except ignorance of grammar."

Table 2.1. *James Parsons' list of cognate numerals (abridged).*

	Irish	Greek	Latin	Italian	French
1	aon	hen	unus	uno	un
2	do	duo	duo	due	deux
3	tri	treis	tres	tre	trois
4	ceathair	tettares	quattuor	quattro	quatre
5	cuig	pente	quinque	cinque	cinq
6	se	hex	sex	sei	six
7	seacht	hepta	septem	sette	sept
8	ocht	okto	octo	otto	huit
9	naoi	ennea	novem	nove	neuf
10	deich	deka	decem	dieci	dix
100	cead	hekaton	centum	cento	cent
	German	Swedish	Russian	Bengali	Persian
1	einz	en	odin	ek	yak
2	zwei	tva	dva	dvi	do
3	drei	tre	tri	tri	se
4	vier	fyra	četyre	car	cahar
5	fünf	fem	pjat'	pac	panj
6	sechs	sex	šest'	chay	shash
7	sieben	sju	sem'	sat	haft
8	acht	atta	vosem'	at	hasht
9	neun	nio	devjat'	nay	noh
10	zehn	tio	desjat'	das	dah
100	hundert	hundra	sto	sa	sad

named for the Latin word for 'god'; compare to Italian *dio*, Spanish *dios*, French *dieu*); Greek *theos*; and Slavic *bog*.[2]

James Parsons expanded his concept to include other languages such as Celtic (Irish, Welsh), Iranian (Persian) and Indic (Bengali). He focused on basic numerals, based on the perfectly sound assumption that "numbers being convenient to every nation, their names were most likely to continue nearly the same, even though other parts of languages might be liable to change and alteration" (cited in Mallory 1989: 10). Even a person untrained in philology could not fail to see the similarities between the different languages in this list (see Table 2.1).

In a very sound methodological move, Parsons also listed the same numerals in four other languages – Turkish, Hebrew, Malay and Chinese – all of which

---

[2] In older forms of Spanish, the word for 'god' was *dio* without the final -*s* as in Modern Spanish – this *s*-less form is retained by Judeo-Spanish (see Section 12.3). The Greek word *theos* 'god' is unrelated to the Romance word for 'god'.

Table 2.2. *Numerals 1–10 in unrelated languages.*

	Turkish	Hebrew	Malay	Chinese
1	bir	'exad	satu	yi
2	iki	šnaim	dua	er
3	üc	šloša	tiga	san
4	dört	'arba'a	empat	si
5	bes	xamiša	lima	wu
6	alti	šiša	enam	liu
7	yedi	šiv'a	tujuh	qi
8	sekiz	šmona	lapan	ba
9	dokuz	tiš'a	sembilan	jiu
10	on	'asara	sepuluh	shi

failed to exhibit similarities with the previous list of Eurasian languages or with each other (see Table 2.2).

Parsons therefore concluded that the languages in the first list (but not in the second) all descended from a common ancestor. Yet, much like his predecessors, Parsons' theory was constrained by the literal interpretation of the biblical book of Genesis whereby all people are descendants of Noah and his three sons: Shem (Semitic peoples of the Middle East and North Africa), Ham (other Africans) and Japheth (Europeans). Naturally, Parsons (1767) hypothesized that the ancestral language of all the ancient and modern languages of Europe, Iran and India was associated with Japheth and his offspring, who had migrated out of Armenia, the resting place of the Ark.[3] He published his study under the long-winded title of *The Remains of Japhet, being Historical Enquiries into the Affinity and Origins of the European Languages*. The book itself is as long-winded and tedious as the title would suggest, which may have been one of the reasons why Parsons' work has remained obscure and largely neglected by subsequent scholarship. The fact that Parsons was a gentleman-scholar who dabbled in plant and human physiology, in addition to philology, might have also contributed to him not being taken seriously. Moreover, Parsons still gullibly accepted the chronicles of the medieval Irish monks, mistakenly included Hungarian in the list of Japhetic languages and assumed that Irish is the purest Japhetic language from which all others are derived.

So the honor of the discovery of the Indo-European language family is traditionally assigned to another eighteenth century Englishman – Sir William Jones, who was the Chief Justice of India and the founder of the Royal Asiatic Society. It was in 1796 during the course of a lecture on Indian culture that Jones made his famous pronouncement on the affinities of Sanskrit (the ancient language of India) and European languages:

---

[3] Curiously, the idea of the Armenian homeland for the Indo-European language family has been more recently revived, as we will see in Section 2.2 below.

Table 2.3. *Partial paradigm of Sanskrit and Latin cases.*

	Sanskrit	Latin
Nominative singular	agnis	ignis
Accusative singular	agnim	ignem
Dative plural	agnibhyas	ignibus

The Sanskrit language, whatever be its antiquity, is of a wonderful struc-
ture; more perfect than the Greek, more copious than the Latin, and more
exquisitely refined than either, yet bearing to both of them a stronger affinity,
both in the roots of verbs and in the forms of grammar, than could possibly
have been produced by accident; so strong, indeed, that no philologer could
examine them all three, without believing them to have sprung from some
common source, which, perhaps, no longer exists. There is a similar reason,
though not quite so forcible, for supposing that both the Gothic and Celtic,
though blended with a different idiom, had the same origin with the Sanskrit;
and the old Persian might be added to the same family.

Although Jones' ideas were not that different from Parsons' (for example, he too believed in the Japhetic source for the Indo-European languages), Jones' eminence as a scholar of languages guaranteed him the attention of the academic world. Still, it was not until the nineteenth century when the study of comparative philology – which by that time had moved to Germany – was developed fully. In particular, it was Franz Bopp and especially August Schleicher who made the comparison of related languages a science in its own right. The main contribution of Franz Bopp (and Rasmus Rask before him) was in extending the object of study from cognate words (such as the basic numerals in James Parsons' study) and sound patterns to include grammatical structures as well. Take, for instance, the Sanskrit and Latin words for 'fire' – *agnis* and *ignis*, respectively. Not only are they similar in sound, but also in how they change in different case forms (see Table 2.3).[4]

While a great deal of evidence for a comparative study of Indo-European languages had been already accumulated by the middle of the nineteenth century, the next step came with August Schleicher's idea that by comparing cognate words and grammatical structures in related languages one can work back through time

---

[4] The idea that affinity between languages – whether in the lexicon or the grammar – is a sign of a family relationship had become so popular by the middle of the nineteenth century that it led Charles Darwin to write in *The Descent of Man*: "If two languages were found to resemble each other in a multitude of words and points of construction, they would be universally recognized as having sprung from a common source" – but as we will see throughout this book, descent from a common source is not the only reason for similarities across languages, and language contact is another power source of cross-linguistic similarities.

and reconstruct the words and structures of the ancestral language (or "proto-language"). In short, Schleicher was the one to develop the so-called comparative reconstruction methodology. Here is how it works for reconstructing the words of the proto-language.

First, one has to compile lists of cognate words, such as the lists of numerals in Parsons' study; another example of a list of Indo-European cognates – all meaning 'night' – is given in (2.1) below:

(2.1)   *night* (English), *nicht* (Scots), *Nacht* (German, Dutch), *natt* (Swedish), *nat* (Danish), *natt* (Norwegian), *nótt* (Icelandic), *nox* (Latin), *nuit* (French), *noche* (Spanish), *noite* (Portuguese, Galician), *notte* (Italian), *nit* (Catalan), *noapte* (Romanian), *nos* (Welsh), *noc* (Czech, Polish), *noč* (Russian), *nič* (Ukrainian), *noć* (Serbian), *naktis* (Lithuanian), *nyx* (Greek), *natë* (Albanian), *nakt-* (Sanskrit)

These cognate terms must come from the basic vocabulary, including body parts ('head', 'heart', 'eye', etc.), kinship terms ('mother', 'father', 'brother', etc.), natural phenomena ('day', 'night', 'star', etc.), basic bodily functions and so on. The reason for restricting the search to basic vocabulary is that such words are not readily borrowed from other languages.

Knights, riders and false friends

One thing to remember in compiling lists of cognates, though, is that cognate words may diverge in meaning: for example, English *dish* and German *Tisch* 'table', or English *starve* and German *sterben* 'die'. Such divergences result from a semantic change that may affect one or both of the cognates. Take, for example, the English word *knight* and its German cognate *Knecht*. Although pronounced slightly differently, these two words seem related, and indeed originally they had a similar meaning, denoting a person low on the social scale. However, the English word underwent a great upward mobility during the Middle Ages and became associated with the aristocracy, while its German cognate retained the humble meaning of 'servant'. The German word for 'knight' is *Ritter*, which is the cognate of another English word: *rider* (in German, but not in English, it carries important social implications). Another example of words that came from the same root but diverged in meaning is the English *loaf* vs. the Russian *xleb* 'bread'. Although the similarity of sound may not be immediately apparent, the English word derives from an earlier form *hlāf* 'bread, loaf of bread' (the macron over a vowel means that it is long): it lost the initial *h* and acquired a more specialized meaning referring to a unit of bread and not to the substance as a whole. Such pairs of words in two languages that sound similar but mean different things are known as **false friends**.

Still, the meanings of the proposed cognates must be related; the mere similarity of sound is not enough to establish cognates. For example, take the following words (roots are separated from suffixes by a hyphen): English *men* (plural of *man*), German *Mähn-e* 'mane', Lithuanian *mèn-uo* 'month', Sanskrit *men-ā* 'female, doe', Russian *men-a* 'exchange', Turkish *men* 'prohibition', Hungarian *mén* 'stallion'. To these nouns we can add a few verbs that have a similar sounding root: French *men-er*

Table 2.4. *English and Latin cognates.*

English	Latin
ten	**d**ecem
two	**d**uo
tow	**d**ūco
tooth	**d**ent-

Table 2.5. *Pronunciation of cognates in several Romance languages.*

	Sardinian	Italian	Romansh	French	(European) Spanish
'100'	kɛntu	tʃɛnto	tsjɛnt	sã	θjen (θjento)
'sky'	kɛlu	tʃelo	tsil	sjɛl	θjelo
'stag'	kɛrbu	tʃɛrvo	tsɛrf	sɛʀ	θjerbo
'wax'	kɛra	tʃera	tsaira	siʀ	θjera

'to drive, lead', Swedish *men-a* 'to think, mean', Ancient Greek *mén-ō* 'I remain', Finnish *men-nä* 'to go'. Despite the similarity of sound, these words are not cognates (note the near-opposite meaning of the English and Sanskrit words).

Even similarity of both sound and meaning do not guarantee that the words are truly cognate. Take, for example, Italian *strano* and Russian *strannyj* – both mean 'strange' and sound similar. Yet, they derive from different roots: the Italian word comes from the Latin *extraneus* 'external, foreign', while the Russian word comes from *strana* 'country'.

Step 2 is to establish regular patterns of sound correspondences between cognates in different languages. For example, the list of cognates in Table 2.4 reveals that the word-initial sound /t/ in English corresponds to /d/ in Latin.

Another example of regular sound correspondences amongst Romance languages is illustrated in Table 2.5: the word-initial /k/ in Sardinian corresponds to the sound /tʃ/ (as the initial sound in the English word *church*) in Italian, /ts/ in Romansch, /s/ in French and /θ/ in European Spanish (the sound /θ/ is pronounced as the *th*- in the English word *thin*).[5]

The third step is to postulate a sequence of regular sound changes which allows the proto-language to be reconstructed from its daughter languages. Since this is the hardest step of all, let's consider it through a specific example. Consider the

---

[5] Other pronunciation symbols here include: /ɛ/ = the vowel in the English word *pet*; /ã/ = the NASAL version of /a/; /ʀ/ = the UVULAR version of /r/. The appearance of /j/ in the Spanish words has to do with the evolution of the following vowel rather than with the changes to the consonants discussed here.

Table 2.6. *Some cognates in English,*
Latin, Greek and Irish.

English	Latin	Greek	Irish
fish	piscis	ikhthys	iasg
father	pater	pater	athair
foot	ped-	pod-	troigh
for	pro	para	do
six	sex	hex	se
seven	septem	hepta	seacht
salt	sal	hal	salann
sweet	suavis	hedys	milis

list of cognates from English, Latin, Greek and Irish in Table 2.6 (the shaded cells mark words which are not cognate to the rest but are included for completeness).

An examination of the first four lines indicates that the word-initial /f/ in English corresponds to /p/ in Latin and Greek. But what does it correspond to in Irish? The answer is nothing, or rather an absence of a consonant. This is what linguists call Ø (zero) for convenience. Looking at the bottom four lines we can see that the word-initial /s/ in English corresponds to /s/ in Latin and Irish as well, but to /h/ in Greek. The correspondence of the Latin /s/ to the Greek /h/ can also be seen in words and morphemes borrowed into English from the two languages: Latin *semi-* (as in *semicircular, semiannual*) vs. Greek *hemi-* (as in *hemisphere*); Latin *sal* 'salt' (as in *saline, salad* and *salami*, the latter two being dishes prepared with salt, *salary*, originally the salt allowance granted to Roman soldiers; the English word *salt* comes from Germanic) vs. Greek *hals* 'salt' (as in *halite* 'rock salt', *halogen*, an element that when combined with a metal, produces a salt); Latin *sol* 'sun' (as in *solar, solstice, solarium*) vs. Greek *helios* 'sun' (as in *heliotropic, heliocentric*); Latin *somnus* 'sleep' (as in *somnolent, somnambulist* 'sleepwalker') vs. Greek *hypnos* (as in *hypnotic*); for more examples, see Solodow (2010: 19).

So in each set of cognates in Table 2.6, which of the sounds is the one inherited from the proto-language (in this case, Proto-Indo-European)? And how do we decide? One possibility is to decide by the "majority vote": in the first case, two out of four languages have /p/, and in the second case, three out of four languages have /s/, so we can decide that these are the sounds from the proto-language. Although this approach is based on a not-unreasonable assumption that the majority of languages will retain what they inherit from the proto-language (rather than introduce a change), it works with only a limited overall success. Another idea is to look for the sounds in older languages, in this case Latin. However, even if we are to trace English to its Proto-Germanic roots, we will already find the same /f/ as in Modern English and not /p/ as in Latin, so this approach is not always successful either.

This kind of pattern may have stumbled early practitioners of the comparative reconstruction methodology; however, as more and more studies have been conducted, philologists (and later, historical and comparative linguists) have developed a sense that certain sound changes are more common than others and therefore a certain directionality of sound change can be assumed. In particular, it appears that the majority of sound changes involve a mutation from a sound that is "harder to pronounce" to a sound that is "easier to pronounce" (in quotes because of the lack of precise measure for the "difficulty to pronounce"). We can call this the Laziness Principle! Actually, the technical term is LENITION.

To illustrate this principle, take the sounds /p/ and /f/: they are similar in that both involve working with the lips (the technical term is LABIAL), and the main difference is in the way the lips are worked. For the /p/ sound, the lips are first pressed tightly together, which prevents the air from escaping, and then the pressure is released, which causes the air to explode out (try it!) – such sounds are called PLOSIVE or STOP CONSONANTS. For the /f/ sound, the lower lip is brought close to the upper teeth, but it is not pressed tightly against the teeth; the air escapes continuously through the narrow opening, creating friction – so such sounds are called FRICATIVE CONSONANTS. Since plosives but not fricatives involve a complete closure and a sharp release, they are considered to be more difficult to pronounce. What about the second pair of sounds: /s/ and /h/? Try pronouncing these sounds: the air escapes continuously through an opening (these are somewhat more difficult to feel in one's mouth because they involve articulation further back in the vocal tract than labial sounds, but trust me on this!). Thus, both /s/ and /h/ are fricative sounds. However, the /s/ sound involves bringing the tip of the tongue just behind the upper teeth, to the area called the ALVEOLAR RIDGE; therefore, this type of sound is known as an ALVEOLAR CONSONANT (or more precisely, a voiceless alveolar fricative, but it is the alveolar part that is important here). The /h/ sound differs from the other consonants described here in that it does not involve an obstruction in the mouth: the air flows through a narrow opening between the VOCAL CORDS (located in the LARYNX). Obviously, creating an obstruction in the mouth is "more work" than not doing so, so /s/ is "harder to pronounce" than /h/. And of course, the easiest sound to pronounce is not pronouncing a sound at all – that is what we referred to as a Ø-sound (zero-sound) above.

Now we can look at the Table 2.6 again and consider which changes would involve going from "harder to pronounce" to "easier to pronounce" sounds. In the first set, the sound that involves the most work is /p/, while /f/ involves less work and the Ø-sound – no work at all. In the second set, /s/ involves more work than /h/. Therefore, we can pretty safely assume that the change went from /p/ to /f/ to the Ø-sound, and from /s/ to /h/. In other words, Proto-Indo-European must have had /p/ and /s/.

Using what we have learned about comparative reconstruction of sounds and words, we can also attempt a reconstruction of grammatical structures of a proto-language, such as case forms (recall the patterns involving *agnis/ignis*,

Table 2.7. *Case forms of the word for 'wolf' in several Indo-European languages.*

	PIE ('wolf')	Sanskrit	Russian	Lithuanian
NOM	*wlk^w-os	vrk-as	volk	vilk-as
VOC	*wlk^w-e	vrk-a	–	vilk-e
ACC	*wlk^w-om	vrk-am	volk-a	vilk-ą[a]
GEN	*wlk^w-osyo	vrk-asya	volk-a	vilk-o
ABL	*wlk^w-od	vrk-ad	–	–
DAT	*wlk^w-oi	vrk-aya	volk-u	vilk-ui
LOC	*wlk^w-ei	vrk-e	volk-e	vilk-e
INST	*wlk^w-o	vrk-a	volk-om	vilk-u

[a] The symbol ą stands in Lithuanian for a nasal /ā/ sound. The nasality of the vowel in this case ending descends from the nasal consonant /m/ in the Proto-Indo-European form of the ending.

The symbol k^w stands for a voiceless labialized velar sound, that is, /k/ pronounced with rounded lips.

in Table 2.3 above). An examination of various Indo-European languages shows that some of these languages have virtually no case system (for example, in English the only thing resembling cases is the paradigm of PERSONAL PRO-NOUNS, such as *he/him/his*), while others – such as Sanskrit, Lithuanian or Russian – have fairly rich case systems (see Table 2.7). Furthermore, Indo-European languages that have case systems exhibit close affinity between the particular case forms. Assuming that change moves in the direction of reducing case systems, the surprisingly similar forms in distinct descendant languages lead us to believe that Proto-Indo-European had a fairly rich case system. Moreover, we can reconstruct its case forms.[6] The Proto-Indo-European case forms reconstructed on the basis of these and other descendant languages are included in the table, and the hyphen is used to separate the noun ROOT from the case SUFFIX.

2.2   The Indo-European controversy

So far, we have seen that a number of languages in Eurasia (classified as belonging to the Indo-European language family) can be shown to have descended from a common ancestral language, which was termed Proto-Indo-European. Moreover, comparative reconstruction methodology has been developed since the middle of the nineteenth century that allows (some) words and even

[6] Note that in historical linguistics, forms that are reconstructed and not attested in historical records are marked by an asterisk in front of the form; as we will see later in the book, this is not the only use of the asterisk symbol.

grammatical forms of Proto-Indo-European to be reconstructed based on words and forms in the descendant languages (recall that such reconstructed words and forms are marked with an asterisk). So historical linguists today know quite a bit about what Proto-Indo-European was like as a language. But where and when was it spoken? By how many people? What were their physical environment and cultural beliefs like? These questions are at the core of Indo-European studies. But the answers are not as clear-cut as one might wish. Especially the issue of the Indo-European homeland remains hotly debated. As Mallory (1989: 143) once put it: "One does not ask 'where is the Indo-European homeland?' but rather 'where do they put it now?'."

Attempts have been made to tie the Proto-Indo-European-speaking people to particular prehistoric cultures identified through archeological remains. Although there is no consensus on where exactly the speakers of Proto-Indo-European lived, the most commonly accepted theory since the 1970s is the Kurgan hypothesis, proposed in 1956 by a Lithuanian-American archeologist Marija Gimbutas. She was one of the first scholars to combine evidence from archeology and linguistics. Specifically, she proposed that the original speakers of Proto-Indo-European were a nomadic tribe in Eastern Ukraine and Southern Russia associated with what archeologists identify as the "Kurgan culture", so named after the distinctive Kurgan burial mounds in the Pontic steppe (flatland). According to this theory, speakers of Proto-Indo-European spread on horseback throughout the Pontic-Caspian steppe around 5,000 BCE and into Eastern Europe by the early third millennium BCE. One strong argument in favor of the Kurgan hypothesis is the fact that Proto-Uralic is the only non-Indo-European language whose lexicon appears to contain loanwords from Proto-Indo-European, such as the words *śata 'hundred' and *porćas 'pig' (Rédei 1986, Koivulehto 1991). For such borrowing from Proto-Indo-European into Proto-Uralic (see Sections 3.1 and 11.2) to be possible Proto-Indo-European must have been spoken in reasonable proximity to Proto-Uralic, which at least some scholars associate with the Pit-Comb Ware culture to the north of the Kurgan culture in the fifth millennium BCE (Carpelan and Parpola 2001: 79).

Marija Gimbutas also speculated about the culture of these Proto-Indo-European speakers, which according to her was male-dominated and hierarchical; this culture supplanted an earlier peaceful goddess- and woman-centered culture of what she referred to as the "Old Europe" (Gimbutas is also credited for founding the field of feminist archeology). This "Old European" culture was based on matrilineal descent, that is, daughters inherited from their mothers, and was thus quite unlike the Proto-Indo-European culture, which followed the more familiar patterns of patrilineal descent where sons inherit from their fathers. Interestingly, although most scholars today do not accept Gimbutas' idea that the pre-Proto-Indo-European culture was matrilineal and woman-centered, this idea has recently received support from genetic studies of bone remains in Neolithic graves in Scandinavia which show that people buried in the same graves were related through the maternal line. While some scholars, notably J. P. Mallory, have questioned Gimbutas' emphasis on the violent or quasi-military nature of the Proto-Indo-European speakers, the Kurgan hypothesis evolved into the mainstream theory among Indo-Europeanists.

However, despite its mainstream status, the Kurgan hypothesis has been challenged by various scholars throughout the years. The main competitor of the Kurgan hypothesis is the Anatolian hypothesis, advanced by Colin Renfrew (1987), a British archaeologist and archeogeneticist. His answers to both the "where" and "when" questions are different to Gimbutas. According to the Anatolian theory, the speakers of Proto-Indo-European lived before the people of the Kurgan culture, about 7,000 BCE, and their homeland was not in the Pontic steppes but further south, in Anatolia (present-day Turkey), from where they later diffused into Greece, Italy, Sicily, Corsica, the Mediterranean coast of France, Spain and Portugal, while another group migrated along the fertile river valleys of the Danube and Rhine into Central and North Europe. This course of diffusion is correlated with the spread of agriculture, which can be traced through archeological remains. One of the main problems facing this theory is the fact that ancient Asia Minor is known to have been inhabited by non-Indo-European people, such as Hattians (later replaced by speakers of Hittite, also an extinct language) and others.

Another alternative theory of the Proto-Indo-European homeland is known as the Armenian hypothesis. Recall that the earliest proposals about the existence of the Proto-Indo-European language family by people like James Parsons and Sir William Jones incorporated the idea that Indo-European languages started in Armenia, the resting place of Noah's Ark. The modern Armenian hypothesis was proposed in the 1980s by Georgian scholar Tamaz V. Gamkrelidze and Russian scholar Vjacheslav V. Ivanov (see Ivanov and Gamkrelidze 1990). They place the Proto-Indo-European speakers in the Armenian Highlands during the fourth millennium BCE, at least a millennium later than the mainstream Kurgan hypothesis and a full three millennia later than the Anatolian hypothesis proposed by Colin Renfrew.

But the alternative hypotheses do not stop there. For example, another old idea given a new life by modern scholarship is that Proto-Indo-European speakers originated in the Indian subcontinent and spread to the remainder of the Indo-European realm through a series of migrations. This "Out-of-India" hypothesis goes back to the work of German poet, critic and scholar Friedrich Schlegel (1772–1829), but has been recently revived mainly by Flemish Indologist Koenraad Elst and Indian author Shrikant Talageri. This idea became the subject of a contentious debate in Indian politics, but it has not gained much support in the academic world. And academics have come up with theories of their own. For example, Johanna Nichols, a professor of linguistics at the University of California at Berkeley, put forward the so-called Sogdiana hypothesis, which places the Proto-Indo-European speakers to the east of the Caspian Sea, in the area of ancient Bactria-Sogdiana in the fourth or fifth millennium BCE (Nichols 1997, 1999). The so-called Paleolithic Continuity Theory, proposed by Mario Alinei in *Origini delle Lingue d'Europa* (1996–2000), maintains that Proto-Indo-European can be traced back to the Paleolithic era, much earlier than the Neolithic estimates in other scenarios of Proto-Indo-European origins. According to this theory, the advent of Indo-European languages should be linked to the arrival of *Homo sapiens* in Europe and Asia from Africa in the Upper Paleolithic. Yet another alternative, the Neolithic Creolisation hypothesis, advocated by Marek Zvelebil in 1995, states that the Indo-European language family resulted from a cultural and linguistic melting pot in the Neolithic Northern Europe, where foreign Neolithic farmers and indigenous Mesolithic hunter-gatherer communities mixed together.

The Proto-Indo-European homeland: where and when?

The various theories about where and when Proto-Indo-European was spoken are summarized in reverse chronological order below:

- **Armenian hypothesis:** the fourth millennium BCE in Armenian Highlands (Gamkrelidze and Ivanov);
- **Sogdiana hypothesis:** the fourth or fifth millennium BCE to the east of the Caspian Sea, in the area of ancient Bactria-Sogdiana (Nichols);
- **Kurgan Hypothesis:** the fifth millennium BCE in the Pontic-Caspian steppe (Gimbutas)
- **Neolithic Creolization hypothesis:** the sixth millennium BCE or later in Northern Europe (Zvelebil)
- **Out-of-India Model:** the sixth millennium BCE in India (Elst)
- **Anatolian hypothesis:** the seventh millennium BCE in Anatolia (Renfrew)
- **Paleolithic Continuity Theory:** before the tenth millennium BCE (Alinei)

Although this wealth of theories as to the origins of the Proto-Indo-European speakers and their language may seem overwhelming, at least some of these theories may prove not to be as mutually exclusive as they seem. This becomes especially true as genetic studies are bringing new elements (and new solutions!) to the puzzle. For example, Luca Cavalli-Sforza and Alberto Piazza have suggested that Colin Renfrew's Anatolian hypothesis and Marija Gimbutas's Kurgan hypothesis need not contradict each other: after all, it is possible – and genetic studies seem to support this – that the same people who originated in Asia Minor had first migrated to the area of the Pontic steppes and from there expanded into Central and Northern Europe. A 3,500-year period would have elapsed between the time of the Proto-Indo-European speakers' sojourn in Anatolia and their appearance in the area of the Kurgans. While Colin Renfrew maintains that the Proto-Indo-Europeans in Anatolia were agriculturalists, it is possible that they could have reverted to a pastoral culture as an adaptation to the environment. Here is how Piazza and Cavalli-Sforza (2006) explain this:

if the expansions began at 9,500 years ago from Anatolia and at 6,000 years
ago from the Yamnaya culture region, then a 3,500-year period elapsed dur-
ing their migration to the Volga-Don region from Anatolia, probably through
the Balkans. There a completely new, mostly pastoral culture developed
under the stimulus of an environment unfavorable to standard agriculture, but
offering new attractive possibilities. Our hypothesis is, therefore, that Indo-
European languages derived from a secondary expansion from the Yamnaya
culture region after the Neolithic farmers, possibly coming from Anatolia
and settled there, developing pastoral nomadism.   (pages 258–259)

Overall, the genetic findings to date provide the strongest support to Gimbutas's
model of Indo-European spread from the southern Russian steppe, and there is
little evidence for a similarly massive migration of agriculturalists directly from
Asia Minor.

So far, we have seen what archeologists and geneticists think about the possible
location and timeframe for the Proto-Indo-European homeland. But what do
linguists say on the matter? And what can they say based solely on the descendant
languages and reconstructions of the Proto-Indo-European language itself? As it
turns out, linguists can weigh in heavily in this debate. First, linguists can place
constraints on where and when the Proto-Indo-European language must have
been spoken, based on what is known of its descendant languages. The leading
idea in locating the homeland of a given language family is to find the area of
the most diversity within the area of the family's distribution. The logic of the
argument is as follows: it is in the area where the given family started (or has
been the longest) that it had the most time to develop new quirks in the language
and therefore to diversify. In the case of the Indo-European languages, the area
of most diversity is clearly in Europe (and possibly in Central or Eastern Europe,
to the extent that these notions are clearly definable geographically). The Indo-
European languages of Iran and India are more closely related to each other than
the Indo-European languages of Europe. Eastern Europe is also the geographic
center of the Indo-European realm, so it stands to reason that speakers Indo-
European languages originated there and then migrated out – in all directions.
Furthermore, based on what we know of modern and earlier Indo-European
languages, the Proto-Indo-European homeland probably extended from 100,000
to 400,000 square miles: if the territory occupied by the speakers of Proto-Indo-
European were larger than that, the language would necessarily diversify. This is
exactly what happened, as the population of the Proto-Indo-European speakers
grew and they expanded to a larger territory.

As to the question of "when", mainstream linguistic estimates hover around
6,000 years ago (or 4,000 BCE): if Proto-Indo-European were much older, we
would expect to see more extensive differences between its descendant languages,
and if it were much younger, we would not be able to explain the differences
between the older descendants of Proto-Indo-European such as Ancient Greek,
Sanskrit and Latin that were already established by the first millennium BCE.

Second, a linguistic reconstruction of a long-dead language can reveal new information about the physical environment and cultural concepts of an actual people who spoke the language. What was the daily life of the Proto-Indo-European speakers like? Were they agriculturalists or nomads? What did they eat, what clothes did they wear and how did they get around? What were their myths and beliefs like? Believe it or not, linguists can shed new light on these questions. For example, linguists working back from the descendant languages have been able to reconstruct many words of Proto-Indo-European; among them the words for 'cold', 'winter', 'snow', 'honey', such trees as 'beech', 'birch', 'pine' and 'ash', and animals like 'wolf', 'bear' and 'deer'. So we must conclude that Proto-Indo-European speakers lived in areas of temperate climate, probably in wooded areas where such trees and animals were to be found. Note that this does not mesh well with the theories that place the original Proto-Indo-Europeans in the steppe or even further south. One solution is to place the Proto-Indo-European homeland further north than is usually assumed, in the Baltic area. Another possibility is that Proto-Indo-European was first spoken in the border zone between the forests and the steppe.

The Proto-Indo-European source of the English word *lox* or Norwegian *lax* (as in the salted fish called *gravlax*) provides an additional example of how linguists develop theories of proto-language homeland location. In the descendant languages the cognates of this Proto-Indo-European word mean 'salmon' and salmon is a fairly northern salt-water fish, not to be found anywhere close to the Pontic steppe (for example, there is no salmon in the Black Sea or the Caspian Sea). So, if the speakers of Proto-Indo-European indeed had a word for 'salmon', they could not have lived in the area of the Kurgans. Problem? Not necessarily. Recall that words may – and often do – change their meaning (see the "Knights, riders and false friends" box). It is possible that this word in descendant languages developed a new meaning of 'salmon' but in Proto-Indo-European it meant something other than 'salmon', for example 'trout' (a kind of fish that is found in rivers and lakes all over Eastern Europe) or even just 'fish'.

Note also that words that were lacking in Proto-Indo-European are as suggestive of the speakers' physical environment as the words that were present in the language. For example, no words have been reconstructed for Proto-Indo-European for trees like 'palm' or 'olive', animals like 'elephant' and 'camel' or even for 'ocean' or 'sea' (the latter is particularly interesting in light of the salmon/ trout dilemma discussed above).

Thus, an examination of the reconstructed vocabulary for Proto-Indo-European (with some representative words listed in (2.2) below) reveals that speakers of the language raised sheep and goats, as well as cows and dogs; had agriculture; probably rode horses and possibly also had wagons and chariots.[7]

---

[7] Recall that nouns in Proto-Indo-European had a rich system of case morphology; that is, depending on where the noun appeared in the sentence, its ending was different. For a list of Proto-Indo-European cases, see Table 2.7. The hyphen at the end of these reconstructed words indicates the position of the case ending.

(2.2) a.   *owi-* 'sheep', *agwhno-* 'lamb', *aig-* and *ghaido-* 'goat', *kapro-* 'he-goat', *su-* 'pig', *porko-* 'young pig', *gwou* 'cow, bull, ox', *kwon-* 'dog', *peku-* 'cattle, wealth'

    b.   *grHno-*, *yewo-* and *pūro-* 'cereal, grain', *wrughyo-* 'rye', *bhares-* 'barley', *al-* and *melH-* 'grind', *sē* 'sow', *arH-* 'plough' (verb), *wogwhni-* 'plough- share', *perk-* and *selk-* 'furrow', *yeug* 'yoke', *serp-* 'sickle', *kerp-* 'gather, harvest', *gwHrHn-* 'hand mill'

    c.   *ekwo-* 'horse', *wegh-* 'convey, go in a vehicle', *kwekwlo-* 'wheel', *aks-* 'axle', *nobh-* 'hub of a wheel'.[8]

To recap, while the exact time and place where the Proto-Indo-European language was spoken remains controversial, advances in archeology and especially genetics, coupled with the magic of reconstructing words in a long-dead language allow us to get a glimpse into the lives of our Proto-Indo-European forbearers.

In the next section, we will examine the present-day Indo-European realm and the internal classification of the Indo-European language family.

2.3   The Indo-European realm

In the previous section we discussed the problem of the Proto-Indo-European homeland: according to the mainstream proposal, Proto-Indo-European speakers originated in the Pontic steppe just north of the Black Sea and the Caspian Sea. By the start of the third millennium BCE, the population of Proto-Indo-European speakers extended to a wider territory and groups living further apart from each other communicated less and less. As a result, the language started to diversify, with clear Northern and Southern dialects (or even dialectal groups) emerging in the northwestern and southeastern parts of the Indo-European realm. This process continued as Indo-European speakers gradually migrated to occupy wider and wider territory. Fast forward another millennium or so, and we are seeing non-mutually-intelligible languages within the Northern and Southern branches: Proto-Germanic, Proto-Italic, Proto-Celtic, Proto-Iranian, Proto-Indic and others. The process of Indo-European expansion and language diversification continues and around 500 BCE we are seeing some familiar languages such as Ancient Greek, as well as languages that would develop into whole families such as Proto-Slavic (the parent language of the present-day Slavic languages, including Russian, Polish and Bulgarian) and languages that would die out well before our time such as Phrygian, Sarmatian and Tocharian. Note that 500 BCE was probably the heyday of Indo-European languages, the time when they occupied the widest territory (before the modern colonial expansion starting in the sixteenth century, of course); the easternmost Indo-European language was Tocharian, which was spoken in western China where Uyghur, a Turkic language, is spoken

---

[8] The exact meaning of the latter word in Proto-Indo-European is debated: it is possible that it originally meant 'navel' and that the meaning was extended to 'hub of a wheel' only later.

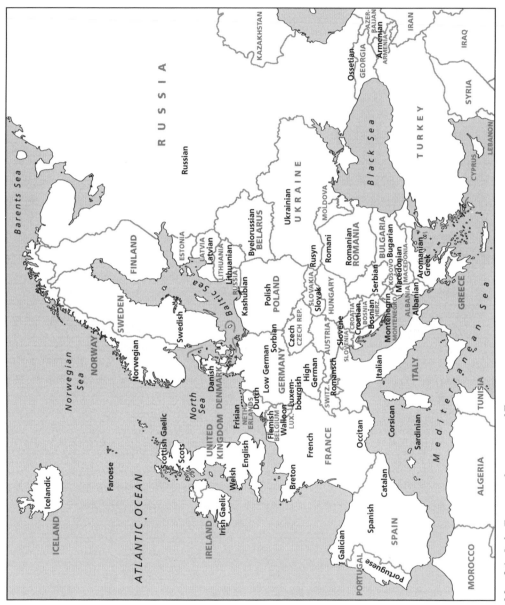

Map 2.1. *Indo-European languages of Europe.*

Note: *Yiddish is not mapped.*

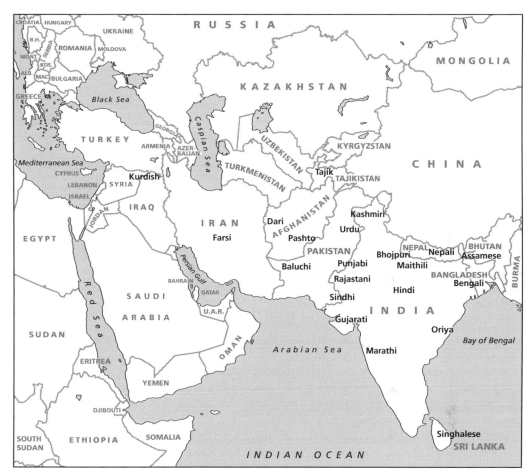

Map 2.2. *Indo-European languages of Asia.*
For Armenian, Ossetian and Romani, see Map 2.1.

today (see Chapter 5). Later, many Indo-European languages once spoken in the great Eurasian steppes were supplanted by languages from a different language family, the Altaic family (see Chapters 5 and 11). Thus, no trace is left today of Sarmatian or Tocharian, only written documents that survive the ravages of time.

Furthermore, migrations and displacements of one group by another involved not just Indo-Europeans vs. non-Indo-Europeans. Even within the Indo-European language family some groups migrated and displaced others: for example, Germanic- and Latin-speaking groups mixed with and displaced speakers of Celtic languages, who once occupied most of Atlantic Europe (large portions of today's France, Spain, Portugal, as well as the whole of the British Isles).

As a result of these gradual migrations, expansions and interactions, we end up with a diverse family of languages that is the Indo-European family. Within it,

Figure 2.1. *Branches within the Indo-European language family.*

languages can be classified into a number of subfamilies, some with a complex internal structure. Figure 2.1 presents a rather simplified picture of the various subfamilies within the Indo-European language family, with a few representative (living) languages listed for each subfamily.

Many of the subfamilies include languages or even whole branches that have become extinct. For example, the Balto-Slavic subfamily once included Old Church Slavonic – the liturgical language of not only the East Slavs, but of other Orthodox Slavs (Serbs, Macedonians, Bulgarians), as well as of Romanians. Likewise, a whole branch of the Italic subfamily – Sabellic – became extinct: these languages, including Oscan and Umbrian, were once spoken in central and southern Italy before Latin replaced them as the power of Rome expanded. In the Celtic family, Gaulish – the language of Asterix and Obelix – likewise was supplanted by Latin (although the people themselves intermixed with the Romans). More recently, two other Celtic languages have become extinct: Cornish and Manx (once spoken in Cornwall and the Isle of Man, respectively); efforts are now being made to revive those languages. And in the Germanic

subfamily a whole branch – East Germanic – died out as well, with its last surviving language, Crimean Gothic, spoken until the sixteenth century. Note that a
whole subfamily can become extinct as well (when all of its languages become
extinct); this happened, for example, to the Illyrian, Thracian, Phrygian, Hittite,
Luwian, Anatolian and Tocharian languages (or language families), not listed in
Figure 2.1. All of this goes to show that language endangerment and extinction
are not new; still, it seems to have accelerated in recent times, as we will discuss
in more detail in the following section and in Chapters 9 and 10.

Let us now consider the different subfamilies one at a time, starting with
the Germanic subfamily. It splits into two surviving branches (as mentioned
above, the third branch – East Germanic – is by now extinct): West Germanic
and North Germanic (or Scandinavian). The West Germanic branch includes
such languages as English, Scots, Frisian, Dutch, Flemish (related to Dutch but
spoken in Belgium), Afrikaans, Luxembourgish, Low German, High German and
Yiddish. The parent language of this branch is known as – you guessed it! – the
Proto-West-Germanic. The North Germanic branch contains the three Mainland
Scandinavian languages – Danish, Swedish and Norwegian – as well as Insular
Scandinavian languages: Icelandic and Faroese (the latter is spoken on Faroe
Islands, halfway between Iceland and Norway).[9] The parent language of this
group is Old Norse.

The next subfamily is Italic, which used to contain several branches but only
one of them – the Romance branch – has any surviving languages. The languages
in this branch all trace their descent from Latin. Within the Romance branch there
are three sub-branches: (1) Eastern Romance, which includes Romanian and
Aromanian – languages that mark the location of the former easternmost outpost
of the Roman empire, the province of Dacia; (2) Italo-Western Romance, which
includes such well-known languages as Italian, French, Spanish, Portuguese, as
well as lesser known languages of Occitan (or Provencal) and Catalan; and (3)
Southern Romance, including Corsican and Sardinian.

The third Indo-European subfamily to be considered here is the Celtic subfamily. Like many others, it too splits into two branches: the Goidelic branch, which
includes the native languages of Ireland and Scotland – Irish Gaelic and Scottish
Gaelic – and the Brythonic branch, which includes the other Celtic languages,
primarily Welsh (spoken in Wales) and Breton (spoken in northwestern corner of
France, the region of Brittany).

Next in Figure 2.1 are listed three subfamilies which contain only one language
each: the Albanian, Hellenic and Armenian subfamilies. These three languages –
Albanian, Greek and Armenian – are isolates within the Indo-European family
showing no closer connection to any other Indo-European languages or to each
other.

---

[9] Whether there are three or four Mainland Scandinavian languages depends on whether the two
Norwegian linguistic varieties – Bokmål and Nynorsk – are considered separate languages or
dialects of the same language.

Yet another subfamily of the Indo-European language family is the Balto-Slavic subfamily, which dominates Eastern Europe. As its name suggests, it too splits into two main branches: Baltic and Slavic. The Baltic group contains just two surviving languages: Latvian and Lithuanian, spoken in two of the three Baltic countries (Estonian is not a Baltic or even an Indo-European language and will be discussed in Chapter 3). The Slavic branch splits into three sub-branches: West Slavic (including Polish, Czech, Slovak, Sorbian, Kashubian and Polabian), East Slavic (including Russian, Ukrainian, Byelorussian and Rusyn[10]) and South Slavic (including Serbian, Bosnian, Croatian, Slovenian, Montenegrin, Bulgarian and Macedonian).

Last but not least are the languages of the Indo-Iranian subfamily, which too splits into two branches: Iranian and Indic (or Indo-Aryan). Languages in the Iranian branch are spoken from the Caucasus to Pakistan and include Persian (or Farsi), with national variants Tajik (in Tajikistan) and Dari (in Afghanistan), as well as Pashto (in Afghanistan and Pakistan), Kurdish (in the border area of Turkey, Iran and Iraq), Baluchi (in Pakistan) and Ossetian (see Section 4.4). The Indic branch contains many languages such as Sanskrit (the classical language of Indian civilization), Pali (the sacred language of Buddhism) and a large number of modern languages including Hindi, Kashmiri, Eastern Punjabi, Gujarati, Rajasthani, Marathi, Bhojpuri, Maithili, Assamese and Oriya in India; Urdu in India and Pakistan; Sindhi and Western Punjabi in Pakistan; Nepali in Nepal; Bengali in India and Bangladesh; Sinhalese in Sri Lanka; and Romani, the language of the Roma or Gypsies (see Section 2.4 below).

While many Indo-European languages are quite well-known, in the next section we turn to the lesser known Indo-European languages.

2.4   Focus on: Lesser known Indo-European languages

While all of you are familiar with English – otherwise you could not read this book! – not everybody has even heard of the closest relative of English, a language called **Scots**. It should not be confused with Scottish English, the dialect of English spoken in Scotland, or with Scottish Gaelic, discussed below. In fact, until the Renaissance period English and Scots were the same language, gradually growing more and more distinct until they were no longer mutually intelligible (at least not easily so). Even though today some people still dispute the language status of Scots and consider it a dialect of English, it is hardly more

---

[10] According to the official Ukrainian policy, Rusyn is considered a dialect of Ukrainian (similar to the Ukrainian Hutsul dialect) rather than a separate language. Nor does Ukraine officially recognize Rusyns as a separate ethnicity, despite the fact that some speakers prefer to consider themselves ethnically distinct from Ukrainians. However, most linguists treat Rusyn is a separate language.

similar to English than Danish is to Norwegian, which are considered distinct languages.

Scots is spoken mostly in the Scottish Lowlands, in southern and central parts of Scotland, as well as in Ulster (Northern Ireland). One familiar example of Scots is the song "Auld Lang Syne", written by Robert Burns in 1788:

> *An sheerly yil bee yur pynt-staup!*
> *an sheerly al bee myn!*
> *An will tak a cup o kyndnes yet,*
> *fir ald lang syne.*

How much of it do you understand without a translation? What is *sheerly*? Or *bee* (it is not the familiar insect!)? Here is a translation to help you:

> And surely you'll buy your pint cup!
> and surely I'll buy mine!
> And we'll take a cup of kindness yet,
> for the sake of old times.

Another poet (or *maker* in Scots) who wrote in Scots is Robert Louis Stevenson. He wrote most of his prose in English, but in *Kidnapped* (written in 1886) he masterfully depicted certain peculiarities of Scots pronunciation, vocabulary and grammar. Moreover, his poetry is written in both English and Scots. By his own admission in "The Maker to Posterity", Scots is a lofty language alongside Greek and Latin (*Lallans* is one of the several names for Scots, and *Tantallon* is a mid-fourteenth-century castle overlooking the Firth of Forth):

> *No bein fit to write in Greek,*
> *I wrote in Lallans,*
> *Dear to my hert as the peat reek,*
> *Auld as Tantallon.*

Let me finish this brief description of Scots by mentioning a few interesting words. Your kin are referred to in Scots as *ilk*, as in *It's yin o ma ilk right enough* ('He is one of my kindred alright'). For 'slobbering' or 'smearing' use *slather*; an extremely exhausted person can be described as *puggled* or *wabbit*, and of course if you study Scots long enough, you will become *knackie* ('adroit, deft, skillful, ingenious') at it!

Scots, a Germanic language spoken in the Scottish Lowlands, is not to be confused with **Scottish Gaelic**, a Celtic language spoken mostly in the Scottish Highlands. Scottish Gaelic exhibits many grammatical features typical of Celtic languages. For example, Scottish Gaelic exhibits the Verb-Subject-Object (VSO) order, found in only about 10% of the world's languages. So the Scottish Gaelic rendition of 'John drank milk' is *dh'òl Iain bainne*, literally 'drank John milk'. Also, Scottish Gaelic and other Celtic languages lack the verb 'have' and use a prepositional construction instead to express possession and ownership. For example, 'I have a house' is *Tha taigh agam*, literally 'Is house at-me'. Note that the verb comes first in this sentence as well. The word *agam* is a preposition expressing agreement with first person singular complement, thus rendering 'at me' in one word. However, Scottish Gaelic "makes up" for the lack of the verb 'have' by having two verbs 'be': one of them – *bi* or *tha*, depending on the form – is used if the predicate is an adjective or a prepositional phrase, while the other – which happens to be *is* – relates two nouns (things are actually a bit more complicated than this statement would have one believe, but we will leave it at that for now). For example, 'I am tired' in Scottish Gaelic is **tha** *mise sgìth*, literally 'am I tired' (note again that the verb is sentence-initial and this is not a question!), while 'I am John' is **is** *mise Iain*, literally, 'am I John', but a different verb 'be' is used here.

For several centuries Scottish Gaelic was losing ground due to both socio-political developments and the generally negative attitudes towards Celtic culture that were common in the past. The most serious socio-political development that affected the status of Scottish Gaelic was the depopulation of the Highlands in the late 1700s and in the 1800s. As a result of the failed Jacobite rising (1688–1746), which was aimed at returning the Stuarts to the thrones of Scotland, England and Ireland and was finally quashed at Culloden in 1746, the Act of Proscription was adopted in 1747, prohibiting Highland dress and the bearing of arms. What followed were Highland Clearances – a series of forced displacements of Scottish Gaelic-speaking population in 1780–1860 – and Ireland's potato famine (caused by potato blight) reaching the Highlands in the mid-1800s. All of these developments led to the destruction of the traditional clan system, a high emigration rate and the near death of the Scottish Gaelic language. Nor did the negative attitudes towards all things Celtic help: in the seventeenth to nineteenth centuries it was common to view Celtic languages, culture and traditions as "corrupt" and "uncivilized", as is evident from the following quote from Matthew Arnold, a literary critic writing for *The Times* in 1867:

> *The Welsh language is the curse of Wales. Its prevalence, and the ignorance of English have excluded... the Welsh people from the civilisation of their English neighbours. An Eisteddfod [the annual Welsh literary and musical festival] is one of the most mischievous and selfish pieces of sentimentalism which could possibly be perpetrated. It is simply a foolish interference with the natural progress of civilisation and prosperity. If it is desirable that the Welsh should talk English, it is monstrous folly to encourage them in a loving fondness for their old language.*

Today, the tides have changed and Celtic languages, traditions, music and crafts are seeing a revival. For example, Scottish music groups like Runrig (named after an old land-usage system) and Capercaillie, and the music festival "Celtic Connections", do a great deal to popularize Celtic culture. Serious efforts are underway to strengthen the Scottish Gaelic language as well: TV and radio programs are broadcast in the language, magazines and books are published, adult language classes are organized. Furthermore, in 1973 a Scottish Gaelic medium college Sabhal Mòr Ostaig was founded near Armadale on the Isle of Skye, and since 1986 Scottish Gaelic has been reintroduced as the language of primary school education. Still, Scottish Gaelic is confined mostly to remote and rural areas of the Highlands, where it is spoken by about 75,000 speakers, of whom about 95% are bilingual in Scottish Gaelic and English.

Another potentially endangered language right in the heart of Europe is the **Corsican** language (also known as Corsu, or Lingua corsa). It is a Romance language, but not closely related to French, Italian or Spanish: unlike those three languages, Corsican belongs to the Southern Romance branch (see Section 2.3 above). It is spoken on the island of Corsica, which was acquired by France in 1768. Since the introduction of the French language in Corsican schools in 1853 and until very recently, the use of Corsican has been declining: in 1980 about 70% of the population had some command of the language, while just ten years later the percentage had declined to 50%, with only 10% using it as a first language. The French government reversed its non-supportive stand and began some strong measures to save the Corsican language. Whether these measures will succeed remains to be seen. Unsurprisingly, the use of Corsican is at its highest in connection with traditional activities, such as polyphonic singing and in other cultural groups (70–80% of those participating), and in hunting and fishing (60–70%); whereas in church it's down to 11% and in night clubs 4%.

One famous Corsican is Napoleon Bonaparte, who, by all accounts, spoke French with a marked Corsican accent. To a French ear, the Corsican accent sounds very much like Italian, although there are some striking differences between Corsican and Italian. For example, in Italian the Latin nominative case ending -*um* became -*o* (e.g. the Latin *annum* 'year' became the Italian *anno* 'year'), while in Corsican it became -*u* retaining the vowel, but dropping the -*m* (cf. the Corsican *annu* 'year').[11] This is also illustrated by the Corsican words *celu* 'heaven' and *regnu* 'reign, kingdom' in the excerpt from the "Our Father" prayer (compare with the Italian *cielo* 'sky, heaven' and *regno* 'reign, kingdom'):

> *Patre Nostru chì sì in celu, ch'ellu sia santificatu u to nome; ch'ellu venga u to regnu, ch'ella sia fatta a to vuluntà, in terra cum'è in celu.*

Another lesser known minority language in Europe is **Romani** (self-name: *rromani ćhib*), spoken by over 3.5 million Řom, or Gypsies, in Central and Eastern Europe.[12] The largest concentrations of Romani speakers are in southeastern

---

[11] To be more precise, the evolution the Latin nominative case ending -*um* in Corsican went through the stage when the vowel was -*o*, as in other Eastern Romance languages (Italian, Sicilian, Romanian and the now-extinct Dalmatian) and then developed back into -*u*.

[12] It is important to distinguish between Romani, which is a fully fledged, everyday family and community language spoken by the people who call themselves Řom, and secret or in-group vocabularies employed by other populations, as well as by some Řom communities, especially in the western margins (Britain, the Iberian Peninsula, Scandinavia). In those areas, formerly Romani-speaking communities often give up their language in favor of the majority language, but retain Romani-derived vocabulary as an in-group code.

Table 2.8. *Romani, Hindi, Bengali,*
Punjabi numerals.

	Romani	Hindi	Bengali	Punjabi
1	ekh	ek	ek	ikk
2	duj	do	dvi	do
3	trin	tīn	tri	tinn
4	shtar	cār	car	cār
5	pandzh	pāñc	pac	pumj
6	shov	che	chay	che
7	ifta/efta	sāt	sat	satt
8	oxto	āṭh	at	aṭhṭh
9	inja/enja	nau	nay	naum
10	desh	das	das	das

and central Europe, especially in Romania, Bulgaria, Macedonia and Slovakia. Several major dialects of Romani are distinguished, among them the Balkan, Baltic, Carpathian, Sinte and Vlax dialects.

The earliest attestation of Romani in Europe is from the fourteenth century, and not much is known about the history of the Řom people from historical records, either their own or by other peoples, so examining the Romani language and its connections to other languages has been instrumental in demystifying the Romani past. The first published work that postulates an Indian origin of the Romani language and its connection to languages of the Indian subcontinent such as Hindi and Bengali is the book by Johann Christian Christoph Rüdiger *On the Indic Language and Origin of the Gypsies* (1782). He used surprisingly modern methodology, collecting his Romani data directly from a Romani speaker (which he admitted to finding "tiresome and boring") and his Hindi data from a manual written by a missionary.[13] Consider the list of numerals from Romani and several other languages in the Indic branch of the Indo-Iranian subfamily of the Indo-European language family in Table 2.8: numerals for 'one' through 'six' and 'ten' are very similar across those four languages (we will return to numerals for 'seven' through 'nine' below).[14]

Nor did Rüdiger limit himself to examining the vocabulary of Romani and other Indic languages. He writes:

> *As regards the grammatical part of the language the correspondence is no less conspicuous, which is an even more important proof of the close relation between the languages.*

[13] Recall that Rüdiger's work was published fourteen years before Sir William Jones's pronouncement about the affinity of Sanskrit, the ancient language of India, with Ancient Greek and Latin.

[14] Dialectal variants in Romani are listed separated by a slash.

The close similarity between Romani and other Indic languages – both in vocabulary and in grammar – indicates that the Řom people originated in the Indian subcontinent, from where they migrated westward. A detailed analysis of Romani phonology and morphology allowed linguists to determine when this migration must have started. For instance, consider the evolution of the grammatical gender system in Indo-Aryan languages. Earlier forms of these languages (known in historical linguistics as Middle Indo-Aryan, or MIA) had three genders: masculine, feminine and neuter. However, by the turn of the second millennium CE, Indo-Aryan languages lost the neuter gender, with most formerly neuter nouns becoming masculine and a few becoming feminine. This phase in the Indo-Aryan language development that took place in the last millennium or so is known as the New Indo-Aryan (NIA) phase. The Romani language fits the profile of a NIA language: it has only two genders, masculine and feminine, and the formerly neuter nouns are now of the same gender as they are in other NIA languages, such as Hindi. For instance, the neuter *agni* 'fire' in the Prakrit language (a MIA language; see also Table 2.3 above) became the feminine *āga* 'fire' in Hindi and likewise a feminine *jag* in Romani. The simplest explanation is that the Romani language was spoken in central India at the turn of the second millennium CE, so that the loss of neuter gender and the reassignment of formerly neuter nouns to masculine or feminine genders occurred **before** the Romani language split off from the rest of the Indic languages. Otherwise, we would have to postulate that Hindi and Romani **independently** reassigned neuter nouns to exactly the same gender classes – a surprising coincidence! Thus, the Romani exodus could not have started before the eleventh century CE. (Unfortunately, linguistic analysis alone does not allow us to figure out why the Řom people left India.)

In recent years, genetic evidence has been brought forward in support of the Indian origin of the Řom people: DNA studies conducted in the late 1990s showed that nearly half of the Romani men carry Y-DNA of haplogroup H-M82 which is rare outside the Indian subcontinent; moreover, nearly 30% of the Romani people carry the mtDNA haplogroup M, most common in Indian subjects and rare outside of Southern Asia (Kalaydjieva *et al.* 2005).[15] Furthermore, genetic studies place the "founding event" (that is, the Romani exodus from India) "approximately 32–40 generations ago", which – assuming 25–30 years per generation – matches the 1,000 CE date derived from linguistic studies (see Morar *et al.* 2004).

Additional linguistic studies of the Romani language and especially of the influences of Greek, Armenian, Turkish and to a lesser extent Persian and Kurdish point to a prolonged stopover that the Řom people made in the Balkans and/or in Anatolia. For instance, Greek has had a strong impact on the Romani lexicon, morphology and syntax, as can be witnessed from the large number of Greek

---

[15] Y-DNA (on Y-chromosomes) is used to trace paternal descent, while mtDNA (mitochondrial DNA) is used to trace maternal descent. Only men carry Y-DNA, but both men and women can be tested for mtDNA analysis.

loanwords in Romani (e.g. *drom* 'road' from the Greek *drómos* 'road'; *zumin* 'soup' from the Greek *zumí* 'soup'; *xoli* 'anger' from the Greek *xolí* 'anger'; as well as grammatical loanwords like *pale* 'again' from the Greek *pale* 'again'; *komi* 'still' from the Greek *akómi* 'still'; and numerals *efta* 'seven', *oxto* 'eight' and *enja* 'nine' – see Table 2.8), as well as from Greek-derived case/number affixes on nouns and tense/aspect affixes on verbs. In syntax, the Greek influence is seen in the emergence of a definite article placed before the noun, and a shift to the Subject-Verb-Object (SVO) order (while Indic languages typically exhibit the Subject-Object-Verb, or SOV, order).[16] However, Romani still shows some of its original Indic word order: for example, instead of prepositions, it uses postpositions (which are essentially the same but follow rather than precede the noun); thus, to say 'for you' both a Romani and a Hindi speaker would say literally 'you for' (note also the similarity between the postpositions themselves):

(2.3) a.   Romani: *tu + ke* 'for you', *la + ke* 'for her'
      b.   Hindi: *tum + ku* 'for you', *uno + ku* 'for her'

---

[16] The reader is referred to Matras (2002) for a more detailed description of the Romani language and history.

3   Non-Indo-European languages of Europe and India

In Chapter 2 we examined the Indo-European languages that are spoken in most of Europe and India. However, it is erroneous to think that all languages in Europe, the Indian subcontinent and in between are Indo-European. In this chapter, we turn our attention to those languages of this region that do not belong to the Indo-European language family. In particular, we will consider two language families – the Finno-Ugric family and the Dravidian family – and a language isolate, Basque.

3.1   Finno-Ugric languages

On the map of non-Indo-European languages in Europe (Map 3.1), three areas stand out: the eastern shores of the Baltic Sea (Finland, Estonia and the neighboring areas of Russia and Sweden), the Great Hungarian Plain and the western Pyrenees area. The latter area is the Basque Country, where Basque (a linguistic isolate) is spoken; we will discuss it in Section 3.2 below. But first we will turn to the other two areas – the eastern Baltic area and the Great Hungarian Plain – where languages of the Finno-Ugric family are spoken.

The first thing to note is that the major languages of this family – Finnish, Estonian and Hungarian – are not similar to the neighboring languages. For example, Finnish shows little resemblance to Swedish (a Germanic language) or Russian (a Slavic language); Estonian is not similar to Russian or Latvian (a Baltic language); and Hungarian stands out among its neighbors: German (a Germanic language), Romanian (a Romance language) and Polish (a Slavic language). The non-cognateness of Hungarian numerals with those in German, Romanian and Polish is illustrated in Table 3.1.

However, Hungarian, Finnish and Estonian resemble each other, as well as other languages spoken in northwestern Russia, as shown by some cognates from these three languages and Mordvin in Table 3.2. Mordvin words are listed both in the traditional orthography using Cyrillic alphabet and in a Roman transliteration.

Several conclusions can be drawn based on this table. First, as pointed out above, the four languages are related. Second, they are not all related to the same degree: Finnish and Estonian appear to be most closely related (they have

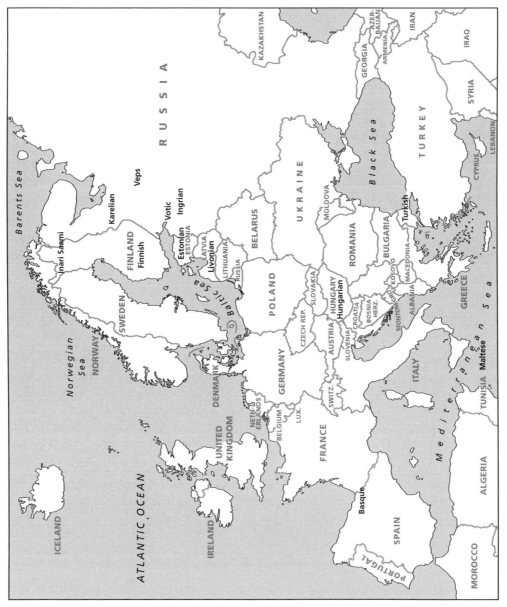

Map 3.1. *Non-Indo-European languages of Europe.*

Table 3.1. *Central European numerals.*

	German	Romanian	Polish	Hungarian
1	eins	uno	jeden	egy
2	zwei	doi	dva	kettő
3	drei	trei	trzy	három
4	vier	patru	cztery	négy
5	fünf	cinci	pięć	öt
6	sechs	şase	sześć	hat
7	sieben	şapte	siedem	hét
8	acht	opt	osiem	nyolc
9	neun	nouă	dziewięć	kilenc
10	zehn	zece	dziesięć	tíz

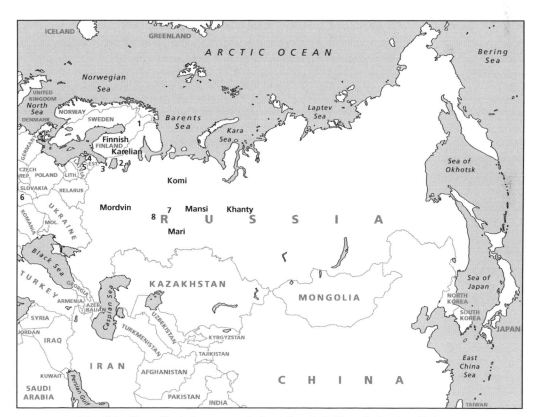

Map 3.2. *Finno-Ugric languages. 1: Inari Saami; 2: Veps; 3: Ingrian, Votic; 4: Estonian; 5: Livonian; 6: Hungarian; 7: Permyak; 8: Udmurt.*

the most cognates that match precisely), and Mordvin is more closely related to Finnish and Estonian than Hungarian is. This is schematized in Figure 3.1.

Recall that the proper comparative reconstruction relies not only on similarity of potentially cognate words, but also on there being recurrent patterns of

Table 3.2. *Some Finno-Ugric cognates.*

	Hungarian	Finnish	Estonian	Mordvin
'hand'	kéz	käsi	käsi	кедь *keď*
'water'	víz	vesi	vesi	ведь *veď*
'blood'	vér	veri	veri	верь *veŕ*
'we'	mi	me	meie, me	минь *miń*
'you (PL)'	ti	te	teie, te	тынь *tyń*
'who?'	ki?	kuka?	kes?	кие? *kije?*
'what?'	mi?	mikä?	mis?	мезе? *meze?*
'2'	kettő	kaksi	kaks	кавто *kavto*
'4'	négy	neljä	neli	ниле *nile*
'eye'	szem	silmä	silm	сельме *seĺme*

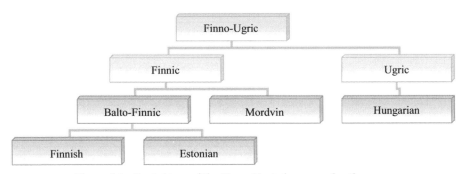

Figure 3.1. *Partial tree of the Finno-Ugric language family.*

differences between cognates. For instance, in Chapter 2 we have established certain patterns of differences between English and Latin (or more generally, Germanic and non-Germanic Indo-European languages; see Table 2.4), as well as between several Romance languages (see Table 2.5). Can we find similarly recurrent patterns of divergence between, say, Finnish and Hungarian? The answer is yes. For example, consider the Finnish and Hungarian words for 'hand', 'water' and 'blood': while the Finnish words have two syllables, the corresponding Hungarian words have only one – the final vowels of the Finnish words are lost in Hungarian. Moreover, the vowel in the first syllable of Hungarian words is lengthened (this is marked in Hungarian orthography by an accent mark, so the word for 'hand' is pronounced /ke:z/, the word for 'water' /vi:z/ and the word for 'blood' /ve:r/).[1]

The two modifications in Hungarian vis-à-vis Finnish – final-vowel deletion and previous-vowel lengthening – are not unrelated. In fact, it is quite common to see a deletion process (typically, a deletion of the following consonant, but

---

[1] Stress in Hungarian always falls on the first syllable, so there is no need to use the accent mark for stress.

Table 3.3. *Additional Hungarian/Finnish cognates.*

	Hungarian	Finnish
'head'	fő	pä
'tree'	fa	puu
'son'	fiú	poika
'nest'	fészek	pesä
'half'	fél	puoli
'six'	hat	kuusi
'three'	három	kolme
'fish'	hal	kala
'death'	halál	kuolema
'hear'	hall	kuulla

sometimes of the next vowel) accompanied by lengthening of the preceding vowel. For example, in Old English words ending in *-ight* were pronounced as /ixt/, so that *night* was pronounced /nixt/ and *knight* – /knixt/.[2] (Recall that the English *knight* and the German *Knecht* are cognates; see the "Knights, riders and false friends" box.) However, later the sound /x/ was lost – and /i/ was lengthened to /iː/ to compensate. Even later, the long /iː/ became the diphthong /aj/ as a result of the process called the GREAT VOWEL SHIFT (note that this change applied to all instances of long /iː/ regardless of whether they resulted from the compensatory lengthening, as with *night* and *knight*, or were original to the word, as with *child* and *rise*).

The final-vowel deletion plus compensatory lengthening is not the only pattern of recurrent sound correspondence between Hungarian and Finnish. Two other patterns concerning consonants can be observed from additional cognates listed in Table 3.3. First, the word-initial /f/ in Hungarian corresponds to /p/ in Finnish (cf. the words for 'head', 'tree', 'son', 'nest', 'half'). Second, the word-initial /h/ followed by /a/ in Hungarian corresponds to /k/ in Finnish (cf. the words for 'six', 'three', 'fish', 'death', 'hear').

But the similarity between Hungarian and Finnish is not limited to the vocabulary: there are many grammatical similarities as well. Four of them that we will discuss here are: (1) vowel harmony; (2) agglutinative morphology; (3) rich case systems; and (4) lack of grammatical gender. First, let us consider VOWEL HARMONY, which is a process by which vowels assimilate to each other across intervening consonants. In particular, vowels in suffixes in Finnish and Hungarian

---

[2] The symbol /x/ is used in transcription to signify a voiceless velar fricative, namely a sound similar to /k/ but pronounced without a complete closure between the back portion of the tongue and the soft palate (velum). The air is pushed through the wide opening between the vocal cords (hence, voiceless) and then through a narrow opening between the back portion of the tongue and the velum (hence, velar fricative). This sound is no longer used in English.

words harmonize to be back or front depending on the vowel of the root (see the "Vowel classification" box). Take, for example, the elative case suffix in Finnish (we will discuss the case system of Finno-Ugric languages in more detail below): it can be pronounced with either [æ] (spelled as *ä* in Finnish) or [a] depending on the vowel of the root (e.g. *tyhmä-stä* 'stupid', *tuhma-sta* 'naughty'). Likewise, the inessive case suffix in Hungarian can be pronounced with either [ɛ] (spelled as *e* in Hungarian) or [a] depending on the vowel of the root (e.g. *egy-ben* 'one', *hat-ban* 'six').[3]

Vowel classification

Vowels used in the world's languages can be classified along several dimensions (try to pronounce the illustrative vowels and pay attention to the position of the tongue and lips!):

- **Back/Front:** depending on the position of the tongue on the horizontal axis (e.g. /i/ in *feel* is a front vowel and /u/ in *fool* is a back vowel);
- **High/Mid/Low:** depending on the position of the tongue and the lower jaw on the vertical axis (e.g. /ɪ/ in *bid* is a high vowel and /ɛ/ in *bed* is a mid vowel and /æ/ in *bad* is a low vowel);
- **Rounded/Unrounded:** depending on the position of the lips – rounded or spread (e.g. /u/ in *fool* is a rounded vowel and /i/ in *feel* is an unrounded vowel);
- **Oral/Nasal:** depending on the position of the velum – for oral vowels, it is raised preventing the air from flowing through the nasal cavity, and for nasal vowels, it is lowered allowing the air to flow through the nasal cavity (e.g. /æ/ in *back* is an oral vowel and /æ/ in *bank* is pronounced as a nasalized vowel); this distinction does not encode meaning in English but it does in French, Portuguese and other languages;
- **Tense/Lax:** depending on the degree of muscle tension in the vocal tract (e.g. /i/ in *feel* is a tense vowel and /ɪ/ in *fill* is a lax vowel).

Another grammatical property characteristic of Finno-Ugric languages is AGGLUTINATIVE MORPHOLOGY, that relies heavily on adding affixes – each expressing one grammatical property – to the root. Examples of agglutinative morphology in Finnish and Hungarian are given below:

(3.1) a.   Finnish: [talo-ssa-ni-kin] lit. 'house-in-my-too' ('in my house, too')
      b.   Hungarian: [haːz-unk-bɔn]   lit. 'house-our-in' ('in our house')

The agglutinative pattern is contrasted with ISOLATING MORPHOLOGY, on the one hand, and with FUSIONAL MORPHOLOGY, on the other hand. In languages with isolating morphology (such as Mandarin Chinese or Thai), grammatical features are expressed through free-standing words, such as particles or auxiliary verbs (this is further illustrated in Chapter 7 below). In languages with fusional morphology, affixes are added to the root, but each affix may

---

[3] For a more detailed discussion of vowel harmony, see van der Hulst and van de Weijer (1995).

express two or more grammatical features, such as tense, aspect and agreement with the subject on verbs, or gender, number and case on nouns. For instance, in the Russian word *kniga* 'book', the affix -*a* expresses simultaneously feminine gender (or declension I), singular number and nominative case.

This brings us to a closer consideration of the case systems in Finno-Ugric languages. Unlike more familiar Indo-European languages with morphological systems of case marking with an average of 6 cases, Finno-Ugric languages have much richer case systems, with 9 cases in Inari Saami (spoken by some 300 speakers in northern Finland), 14 cases in Estonian, 15 cases in Finnish, 21 cases in Hungarian (according to some linguists; see Tompa 1968: 206–209) and up 27 cases in certain dialects of Komi.[4] The various case forms of the Hungarian word *hajó* 'ship' are given in (3.2) below. Note that many of these cases, such as inessive, elative, illative, adessive, ablative, allative and others, express locative relations typically encoded in Indo-European languages by the use of prepositions instead of case marking.

(3.2)			
	Nominative:	hajó	'ship' [subject]
	Accusative:	hajó-t	'ship' [object]
	Inessive:	hajó-ban	'in a ship'
	Elative:	hajó-ból	'out of a ship'
	Illative:	hajó-ba	'into a ship'
	Superessive:	hajó-n	'on a ship'
	Delative:	hajó-ról	'about a ship'
	Sublative:	hajó-ra	'onto a ship'
	Adessive:	hajó-nál	'by a ship'
	Ablative:	hajó-tól	'from a ship'
	Allative:	hajó-hoz	'to a ship'
	Terminative:	hajó-ig	'up to a ship'
	Dative:	hajó-nak	'ship' [indirect object]
	Instrumental-comitative:	hajó-val	'with a ship'
	Formal:	hajó-képp	'as a ship'
	Essive:	hajó-ul	'by way of a ship'
	Essive-formal(-similitive):	hajó-ként	'in the capacity of a ship'
	Translative-factitive:	hajó-vá	'[turn] into a ship'
	Causal-final:	hajó-ért	'for the purpose of a ship'
	Distributive:	hajó-nként	'per ship'
	Sociative:	hajó-stul	'together with a ship'

Finally, Finno-Ugric languages also lack grammatical gender, even in their pronouns. As a result, the same pronoun is used for 'he' and 'she': *hän* in

---

[4] Languages with a small number of cases include languages with no case marking at all (e.g. English, which has no cases for nouns), languages with two cases, usually called direct and oblique (e.g. Old French), languages with three cases (e.g. Modern Standard Arabic and Romanian), languages with four cases (e.g. German), languages with five cases (e.g. Ancient Greek). Languages with rich case systems – which typically include a number of locative-directional cases, as do case systems of Finno-Ugric languages – are found also in the Caucasus region (see Chapter 4), especially in Dagestan: Lezgin has 18 cases and Tabasaran has a record of 46 cases (Plungian 1996: 118).

Table 3.4. *Ugric numerals.*

	Mansi	Khanty	Hungarian
1	akʷa	yit, yiy	egy
2	kitiɣ	katn, kat	kettő
3	χūrəm	xutəm	három
4	ńila	nyatə	négy
5	at	wet	öt
6	χōt	xut	hat
7	sāt	tapət	hét
8	ńololow	nəvət	nyolc
9	ontolow	yaryaŋ	kilenc
10	low	yaŋ	tíz

Finnish, *tämä* in Votic (an endangered language spoken by only about a dozen speakers in northwestern Russia), *tema* in Estonian, *ő* in Hungarian.

To recap, we have seen that Finno-Ugric languages, such as Finnish, Estonian and Hungarian, exhibit strong affinity both in their vocabularies and in their grammars. Moreover, various Finno-Ugric languages exhibit different degrees of affinity to each other: for example, Finnish and Estonian are more closely related to each other than to Hungarian. In fact, all the Finno-Ugric languages mentioned so far, including not only Finnish and Estonian, but also Votic, Inari Saami, Mordvin and Komi, constitute the same branch of the Finno-Ugric family: the Finnic branch. So is Hungarian an isolate within the Finno-Ugric family (just as Greek or Albanian are isolates within the Indo-European family; see Figure 2.1)? The answer is no, but the closest linguistic relatives of the Hungarians are not their geographic neighbors. In fact, they live about 2,500 miles to the northeast, east of the Ural Mountains. These are people called Khanty and Mansi (the administrative division of the Russian Federation where they live is called the Khanty-Mansi Autonomous Okrug and its capital is Khanty-Mansiysk, an oil boom town and a center of alpine skiing). Approximately 13,600 people speak Khanty and under 3,000 speak Mansi (generally, Mansi have been more assimilated by the Russians than the Khanty). To illustrate the affinity of Hungarian with Khanty and Mansi, Table 3.4 presents numerals 1–10 from the three languages.

A more complete tree of the Finno-Ugric family is shown in Figure 3.2 (the symbol ℂ indicates "waning" languages, spoken by relatively small groups of mostly bilingual speakers and not passed on regularly to the children; if nothing is done to change the situation these languages will become extinct in a couple of generations at the most).

This brings us to the question of the geographic distribution of the Finno-Ugric family. Most language families are spoken in geographically contiguous areas, but this is not true of the Finno-Ugric family, whose languages is spoken over three non-contiguous areas: (1) the Ural Mountains and the upper reaches of the

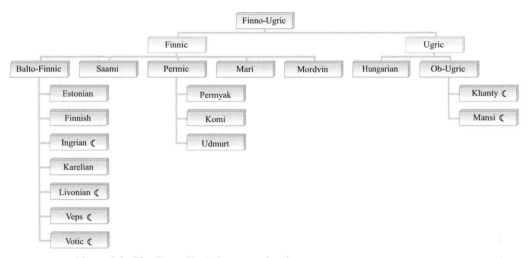

Figure 3.2. *The Finno-Ugric language family.*

Volga River and its tributaries, (2) eastern Scandinavia and the eastern shores of the Baltic Sea and (3) the Great Hungarian Plain. Why these three locations? The first location – around and just south of the Ural Mountains – is probably the area of the original Finno-Ugric homeland: historical linguists argue as to whether Finno-Ugric languages were originally spoken on the eastern or the western slopes of the Ural Mountains, but it is fairly clear that it was somewhere close to the Urals. The other two locations resulted from different paths of development in the Finnic and Ugric branches of the Finno-Ugric family. Curiously, the two branches exemplify two different reasons why a certain linguistic group, family or branch may be spread over a non-contiguous territory.

In the case of the Finnic branch, its geographic non-contiguity resulted from language withering and extinction in the center of the original Finnic realm. Finnic languages were once more extensively spoken in what is today northwestern and central parts of European Russia. However, in the late eleventh and early twelfth centuries CE, several Finnic-speaking groups – Merya, Muroms and Meshchera – gradually disappeared through acculturation to the Slavic-speaking Russians, who, under the pressure of Turkic-speaking nomads, were themselves pushing into the upper Volga territories previously inhabited by Finnic speakers. Thus, gradually the Russian language has supplanted several Finnic languages in what is now central Russia.

In contrast, the geographic non-contiguity of the Ugric branch resulted from a very different development: the Magyar migration. The original homeland of the Hungarians (or Magyars, as they call themselves) – Magna Hungaria – was located in the Kama basin, but by the turn of the ninth century CE, they moved to the Pontic steppe, north of the Black Sea. In the next century, they moved yet further west, pushed by another group: the Pechenegs (who spoke one of the Turkic languages; see Chapter 5). The Magyars crossed the Carpathian Mountains and by the end of the ninth century settled in the Great Hungarian Plain, the one place in Europe where pastoralist lifestyle could be easily maintained. There, the Magyars encountered a population speaking mostly a Slavic language (probably not unlike an older form of Serbo-Croatian), as well as some Romance-speaking groups, and imposed their Ugric language on them.

Interestingly, the number of the Magyar conquerors was relatively small, about 30% of the resulting population, and their genes were further diluted by subsequent exchanges with their neighbors. That is why the genetic maps of Europe, such as the map that shows the distribution of PC2 (the second principal component of genetic variation among Europeans) presented in Cavalli-Sforza and Cavalli-Sforza (1995), Cavalli-Sforza (2000), do not highlight Hungary. In contrast, Finns, Estonians, Karelians and especially the Saami do stand out on that map. This genetic uniqueness of Finns (and related peoples) has been recently supported by the findings of the study conducted by the Institute for Molecular Medicine Finland (FIMM), which compiled the Finnish Gene Atlas based on DNA from more than 40,000 Finns.[5] Unlike the Hungarians, speakers of Finnic languages managed to retain their special genetic profile because they descended from a more extensively Finno-Ugric founding population.

3.2   Basque

Unlike the Hungarians, who live in the heart of Europe, but whose original homeland is in the area more peripheral to the Indo-European realm, Basque speakers did not come to the Iberian Peninsula from elsewhere in historical times. Quite the opposite is true: they are the original inhabitants of the area, from the times before Celtic and Romance speakers came to inhabit Atlantic Europe.[6] The name of the language – Basque (self-name: *Euskara*) – and of the postulated related Vasconic languages, by now extinct, comes from the Latin word *vascones* meaning 'foresters'; Vasconia was the name the Romans gave to the up-country of the western Pyrenees. It is by now a widely accepted view that speakers of Basque (or related Vasconic languages) once inhabited a much wider territory, stretching from the British Isles in the north to Gibraltar in the south through the western half of today's France and Belgium. Gradually, the Basque-speaking area has been shrinking relentlessly, although today its border

---

[5] See: www.fimm.fi/en/scientific_highlights/the_new_finnish_gene_atlas_places_finns_on_the_world-s_genetic_map/

[6] There are several other known but by now extinct languages that were survivors of Indo-European invasions: Minoan on Crete, Etruscan in today's Tuscany and possibly Pictish in Scotland (the exact nature of the latter is still very controversial). Also, scholars of Ancient Greek find many words in that language that probably survive from the languages spoken in that area before the arrival of Indo-Europeans.

has become relatively stable, especially in the north, where the neighboring language is not Spanish or French, but Gascon, a very distinct variety of Occitan. Still, even within the borders of the Basque-speaking area, far from everybody speaks the language: it is spoken by about 580,000 people in the Basque Country (Euskadi), an autonomous community in the Pyrenees in North-Central Spain, Southwestern France, and in the autonomous community of Navarre in Spain. This constitutes about a fourth of the inhabitants of the Basque country and slightly less than half of the inhabitants of the Basque-speaking area in the northern third of the Basque country. As is the case with many other minority languages of Europe, efforts are underway to stabilize the status of Basque by including it in the school curriculum, publishing books and newspapers in the language, using it in the media and so on. Today, Basque has the status of an official language along with Spanish in the Basque regions of Spain, in the Basque Country and in some parts of Navarre, but it has no official status in the Basque Country of France.

The Vasconic Retreat hypothesis has received confirmation from genetic studies as well. For example, Cavalli-Sforza's work on principle components (Cavalli-Sforza and Cavalli-Sforza 1995, Cavalli-Sforza 2000) suggests that PC5 (the fifth principle component) maps the retreat of the Vasconic speakers: the highest degree of PC5 is found in the Basque Country. More recently, Y-DNA studies show that the highest concentration of the Y-haplogroup R1b is found in the Basque Country, as well as in the western parts of the British Isles: this further supports the idea that Vasconic speakers were once spread much further north along the Atlantic coast of Europe.

Genetic studies have helped not only to support the Vasconic Retreat theory – originally proposed by a German linguist Theo Vennemann – but also to discredit the alternative hypotheses, such as the Caucasian–Basque connection theory which maintained that Basque is related to the languages of the Caucasus (see Chapter 4), such as Georgian or Chechen. Neither studies of classical markers (that is, blood groups and protein electromorphs) nor of mtDNA found any genetic link between Basques and Caucasians (Bertorelle *et al.* 1995, Nasidze and Salamatina 1996, Comas *et al.* 2000).

Not only are Basques an outlier population within Europe from the genetic point of view, but the Basque language is also quite distinct from the surrounding European languages.[7] Unlike the Indo-European languages (but like Finno-Ugric languages discussed in the previous section), Basque is an agglutinative language. Also, it features a vigesimal number system (also found in Celtic languages and Caucasian languages), that is, a number system based on 20 rather than 10. For

---

[7] Note, however, that Basque has had an effect on some neighboring Romance languages, particularly Catalan and Gascon. For example, both Basque and Gascon lack word-initial [r] sound which is replaced by *err-/arr-*. Unlike French and like Basque, Gascon has a simple five-vowel system. Also, Catalan and even Spanish have lost the word-initial /f/ and replaced it by "mute" *h*, as in the Latin *fablar* 'to speak' which turned in Spanish into *hablar*.

example, 31 in Basque is *hogeita hamaika*, literally '20 + 11'; 50 is *berrogeita hamar*, literally '(2 × 20) + 10'; and 80 is *laurogei*, literally '4 × 20'.[8]

But the most "exotic" – for an Indo-European language speaker – feature of Basque is its case and agreement system. Like Finno-Ugric languages, Basque has a very rich case system, with thirteen cases, some of which – such as inessive, allative, ablative, terminative, instrumental, comitative – express relations typically expressed through prepositions in Indo-European languages. But even the core grammatical cases in Basque are different from the more familiar case systems of Indo-European languages. Recall from Table 2.7 in Chapter 2 that in addition to oblique cases such as ablative, dative, locative, genitive and instrumental, Indo-European languages have two core grammatical cases: nominative and accusative. Let's consider more closely how these cases are used in Indo-European languages.

Take, for example, Latin. Although the most canonical order in Latin was Subject-Object-Verb (SOV), these three elements could come in any order, depending in large part on the context. Thus, the six logically possible orders of subject, object and verb are all possible in Latin, so to say 'The carpenter looked at the senator' any of the following permutations could be used:

(3.3) a.   **Structor**   aspexit   **senatorum**.
        carpenter   looked.at   senator

    b.   **Senatorum** aspexit   **structor**.
        senator   looked.at   carpenter

    c.   **Senatorum structor**   aspexit.
        senator   carpenter   looked.at

    d.   Aspexit   **senatorum structor**.
        looked.at   carpenter   senator

    e.   Aspexit   **structor**   **senatorum**.
        looked.at   carpenter   senator

    f.   **Structor**   **senatorum** aspexit.
        carpenter   senator   looked.at

So how would a Latin speaker encode (and a Latin listener decode!) who looked at whom? The answer is by paying attention to case markers, such as the accusative marker *-um* on *senator* 'senator' in (3.3). The lack of *-um* marks the masculine noun *structor* 'carpenter' as nominative (other types of nouns – called DECLENSIONS – have overt markers for the nominative case). To recap, in a TRANSITIVE SENTENCE; that is, a sentence with both a subject and an object, the subject is marked with nominative case and the object with accusative case.

But what about an INTRANSITIVE SENTENCE, that is a sentence with just a grammatical subject, such as 'John left' or 'Mary worked'? From a purely communicative point of view, there is no need for case marking in intransitive sentences, but natural language does not work that way: if nouns are marked for

---

[8] The French *quatre-vingt* '80', literally '4 × 20', is probably a remnant of the old influence of Basque on (southern dialects of) French.

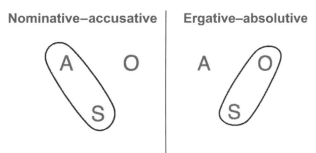

Nominative–accusative | **Ergative–absolutive**

Figure 3.3. *The nominative–accusative case system of Latin and the ergative–absolutive case system of Basque.*

case in some instances in a given language, they typically must be marked for case in all types of sentences. So in Latin, subjects of intransitive sentences are marked exactly like subjects of transitive sentences: they are nominative.

(3.4)   **Dominus   servos**   vituperabat quod   non laborabant.
        master.NOM slaves.ACC cursed   because not worked.they
        'The master cursed the slaves because they were not working.'

(3.5)   **Dominus**   ad villam ambulat.
        master.NOM to house   walks
        'The master walks to the house.'

However, in principle nothing prevents a language from marking subjects of intransitives just like objects – rather than subjects – of transitives. This is exactly how the case system of Basque works. The technical term for a system like that is ERGATIVE, and it is also the name of the case used in such a language for subjects of transitives (but not of intransitives). The other case – the one used for both objects of transitives and subjects of intransitives – is called ABSOLUTIVE (although sometimes the term "nominative" is used for this case as well). The two systems – the nominative–accusative system of Latin and other Indo-European languages and the ergative–absolutive system of Basque – are schematized in Figure 3.3, where A stands for Actor or subject of transitive, O stands for object (of transitive) and S for subject of intransitive:[9]

Let's turn now to specific examples of how the case system works in Basque. The absolutive case is not marked overtly (as is true of nominative case for nouns like *structor* 'carpenter' in Latin); the ergative case is marked by the suffix *-k*. Thus, in a transitive sentence the subject is marked with the suffix *-k* and the object appears in its base form, with no overt case marker (linguists refer to this as a ZERO-MARKER, or Ø-marker); in an intransitive sentence the subject is likewise in its base form, with no overt case marking.[10]

---

[9] Note that Finno-Ugric languages, discussed in the previous section, too have nominative–accusative case systems.

[10] The suffix *-a* in these examples is the definiteness marker, similar in function to the English article *the*.

(3.6)   **ehiztari-a-k**   **otso-a-Ø**   harrapatu du.
         hunter-DEF-ERG wolf-DEF-ABS caught   has
         'The hunter has caught the wolf.'

(3.7)   **otso-a-Ø**   etorri   da.
         wolf-DEF-ABS arrived is
         'The wolf has arrived.'

There are some additional complications with respect to the case and agreement system of Basque, which we will not go into here (but see Saltarelli 1988, Hualde and de Urbina 2003, Rijk 2008); the chief complication involves verbs that are intransitive in English and many other languages, but translate as transitive-verb-plus-noun constructions in Basque (Levin 1983). As we will see in Chapter 4 below, many languages of the Caucasus are likewise ergative, which was one of the strongest grammatical parallels between the two groups of languages (vigesimal number system and agglutinative morphology are also found in Caucasian languages), which led to the postulation of the Caucasian–Basque connection, mentioned above and by now largely discredited.

3.3   Dravidian languages

Just as Basque speakers are remnants of the population that used to inhabit this part of the world prior to the arrival of Indo-Europeans, Dravidian speakers are remnants of the formerly larger population that inhabited all of the Indian subcontinent before the beginning of the Christian Era. The Indo-Aryan languages, such as Hindi, Bengali and Marathi, were not native to India; rather they were introduced by Indo-European speakers from the north, who either displaced or else conquered and acculturated Dravidian speakers. But according to genetic studies such as Cavalli-Sforza's (2000: 157):

> The center of origin of Dravidian languages is likely to be somewhere in the Western half of India. It could be also in the South Caspian ... or in the northern Indian center ... This language family is found in northern India only in scattered pockets, and in one population (Brahui) in western Pakistan.

Today, the Dravidian language family consists of 85 languages, spoken by over 200 million speakers, mostly in southern India, as well as in northeastern Sri Lanka and in Pakistan. The best known among Dravidian languages are Tamil, Telugu, Kannada and Malayalam. Since the country's provincial boundaries were redrawn along linguistic lines in 1956, each of these four languages has been spoken (and has a co-official status) in a single state. Telugu is the most widely spoken Dravidian language with 70 million people in the southeastern province of Andhra Pradesh (capital: Hyderabad). Tamil is spoken by over 60 million speakers in the southern state of Tamil Nadu (capital: Madras) and by nearly

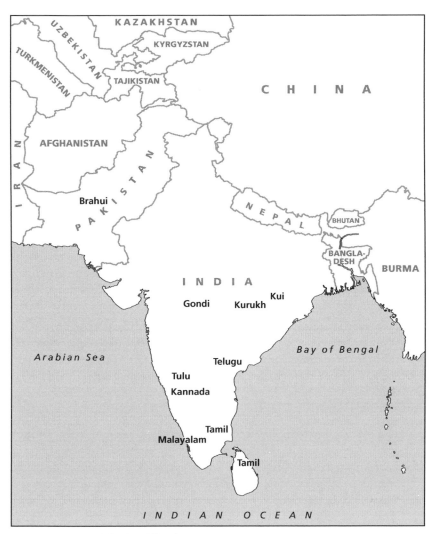

Map 3.3. *Dravidian languages.*

4 million in northeastern Sri Lanka. Kannada is spoken by over 35 million people on the west coast in Karnataka (capital: Bangalore), and Malayalam is spoken by over 35 million people in the southwestern state of Kerala (capital: Trivandrum). Tamil, Malayalam and Kannada are closely related and belong to one branch of the Dravidian family (the Southern branch), while Telugu is quite different from the others and belongs to the Central branch.

Other Dravidian languages, such as Gondi, Kui and Kurukh, are spoken in central India, where Indo-European languages are dominant: Gondi is spoken by over 2 million people in Madhya Pradesh and northeastern Maharashtra; Kui is spoken by 765,000 people in southern Orissa; and Kurukh is spoken by over 2 million people in Bihar, Orissa and Madhya Pradesh. The few pockets

Table 3.5. *Numbers in Dravidian languages and Bengali.*

	Malayalam	Tamil	Telugu	Bengali
1	onnu	onru	okati	ek
2	rantu	irantu	rendu	dvi
3	mûnnu	mûnru	mûdu	tri
4	nâlu	nânku	nâlugu	car
5	añju	aintu	aidu	pac
6	âru	âru	âru	chay
7	êru	êlu	êdu	sat
8	ettu	ettu	enimidi	at
9	onpatu	onpatu	tommidi	nay
10	pattu	pattu	padi	das

of Dravidian speakers in those parts of central India lend weight to the theory that in the past, prior to the arrival of Indo-Europeans, Dravidian languages were spoken in a much wider area of central and northern India. Another Dravidian language – Tulu – is spoken by nearly 2 million people in the southern state of Karnataka, alongside Kannada, while Brahui is the only Dravidian language spoken in Pakistan (more precisely, in the southwestern province of Baluchistan); in addition to 2 million speakers in Pakistan, Brahui also has 200,000 speakers in Afghanistan and another 20,000 in Iran.

The existence of the Dravidian language family was first recognized by a British civil servant in India, Francis W. Ellis, in 1816, only 20 years after Sir William Jones' pronouncement that is taken to mark the recognition of the Indo-European language family. It was Ellis too who realized that Dravidian languages are not related to Indo-European ones. In his *Dissertation on the Telugu Language* (cited in Krishnamurti 2003: 16) he wrote:

> the high and low Tamil; the Telugu, grammatical and vulgar; Car-
> natake or Cannadi, ancient and modern; Malayalma or Malayalam and
> Tuluva... constitute[e] the family of languages which may be appropriately
> called the dialects of South India... with which [Sanskrit] has no radical
> connection.

But as you can see from the quote above, Ellis did not use the term Dravidian. In fact, this term was not used in print until the publication of Robert A. Caldwell's *Comparative Grammar of the Dravidian or South Indian Family of Languages* in 1856. The name comes from the Sanskrit word *dravida*, which historically referred to the Tamil language and people.

The affinity of Dravidian languages in the vocabulary can be illustrated by their words for basic numbers. In Table 3.5, these are contrasted with numbers in Bengali, an Indo-Aryan language spoken in northeastern India. As can also be seen from this table, not all Dravidian languages are related to each other to the same degree. Thus, Malayalam and Tamil are more closely related to each other than to Telugu: as mentioned above, Telugu is a member of the Central branch of the Dravidian family, while Malayalam and Tamil are members of the family's Southern branch.

Both the sound system and grammar of Dravidian languages also make them quite distinct from the neighboring Indo-Aryan languages. Unlike Indo-European languages – but like many Finno-Ugric languages – Dravidian languages do not distinguish between voiced and voiceless stops. For example, the contrast between /p/ and /b/ is not used to differentiate meaning. Instead of distinguishing consonants by voicing, Dravidian languages employ more places of articulation for consonants, making a three-way distinction between DENTAL, ALVEOLAR and RETROFLEX PLACES OF ARTICULATION. Dental consonants are pronounced with the tip of the tongue pressed against or brought close to the upper teeth; for alveolar consonants, the tip of the tongue is pressed against or brought close to the alveolar ridge, just behind the upper teeth; and for retroflex consonants, the tip of the tongue curls back behind the alveolar ridge. For example, in Malayalam /kʌnni/ with an alveolar nasal consonant means 'virgin', while /kʌɳɳi/ with a retroflex nasal consonant means 'link in a chain'. Note that some Indo-Aryan languages have retroflex consonants too, as a result of diffusion from Dravidian languages.

From a morphological point of view, Dravidian languages are agglutinative, once again unlike Indo-European languages, but like Finno-Ugric languages (and Basque). Thus, grammatical relations in Dravidian languages are indicated by the addition of suffixes to roots, and these suffixes are strung one after another, resulting on occasion in very long words. Dravidian languages generally do not use prefixes.

Dravidian languages, such as Tamil, also exhibit a distinct system of noun genders. Unlike the more familiar systems in Indo-European languages that have masculine, feminine and sometimes neuter gender (see the discussion of Romani in Section 2.4), Tamil nouns (and pronouns) are classified into two major gender-like classes: "rational", including nouns referring to humans (in some dialects, only to men) and deities, and "irrational", including nouns referring to children, animals, objects, as well as abstract concepts. "Rational" nouns distinguish masculine and feminine sub-genders, based on the sex of the referent, and both "rational" and "irrational" nouns distinguish singular and plural number. The case system of Dravidian languages follows the nominative–accusative pattern, found in both Indo-European and Finno-Ugric languages (but not in Basque): the core structural cases are nominative, used for subjects of transitives and intransitives alike, and accusative, used for objects.

In syntax, Dravidian languages exhibit a rigid Subject-Object-Verb (SOV) order (as does Basque, as mentioned above). As is typical of languages with the SOV order, main verbs in Dravidian languages precede the auxiliaries (note the same pattern in Basque in (3.6) and (3.7) above). Moreover, possessors typically precede nouns they modify (as with the *s*-genitives in English and unlike the *of*-genitives: ***John's** friend*, but *a friend **of my sister***). These patterns are considered in more detail in the following section.

3.4   Focus on: Universals and the parametric theory of language

Let's start our discussion of the parametric theory of language by considering one Finno-Ugric language – Udmurt – and one Dravidian language – Telugu. We shall focus in particular on certain word order patterns observable in these languages. But first let's introduce some basic geographic and demographic information about these two languages.

Udmurt, as mentioned above, is a Finno-Ugric language (more specifically, it belongs to the Permic sub-branch of the Finnic branch). It is spoken in the Russian republic of Udmurtia (capital: Izhevsk), about 600 miles northeast of Moscow, where it is a co-official language alongside Russian. The number of Udmurt speakers is estimated at 464,000; however, many younger people, especially in cities, do not speak Udmurt since their parents think that knowing Russian will give their children better educational and economic opportunities.[11] This causes worry about the future survival of the language. Yet, in rural areas, Udmurt is spoken by a much higher proportion of ethnic Udmurts; it is also used as a language of instruction, at least in primary schools in rural areas. In addition, Udmurt has a niche in the media as well: every morning one can listen to the news and weather in Udmurt, and in the evenings watch Udmurt programs on TV.

The closest relatives of Udmurt are Komi(-Zyrian) and (Komi-)Permyak (see Figure 3.2 above). However, unlike these and other Finno-Ugric languages, Udmurt does not distinguish short and long vowels and does not have vowel harmony; moreover, it is characterized by stress falling on the last syllable of a word. Other un-Finno-Ugric features of Udmurt include a large number of loanwords from Tatar (a Turkic language) and Russian; Tatar has also influenced Udmurt phonology and syntax. But like other Finno-Ugric languages, Udmurt has agglutinative morphology, lacks gender distinction even in personal pronouns (e.g. *so* 'he/she/it') and has fifteen cases, among them seven are the so-called locative cases, such as inessive, illative, elative, egressive, terminative, prolative and approximative (curiously, animate nouns distinguish only eight cases).

On the Dravidian side, we will illustrate things with **Telugu**, the language of nearly 70 million people in India's Andhra Pradesh and the neighboring states of

---

[11] Because of the influx of Russian industrial workers who were moved to the Urals region with their weapons factories during World War II, the population of Udmurtia is now 58% Russian. It is in Udmurtia that Russia's great composer Peter Ilyich Tchaikovsky was born in 1840 and another Russian, Mikhail Kalashnikov, invented the sub-machine gun named after him in 1947.

Karnataka, Tamil Nadu, Orissa, Maharashtra and Chattisgarh. It is also spoken by émigré communities in Bahrain, Canada, Fiji, Malaysia, Mauritius, Singapore, South Africa, United Arab Emirates and the United States. Despite being the third most widely spoken language in India and fifteenth in the *Ethnologue* list of most-spoken languages worldwide, Telugu is relatively unfamiliar outside of India.

The oldest extant inscriptions in Telugu are dated 575 CE and the first literary work, a poetic translation of a part of the *Mahābhārata*, belongs to the eleventh century CE. As mentioned above, Telugu is not very closely related to Tamil, Malayalam or Kannada and belongs to a different branch of the Dravidian family. However, Telugu has had a lot of give-and-take with Kannada, and the two languages share a common stage of evolution in their script called the Telugu-Kannada script (seventh–thirteenth centuries CE). There are four regional dialect groups of Telugu: northern, southern, eastern and coastal; the latter is the basis for the Modern Standard Telugu. Like other Dravidian languages, Telugu uses a number of retroflex consonants and has agglutinative morphology.

Let's now turn to the patterns of word order. Perhaps surprisingly, both Udmurt and Tamil exhibit several similar patterns. First of all, both languages have the **Subject-Object-Verb** (SOV) order.

(3.8)   Udmurt
         nʲulsekašʲjos gondïr kutiⱼⁱʲam.
         hunters   bear   caught
         'The hunters have caught a bear.'
                    (Csúcs 1998: 297)

(3.9)   Telugu
         rāmu ninna   kamala-ku   pustakam icc-ǣ-ḍu.
         Ramu yesterday Kamala-DAT book   give-PST-3SG.M
         'Ramu gave a book to Kamala yesterday.'
                    (Krishnamurti 2003: 427)

In addition, both of these languages feature **postpositions** rather than prepositions:

(3.10)   Udmurt
         universitet **bere**
         university after
         'after university'

(3.11)   Telugu
         bomma **kōsam**
         doll   for
         'for the sake of the doll'
         (Krishnamurti 2003: 431)

Moreover, if we look closer at the NOUN PHRASES in these languages, we
will observe that **genitives/possessors, demonstratives, numerals and adjectives** precede the nouns that they modify. The Udmurt examples in (3.12) below
illustrate the genitive/possessor preceding the noun, the numeral preceding the
noun and the adjective preceding the noun; the Telugu examples illustrate the
genitive/possessor preceding the noun, the demonstrative preceding the noun,
the numeral preceding the noun and the adjective preceding the noun in (3.13).

(3.12)   Udmurt
   a.   genitives/possessors
      dïšetišʲ-len   knʲigaosïz
      teacher-GEN books
      'the teacher's books'
          (Csúcs 1998: 295)

   b.   numerals
      das studentʲos
      ten students
      'ten students'

   c.   adjectives
      tëdʲï derem
      white shirt
      'white shirt'
      (Csúcs 1998: 295)

(3.13)   Telugu
   a.   genitives/possessors
      nā pustakam
      my book
      'my book'

   b.   demonstratives, numerals, adjectives
      ā   reṇḍu manic kotta tellaṭi pedda pustakālu
      those two   good new white big   books
      'those two good big new white books'
          (Krishnamurti 2003: 429)

The same word order patterns are typical of many other Finno-Ugric and
Dravidian languages: Subject-Object-Verb order in sentences; noun followed by
postposition; the genitive preceding the noun; the demonstrative preceding the
noun; the numeral preceding the noun; and the adjective preceding the noun.
The question that arises at this point is whether these identical patterns provide
evidence for a family relationship between Finno-Ugric and Dravidian languages;
according to this hypothesis these languages would form a Finno-Ugro-Dravidian
macro family.[12] After all, it is exactly those sorts of deep grammatical similarities
(coupled with affinity in the basic vocabulary) that are taken as proof of family
relationships among languages.

---

[12] Other macro family proposals are discussed in Chapter 11.

Yet, the Finno-Ugro-Dravidian hypothesis cannot be sustained. The main problem is that these properties tend to occur together across languages. Moreover, the opposite word order patterns tend to occur together as well. Thus, languages with OV order, regardless of their family affiliation, tend to have postpositions and prenominal modifiers (such as demonstratives, genitives/possessors, numerals and adjectives). Conversely, languages with VO order tend to have prepositions and postnominal modifiers – again, regardless of their family affiliation. These tendencies have been formulated as the so-called Greenberg's Universals, named after Joseph Greenberg (1915–2001), who led a typology project at Stanford University. Here are some of the relevant universals, proposed by Greenberg (1966):

(3.14) a. **Greenberg's Universal 2**:
In languages with prepositions, the genitive almost always follows the governing noun, while in languages with postpositions it almost always precedes.

b. **Greenberg's Universal 3**:
Languages with dominant VSO order are always prepositional.

c. **Greenberg's Universal 4**:
With overwhelmingly greater than chance frequency, languages with normal SOV order are postpositional.

(Greenberg 1963/1966: 79)

d. **Greenberg's Universal 18**:
When the descriptive adjective precedes the noun, the demonstrative and the numeral, with overwhelmingly more than chance frequency, do likewise.

According to Greenberg's Universal 2, it is unsurprising that in languages with postpositions, such as Udmurt or Telugu, the genitive precedes the noun. This correlation between postpositions and the genitive preceding the noun is found in many other languages as well, for example in Turkish (Turkic; see Chapter 5), which – like Udmurt and Telugu – also features the OV order and the adjective preceding the noun:

(3.15)   Turkish
a.   postposition:
vapur **ile**
boat   with
'with a boat'

b.   genitive/possessor preceding noun:
müdür-ün   ev-i
director-GEN house-ACC
'the house of the director'

c.   OV:
ev-i   gör-dü-m.
house-ACC see-PST-1SG
'I saw the house.'

d.   adjective preceding noun:
güzel   ev
beautiful house
'a beautiful house'

The opposite pattern – a language with prepositions and genitive following the noun – is illustrated with Russian (Slavic, Indo-European):

(3.16)   Russian
a.   preposition:
v   dom
into house
'into a/the house'

b.   noun preceding genitive:
dom   Tani
house Tanya.GEN
'Tanya's house'

However, this correlation between postpositions and the genitive preceding the noun is a strong tendency but not an absolute rule: consider English, which like Russian has prepositions, but where genitives precede rather than follow the noun they modify, as in *into John's house* (not **into house John's*). Of course, English also has a different kind of possessor, marked by the preposition *of*, as in *the house of mine*. Still, the *'s*-genitives in English present a problem for Greenberg's Universal 2.

Greenberg's Universal 18 also governs the order of nominal modifiers. According to this universal, we would expect a language with prenominal adjectives to have likewise prenominal demonstratives and numerals. Again, Udmurt and Telugu do not disappoint. Nor does English this time: consider *those five cute puppies*. Here, the adjective *cute*, the demonstrative *those* and the numeral *five* all precede the noun *puppies*.

According to Greenberg's Universal 4, we would expect a language with the SOV order – such as Udmurt or Telugu – to have postpositions, and they do indeed. As do many other languages with the SOV order: Basque, Hindi and Japanese, to name just a few. In fact, exceptions to this universal are quite rare: according to the World Atlas of Language Structures Online (http://wals.info/), 427 out of 437 languages (98%) in their sample fit this pattern, while only 10 languages are exceptions. These exceptional languages have the OV order but also prepositions, rather than postpositions. Among these languages are Farsi/Persian (Indo-European), Tigré (Semitic; see Chapter 5) and Mangarrayi (Gunwingguan; Australia; see Chapter 9).

The opposite pattern is considered in Greenberg's Universal 3; however, it is not formulated for all languages with VO order, but only for those with VSO order. Such languages are expected to be prepositional. Yet, among languages with SVO order there are a few languages with postpositions, among them several

Finno-Ugric languages, including Finnish, Komi-Zyrian (a close relative of Udmurt) and Mordvin (Erzya).

To recap, certain word order patterns appear to occur as a package: for example, the OV order in sentences typically co-occurs with postpositions, the genitive preceding the noun and the adjective preceding the noun. The combination of all these features is found in Udmurt and Telugu, as well as in Hindi and Armenian (both Indo-European), Burushaski (isolate), Chechen (Northeast Caucasian; see Section 4.2 below), Georgian (Kartvelian; see Section 4.3 below), Amharic (Semitic; Ethiopia; see Section 5.2 below), Korean and Japanese (see Chapters 7, 11), among countless others. Consider the following data from Japanese:[13]

(3.17)   Japanese
     a.   OV:
           Taroo-ga   hon-o   kat-ta.
           Taro-NOM   book-ACC   buy-PST
           'Taro bought a book.'

     b.   postposition:
           nihon **ni**
           Japan in
           'in Japan'

     c.   genitive/possessor preceding noun:
           Taroo-no   hon
           Taro-GEN   book
           'Taro's book'

     d.   adjective preceding noun:
           kuroi neko
           black cat
           'a black cat'

Conversely, the VO order typically co-occurs with prepositions, the noun preceding the genitive and the noun preceding the adjective. This combination is attested in Spanish (Romance, Indo-European; illustrated below), Breton (Celtic, Indo-European), Modern Standard Arabic (Semitic; see Chapter 5), Chichewa (Niger-Congo; Mozambique; see Chapter 6), Fijian (Austroneasian; Fiji; see Chapter 8), to name just a few.

(3.18)   Spanish
     a.   VO:
           Yo comí el   arroz.
           I ate the rice
           'I ate the rice.'

     b.   preposition:
           con Pedro
           with Pedro
           'with Pedro'

[13] Examples in (3.17a, c) are from Shabatani (1990: 257–258).

c.   noun preceding genitive/possessor:
la   hermana de David
the sister   of David
'David's sister'

d.   noun preceding adjective:
la   casa   roja
the house red
'the red house'

The most important conclusion to be drawn from this is that such correlations between word order patterns cannot be taken to support family relationships between languages. Instead, certain grammatical patterns must be considered as overt realizations of a single underlying rule, which linguists call a "parameter". This idea underlies the parametric theory of language, developed by Noam Chomsky and his colleagues. According to Baker (2001a: ix), "parameters . . . play the same foundational role in scientific theories of linguistic discovery that atoms play in chemistry" because "these parameters combine and interact with each other in interesting ways to create the wide variety of languages that we can observe around us".

Which way are you headed?

According to the parametric theory of language, certain grammatical properties of language that always "go in a package" are considered to be overt realizations of a single underlying factor, called a parameter. So what about the word order patterns discussed here, such as OV vs. VO and postpositions vs. prepositions? As mentioned in the text, OV languages typically have postpositions, and VO languages tend to have prepositions. In fact, there are additional word order patterns that correlate with those. For example, OV languages tend to have postverbal auxiliaries, while VO languages tend to have preverbal auxiliaries (compare Basque examples in (3.6) and (3.7) in Section 3.2 above with their English translations). But what is the single underlying rule that explains these three word order patterns?

To understand this, let's consider the three patterns more closely:
- the OV/VO pattern: the order of a verb (word) + an object (noun phrase):
     eat + [an apple]
- the postposition/preposition pattern: the order of an adposition (word) + a noun phrase:
     in + [the book]
- the V-Aux/Aux-V pattern: the order of an auxiliary (word) + a verb phrase:
     has + [done so]

In all three cases, we are concerned with the order of a word (which linguists call a HEAD) and a phrase that complements it (linguists call such a phrase COMPLEMENT). The parameter that controls this order is called the **Headedness Parameter** (Travis 1984). As is the case with many other parameters proposed to date, this parameter has two options: the head preceding the complement and the complement preceding the head. Languages with the former "setting" (or "value") of the parameter are called Left-Headed and languages with the latter "setting" are called Right-Headed (in a eurocentric way, linguists use "left" to mean "before or first" and "right" to mean "after or later", even when talking about languages written from right to left or from top down; Baker 2001a uses "head first" and "head last", respectively).

Let's review: in a Left-Headed (or head-first) language, the head precedes its complement and we get VO, prepositions and auxiliaries before verb phrases; conversely, in a Right-Headed (or head-last) language, the head follows its complement and we get OV, postpositions and auxiliaries after verb phrases. Before reading on, can you name three Left-Headed and three Right-Headed languages?

Answer: Left-Headed languages include English, Spanish, Russian, Chichewa, Fijian, Breton and others; Right-Headed languages include Udmurt, Telugu, Hindi, Basque, Japanese, Turkish, Georgian, Amharic and others.

The parametric theory of language has significant implications not only for the study of individual languages but also for our understanding of human thought and culture. While it is difficult to believe that all languages are alike, many people have overemphasized the differences between languages, claiming that "languages are incomparably different and thus their speakers are incapable of truly understanding each other" (Baker 2001a: x). This is the view often referred to as the Whorf–Sapir Hypothesis, according to which the varying cultural concepts inherent in different languages affect the way in which speakers of these languages classify and experience the world around them. The parametric theory of language takes the middle ground by treating languages as "different but commensurable" (Baker 2001a: x).

4   Languages of the Caucasus

The Caucasus region straddles the border between Europe and Asia and is dominated by the imposing Great Caucasus mountain range, which stretches between the Black Sea and the Caspian Sea and includes Europe's highest mountain, Mount Elbrus. This region has been known for a long time as one of the world's ethnically and linguistically most diverse areas. According to the Roman historian Pliny, when the Romans came to the Caucasus, they needed 134 interpreters to deal with the jumble of languages they found; the tenth century Arab geographer and historian al-Azizi referred to the area as the "mountain of languages". Today, this relatively small area (about the size of New England) is home not only to over 100 languages, but to three distinct language families unique to the Caucasus region which have no kin elsewhere: the Northwest Caucasian family, the Northeast Caucasian family and the South Caucasian (or Kartvelian) family. These families are quite old, especially the South Caucasian and the Northeast Caucasian families (Nichols 1992: 14).

All three language families indigenous to the Caucasus are known for their complex systems of consonants (including some "exotic" consonants such as ejectives; see Section 4.2 below), complex agglutinative morphology and ergative case systems (see Section 3.2 above). These similarities led some linguists to consider those three families as branches of a larger Ibero-Caucasian macro family (this was originally proposed by a Georgian linguist, Arnold Chikobava); some other linguists – most notably a Russian historical linguist Sergei Starostin – believe that only Northwest Caucasian and Northeast Caucasian languages, are related. However, grammatical differences between the three groups of languages are considerable. For instance, even though all three groups have ergative systems of marking who did what to whom, they use very different morphological means to express such grammatical relations: Northeast Caucasian languages, such as Chechen, signal grammatical relations by case markers on nouns; Northwest Caucasian languages, such as Abkhaz, mark grammatical relations by complex agreement prefixes on verbs; and South Caucasian languages, such as Georgian, use both case markers on nouns and agreement markers on verbs. Moreover, while Northwest Caucasian languages such as Abkhaz inflect postpositions and possessed nouns, South Caucasian languages such as Georgian and Northeast Caucasian languages such as Chechen use a genitive case for possession. These differences force the more conservative historical linguists to treat the three language families of the Caucasus as unrelated.

Map 4.1. *Languages of the Caucasus.*

In addition to those three language families indigenous to the Caucasus region, other languages are spoken here that belong to other language families, not unique to the Caucasus: Indo-European (e.g. Russian in Northern Caucasus, Armenian in the Trans-Caucasian region) and Turkic languages (e.g. Karachay-Balkar and Kumyk in Northern Caucasus, Azerbaijani in the Trans-Caucasian region). As we will see in Section 4.4 below, some of these languages have been rather heavily influenced by languages indigenous to the Caucasus region.

The linguistic mosaic of the Caucasus is further complicated by the fact that there is no single lingua franca for the entire region (at least until the recent arrival of the Russians). In the north Caucasus in particular, the situation involves the so-called local bilingualism with a clear vertical pattern, described by Joanna Nichols (1992: 15) as follows:

> *residents of highland villages generally know the language of a lower village, but not vice versa; languages of lowlands regions offering markets and seasonal employment may be known by residents of several higher levels... Prior to the recent spread of Russian, the lowlands to the north and southeast of the mountains were Turkic-speaking, so that various Turkic languages served as local (vertical) lingua francas, and they are sufficiently closely related that Turkic can loosely be said to have functioned as a lingua franca of the north Caucasus; but this is an accident of the genetic closeness of the Turkic languages. Before the appearance of Turkic languages on the North Caucasian steppe, the lowlands languages that served as lingua*

*francas – some of them Iranian and some Northeast Caucasian, to judge
from the languages which now have extended vertical distributions (Ossetic,
Chechen-Ingush, Avar, Lak, Dargi) – were quite different from one another.*

In the next three sections, we will consider each of the three language families
unique to the Caucasus.

4.1   Northwest Caucasian languages

The Northwest Caucasian language family (also known as the
Abkhaz-Adyghe or the Abkhaz-Circassian family) includes such languages as
Abaza, Abkhaz, Adyghe and Kabardian. Sometimes speakers of Adyghe and
Kabardian are referred to as Circassians, and sometimes this term applies to
speakers of all four Northwest Caucasian languages. Another language classified
as a Northwest Caucasian language is Ubykh, which became extinct in the early
1990s. Today, speakers of Northwest Caucasian languages are mostly Muslims;
they live in three autonomous republics of the Russian Federation: Kabardino-
Balkaria, Karachay-Cherkessia and Adygea. Note that two of the three republics
have hyphenated names because they include not only speakers of Northwest
Caucasian languages but also speakers of unrelated Turkic languages: Balkar and
Karachay. This is a result of the Soviet policy of ethnic gerrymandering under
Stalin: placing two peoples with distinct ethnic and linguistic history together
in one administrative unit created republics that lacked a true ethnic core and
were thus more easily governed from Moscow. The Soviet ethnic policy in the
Caucasus was a continuation of the earlier conquest of the region by the Russian
empire under the Tsars, which resulted in the creation of sizable diasporic communities of Circassians in Turkey and elsewhere in the former Ottoman lands.
These communities retain their ancestral languages to differing degrees.

As mentioned above, Northwest Caucasian languages, such as Abkhaz, are
agglutinative, meaning that grammatical features are expressed through adding
prefixes and suffixes each of which expresses only one feature. In the case of
Northwest Caucasian languages, the morphological "action" is centered on the
verbs, which are marked for tense, as well as for agreement with not only subjects
(as in more familiar indo-European languages; cf. English: *The children play* but
The child plays) but with other arguments: direct objects and indirect objects. The
noun system is much simpler: for instance, Abkhaz distinguishes just two cases,
the nominative and the adverbial. In other words, grammatical relations, such as
subject, object and indirect object, are expressed on the verb and not on the nouns
themselves. Consider the following example from Abkhaz (from Hewitt 1979:
36). The verb *te* 'give' has a suffix *-yt'* expressing tense, as well as three prefixes:
ø-, which expresses agreement with the direct object *a-šq'wəi* 'the book', *lə-*,
which expresses agreement with the indirect object *a-pħwəs* 'the woman', and

y-, which expresses agreement with the subject *a-xac'a* 'the man'. The nouns themselves are not marked for case; the prefix *a-* marks them as definite (and translates as 'the' in English). Note also the Subject-Object-Verb (SOV) order, characteristic of Abkhaz and other Northwest Caucasian languages.

(4.1) a-xàc'a a-pħwəs   a-šq'wə Ø-lə-y-te-yt'
       the-man the-woman the-book it-her-he-give-TENSE
       'The man gave the book to the woman.'

Finally, another interesting property that Abkhaz is known for is the highest ratio of consonants to vowels: it has 58 consonants but only 2 vowel PHONEMES (a phoneme is a sound that is used in a given language to distinguish meaning): an open vowel /a/ and a closed vowel /ə/ (Maddieson 2008). Ubykh – now extinct – had possibly the most skewed consonant/vowel ratio of all languages: like Abkhaz, it had only two vowel phonemes but a whopping 80 consonant phonemes![1]

4.2   Northeast Caucasian languages

The Northeast Caucasian language family (also known as Nakh-Daghestanian) includes over 30 languages, spoken in the central and eastern Caucasus, the best known among them being Chechen, Ingush and Lezgin. As with speakers of Northwest Caucasian languages, speakers of Northeast Caucasian languages are mostly Muslim; however, the 4,200 speakers of Udi, who now inhabit three villages in Azerbaijan and Georgia and are remnants of a larger pre-Georgian population, are monophysite Christians. In addition to their homeland in the North Caucasus, there are sizeable diasporic communities of Chechen and Ingush people in Turkey and Jordan. They are descendants of emigrants and deportees from the Russian conquest of the Caucasus in the nineteenth century; despite the long-term diaspora, they retain the language quite well.

As is the case with most other languages families, the Northeast Caucasian language family has a complex internal structure, with some languages more closely related to each other than others; for instance, Chechen and Ingush are more closely related to each other than to any other languages in the family. The structure of the Northeast Caucasian language family according to the *Ethnologue* is shown in Figure 4.1. However, there is a substantial controversy as to the exact relationships among the Northeast Caucasian languages; for example, some linguists (Nichols 2003, Schulze 2009) combine Avar-Andic and Tsezic into one branch. Nichols also combines Lak and Dargi into one branch, and Lezgic and Khinalugh into another branch. Schulze combines Lak, Dargi, Lezgic, Khinalugh and Nakh into the same branch.

---

[1] See Campbell (1991: 10).

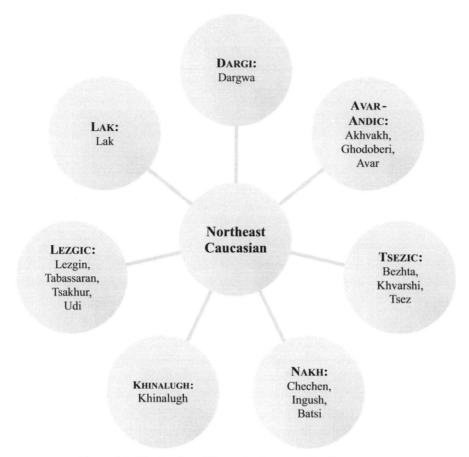

Figure 4.1. *The Northeast Caucasian language family.*

From the linguistic point of view, the Northeast Caucasian family is known for the complex sound inventories (up to 70 consonants and up to 30 vowels in some languages!), agglutinative morphology and ergative systems of expressing grammatical relations (i.e. who did what to whom). Note that these languages use case morphology on nouns to express grammatical relations, unlike Northwest Caucasian languages, which use verbal agreement morphology instead (see (4.1) and the corresponding discussion above).

Let's illustrate these properties with Chechen. Like most other languages indigenous to the Caucasus, Chechen has a large number of consonants: about 40 to 60, depending on the dialect and the analysis (compare this to 24–26 consonants in English). Included in that large inventory of consonants are the so-called EJECTIVE CONSONANTS. These are the /p, t, k, q/-like sounds with a certain "spat" quality to them.[2] Let's see what that means. Recall from

---

[2] In IPA the symbol /q/ denotes a UVULAR stop. Its articulation is similar to that of /k/, but the back of the tongue presses against the uvula rather than the soft palate (velum). The uvula is a small,

Chapter 1 that to pronounce a "plain" (i.e. non-ejective) stop sound we "close-and-release": first, close the oral articulators, which prevents the air from escaping the mouth for a short moment, and then release abruptly, which lets the air explode out of the mouth.[3] The ejective counterparts of these stop consonants are pronounced with a simultaneous closure of the GLOTTIS (that is, the space between the vocal cords in the larynx), which greatly raises air pressure in the mouth, so that when the oral articulators separate, there is a dramatic burst of air.[4] Ejective consonants are relatively rare cross-linguistically: they are found in about 15% of the world's languages and not in any widely spoken ones. Among Indo-European languages ejective consonants are found in Ossetic and some dialects of Armenian, but both of these languages most likely borrowed ejective consonants from the neighboring Caucasian languages (e.g. Georgian). Other language families that have ejective consonants include Athabaskan, Siouan and Salishan languages in North America; Quechua and Aymara (spoken in Bolivia); Amharic (spoken in Ethiopia); Hadza and Sandawe (spoken in Tanzania); Khoisan languages of southern Africa; and Itelmen (spoken in Kamchatka).

As if the distinction between "plain" and ejective stops is not enough, Chechen also distinguishes consonants by length or, more precisely, by the degree of muscular tension involved: the tense consonants are pronounced longer.

In addition to its complex consonant inventory, Chechen also has a relatively extensive inventory of vowels (up to 44, depending on the dialect and analysis). Besides the familiar front unrounded vowels (such as /i/ in *bead* or /æ/ in *bad*) and back rounded vowels (such as /u/ in *fool* or /a/ in *father*), Chechen also has front rounded vowels: /y/ as in the French *chute* 'fall' and /ø/ as in the French *peu* 'few'. Moreover, like in French, the distinction between oral and nasal vowels is used to encode meaning.

From the grammatical point of view, Chechen – like other Northeast Caucasian languages – is agglutinative and ergative. Chechen nouns belong to one of several genders or noun classes, each with a specific prefix with which the verb or an accompanying adjective agrees. However, the verb does not agree with the subject or object in person or number. Apart from the gender agreement, the only verbal morphology in Chechen encodes tense, mood and other verbal categories. In other words, grammatical relations – subject, object, indirect object – are expressed by case marking on nouns themselves rather than by verbs, in stark contrast to Northwest Caucasian languages. Chechen has eight cases – nominative, genitive, dative, ergative, instrumental, substantive, comparative and locative – and a large

---

tongue-like projection hanging down from the back edge of the middle of the soft palate. This is the organ that vibrates when you gargle your throat or attempt to say /r/ in a French manner.

[3] Which oral articulators are involved depends on whether you are trying to pronounce a [p], a [t], a [k] or a [q]: for a [p], it is the lips that are pressed tightly against each other; for a [t], the tip of the tongue is pressed tightly behind the upper teeth; and for a [k] or a [q], the back portion of the tongue is pressed against the soft palate or the uvula, respectively.

[4] By definition, all ejective sounds are voiceless. You can hear ejective sounds pronounced here: www.paulmeier.com/ipa/nonpulmonics.html.

number of postpositions to indicate the role of nouns in sentences. Consider the following illustrative example. Here, the only morphology on the verb is the prefix *d-* which encodes agreement with the direct object *aaxča* 'money'. Grammatical relations are expressed through suffixes on the nouns: the ergative suffix *-s* on the subject (this is a transitive sentence), the dative suffix *-na* on the indirect object and the zero-marker for the absolutive on the direct object.

(4.2)   Muusaa-s   šien   woʔa-na   aaxča   d-elira
          Musa-ERG   his.REFL son-DAT   money-ABS *D*-gave
          'Musa gave his son money.'

Note also the Subject-Object-Verb (SOV) order; as is typical of languages with the SOV order, adjectives and demonstratives precede the nouns they modify (as discussed in Section 3.4).

A similar pattern occurs in Lezgin (a Lezgic, Northeast Caucasian language spoken by 397,000 in southeastern Dagestan and along the west Caspian Sea coast), which too is an SOV language with grammatical relations marked through ergative–absolutive case marking on nouns (and no agreement on the verb), and with adjectives and demonstratives preceding the nouns they modify.

(4.3) a. Ada   abur   k'wal.i-z   raqur-na.
          she.ERG they.ABS house-DAT   send-AOR
          'She sent them home.'
                                          (Haspelmath 1963: 6)

     b.   i   güzel   cükw-er
          this beautiful flower-PL
          'these beautiful flowers'
          (Haspelmath 1963: 262)

Another interesting thing about case marking in Northeast Caucasian languages is the rich and yet streamlined inventory of case markers to encode location and direction of movement. But before we examine these systems in Northeast Caucasian languages, let's consider how location and direction are encoded in a more familiar language. In English, the main tool for expressing location and direction is prepositions:

(4.4) a. Mary is [**in** the house].   (location)
     b.   Mary ran [**into** the house].   (destination)
     c.   Mary ran [**out of** the house].   (source)
     d.   Mary ran [**past** the house].   (path)

In (4.4a) the bracketed prepositional phrase encodes a location that Mary is at; in (4.4b–d) the bracketed prepositional phrase encodes direction of motion. But in those three sentences the direction is encoded in different ways. In (4.4b), Mary moves by running from a place that is not in the house to a place that is inside the house; in other words, the house is the destination of Mary's running. In (4.4c), Mary runs from a place inside the house to a place outside the house, so the house is the source (or the point of origin) of Mary's running. Finally, in (4.4d) the house is neither a destination nor a source; instead, Mary runs from a place that is not at the house to a place that is at the house and then again to a place that is not at the house. Furthermore, in English there are several prepositions that encode destination depending on the relation of the Figure (in the examples above, Mary) to the Ground (in the examples above, the house). For example, if a squirrel (Figure) jumps *into the box*, it ends up **in** the box (Ground); if it jumps *onto the box*, it ends up **on** the box; and if it jumps *to the box*, it ends up **at** the box. To recap, we can break up the meaning of various location/direction prepositions into two components: the location of the Figure with respect to the Ground (e.g. 'in', 'at', 'on', 'under') and type of movement with respect to the location (e.g. 'to', 'from', 'through', or no movement, that is stationary location).[5]

Generally speaking, languages differ as to what they choose to lexicalize (that is, assign words or case markers to): which types of locations, which types of movement and which combinations of the two. For example, English has different words *on* and *over*, depending on whether the Figure is touching the Ground, but only one word *under*, regardless of whether the Figure is touching the Ground. Moreover, English lexicalizes movement that starts or ends in a particular location (e.g. *into* and *out of*), but not movement in the direction of a certain location (e.g. 'in the direction of on top of X'). Finally, while English has a dedicated preposition for certain destinations (e.g. *to*, *into*, *onto*), it does not have one for 'to under X', 'to behind X' or 'to over X'. Nor are there dedicated prepositions in English for such sources as 'from behind X' or 'from under X' or for such paths as 'past under X' or 'past behind X'.

In comparison to English, and even to the Finno-Ugric languages, Northeast Caucasian languages have a more complex yet streamlined system of markers to express both location (i.e. 'in', 'on', 'at') and direction of motion ('to', 'from' or 'past'). Let's illustrate this with Avar (an Avar-Andic language spoken by 788,000 in Western Dagestan and Azerbaijan). First of all, Avar (and other Northeast Caucasian languages) use case suffixes which attach to nouns rather than prepositions (separate words preceding the noun) to indicate location or direction. As shown in Table 4.1, Avar has 20 distinct markers of location and direction of motion, but these markers comprise 5 series of 4 markers each (the terms in parenthesis are the names of the cases). The first suffix that attaches to the noun root encodes the type of location ('on', 'in', etc.) and the second

---

[5] Recall that in Finno-Ugric languages, like in Northeast Caucasian languages, these distinctions in location and direction of movement are encoded through case marking. For example, location is rendered by the inessive case, destination – by the illative case, source – by the elative case; the relevant forms of the Hungarian *hajó* 'ship' are: *hajó-ban* in a ship', *hajó-ba* into a ship', *hajó-ból* out of a ship'. See Section 3.1 for more details.

Table 4.1. *Location and direction case markers in Avar.*

	On	At	In$_1$	Under	In$_2$
Location (locative)	-d-a (superessive)	-q (apudessive)	-t (interessive)	-L' (subessive)	-Ø (inessive)
Destination (allative)	-d-e (superlative)	-q-e (apudlative)	-t-e (interlative)	-L'-e (sublative)	-Ø-e (illative)
Source (ablative)	-da-sa (superelative)	-q-a (apudelative)	-t-a (interelative)	-L'-a (subelative)	-Ø-ssa (inelative)
Path (perlative)	-da-san (supertranslative)	-q-an (apudtranslative)	-t-an (intertranslative)	-L'-an (subtranslative)	-Ø-ssan (intranslative)

Table 4.2. *Location and direction case markers in Lezgin.*

	On	At	Behind	Under	In
Location (locative)	-l (superessive)	-v (adessive)	-qh (postessive)	-k (subessive)	-a or -e (inessive)
Destination (directive)	-l-di (superlative)	-v-di (addirective)	-qh-di (postdirective)	-k-di (subdirective)	–
Source (elative)	-l-aj (superelative)	-v-aj (adelative)	-qh-aj (postelative)	-k-aj (subelative)	-aj or -ej (inelative)

suffix encodes the type of direction ('at', 'from', 'to', etc.).[6] Thus, -de means 'onto', -qe means 'to' and -te means 'into'. However, there is no single English preposition corresponding, for instance, to the Avar -L'a (although Russian, for example, does have a preposition like that: iz-pod 'from under').

Table 4.2 shows a similarly complex system of marking location and direction of motion exists in Lezgin, which has 14 locative cases (note that one cell in Table 4.2 is empty: there is no corresponding form in Lezgin).

Note that while Avar and Lezgin lexicalize five types of location each ('on', 'in', 'at' and 'under' in both languages, with an additional 'in' in Avar and 'behind' in Lezgin), other Northeast Caucasian languages may lexicalize as many as seven types of location. For example, Tsez (also known as Dido; a Tsezic language spoken by 15,400 people in Southern Dagestan) has separate markers for the two kinds of 'in' (in substances and in receptacles), 'at', 'on', 'under', 'behind' and 'near'. Bezhta (another Tsezic language, spoken by 6,200 people in Southwestern Dagestan) has separate markers for such locations as 'on', 'under', 'inside', 'next to and touching', 'next to but not touching', 'next to but in

---

[6] The basic meaning of the two series labeled here In1 and In2 is currently described as involving the distinction 'in dense space' vs. 'in empty space'. For more detailed descriptions of the location/direction marking in Avar and similar languages, the reader is referred to Charachidzé (1981), Comrie (1999), Creissels (2008), Pantcheva (2009) and the references cited there.

ა	ბ	გ	დ	ე	ვ	ზ	ჱ	თ	ი
an	ban	gan	don	en	vin	zen	e-merve	tan	in

კ	ლ	მ	ნ	ჲ	ო	პ	ჟ	რ	ს
k'an	las	man	nar	ie	on	p'ar	zhan	rae	san

ტ	ჳ	უ	ფ	ქ	ღ	ყ	შ	ჩ	ც
t'ar	vie	un	par	kan	ghan	q'ar	shin	chin	tsan

ძ	წ	ჭ	ხ	ჴ	ჯ	ჰ	ჵ	
dzil	ts'il	ch'ar	xan	qar	jan	hae	hoe	

Figure 4.2. *The Mxedruli alphabet.*

a nonspecific position relative to' and 'in complete contact with'. Furthermore, in addition to lexicalizing such types of movement as destination (e.g. 'into'), source (e.g. 'out of') and path (e.g. 'through'), some Northeast Caucasian languages have dedicated markers for movement 'in the direction of in/on/under X' and 'in the direction from in/on/under X'. One may only wonder if the complex topography of the region where these languages are spoken has had any connection to these complex systems of marking location and direction of movement.

4.3   Kartvelian languages

The Kartvelian language family (also known as South Caucasian) comprises Georgian and its three sister languages: Svan, Laz and Mingrelian. It is believed that Svan, which is the most conservative of the Kartvelian languages, preserving many archaic characteristics, separated from the other languages in the family in the second millennium BCE, with Georgian separating from Laz and Mingrelian about a thousand years later. Today, Laz is spoken by about 30,000 people in the Asian part of Turkey, just south of the Caucasus region; the other three languages are spoken in Georgia (but the Ingilouri dialect of Georgian is spoken in the neighboring country of Azerbaijan). Mingrelian counts 500,000 speakers, Svan 15,000 speakers and Georgian nearly 4 million speakers. Most speakers of Kartvelian languages are Christian (Georgian Orthodox), but there are smaller groups of Kartvelian speakers in southern Georgia who are Muslim.

Unlike most other languages indigenous to the Caucasus, Georgian has an old writing system and a long-standing literary tradition. It uses its own alphabet, illustrated in Figure 4.2, called *mxedruli* (or *mkhedruli*), which was created after Georgia became Christianized in the fourth century CE. The word *mxedruli* literally means 'cavalry' or 'military', which highlights the civil origin of this alphabet: up until the eighteenth century, this alphabet was used only for non-religious purposes, alongside two other alphabets, *asomtavruli* and *nusxuri*. The *asomtavruli* was the oldest form of Georgian writing, used primarily for historical monumental inscriptions (the oldest uncontested example of Georgian writing using the *asomtavruli* alphabet is an inscription from 430 CE in a church in Bethlehem). The *nusxuri* alphabet first appeared in the ninth century and was used mostly for ecclesiastical works. The modern *mxedruli* alphabet contains 33 symbols each of which is used to represent a phoneme (i.e. meaningful sound of the language). Another interesting thing to note about the *mxedruli* alphabet is that it is purely unicameral, meaning that there is no distinction between lower case and upper case letters. While there are some Georgian inscriptions dating from as early as the fifth century CE, the earliest extant Georgian manuscripts survive from the seventh century, and the first Georgian book was printed in the seventeenth century. A significant body of documents survive from both the Old Georgian period (fifth–twelfth centuries) and the Medieval Georgian period (twelfth–eighteenth century); these are mostly religious documents and epics. The oldest surviving literary text in Georgian is the "Martyrdom of Saint Shushaniki, the Queen" (*Tsamebay tsmindisa Shushanikisi, dedoplisa*) by Iakob Tsurtaveli, and the best known Georgian national epic, "The Knight in the Panther's Skin" (*Vepkhistqaosani*), by Shota Rustaveli, dates from the twelfth century.

As do other Caucasian languages, Georgian has a relatively complex inventory of consonants, including ejective stops (see Section 4.2 above), featured in such words as *p'uri* 'bread', *t'alaxi* 'mud', *k'udi* 'tail', *ts'ero* 'crane' and *tʃ'ikʰa* 'cup'. Moreover, there are three uvular consonants: a voiceless uvular fricative /χ/ (the final sound in the German *Dach* 'roof'), a voiced uvular fricative /ʁ/ (the initial sound in the French *roue* 'wheel') and an ejective uvular stop /q'/ – the most "exotic" consonant sound of Georgian (at least, for an English speaker), but you would need to learn it to say *miq'varxar* 'I love you'! Other words with uvular consonants include *xari* 'bull' (pronounced [χari]), *xaribi* 'poor' (pronounced [ʁaribi]) and *q'ava* 'coffee'.

As if to compensate for "exotic" consonants, Georgian has a relatively modest vowel system, with only five vowel phonemes: /a, ɛ, i, ɔ, u/. Moreover, Georgian allows some very complex combinations of consonants (i.e., consonant clusters), especially word initially. Words with two initial consonants include **ts'q'ali** 'water', **sts'ori** 'correct', **rdze** 'milk', **tma** 'hair', **mta** 'mountain', **tsxeni** 'horse'.[7] Think also of the name of Georgia's capital **Tbilisi**, which many English

---

[7] In Georgian (and elsewhere), /ts/, /dz/ and /tʃ/ are not combinations of two sounds but rather single sounds called AFFRICATES. The articulation of an affricate combines a stop and a fricative: as with a stop sound, the articulators are closed, but the release is not abrupt, leading into a fricative stage when the air escapes through a narrow opening. While /ts/ and /dz/ are rather rare in English, /tʃ/ is very common: think about words like *church* and *chapter*. The symbol /ʃ/ in isolation indicates the voiceless palato-alveolar fricative, as in the English words **ship, nation** and **chaperone**. To articulate it, the vocal cords are spread wide letting the air escape the glottis unimpeded, while the blade of the tongue is brought behind the alveolar ridge leaving a narrow opening for the air to escape.

speakers pronounce with a vowel between the two initial consonants, making it a four-syllable "Te-bi-li-si", rather than a three-syllable word, as in the Georgian pronunciation. Georgian also allows three initial consonants, as in *tkven* 'you (plural)', *mts'vane* 'green', *tsxviri* 'nose', *t'k'bili* 'sweet', *mt'k'ivneuli* 'painful' and *tʃrdiloeti* 'north'. Even more interestingly, Georgian allows four, six or even eight (!) initial consonants, as in *mk'vleli* 'murderer', *mtsvrtneli* 'trainer' and *gvbrdgvni* 'you tear us', respectively. Imagine pronouncing those when *mtvrali* 'drunk'!

As far as morphology is concerned, Georgian – and Kartvelian languages in general, as well as other languages indigenous to the Caucasus – is an agglutinative language so that words may contain as many as eight morphemes, as in *a-g-e-ʃen-eb-in-a-t* 'you (plural) had built' (hyphens here indicate morpheme breaks). The inflectional morphemes are attached to the root not in a haphazard fashion but rather follow the template in (4.5):

(4.5)   preverb > personal prefix > character or version vowel > VERBAL ROOT > passive suffix > thematic suffix > causative suffix > imperfective suffix > nominal suffix > auxiliary verb > plural suffix

The preverb in the first position in the template encodes directionality or an arbitrary meaning (that is, a different meaning for different verbs); the version marker may be added to encode additional lexical meaning. The verbal root may be followed by a number of suffixes, including a passive marker (similar to the English *-en* in *eaten*), a thematic suffix, which can also mark passives or add an arbitrary meaning. Causative marker distinguishes causative from inchoative verbs (e.g. 'break' in the Georgian counterpart of the English 'John broke the vase' would have it, but 'break' in the Georgian counterpart of the English 'The vase broke' would not). After the causative marker may come the imperfective marker which is present in imperfective forms, present and future subjective and conditional forms. Finally, an auxiliary verb, which in Georgian is suffixed onto the lexical verb (unlike in English, where auxiliaries stand free) and plural marker conclude the verbal template in Georgian. Georgian verbs also encode agreement with both subject and object by using a complex system of prefixes and suffixes for different person and number combinations.

Unlike Northwest Caucasian languages, which too have fairly complex systems of verbal morphology, Kartvelian languages such as Georgian also have complex systems of nominal case morphology, not unlike those in Northeast Caucasian languages. Georgian nouns distinguish seven cases: nominative/absolutive, vocative, ergative, genitive, dative, instrumental and adverbial. The table below illustrates the forms of the noun *kali* 'woman', both in the singular and in the plural. Before reading on, can you figure out what is the plural marker in Georgian, corresponding to the English *-s*, as in *cats*?[8]

---

[8] **Answer:** the plural marker in Georgian is the suffix *-eb*. Note that it attaches before the case suffix. This is another example of agglutinative morphology in Georgian: number (singular vs. plural) and case are expressed by separate suffixes rather than by the same suffix (as in Russian where the suffix *-ov*, for example, expresses both plural number and genitive case).

Table 4.3. *Case forms of the noun* kali
'woman' in Georgian.

	Singular	Plural
Nominative (Absolute)	kali	kalebi
Vocative	kalo	kalebo
Ergative	kalma	kalebma
Genitive	kalis	kalebis
Dative	kalsa	kalebsa
Instrumental	kalit	kalebit
Adverbial	kalad	kalebat

As you can figure out from the names of cases in Table 4.3, Georgian case system is ergative: the subjects of intransitives are marked the same as the objects – rather than subjects – of transitives, while the subjects of transitives are marked differently.[9] For example, in (4.6) we have a transitive sentence with the verb in the aorist (past) tense: the subject is marked with the ergative case suffix -*ma*, while the object is marked with the nominative/absolutive case suffix -*i*. In (4.7), we have an intransitive sentence (the verb is still in the aorist tense), and its subject is marked with the nominative/absolutive case suffix -*i*.

(4.6)   bitʃ'-ma dzaghl-i   bagh-ʃi   damala.
         boy-ERG dog-NOM garden-DAT.in hid.AOR
         'The boy hid the dog in the garden.'

(4.7)   dzaghl-i   bagh-ʃi   daimala.
         dog-NOM garden-DAT.in hid.AOR
         'The dog hid in the garden.'

Note also that even though the case system in Georgian is ergative, the agreement system (i.e. the morphological markers of grammatical relations on the verb) work in the nominative–accusative fashion: subjects of both transitive and intransitive sentences are reflected in the verb through exactly the same affixes; the exact choice of affix depends on the person/number combination of the subject. The person/number of the object likewise must be reflected on the verb, but object agreement markers are a distinct set from the subject agreement markers. Before reading on, look at Table 4.4. Can you figure out what the prefixes *g*- and *v*- encode?[10]

To recap, Georgian uses both nominal case morphology and verbal agreement morphology to encode grammatical relations (the "who did what to whom"); the

[9] This is true only in some grammatical tenses, such as the aorist (or past) tense. In other tenses, such as the future tense, the case system is nominative–dative. Moreover, some intransitive verbs (e.g. *daatsemina* 'sneezed') appear with nominative/absolutive subjects, contrary to expectations. These are complications we will not discuss in detail here.

[10] **Answer:** the prefix *g*- encodes agreement with the second person object and the prefix *v*- encodes agreement with the first person subject.

Table 4.4. *Subject and object agreement markers in Georgian.*

	Subject		Object	
	Singular	Plural	Singular	Plural
first	v-	v- -t	m-	gv-
second	Ø/x-	Ø/x- -t	g-	g- -t
third	-a/o/s	-n	Ø-	Ø- -t

case system works in the ergative–absolutive way, while the agreement system works in the nominative–accusative way.

4.4 Indo-European languages in the Caucasus

In addition to the three language families indigenous to the Caucasus, some Indo-European and Turkic languages are also spoken in the region. While Turkic languages are discussed in more detail in Chapter 5, here we will discuss briefly three lesser known Indo-European languages spoken in the Caucasus region: Ossetic, Talysh and Tat. All three of these languages belong to the Iranian branch of the Indo-European language family: these populations are descendants of the Iranian-speaking population that was dominant in Azerbaijan before the arrival of Turkic languages to the region.

One language from the Iranian branch of the Indo-European family that is spoken in the Caucasus region is **Ossetian**, also known as Ossetic, Ossete and Osetin. There are two main hypotheses concerning the origin of Ossetians. The first hypothesis (Miller 1992) describes the Ossetians as descended from the Alani, an Iranian-speaking warrior Scythian-Sarmatian tribe. According to the second hypothesis, the Ossetians are descendants of one of the autochthonous groups from the Caucasus, which adopted an Iranian language in the early Middle Ages or possibly even earlier; according to this theory, prior to the adoption of an Iranian language, the Ossetians spoke a Caucasian language. Recent genetic studies provide evidence for the first hypothesis, especially when mtDNA is considered; Y-DNA shows more contact with other Caucasian groups (Nasidze *et al.* 2004), which may be explained by the influx of Caucasian men into the otherwise Iranian population.

Today, Ossetian is spoken by about 500,000 speakers in North Ossetia-Alania (part of the Russian Federation, where it has a co-official status alongside Russian) and by another 100,000 speakers in Georgia (more specifically in South Ossetia, where it has a co-official status alongside Russian and Georgian).[11] In both areas

---

[11] As of the time of writing, South Ossetia is recognized by Russia, Nicaragua, Venezuela and Nauru as an independent state but by the rest of the international community as part of Georgia.

Table 4.5. *Cognates in Ossetian and other Indo-European languages.*

Ossetian	Pashto	Persian	Urdu	Russian	English
mæj	myāsht	māh	māh	mes'jats	month
næwæg	nəvay	nou	nayā	novyj	new
mad	mōr	mādar	mā	mat'	mother
æxshæv	shpa	šab	rāt	noč	night
ærtæ	dre	se	tīn	tri	three
shyrx	sur	sorx	surkh	krasnyj	red

of Ossetia, the Ossetian language is used as the linguistic medium in primary schools and is taught as a subject at the middle/high school level, as well as at the college level. There are newspapers, magazines and books published in Ossetian; it is used in the media, theaters, etc.

The closest relatives of Ossetian are northeastern Iranian languages, such as Pashto and Yaghnobi; however, Ossetian has been in contact with the neighboring Caucasian languages for so long that it exhibits many features characteristic of those Caucasian languages. An Ossetian linguist Vaso Abaev (1964) writes:

> In the course of centuries-long propinquity to and intercourse with Caucasian languages, Ossetian became similar to them in some features, particularly in phonetics and lexicon. However, it retained its grammatical structure and basic lexical stock; its relationship with the Iranian family, despite considerable individual traits, does not arouse any doubt.

An example of the Caucasian influence on Ossetian phonetics is the presence of ejective stops /p', t', k', ts', tʃ'/ as in *p'a* 'kiss', *t'æpp* 'blow', *k'us* 'basin', *ts'iu* 'little bird' and *uatʃ'i* 'neck' (for an explanation of how ejective sounds are pronounced, see Section 4.2 above). Lexical borrowings from languages indigenous to the Caucasus are numerous and include words from the basic vocabulary stock such as *žač'e* 'beard' from the Kabardian *žak'e* (Abaev [1958] 1984: 285, Bielmeier 1977) and words for cultural terms like *zwar* 'cross, sanctuary' from the Georgian *ʒwari* 'cross' (Abaev [1958] 1984).

Still, when it comes to the basic lexical stock, Ossetian has more numerous cognates with other Indo-European languages, especially Iranian ones, as illustrated in Table 4.5 (items in the shaded cells are not cognates but are included for completeness).[12]

Unlike languages indigenous to the Caucasus, Ossetian shows no trace of ergativity. The grammatical relations of subject, object and indirect object are

---

[12] The apostrophe in Ossetian words indicates ejective pronunciation of the preceding stop, while in Russian words it indicates the PALATALIZATION of the preceding consonant (that is, articulation where the body of the tongue rises towards the hard palate, in addition to whatever the other articulators are doing).

reflected through cases on nouns (and partially reflected in the verbal morphology). The case system of Ossetian consists of nine cases: nominative, genitive, dative, allative, ablative, inessive, adessive, equative and comitative. While the core cases follow the nominative–absolute schema (unlike those in Caucasian languages), the relatively rich system of locative cases may well be a borrowed Caucasian trait (see Section 4.2 above). Subjects of both transitive and intransitive sentences are marked the same – nominative, which does not have an overt marker (zero-marker) in the singular, but is marked overtly in the plural. Interestingly, a direct object is marked nominative as well when it is indefinite (see (4.8) below); if definite, the direct object is marked by the genitive suffix -*y* (see (4.9) below).[13]

(4.8)   Xishtær-t-æ   læppu-jyl   nom   shæværdtoj.
        elder-PL-NOM   boy-ADESS   name-NOM   they.put
        'The elders gave a name to the boy.'

(4.9)   Mæ mad-y   ragæj   nal   fedton.
        my   mother-GEN long time   no more   I.saw
        'I haven't seen my mother for a long time.'

A similar pattern – overt case marking only for definite direct objects – is found in several other languages, such as Turkish (Turkic) and Modern Hebrew (Semitic); for a more detailed discussion of both of these languages see Chapter 5 below.

(4.10)   Turkish
    a.   indefinite object:
         ağaç gördük.
         tree saw.1PL
         'We saw **a** tree.'

    b.   definite object:
         ağac-ı   gördük.
         tree-ACC   saw-1PL
         'We saw **the** tree.'

(4.11)   Modern Hebrew
    a.   indefinite object:
         ra'inu   'ets.
         saw-1PL   tree
         'We saw **a** tree.'

    b.   definite object:
         ra'inu   **'et**   ha-'ets.
         saw-1PL   ACC   DEF-tree
         'We saw **the** tree.'

---

[13] Examples from Abaev (1964: 18, 121). The exact generalization about what is or is not marked with the genitive suffix -*y* is more complicated than described in the text above and involves not just definiteness but also animacy, noun versus pronoun and proper name versus common noun distinctions.

Table 4.6. *Talysh and Persian cognates.*

	Talysh	Persian
'cat'	piš	piši
'day'	rüž	ruz
'eye'	čâš	čašm
'food'	xerâk	xorāk
'language, tongue'	zivon	zabān
'moon'	mâng	māh
'night'	šav	šab
'woman, wife'	žēn[a]	zan
'to eat'	hardē	xordan
'to fear'	târsē	tarsidan

[a] Compare Russian *žena* 'wife', *ženščina* 'woman'.

Going back to Ossetian, note that nominal morphology is agglutinative, which is rather unusual for an Indo-European language. In particular, the case suffixes and the plural suffix -*t* are separate: the case suffixes are the same for both numbers and the number suffix is the same for all cases. Yet, verbal morphology follows the expected Indo-European fusional pattern: the same morpheme expresses tense, mood and agreement in person and number.

As in other Iranian languages, there is no grammatical gender system in Ossetian and the tense system is based on two verbs stems: present and past. Note also that the word order in Ossetian is Subject-Object-Verb (SOV), as in other Iranian languages. In this respect, Iranian and closely related Indic languages are unlike most other Indo-European languages which tend to have VO rather than OV order. Finally, as do most other SOV languages, Ossetian has postpositions rather than prepositions. To recap, Ossetian has a grammatical structure of an Iranian language, despite three millennia of sojourn in the Caucasus.

Two other Iranian languages spoken in the Caucasus are Talysh and Tat. **Talysh** belongs to the northwestern Iranian branch and is spoken by 800,000 speakers in southeastern Azerbaijan, mostly in rural areas and along the Caspian coast, with another 112,000 speakers in Iran. The affinity of Talysh to Persian (Farsi), the official language of Iran, is obvious from the Table 4.6 presenting some cognates from Talysh and Persian. In the grammar, Talysh also exhibits significant similarities with Persian.

Another linguistic group that descends from the pre-Turkic Iranian-speaking population is **Tat**. This is a southwestern Iranian language spoken by approximately 18,000 people in northeastern Azerbaijan and along the Caspian littoral; additional groups of Tat speakers live in Russia and Iran, totaling another 10,000 speakers. Most Tat speakers are Muslim, but there is a variety of Tat, called Juhuri or Judeo-Tat, spoken by the Mountain Jews of the eastern Caucasus Mountains, especially in northern Azerbaijan and southern Dagestan (most Mountain Jews have by now immigrated to Israel).[14] According to most linguistic descriptions, Muslim and Judeo-Tat are mutually intelligible; however, the speakers themselves consider those two separate languages because of the religious divide between the two groups.

The status of both Talysh and Tat is vulnerable at best. The main reasons for the worry about the future of Tat (and Talysh) have to do with high levels of bilingualism with Azeri and Russian; for example, Grjunberg and Davidova (1982: 231, translated from Russian) state that "an overwhelming majority of Tats who live in Azerbaijan consider themselves Azerbaijanis, and the Azerbaijani language, equally with Tat, as their mother tongue". As a result, the use of Talysh and Tat is severely restricted: while Talysh is taught in primary schools and used in the media, Tat is mostly limited to use at home. But most worrisome is that those languages are not passed on to children on a regular basis: without this intergenerational transmission, those languages may become extinct very soon. Still, the actual situation differs from region to region and from community to community (see Clifton *et al.* 2005, Clifton 2009).

4.5   Focus on: Field linguistics

As you read this book, I hope you are developing a sense of wonderment at the rich diversity of human languages: what sounds different languages use, what they do or do not have words for, how words are put together to express meaning – all of this differs widely across languages. But how do we linguists find out about different languages, where and by whom they are spoken and, most importantly, what they are like, linguistically speaking?

While today much knowledge about the world's languages can be gleaned from grammatical descriptions in books, scholarly journals and conference presentations, not to mention the internet, the primary method of collecting information about various languages has been, and still is, conducting fieldwork. As with many other terms in linguistics, "field linguistics" means different things for different people. But at the core of field linguistics is the research work of documenting a language in the area where it is spoken through communication with its native speakers, which can take the form of conversations, interviews, experiments or simply listening to the speech of the locals. You may wonder why it is necessary to document the world's languages at all, and why it is necessary to do so "in the field"? How is it done? Is it necessary for a field linguist to speak the language he or she studies? A full and satisfying answer to these questions requires a book of its own, and many such books have been written (see Payne 1997, Newman and Ratliff 2001, Crowley 2007, Vaux *et al.* 2007, Bowern 2008, among others).

---

[14] For a more detailed discussion of Jewish mixed languages, see Chapter 12 below.

This growing body of scholarship in field linguistics and the general resurgence of interest in doing fieldwork in recent years is due in part to the growing concern about documenting endangered languages. It has become clear that many of the world's languages will soon disappear from the face of the earth, many within the next 30–40 years. Thus, it is crucial that we describe and record as many languages as we can before they are gone forever. And in many cases language documentation of this sort becomes the first step in a language maintenance program which attempts to keep the language from disappearing in the first place.

But it is not only endangered languages that need to be documented. We know precious little about most of the world's languages, regardless of whether they are about to disappear or not. Many languages have not been described at all and many of those that have been described have been described only patchily and without regard to contemporary linguistic theories. These older grammatical descriptions, valuable as they are, often contain gaps in understanding or even outright errors, which can be corrected only through further fieldwork. Moreover, as linguistic theory develops, it develops new tools for description and analysis of – and raises new questions about – human languages, thus giving new opportunities and setting new goals for field linguists. On the other hand, linguistics as a discipline cannot grow without the continuing fieldwork because describing particular languages is a necessary prerequisite for developing an increased understanding of the general linguistic typology, without which we cannot build a better theory of language and, more generally, understand human cognition.

But even if the importance of documenting languages is clear, you may still question the necessity of doing so in the field. After all, with so much information about languages available in published form and online, why travel to a remote part of the globe to do fieldwork? One good reason is that many languages are spoken in small, contained areas; often, speakers of a language of interest are not to be found outside that area and cannot be accessed through the internet (besides, there is always the danger that those who live elsewhere or use modern communication technologies speak differently from the core group of speakers who do not). In addition, working in the field allows a researcher to work with more speakers that may be available in diaspora, which is often necessary to describe the language in enough detail. After all, field linguists work with people who have lives of their own and can dedicate only so much of their time to interactions with a linguist; events such as harvest times, weddings and funerals often interfere with linguistic fieldwork. But having access to a significant number of speakers has another benefit as well: it allows us to separate general patterns of speech common to a linguistic community from individual linguistic peculiarities of any given speaker. But while figuring out the general patterns is important, it is equally crucial to control for dialectal variation, and working in one spot (i.e. one village or town) allows researchers to do just that. Finally, working in the field naturally leads to the researcher and the speakers of the language being studied to develop a human bond, which is extremely valuable for both sides: it allows the researcher to place the language in its cultural and human context and it gives the speakers a new sense of importance of and pride in their cultural and linguistic identity.

While knowing about the language to be studied, its speakers and its social and cultural context is very helpful for a field linguist, most typically, a field linguist is not himself or herself a speaker of the language studied. Sometimes, a field linguist may know something about the language or may even speak it to some degree; other field linguists prefer to start from scratch and work with a language they do not speak and perhaps even know nothing about. In yet other cases, starting from scratch is a necessity: after all, someone must always be the first one to document any given language!

How much is known about the language to be studied beforehand also determines in part how one goes about doing fieldwork on that language. If nothing is known about the language, one has to start from identifying the sounds used in the language and figuring out their relationships and the patterns that govern their distribution. Another task early on is to compile a dictionary of the language (at least a rudimentary one). Only after the phonology (sound patterns) and some basic vocabulary have been documented can a field linguist start figuring out the rules for putting words together into meaningful phrases and sentences (morphology and syntax). But what is to be done during fieldwork and how it is to be done also depends on the scholarly goals and the framework a particular researcher adopts: typology- and description-oriented linguists ("D-linguists" in Evans and Levinson's 2010 terminology) typically attempt to create a broad grammatical description of a language, whereas theoretical linguists ("C-linguists" in Evans and Levinson's 2010 terminology) may be more interested in a particular phenomenon or set of phenomena.

Thus, fieldwork is an important component of the work of different types of linguists. And, unsurprisingly, many distinguished linguists have done fieldwork of their own. To give but a few examples, Nancy Dorian conducted fieldwork on the East Sutherland dialect of Scottish Gaelic (see Section 2.3); Shobhana Chelliah has studied Meithei, a Tibeto-Burman language spoken in northeastern India and is now working on the endangered language of Lamkang, another Tibeto-Burman language, spoken by 10,000 in Southeast Manipur, India (see Chapter 7); Richard M. W. Dixon has spent many years working with the Dyirbal people in Australia (see Chapter 9); and Daniel L. Everett has worked with the Pirahã tribe in the Amazonian rainforest of northern Brazil (see Chapter 10). Among theoretical linguists who have done significant fieldwork are: Mark C. Baker, who has worked on Mohawk (see Chapter 10), among other languages; Christopher Collins, who has done fieldwork on several Khoisan languages, including N|uu and ‡Hoan (see Chapter 6.3); Sandra Chung, who has been conducting fieldwork on various Austronesian languages, including Maori, Tongan, Samoan, Indonesian and most notably Chamorro (see Chapter 8); Jonathan Bobaljik and Susi Wurmbrand, who have traveled to Kamchatka Peninsula in the Russian Far East to work on Itel'men, a Chukotko-Kamchatkan language (see Chapter 11).

And of course the reason for discussing fieldwork in the chapter on languages of the Caucasus is that this region has served as the location for many linguistic fieldwork projects. As you know from the earlier sections of this chapter, the Caucasus region is one of the most linguistically diverse regions in the world and this is especially true of Dagestan in the Northeastern Caucasus. With the area about the size of Pennsylvania and population about one third that of Massachusetts, Dagestan is home to dozens of languages and dialects, some spoken in one village only. So it is unsurprising that Dagestan has served as a magnet to many field linguists, both in the former Soviet Union (and now in Russia) and in the West. But while most Western field linguists tend to work alone or in small teams of two-three researchers, linguists from Moscow State University established a tradition of summer linguistic expeditions, in which a group of linguists would go to a chosen locale and conduct fieldwork on a given language together as a team (some expeditions were as large as 35–37 people, with the average expedition size being 15 participants). Originally, the idea of such expeditions was conceived by a Moscow linguist Alexander Kibrik; he also continued to served as both the academic director and the expedition manager for over 25 years. The first expedition under Kibrik's guidance went out – where else? – to Dagestan in the summer of 1967. In over 40 years since, more than 600 participants – professors and students from the Department of Theoretical and Applied Linguistics at Moscow State University, as well as guest researchers from other universities worldwide – participated in more than 65 linguistic expeditions. In addition to Dagestan, where about a third of the expeditions went, Kibrik's teams also traveled to other regions in the Caucasus, where languages such as Udi, Svan, Abkhaz, Kurdish and others have been studied. Additional expeditions went to the Tuva and Altai regions in Southern Siberia, to the Kamchatka Peninsula and the Far East of Russia, to Tatarstan and Mari-El republics in the central Volga region of European Russia and to the Yamalo-Nenets Autonomous Okrug in Western Siberia. After nearly 100,000 miles on road, Kibrik's expeditions studied 63 languages from 8 language families, resulting in over 250 scholarly publications, as well as dictionaries of several of the languages and many undergraduate and graduate theses. In the Dagestan expeditions alone many languages have been studied, among them: Agul, Akhvakh, Andi, Archi, Avar, Bagvalin, Bezhta, Budukh, Chamalal, Darghi, Ghinukh, Ghodoberi, Gunzib, Khinalug, Khvarshi, Kryz, Lak, Lezgin, Rutul, Tabasaran, Tindi, Tsakhur and Tsez.

But I would like to stress not only the scholarly significance of these expeditions, conceived and conducted by Alexander Kibrik, but also their pedagogical importance. According to Sergei Tatevosov, who has participated in twenty of these expeditions and has been heading them since 1999, among the undergraduate students in the department who continue to graduate school and become professional linguists, at least 80% have at some point participated in Kibrik's expeditions and many developed their true interest in languages through these projects. The expeditions – and the continuing work of analysis and write-up based on the materials gathered in the field – serve as an excellent practical school where older, more experienced linguists train students who may have as little as two years of education in linguistics. For example, Sergei Tatevosov himself went to his first expedition as an undergraduate student, continued as a graduate student (he collected most of the data for his doctoral thesis through fieldwork in these expeditions) and now trains the next generation of undergraduate and graduate students to do the same. And as much as these expeditions are important for language documentation and education, they are not without fun: their participants get to see beautiful landscapes, meet interesting people and immerse themselves in diverse cultures.

But while the intellectual and emotional rewards of linguistic expeditions are immense, there are dangers inherent in them as well. Some are as trivial as an occasional food poisoning or a forced drinking binge (many participants of the Caucasian expeditions recall having to drink huge quantities of home-brewed alcohol since a refusal to participate in such "festivities" is taken as an offense by the hospitable Caucasian hosts). Other dangers are more disturbing: for example, the Tatevosov-led expedition to North Ossetia in August 2008 became an unwitting witness to the events of the Russo-Georgian War: the establishment of field hospitals and refugee centers, military aircraft flying overhead, etc. But such is life and linguistics would have been much poorer if it were not for the linguists who brave the dangers of fieldwork in the name of science!

5 Languages of Northern Africa, Middle East and Central Asia

In the previous chapter, we discussed languages of the Caucasus; in this chapter, we are moving to the region immediately south of the Caucasus – the Middle East – and the geo-linguistically related Near East, North Africa and Central Asia. In addition to Iranian languages from the Indo-European family, already discussed in Chapter 2, we encounter two other major language families in this region: Turkic and Semitic, each to be discussed in a separate section below.

5.1 Turkic languages

Turkic languages constitute a large language family of some 40 languages, spoken by approximately 120 million people as a native language across a vast area stretching from the Balkans in the west through the Caucasus and Central Asia and into Siberia and Western China. Recall that we have already encountered several Turkic languages in previous chapters, such as Yakut in northeastern Siberia (Chapter 1) and Karachay-Balkar, Kumyk and Azerbaijani in the Caucasus (Chapter 4).

While Turkish – the Turkic language with the greatest number of speakers, over 46 million, or about 40% of all Turkic speakers – is quite well known, many other Turkic languages, even those that count over a million speakers, are much less known. Among such large but largely unknown Turkic languages are: Chuvash with 1,640,000 speakers (spoken in the upper Volga basin), Uyghur with 8,400,000 speakers (spoken in China), Azerbaijani (or Azeri) with 6,100,000 speakers (spoken in Azerbaijan), Turkmen with 3,430,000 speakers (spoken in Turkmenistan), Kazakh with 5,290,000 speakers (spoken in Kazakhstan), Kyrgyz with 2,450,000 speakers (spoken in Kyrgyzstan) and Tatar with 5,350,000 speakers (spoken in the Tatarstan and Bashkortostan Republics of the Russian Federation).

As with other language families, the Turkic family can be broken down into branches, with languages within each branch exhibiting higher degree of similarity and mutual intelligibility.[1] For example, there is a high degree of

---

[1] It should be noted, however, that classification of Turkic languages is rather difficult, in part because the languages are very close to one another linguistically, and in part because population movements and language politics have overlaid new distinctions on old ones.

Map 5.1. *Turkic languages. Balkan Gagauz Turkish is not mapped. 1: Kumyk;*
2: Azerbaijani; 3: Karachay-Balkar; 4: Karakalpak.

mutual intelligibility between languages in the Southern Turkic (or Oghuz)
branch, such as Turkish, Azeri (or Azerbaijani), Turkmen, Kashkay, Gagauz and
Balkan Gagauz Turkish. Similarly, languages in the Western Turkic (or Kipchak)
branch, such as Karakalpak, Kazakh, Tatar, Kyrgyz, Balkar, Karaim are more
closely related to each other than to the rest of the Turkic family. The internal
structure of the Turkic family as a whole is shown in Figure 5.1.

As we would expect from languages in a family, Turkic languages exhibit
certain similarities both in their basic vocabularies and in grammars. The overall
affinity of Turkic languages, as well as the closer affinity within the Southern
Turkic branch (cf. Turkish, Azeri and Turkmen) are illustrated with the selection
of cognates in Table 5.1.

Cognates like those in Table 5.1 also allow us to see some patterns of recurrent
sound correspondences. For example, words for 'knee', 'full' and 'four' illustrate
the correspondence between word-initial /d/ in Southern Turkic (cf. Turkish,
Azeri and Turkmen) and /t/ in other branches of the Turkic family. Before reading
on, can you find one exception to this generalization?[2] Similarly, words for 'eye',

---

[2] **Answer:** the word for 'four' in Tatar has a /d/ rather than a /t/ as expected from the above
generalization.

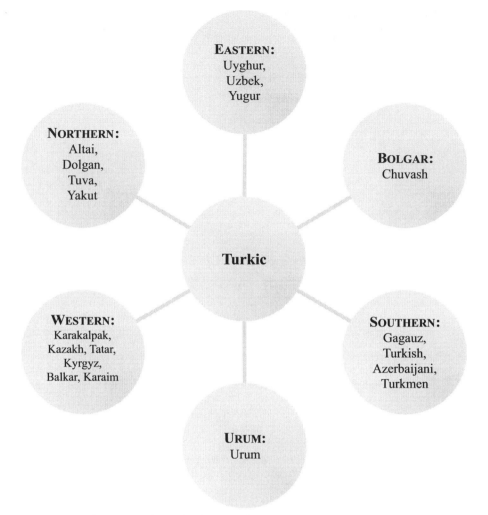

Figure 5.1. *The Turkic language family.*

'ship' and 'sky' illustrate the correspondence between word-initial /g/ in Southern Turkic and /k/ in other branches of the Turkic family. Note that the reverse is not true: not all instances of /k/ in non-Southern Turkic languages correspond to /g/ in Southern Turkic (cf. the words for 'bridge').

The affinity among Turkic languages extends beyond their vocabularies to their grammars. The following six properties are (nearly) universal within the Turkic family. First, Turkic languages exhibit **vowel harmony** (see Chapter 3).[3] For example, in Turkish, vowels within a word harmonize along two dimensions: back/front and rounded/unrounded (as in Finno-Ugric languages, the back/front

---

[3] Standard Uzbek is rare among Turkic languages in that it does not have vowel harmony (see Section 5.3 below).

Table 5.1. *Cognates in several Turkic languages.*

	Turkish	Azeri	Turkmen	Tatar	Uyghur	Yakut	Chuvash
'son'	oğul	oğul	oğul	ul, uğıl	oghul	uol	yvăl, ul
'girl'	kız	qız	gyz	qız	qiz	ky:s	hĕr
'heart'	yürek	ürək	ýürek	yöräk	yürek	süreq	čĕre
'knee'	diz	diz	dy:z	tez	tiz	tüsäχ	čĕrpuśśi
'belly'	karın	qarın	garyn	qarın	qerin	qaryn	hyrăm
'eye'	göz	göz	göz	küz	köz	kos	kuś
'fish'	balık	balıq	balyk	balıq	beliq	balyk	pulă
'bridge'	köprü	körpü	köpri	küper	kövrük	kürpe	kĕper
'ship'	gemi	gəmi	gämi	köymä	keme	–	kimĕ
'sky'	gök	göy	gök	kük	kök	küöq	kăvak/koak
'new'	yeni	yeni	yany	yaña	yengi	sana	śĕnĕ
'full'	dolu	dolu	do:ly	tulı	toluq	toloru	tulli
'four'	dört	dörd	dö:rt	dürt	tört	tüört	tăvattă

dimension is more basic). Typically, vowels in suffixes adjust to the properties of vowels in the root. Take, for example, the locative case suffix, which has two forms: *-da* and *-de*. The form is chosen depending on the vowels of the noun root: if the vowels in the root are back vowels, as in *kapı* 'door', the form *-da* is chosen (*kapıda* 'at the door'); if the vowels in the root are front vowels, as in *Türkiye* 'Turkey', the form *-de* is chosen (*Türkiyede* 'in Turkey'). High unrounded vowels in suffixes such as /i/ and /ɨ/ (high back unrounded vowel spelled in Turkish orthography as *ı*) also harmonize for rounding: if the vowels in the root are rounded, /i/ and /ɨ/ become /y/ (spelled in Turkish orthography as *ü*) and /u/, respectively. Consider the following example, where the suffix has four forms, depending on both backness and rounding of the vowels in the root:

(5.1)   Türkiye'**dir**   'it is Turkey'
          kapı**dır**   'it is the door'
          gün**dür**   'it is day'
          palto**dur**   'it is the coat'

Similarly, in Kazakh (Western Turkic) the accusative case suffix can be realized as either *-ni* or *-nı* depending on the backness of the vowels of the root: compare *kemeni* 'ship.ACC' (all front vowels) with *ajanı* 'air.ACC' (all back vowels). And in Chuvash (Bolgar) the locative suffix can be realized as either *-ta* or *-te* depending on the backness of the vowel of the root, as in *ʃupaʃkarta* 'in Cheboksary' (all back vowels), but *kilte* 'at home' (all front vowels), while in Bashkir (Western Turkic), the locative suffix can also be realized as either *-ta* or *-tæ* depending on the backness of the vowels of the root, as in *atta* 'at the horse' (all back vowels), but *ɛtte* 'at the dog' (all front vowels).[4]

---

[4] Chuvash data are from Róna-Tas (2007) and Bashkir data are from Poppe (1964).

The second property that is common to all Turkic languages is extensive **agglutinative morphology**, meaning that suffixes (each denoting one grammatical feature) can be strung one after another to create sometimes very long words. Take, for example, the Turkish word *evlerinizden*. It is composed of four morphemes: the root *ev* 'house' and three suffixes, *-ler* encoding plural number, *-iniz* 'you (plural)' and *-den* encoding ablative case (which can be translated into English as 'from'). Putting it all together, *evlerinizden* means 'from your (plural) houses'. But Turkish morphology does not stop there: other suffixes can be attached to *evlerinizden* 'from your (plural) houses'; for instance, *evlerinizdendi* means 'he/she/it was from your (plural) houses' and *evlerinizdenmiş* means 'he/she/it was (apparently/said to be) from your (plural) houses'. Thus, words in Turkish can express what in English we would render with a whole sentence, as in the following example:

(5.2)   *Avrupa-lı-laş-tır-ıl-amı-yan-lar-dan-sınız*
Europe-from-become-cause-PASS-unable-one who-PL-from-you
'You are of those who are unable to be caused to become European.'
or more colloquially: 'You are one of those we can't make a European out of.'

Similarly, the Uyghur (Eastern Turkic) word *öyingizge* 'to your house' is composed of three morphemes: the root *öy* 'house', the second person possessive suffix *-ingiz* and the dative case marker *-ge* (see Engesæth *et al.* 2009).

The third property common to all Turkic languages is the **lack of grammatical gender** distinction. Thus, unlike in Spanish, French, German or Russian, nouns and even personal pronouns do not distinguish masculine, feminine and neuter. For example, English third person singular pronouns 'he', 'she', and 'it' all correspond to a single pronoun: *o* in Turkish (Southern Turkic), *ol* in Kazakh (Western Turkic), *al* in Kyrgyz (Western Turkic), *u* in Uyghur (Eastern Turkic), *kini* in Yakut (Northern Turkic) and *un* in Chuvash (Bolgar).

The fourth property shared by Turkic languages is the **Subject-Object-Verb (SOV)** order (compare to the Subject-Verb-Object, or SVO, order in English or Spanish), as shown by the following examples from Turkish and Uyghur (Uyghur data is from Engesæth *et al.* 2009):

(5.3) a.   Turkish
Hasan pasta yedi.
Hasan cake   ate
'Hasan ate cake.'

    b.   Uyghur
Men Uyghurche oquymen.
I   Uyghur   study
'I study Uyghur.'

As is typical of languages with the SOV order (see Section 3.4 above), Turkic languages have **postpositions** rather than prepositions. For example, consider the

Turkish *benimle* 'with me' (literally, 'me with'), Kyrgyz *kol menen* 'by hand' (literally, 'hand by') or Bashkir *balahy hymak* 'like his child' (literally, 'child-his like').[5]

Finally, Turkic languages use special markers – typically, suffixes – to encode what linguists call **evidentiality**, that is the speaker's mental attitude towards what he or she asserts in speech, specifically the degree of surety in the truth of the asserted proposition. Thus, one may be sure that what one says is true because one has reliable evidence for that or because one has unquestionable faith in what one says being true. Conversely, one may be less sure either because one has only partial evidence or because one makes deductions on the basis of one's experience from previous situations. In familiar languages like English, this distinction is not necessarily expressed and when it is expressed, it is typically done by adverbs, such as *allegedly*, *probably*, *apparently* as in *John allegedly/probably/apparently robbed the bank*. But in Turkic languages this distinction may be expressed through grammatical rather than lexical means. For instance, in Turkish a suffix *-mIş* may be added to express evidentiality as in the following examples (from Aksu-Koç 2000):[6]

(5.4)   Ali Ankara-dan   ayrıl-ıyor
         Ali Ankara-ABL   leave-IPFV
         'Ali is leaving Ankara.'

(5.5)   Ali Ankara-dan   ayrıl-ıyor-**muş**
         Ali Ankara-ABL   leave-IPFV-EVID
         'Ali is evidently leaving Ankara.'

According to Aksu-Koç (2000: 17), "depending on context, the presence of *-mIş* indicates that the information is novel for the speaker's consciousness, that the assertion is based on partial evidence which is either physical or linguistic, or that it belongs totally to the realm of the imaginary". Another evidential suffix *-DIr* is used "in the absence of any physical or linguistic evidence, in evaluative statements". Similar suffixes are found in other Turkic languages: Salar (Southern Turkic branch, spoken by 60,000 people in China; see Dwyer 2000), Khalaj (Southern Turkic branch, spoken by 42,100 people in Iran; see Kıral 2000), Gagauz (Southern Turkic branch, spoken by 138,000 people in Moldova; see Menz 2000), Yakut (Northern Turkic branch, spoken by 363,000 people in the Sakha region, near the Arctic Ocean, the length of middle Lena River, Aldan and Kolyma rivers; see Buder 1989) and others.

---

[5] Kyrgyz data from Hebert and Poppe (1963) and Bashkir data from Poppe (1964).

[6] Here and below, the upper-case I indicates that the vowel may be realized as /i/, /ı/, /y/ or /u/ (or in Turkish orthography: i, ı, ü or u); see the discussion of vowel harmony in the main text above. The upper-case D indicates that the consonant may be realized as either /d/ or /t/ depending on last consonant of the stem to which the suffix is attached. IPVF is an imperfective suffix.

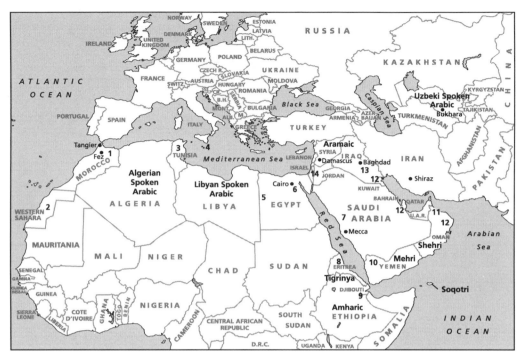

Map 5.2. *Semitic languages. 1: Moroccan Spoken Arabic; 2: Hassaniyya Spoken Arabic; 3: Tunisian Spoken Arabic; 4: Maltese; 5: Western Egyptian Bedawi Spoken Arabic; 6: Egyptian Spoken Arabic; 7: Hijazi Spoken Arabic; 8: Tigré; 9: Harari; 10: Sanaani Spoken Arabic; 11: Omani Spoken Arabic; 12: Gulf Spoken Arabic; 13: Mesopotamian Spoken Arabic; 14: Hebrew.*

5.2   Semitic languages

Semitic languages are among the best studied language families with a long history of scholarship by linguists and Bible scholars alike. The Semitic family consists of 70 languages spoken by more than 467 million people across much of the Middle East, North Africa and the Horn of Africa. Over 206 million of those who speak a Semitic language speak some form of Arabic; Amharic is spoken by over 17 million people in northwestern Ethiopia, Hebrew by nearly 5 million in Israel, and Tigrinya by over 3 million in northern Ethiopia.

Since the Middle East has been one of the cradles of writing, Semitic languages are attested in a written form from a very early date: texts in Eblaite and Akkadian written in a script adapted from Sumerian cuneiform are dated from around the middle of the third millennium BCE.[7] Other writing systems used for early Semitic languages were alphabetic in nature. Among them are the Ugaritic, Phoenician, Aramaic, Hebrew, Syriac, Arabic, South Arabian and Ge'ez

---

[7] Sumerian was, as far as we can tell, an isolate and not a Semitic language.

alphabets. Because of this wealth of written documents in Semitic languages, we know a great deal about the history and development of these languages, including several now extinct Semitic languages: Jewish Babylonian Aramaic (language of the Babylonian Talmud, extinct since the eleventh or twelfth century CE), Mlahsö (the last speaker of which died in 1998), Classical Mandaic (the liturgical language used by followers of the Mandaean religion), Syriac (which became extinct in the tenth to twelfth centuries CE, but is used as the liturgical language of Syrian Christian churches), Samaritan Aramaic (became extinct in the tenth–twelfth centuries CE), Samaritan and Ancient (or Biblical) Hebrew (the language of the Hebrew Bible).

Buried treasures

The cornucopia of written documents in various earlier Semitic languages is further supplemented by the documents written in the Hebrew script found in the so-called *genizot* (plural of *genizah*). These are depositories for worn-out books and papers stored there until they could receive a proper cemetery burial since in the Jewish tradition it is forbidden to throw away writings containing the name of God. In practice, *genizot* contained writings of both religious and secular nature (including personal letters or legal contracts opening with the customary invocation of God) and even writings in languages other than Hebrew but written in the Hebrew script: Judeo-Arabic, Judeo-Persian, Judeo-Spanish, Yiddish, Old French, Arabic, etc. (for a more detailed discussion of Jewish languages, see Chapter 12). By far the best-known *genizah*, which is famous for both its size and spectacular contents, is the Cairo Genizah, discovered in 1864 by Jacob Saphir. It contained almost 280,000 manuscript fragments dated from about 870 CE to as late as 1880. These documents allowed scholars to study social and economic history, especially for the period between 950 and 1250 CE (this is the period that most documents date from), as well as the development of Semitic languages (especially Hebrew and Arabic). Even conclusions about the development of some Indo-European languages can be drawn from an examination of how words in other languages (such as Old French) are rendered in the Hebrew script.

Today, Hebrew is an official language of Israel, yet it is quite different from Ancient (or Biblical) Hebrew. The official story is that Modern Hebrew is a revived form of Biblical Hebrew, which has been used (and is still used) as a liturgical and religious language of Judaism. However, "revived" may not be the proper word, as much as "constructed on the basis of". Some scholars go even as far as claiming that Modern Hebrew (or "Israeli", as Zuckermann forthcoming, calls it) is a descendant of Yiddish or even a Slavic language (Wexler 1990). Still, the connection between Modern Hebrew and Biblical Hebrew is strong enough to see them as related languages (Hoffman 2004).

Another important – and the most widely spoken – Semitic language is Arabic. However, it is important to understand that Arabic is not one monolithic language but rather a collection of about 40 languages, from Moroccan Spoken Arabic in the west to Omani Spoken Arabic in the east, from Uzbeki Spoken Arabic in Uzbekistan to Sanaani Spoken Arabic in Yemen. These Arabic varieties are not always mutually intelligible; thus, a speaker of Moroccan Spoken Arabic from lowlands of Morocco and a Dubai-native speaking Gulf Spoken Arabic would not be able to understand each other, at least not easily. These differences between local varieties of Arabic arose as a result of contact with languages spoken in different parts of the Arabic-speaking world prior to the arrival of the Arabs, as well as with the neighboring and colonial languages. As a result, many of these local varieties of Arabic are not mutually comprehensible at all, so the lingua franca of the Arab world is the Modern Standard Arabic, which is used in administration and education and has a written form (spoken varieties of Arabic are not typically written down although the Arabic script can be used to write them down). But Modern Standard Arabic is not a native language for anybody; rather, Arabic speakers grow up acquiring a local spoken variety from their parents. This situation, where every educated Arabic speaker is bilingual in Modern Standard Arabic and in some local spoken Arabic, is called DIGLOSSIA: the two languages coexist both in the minds of the speakers and in terms of use. Specifically, Standard Arabic is used for education, official purposes, written materials and formal speeches, while spoken varieties are used in informal situations.

Arabic is also the language of the Qur'an, but that holy book is written in Classical Arabic, which became the language of scholarship and religion with the spread of Islam. Its relation to the modern spoken varieties is similar to that of Latin to the modern Romance languages. Today, Classical Arabic – pretty much unchanged in its grammar and vocabulary since the seventh century CE – is used for religious and ceremonial purposes and is learned formally in school (like Modern Standard Arabic). Because of the influence of Islam, Classical Arabic is studied in the non-Arabic-speaking Muslim world as well.

Yet another Semitic language important from the religious point of view is Aramaic. Portions of the Bible were written in this language (and parts of the dialogue in Mel Gibson's film *The Passion of Christ* are done in Aramaic as well). Several small ethnic groups, in particular in northeast Syria, as well as in the mountains of northern Iraq, eastern Turkey and northwestern Iran, continue to speak Aramaic dialects (especially Western Neo-Aramaic, which has about 15,000 speakers). Syriac – extinct as a spoken language – continues to be the liturgical language for several Christian groups, including the Maronites, Syrian and Iraqi Christians.

On the southern rim of the Arabian Peninsula, in Arabic-dominated Yemen and Oman, a very different group of languages is spoken – Modern South Arabian languages, such as Mahri (70,600 speakers in Yemen; 50,800 in Oman; 14,400 in Kuwait), Shehri (25,000 speakers in Oman) and Soqotri (57,000 speakers in Yemen).

Table 5.2. *Cognates in Semitic languages.*

	Arabic	Hebrew	Aramaic	Geez	Mehri
'father'	ʻab-	ʼāb-	ʼab-āʼ	ʻab-	ha-yb
'heart'	lubb-	lēb(āb)	lebb-āʼ	libb	ha-wbēb
'house'	bayt-	báyit, bêt	bayt-āʼ	bet	beyt, bêt
'peace'	salām-	šālôm	šlām-āʼ	salām	səlōm
'tongue'	lisān-	lāšôn	leššān-āʼ	lissān	əwšēn
'water'	māʼ-/māy	máyim	mayy-āʼ	māy	hə-mō

Ethiopia and Eritrea is another region where many Semitic languages are spoken, including Amharic (17,400,000 speakers in Ethiopia), Tigré (1,050,000 speakers in the northern and central Eritrean lowlands and parts of eastern Sudan), Tigrinya (3,220,000 speakers in Ethiopia and 2,540,000 speakers in Eritrea). Amharic and Tigrinya are official languages of Ethiopia and Eritrea, respectively. A number of Gurage languages are spoken by populations in the semi-mountainous region of southwest Ethiopia, while Harari is restricted to the city of Harar. Ge'ez, the ancient language of the Aksumites, remains the liturgical language of Ethiopian Orthodox Church.

The structure of the Semitic language family is depicted in Figure 5.2. As with other language families the affinity of Semitic languages can be witnessed both in their vocabularies and in their grammars. Table 5.2 illustrates some cognates in Arabic and Hebrew (both belonging to the South Central branch), Aramaic (the Aramaic branch), Geez (the Ethiopian branch) and Mehri (the South Arabian branch).

There are also plenty of cognates of the "false friends" kind in Semitic languages (see "Knights, riders and false friends" box, Chapter 2). For example, the root √L-B-N means 'milk' in Arabic, but the color 'white' in Hebrew (although the Hebrew word *leben* also refers to a low-fat fermented milk product). The root √L-Ḥ-M means 'meat' in Arabic, but 'bread' in Hebrew and 'cow' in Ethiopian Semitic languages; the original meaning was most probably 'food'. The word *medina* (root: √M-D-N) has the meaning of 'metropolis' in Amharic and 'city' in Biblical Hebrew[8] and Arabic,[9] but in Modern Hebrew it means 'state' (as in the name of the State of Israel, *medinat Isra'el*).

Note that the roots in the examples above are presented as √X-Y-Z: this is because lexical roots; that is, roots of nouns, verbs and adjectives in Semitic languages, typically consist of three consonants – and no vowels! This brings us to consider the most characteristic property of Semitic grammars: their non-concatenative, or "root-and-template", morphology. But first, let's consider how

[8] At least as close to a city as you could get in Biblical times.
[9] Think of the holy city of Medina in Saudi Arabia.

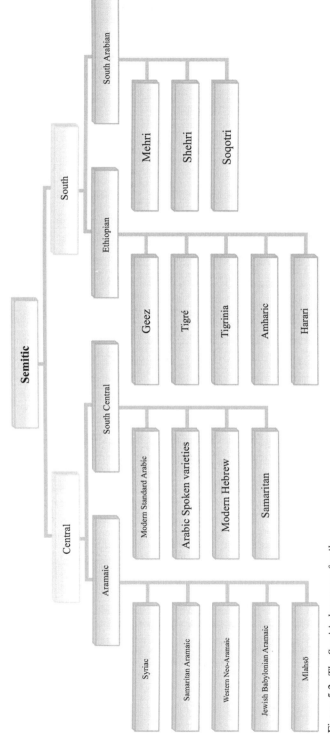

Figure 5.2. *The Semitic language family.*

grammatical meanings – for example, plural number on nouns or past tense on verbs – are expressed in more familiar languages such as English, Spanish or Russian. In such concatenative languages, morphemes are typically (but as we will see immediately below, not always) contiguous chunks of sounds, placed one after another. For example, the plural of the English word *book* is *book + s* and the past tense of *play* is *play + ed*. However, not all English nouns and verbs form plural number or past tense in this way: for instance, the plural of *man* is *men* (not **mans*), the plural of *mouse* is *mice* (not **mouses*), the past tense of *sit* is *sat* (not **sitted*) and the past tense of *run* is *ran* (not **runned*).[10] Instead of adding a suffix to a contiguous root, the vowel in the root/stem is changed. This is – technically – an example of non-concatenative morphology. Thus, you can think of the Semitic "root-and-template" morphology as the *man–men* or *sit–sat* alternation – on steroids!

However, instead of thinking of the Semitic non-concatenative morphology as a massive vowel alternation pattern, most linguists analyze it by considering only consonants as part of the noun or verb root, while vowels – and where they are placed in relation to the consonants of the root – constitute the "template". To treat the English alternations above in a similar fashion we would have to consider the root for 'man' to be $\sqrt{}$M-N, the root for 'mouse' to be $\sqrt{}$M-S, the root for 'sit' to be $\sqrt{}$S-T and the root for 'run' to be $\sqrt{}$R-N, with the vowels being part of the template indicating singular vs. plural number, or present vs. past tense. Note that the roots $\sqrt{}$M-N and $\sqrt{}$M-S would have to belong to different inflectional classes (declensions), since we do not want to have *moun–mine* for 'man–men' or *mas–mes* for 'mouse–mice'. So English has the beginnings of a non-concatenative Semitic language!

The real difference between English and Semitic languages is in the predominance of the concatenative (suffix-adding) and non-concatenative ("root-and-template") morphology: most English nouns and verbs follow the concatenative pattern, while the majority of nouns and/or verbs in a Semitic language follow the non-concatenative pattern.

Various noun or verb forms in Semitic are created from noun or verb roots (typically consisting of three consonants, although 2- and 4-consonant roots also exist) in different ways: by inserting vowels, doubling consonants, lengthening vowels and sometimes even by adding prefixes or suffixes in conjunction with the other methods. Consider what can be done with the Semitic root $\sqrt{}$K-T-B meaning 'write' in Modern Standard Arabic (see (5.6)) and Modern Hebrew (see (5.7)).[11]

---

[10] Note a different use of the asterisk symbol here: while in historical linguistics the asterisk is used to mark reconstructed forms (see Chapter 2), in synchronic linguistics the same symbol is used to mark forms that are ungrammatical (i.e. not part of the language under consideration).

[11] This root appears in Modern Hebrew in most cases as $\sqrt{}$K-T-V because of a regular phonological alternation between [b] and [v] that need not concern us here.

(5.6)   **katab**a 'he wrote' (masculine)
          katabat 'she wrote' (feminine)
          katabtu 'I wrote' (feminine and masculine)
          a**ktub** 'I write' (feminine and masculine)
          kutiba 'it was written' (masculine)
          kitāb- 'book' (the hyphen shows end of stem before various case endings)
          kutub- 'books' (plural)
          kutayyib- 'booklet' (diminutive)
          kātib- 'writer' (masculine)
          kātibat- 'writer' (feminine)
          ma**ktab**- 'desk' or 'office'
          ma**ktab**at- 'library' or 'bookshop'

(5.7)   **katav** 'he wrote'
          katva 'she wrote'
          katavti 'I wrote'
          kotev 'I, you(singular), he writes' (masculine)
          katuv 'written' (masculine)
          ktuva 'written' (feminine)
          ktuba 'ketubah (a Jewish marriage contract)' (note [b] here, not [v])
          kattav 'reporter' (masculine)
          kattevet 'reporter' (feminine)
          kattava 'article'
          ktovet 'address'
          ktav 'handwriting'

Various templates are used in Arabic and Hebrew to form nouns and verbs with a particular lexical meaning. For example, in Arabic the C1aC2C2āC3 template denotes a practitioner of an action denoted by the verbal root, as in *najjār-* 'carpenter' and *zubbāz-* 'baker', while the template *ma*C1C2aC3 denotes a noun of place, as in *madras-* 'school' and *matbax* 'kitchen'. Templates can also be used to express grammatical meaning: for example, the C1aC2āC3 template is used to form plurals, as in *ħakaam* 'judgments' from *ħukm* 'judgment' and *ʕanaab* 'grapes' from *ʕinab* 'grape' (note that the vowels of the singular are simply disregarded when plural is formed). Another example of a template with a grammatical meaning is the C1uC2ayC3 template used for diminutives: *ħukaym* is the diminutive of 'judgment' and *ʕunayb* is the diminutive of 'grape'.

Similarly, the template C1aC2eC3*et* in Hebrew denotes a name of a disease, as in *sakeret* 'diabetes' (from *sukar* 'sugar') and *tsahevet* 'jaundice' (from *tsahov* 'yellow'). One of the cutest novel words in Modern Hebrew is also formed by applying this template: from *neyar* 'paper' we get *nayeret* 'paperwork' – or 'paper-disease'!

Note that this "root-and-template" morphology can be applied to loanwords as well. For example, one of the common verbal templates in Modern Hebrew is the so-called "pi'el" template (all verbs are given here not in the infinitive but in the third person singular past tense form), typically written as C1iC2C2eC3. In other words, the vowel /i/ is inserted after the first consonant of the root, the vowel /e/ is inserted after the second consonant of the root and the second consonant is doubled. For example, the root √D-B-R in this template gives us *dibber* 'he spoke', the root √G-D-L gives us *giddel* 'he grew/raised' and the root √L-M-D – *limmed* 'he taught'. If the root happens to have four rather than three consonants, the second consonant is not doubled and the vowel /e/ is inserted after the third consonant: C1iC2C3eC4 (e.g. the root √K-R-S-M gives us *kirsem* 'he gnawed' and the root √P-R-S-M gives us *pirsem* 'he advertized'). Many loanword verbs in Modern Hebrew fit into this template: for example, *tilpen* 'he phoned' (from *telephone*), *pitrel* 'he patrolled' (from *patrol*), *tirped* 'he torpedoed' (from *torpedo*), as well as the tricky cases of *fikses* 'he faxes' (from *fax*) and *fikkes* 'he focused' (from *focus*). Before reading on, can you figure out what English word does the Hebrew verb *sindel* come from?[12]

5.3   Focus on: Language contact

In the previous sections, we discussed Turkic and Semitic languages. In this section, we will discuss one lesser known language from each of these two families: Maltese (Semitic) and Uzbek (Turkic). Unlike languages discussed so far and used to illustrate the characteristic properties shared by languages in these families, Maltese and Uzbek are less typical members of their families. The reason for this uncharacteristic nature of these two languages is the same in both cases: language contact with other neighboring languages, which in both cases happen to be from the Indo-European family. In the case of Maltese, it is Italian and to a lesser degree French; in the case of Uzbek, it is Tajik (an Iranian language).

Let's start with **Maltese**, a member of the Semitic family. In general, Malta – a small island 93 km south of Sicily – is a fascinating place from a linguistic point of view. It is the only country in Europe where a Semitic language has an official status and it also boasts one of the highest levels of multilingualism in Europe if not in the world. If the official statistics are to be believed, the Maltese language is spoken by 100% of the people in Malta. In addition, 88% of the population speak English (which serves as a co-official language of Malta), 66% speak Italian (which used to be a co-official language as well) and 17% also speak French.

Genetically speaking, the population of Malta is predominantly southern-European in origin: according to the Maltese population census, about 97% of the island's population are ethnic Maltese people (and most of the remaining

---

[12] **Answer:** *sindel* comes from the English word *sandal* and refers not to putting on a type of footwear, but to encasing the wheels of an illegally parked car into a special contraption.

3% are retired Brits). Genetic studies further indicate close ties of the Maltese people with southern Europeans and a less close connection with the peoples of the Middle East or North Africa. Apparently, whatever genetic ties may exist between the Maltese and the Middle East/North Africa go back to the time of the Phoenicians (who spoke a Semitic language too).

Yet, the Maltese language is a Semitic language, a close relative of the Arabic varieties spoken in North Africa and a descendant of Siculo-Arabic, the language of the Arab rulers of Malta in the ninth–eleventh centuries CE. However, unlike all other Semitic languages, Maltese is written using a modified form of the Roman alphabet, with certain digraphs and diacritics introduced to represent sounds of Maltese that are not found in Latin and similar languages. For example, ċ is used to represent the sound commonly rendered in English with the digraph "ch" (as in *church*) and ġ represents the sound commonly rendered in English with "j" or "dg" (as in *judge*). Furthermore, the symbol ħ represents the voiceless pharyngeal fricative. It is pronounced by creating a narrow opening between the root of the tongue (where the tongue attaches to the lower jaw) and the pharynx, the upper part of the throat. This type of sound is not found in familiar Indo-European languages, but is quite typical of the Semitic languages: Arabic, (certain dialects of) Hebrew and others.[13]

Moreover, much of the Maltese vocabulary (up to 70%, according to some estimates) has been borrowed from Italian, French and English – this makes reading the title page of the Maltese Wikipedia a breeze even for someone with no knowledge of Arabic or any other Semitic language (see Figure 5.3). Note also that some of these Romance loanwords are derived from Sicilian rather than Italian or French and thus exhibit Sicilian characteristics, such as /u/ in place of the Italian /o/, as in *teatru* 'theater' (compare with the Sicilian *tiatru* and Italian *teatro*). Before reading on, do you remember what other language we have discussed that exhibits the same characteristic?[14]

Still, Maltese retains much of its basic vocabulary and FUNCTION WORDS (articles, prepositions, pronouns, auxiliaries, conjunctions) from Arabic. Among the many words retained from Siculo-Arabic are *kapunata* (a dish of eggplants, olives, raisins, etc.), *qassata* (a savory pastry pie), *ġunġlien* 'sesame seed', *żaffran* 'saffron' and *żbib* 'raisins' – all featured prominently in Maltese cuisine, which shows strong Arabic and North African influences.

Moreover, Maltese also retains many grammatical features of a classical Semitic language, such as its heavy reliance on non-concatenative, or "root-and-template", morphology. Consider some native Maltese nouns: the plural of *tifel* 'boy' is *tfa:l* 'boys', the plural of *shahar* 'month' is *shhu:r* 'months', the plural of *felli* 'slice' is *flieli* 'slices', and the plural of *nbi:d* 'wine' is *nbeyyed* 'wines'. Interestingly, even some loanwords from Romance languages or English follow

---

[13] This sound is also found in many languages of the Caucasus, such as Abkhaz and Kabardian (Northwest Caucasian), Avar, Agul and Chechen (Northeast Caucasian).

[14] **Answer:** the Corsican language (see Section 2.4).

Werrej

Xjenzi matematiċi, fiżiċi u naturali

Astronomija · Bioloġija · Ekoloġija · Entomoloġija · Fiżika · Ġometrija · Kimika · Matematika · Statustika · Xjenza Naturali

Xjenzi soċjali, storja, ġeografija

Antropologija · Arkeoloġija· Drittijiet · Edukazzjoni · Ekonomija · Finanza · Filosofija · Ġeografija · Mużikologija · Politika · Psikoloġija · Soċjoloġija · Storja

Teknoloġija u xjenzi applikati

Agrikoltura · Arkitettura · Astronomija · Komunikazzjoni · Elettronika · Industrija · Informatika · Inġinerija · Internet · Mediċina· Teknoloġija · Transport

Reliġjon, arti, letteratura, lingwi

Reliġjon · Arti · Ċinema · Letteratura · Lingwa u Lingwistika · Mużika · Pittura · Skultura · Teatru · Żfin

Passatempi u soċjetà

Divertiment · Ġonna · Kċina · Logħob · Passatempi · Saħħa · Spettaklu · Sport · Televiżjoni · Turiżmu

Werrej

Alfabetiku · Alternattiv (Aa - Zz) · Biografiji · Kategoriji · Portali

Figure 5.3. *Wiki subjects in Maltese.*

the non-concatenative pattern: for instance, the plural of the Romance loanword *forn* 'oven' is *fra:n* 'ovens' (analogous to the plural 'boys') and the plural of the Romance loanword *vers* 'poem' is *vru:s* 'poems' (analogous to the plural 'months'). Similarly, the plural of the English loanword *kitla* 'kettle' is *ktieli* 'kettles' (analogous to the plural 'slices') and the plural of the English loanword *skuna* 'schooner' is *skejjen* 'schooners' (analogous to the plural 'wines'). Thus, not only do most native Maltese nouns follow the non-concatenative pattern but loanwords can do so too. Note that the same cannot be said of the irregular *man/men*-type alternations in English: only native Germanic words ever fit into the "irregular" (vowel-changing, rather than suffix-adding) pattern.

The same is true of verbs in Maltese: like verbs in other Semitic languages, they consist of a (typically) tri-consonantal root and a template that encodes tense and agreement with the subject. Verbs borrowed from Romance languages fit into the same templates as native Maltese verbs: for instance, *iddecidejna* 'we decided' comes from a Romance verb (compare with Spanish *decidir*, French *decider*, Italian *decidere*) plus the Maltese first person plural perfect marker *-ejna*.

Like Maltese, **Uzbek** has been heavily influenced by its Indo-European neighbors. But before we discuss Uzbek vocabulary and grammar more closely, it is important to clarify some intricacies of the ethno-linguistic situation in Uzbekistan. The ethnonym "Uzbek" today refers to a mix of three distantly related ethnic groups: Kipchak Uzbeks, who speak a Western Turkic language similar to Kazakh and Kyrgyz, Oghuz Uzbek, who live in Khwarezm, along the lower Amu Darya river and speak a Southern Turkic language, most closely related to Turkish and Turkmen, and a group previously referred to as "Sart", who live mostly in the eastern parts of Uzbekistan, especially in the Fergana Valley and speak a language classified as Eastern Turkic. The Soviets – who muddled the ethno-linguistic distinctions in various parts of their vast empire (see also Chapter 4) – decided in the mid-1920s that "Sart" was a derogatory term and replaced it with "Uzbek", thus creating an umbrella term for all Turkic-speaking peoples in the newly formed Soviet republic of Uzbekistan. However, the Standard Uzbek, which became the official language of Uzbekistan, institutionalized through educational institutions, government and the media, was derived mostly from the language of the Sart group. It has been heavily influenced by Tajik (an Iranian language) and exhibits a close affinity with Uyghur (spoken in Xinjiang Uygur Autonomous Region of China).[15]

Uzbek is the second Turkic language after Turkish both in cultural importance and number of speakers. It is spoken by 16.5 million speakers in Uzbekistan, as well as by 350,000 speakers in Kazakhstan, 317,000 speakers in Turkmenistan and 5,000 speakers in Xinjiang (China). Because language contact has been such an important factor in defining many features of Modern Uzbek, it is important to mention other ethno-linguistic groups in Uzbekistan: 934,000 speakers of Tajik

---

[15] Sometimes Standard Uzbek is also referred to as Northern Uzbek, to distinguish it from a related language, Southern Uzbek, spoken by 1,400,000 speakers in northern areas of Afghanistan.

Table 5.3. *Cognates in Uzbek and some other Turkic languages.*

	Uzbek	Uyghur	Kyrgyz	Turkmen
'eye'	ko'z	köz	köz	göz
'bridge'	ko'prik	kövrük	köpürö	köpri
'heart'	yurak	yürek	jürök	ýürek
'sun/day'	kun	kün	kün	gün
'girl'	qiz	qiz	kız	gyz
'belly'	qorin	qerin	karyn	garyn
'fish'	baliq	beliq	balık	balyk
'blood'	qon	qan	kan	ga:n
'head'	bosh	baş	bash	baş
'mother'	ona	ana	ene	ene

(an Iranian language) mostly in the oases of Samarkand and Bukhara and in the Fergana Valley in the East; 808,000 speakers of Kazakh (Western Turkic) in the north; 407,000 speakers of Karakalpak (Western Turkic) along the lower Amu Darya river, south of the Aral Sea; 150,000 speakers of Crimean Tatar (Southern Turkic) around Samarkand; and speakers of Russian, who live mostly in major urban areas, such as the capital Tashkent.[16]

As mentioned above, Standard Uzbek was created on the basis of the dialect spoken in the Fergana Valley. Curiously, in certain respects Standard Uzbek appears decidedly un-Turkic. For example, it lacks the rules of vowel harmony, characteristic of most other Turkic languages, including the dialects of other ethnic groups subsumed under the term "Uzbek", such as Kipchak Uzbek and Oghuz Uzbek. Recall from our discussion of vowel harmony in Section 5.1 that the presence of vowel harmony in a language restricts the possible qualities of vowels in a word: all vowels in a word must be either front or back. In Standard Uzbek this rule does not hold, and the *o* and *ö* of other Turkic languages are both pronounced as [o] (see the words for 'eye' and 'bridge' in Table 5.3), the *u* and *ü* – as [u] (see the words for 'heart' and 'sun/day' in Table 5.3), and *i* and *ı* – as [i] (see the words for 'girl', 'belly' and 'fish' in Table 5.3). The lack of vowel harmony results in that suffixes in Standard Uzbek typically have just one form, rather than two or even four, as in Turkic languages with vowel harmony (see Section 5.1). Moreover, in many cases where other Turkic languages have [a], Standard Uzbek has [o] (see the words for 'blood' and 'head' in Table 5.3). Finally, Standard

---

[16] Because Uzbekistan government has long tried to force Tajiks to drop their ethnic identity and to become Uzbeks, some think that the real number of Tajiks in Uzbekistan is much higher than the official statistics would have us believe. For example, the Tajikam website dedicated to Tajiks of Uzbekistan (http://tajikam.com/index.php?option=com_content&task=view&id=68&Itemid=36) states that "the real number of Tajiks living in Uzbekistan is believed to be nearly 42 percent (11–14 millions) of the population".

Uzbek stands out among other Turkic languages in its vocabulary and grammar as well, where it exhibits strong influences of Iranian languages, such as Tajik and Persian (many originally Arabic words have been borrowed into Uzbek through Persian).

But despite some non-Turkic features, Standard Uzbek exhibits many characteristics of a Turkic language. Its basic vocabulary is Turkic, as can be seen in Table 5.3. Moreover, like other Turkic languages, Standard Uzbek is an agglutinative language; also, it lacks the grammatical gender distinction. Even certain grammatical morphemes are cognate with those in other Turkic languages; for instance, the accusative case morpheme in Standard Uzbek is *-ni*, as in *kitob**ni*** 'book.ACC' (cf. the Kazakh *kemeni* 'ship.ACC'), and the locative case morpheme in Standard Uzbek is *-da*, as in *uyda* 'at the house' (cf. the Tukish *kapıda* 'at the door', Chuvash *ʃupaʃkarta* 'in Cheboksary' and Bashkir *atta* 'at the horse'). Similarly, the plural number is expressed on Uzbek nouns and verbs by the suffix *-lar*, as in *kitob* 'book' vs. *kitob**lar*** 'books' and *keldi* 'he came' vs. *keld**ilar*** 'they came'; it is cognate with the Turkish plural suffix *-lar/-ler* and the plural suffixes in many other Turkic languages.

Also like other Turkic languages, Standard Uzbek has the Subject-Object-Verb (SOV) order in sentences (see (5.8)) and uses postpositions rather than prepositions (see (5.9)):

(5.8)   Men kitob yozdim.
         I   book   wrote
         'I wrote a book.'

(5.9)   Biz non   haqida gapirdik.
         We bread about   talked
         'We talked about bread.'

To recap, while Standard Uzbek has many non-Turkic features as a result of contact with other languages, most notably Tajik, it retains the basic vocabulary and grammatical features of a Turkic language.

6   Languages of sub-Saharan Africa

According to most recent studies, sub-Saharan Africa is genetically the most diverse part of the world: the genetic diversity here is greater than in the rest of the world combined. This is not surprising given the Out-of-Africa theory, which postulates East Africa (researchers disagree as to the exact location) as the cradle of anatomically modern humans. It is highly probable that sub-Saharan Africa is also where human language first began to develop. Thus, it should come as no surprise to discover that Africa is possibly the most linguistically diverse continent on the planet.

So what languages are spoken in Africa? In Chapter 5, we discussed Semitic languages, which are considered as part of the Afro-Asiatic macro family (see Chapter 11); these languages occupy the northern part of the African continent. There are also some Indo-European languages (see Chapter 2) spoken in Africa; they have been brought to this continent by the European colonizers, with the exception of Afrikaans, which was born on the African soil as an offshoot of Dutch. One other language born on African soul and spoken in Africa – Malagasy – will be discussed in Chapter 8, where other Austronesian languages, to which it is related, are examined. In this chapter we will discuss several of the other languages found in Africa. Specifically, three language families are the subject of the following three sections. Two of these families are very large – the Niger-Congo family with 1,514 languages and the Nilo-Saharan family with 204 languages, and the third – the Khoisan family – comparatively small, with only about 30 languages.

As we shall see throughout this chapter, languages of sub-Saharan Africa share many common features, especially in their sound systems. This is not because these languages are all related but because of language contact. Among these sub-Saharan areal features are "exotic" sounds such as implosives, doubly articulated consonants, prenasalized consonants and click sounds (you will find explanations of how these sounds are pronounced in Sections 6.2 and 6.3 below). Another property that many sub-Saharan languages share is the use of tones (these are explained in Chapter 7 on East Asian languages): most languages in the Nilo-Saharan and the Khoisan families are tonal and the large majority of the Niger-Congo languages are tonal as well.

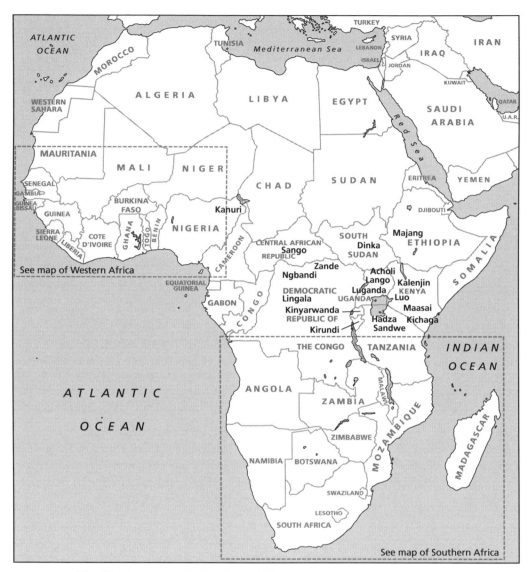

Map 6.1. *Languages of sub-Saharan Africa.*

6.1   Nilo-Saharan languages

As seen in the hyphenated name, Nilo-Saharan is primarily a family of the African interior, including the greater Nile basin and its tributaries, as well as the central Sahara desert. Roughly speaking, Nilo-Saharan languages are sandwiched between Afro-Asiatic languages (including the Semitic ones; see Sections 5.2 and 11.1) to the north and the Niger-Congo languages (see next section) to the south. There are over 200 languages in the family, spoken by over 10 million people, mostly in East Africa, in the upper reaches of the Nile,

Map 6.2. *Languages of Western Africa.*

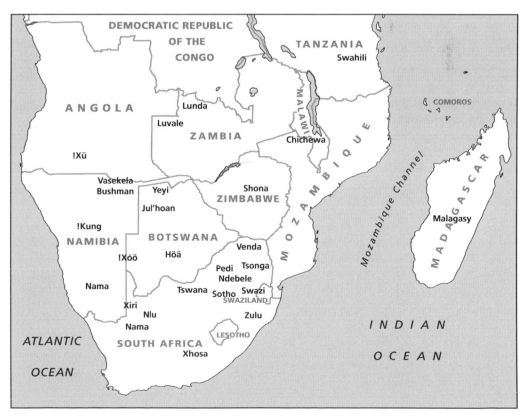

Map 6.3. *Languages of Southern Africa.*

especially in Sudan, Kenya and Uganda. At the outset, it is important to bear in mind that Nilo-Saharan is one of the lesser studied families, and there are scholars who doubt that all of the languages included in this family are really related. Disagreements also exist about the internal classification within the Nilo-Saharan family.

Although few Nilo-Saharan languages are known outside of the area where they are spoken, several of them have over a million speakers. These include Luo (an Eastern Sudanic language with over 4 million speakers in Kenya, northern Uganda and Tanzania; Luo is Kenya's third largest linguistic group); Kalenjin (1.6 million speakers in Kenya); Kanuri (about 3.5 million speakers in Nigeria, Cameroon, Chad, Niger and Sudan); Dinka (nearly 1.4 million speakers in Southern Sudan, where the Dinka constitute one of the most powerful ethnic groups); Lango (nearly 1.5 million speakers in Uganda); and a closely related language Acholi (1.2 million speakers in Uganda and Sudan).

But the best known Nilo-Saharan language is Maasai, also known as Maa, not to be confused with another language by that name spoken in Vietnam! As its name suggests, Maasai is spoken by the Maasai people, the tall warrior-herdsmen of East Africa. At present, there are 590,000 speakers of Maasai in Kenya and another 455,000 in Tanzania, and the Maasai population is reported to be increasing. Most of the Maasai speakers are semi-nomadic pastoralists raising cattle and goats, but there are also agriculturalist groups who speak Maasai.

Another relatively well-known group of Nilo-Saharan languages is the Songhai branch. Over 3 million speakers of the various Songhai languages live not in East Africa like other Nilo-Saharan speakers but in Central and West Africa, in today's Mali, Niger, Benin and Burkina Faso. The largest Songhai variety is Zarma, with 2.4 million speakers in Niger, Nigeria, Burkina Faso and Mali. Songhai languages are very important historically, as it was speakers of these languages who established the powerful Songhai Empire, with the capital Gao and the well-known city of Timbuktu. This empire existed almost until the arrival of the French colonizers: it was destroyed by the Moroccan sultan only at the end of the sixteenth century.

Generally speaking, Nilo-Saharan languages are quite diverse: some of them are tonal (see Chapter 7 for a more detailed discussion of tonal systems), but others – such as Koyraboro Senni Songhay – are not. They have complicated morphology including internal vowel alternations of the English *foot–feet* and *sing–sang–sung* type. Some Nilo-Saharan languages have grammatical gender but none have the complex noun class systems of the kind found in many Niger-Congo languages (see next section).

Another morphological property that is considered by some to be the hallmark of the Nilo-Saharan family is the singulative–collective–plurative number system: unlike in English, where the singular number is unmarked and the plural has a special morpheme associated with it (e.g. *dog* vs. *dog-s*), in a language with a singulative–collective number system, it is the grammatical number for multiple items that is the morphologically unmarked form of a noun, and the noun is specially marked with a singulative morpheme to indicate a single item. For example, Majang (an Eastern Sudanic language, 15,300 speakers in Ehtiopia) has the morphologically unmarked collective form ŋɛɛti 'lice' contrasting with the morphologically marked singulative form ŋɛɛti-*n* 'louse' (Bender 1983: 124).[1] Some languages with a collective–singulative system do mark plural number overtly, in which case that form is called the plurative.

In syntax, most Nilo-Saharan languages have SVO word order, but a few – for example, Songhai – have the SOV order, and some other Nilo-Saharan languages have VSO order, which is common in their Afro-Asiatic neighbors to the north. For example, Maasai is a VSO language. Adjectives typically follow the nouns they modify, as would be expected in VO languages (see Section 3.4).

6.2   Niger-Congo languages

By the number of languages, the Niger-Congo family is the largest language family not only in Africa but in the world as a whole. Over 1,500 languages spoken in most of sub-Saharan Africa are grouped into this family. The Niger-Congo family is typically divided into three branches: Atlantic-Congo, Kordofanian and Mande. However, this classification is not uncontroversial: some researches treat Atlantic-Congo and Mande as the same branch and, perhaps confusingly, reserve the term Niger-Congo for this branch, referring to the family as a whole as Niger-Kordofanian. The internal classification of the Atlantic-Congo branch is also uncertain, with the same languages classified alternatively as members of different sub-branches. For example, some scholars assign Igbo and Ijo to the Kwa sub-branch and others to the Benue-Congo sub-branch. Other language groupings inside the Atlantic-Congo branch include Kru, Gur, Adamawa-Ubangi and others. The largest grouping within the Benue-Congo branch is the Bantu languages; over 160 million people speak a Bantu language.

Among the individual languages in the Niger-Congo family are: **Fula** (also known as Fulfulde; the *Ethnologue* treats its varieties as separate languages), a

---

[1] Special singulative morpheme may exist in languages with otherwise familiar singular–plural number systems. For example, in Russian – like in English – the singular is typically unmarked and the plural has a special morpheme (e.g. *stol* 'table' – *stoly* 'tables'). However, a few lexical classes, for instance words for various berries, have an unmarked collective form (referring to the kind of berry in general or to some amount of berries), and the suffix -*in* functions as a singulative, making words to refer to one berry. For example:

(i) a.   Vanya jest klubnik-u.
           Vanya eats strawberry-ACC
           'Vanya is eating some strawberries.' or 'Vanya eats strawberries (in general).'

    b.   Vanya jest klubnič-in-u.
           Vanya eats strawberry-SGL-ACC
           'Vanya is eating a single strawberry.'

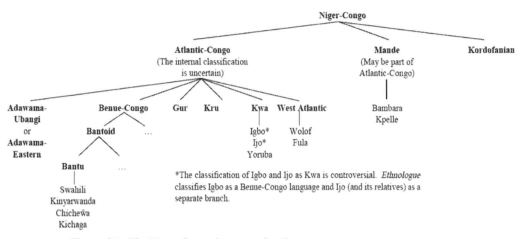

Figure 6.1. *The Niger-Congo language family.*

Fulani-Wolof (or West Atlantic) language spoken by nearly 20 million pastoralists in Niger, Nigeria, Cameroon, Benin and neighboring countries; **Wolof**, another Fulani-Wolof (aka West Atlantic) language spoken by nearly 4 million people in Senegal and Mauritania; **Yoruba**, a language alternatively classified either as Kwa or as Benue-Congo, spoken by 18,900,000 in Nigeria and another 465,000 in Benin; **Igbo**, another Benue-Congo language spoken by 18 million in Nigeria; **Éwé**, a Kwa language spoken by 2,250,000 in Ghana and another 862,000 in Togo; **Akan**, another Kwa language spoken by over 8 million people in Ghana. The Bantu grouping includes such languages as **Swahili**, spoken by nearly 690,000 people in Tanzania, Kenya and neighboring countries (it also serves as the lingua franca for much of East Africa); **Kinyarwanda**, spoken by 7.5 million people in Rwanda, DRC and Uganda; **Chichewa** (also known as Nyanja), spoken by nearly 8.5 million in Malawi, Mozambique, Zambia and Zimbabwe; **Kichaga** (again, the *Ethnologue* treats it as a number of distinct languages), spoken by some 1.2 million people in Tanzania; **Zulu**, spoken by nearly 10 million people in South Africa and neighboring countries; and **Xhosa**, spoken by nearly 8 million people in South Africa and Lesotho. The Mande branch includes **Bambara**, spoken by 2.7 million people in Mali, and **Kpelle**, spoken by 487,000 in Liberia. These groupings and languages are schematized in Figure 6.1.

Overall, there is a great deal of diversity among languages in the Niger-Congo family. As with Nilo-Saharan languages, many but not all Niger-Congo languages are tonal (see Chapter 7). For example, while most Bantu languages are tonal, Swahili – perhaps the best-known Bantu language – is not.

Another interesting property of sound systems in Niger-Congo languages is their large inventories of consonants, including some "exotic" sounds, such as doubly articulated stops, prenasalized consonants, implosives and even clicks.

DOUBLY ARTICULATED STOPS are pronounced by creating a closure simultaneously at the velum and the lips. For example, the names of the languages Kpelle and Igbo contain such doubly articulated stops /k͡p/ (a voiceless oral doubly articulated stop) and /g͡b/ (a voiced oral doubly articulated stop). Some languages have doubly articulated nasals in addition to doubly articulated oral stops.

PRENASALIZED CONSONANTS are sequences of a nasal and an obstruent (most commonly a stop) that behave like single consonants, as far as phonological rules of the language are concerned. Such consonants are relatively uncommon in languages of the world: in addition to African languages, prenasalized consonants are also found in the Southern Min and Loloish grouping in the Sino-Tibetan language family (see Chapter 7), in Indic languages such as Sinhalese and Maldivian (recall from Chapter 2 that Indic languages are a grouping within the Indo-European language family) and in Fijian (an Austronesian language; see Chapter 8). But it is in sub-Saharan Africa where prenasalized consonants are particularly common, especially in Bantu languages: for example, the /ⁿt/ in the middle of *Bantu* and /ᵐb/ in the beginning of *Mbuti*, the name of pygmy groups in the Congo region who speak a Bantu language. Other familiar instances of prenasalized stops include the name of Si**mb**a from Disney's *The Lion King* (*simba* is the Swahili word for 'lion'), the name of Ghana's politician Kwame **Nk**rumah and the capital of Chad, **N'Dj**amena.[2]

IMPLOSIVES are sounds that are pronounced by inhaling rather than exhaling the air. For example, Swahili has four implosive consonants: bilabial implosive /ɓ/, alveolar implosive /ɗ/, palatal implosive /ʄ/ and velar implosive /ɠ/. Finally, some Niger-Congo languages, especially the Bantu languages spoken in South Africa, have click sounds which they probably acquired through diffusion from the neighboring Khoisan languages (see next section).

Morphologically, Niger-Congo languages are agglutinative. Unlike many other agglutinative languages we have encountered in previous chapters (e.g. Finno-Ugric languages in Section 3.1, Dravidian languages in Section 3.3 and Turkic languages in Section 5.1), Niger-Congo languages use both suffixes and prefixes. In fact, Swahili uses mostly prefixes rather than suffixes. For example, both tense and agreement – and Swahili verbs must agree with both the subject and the object – are expressed by prefixes. In (6.1a), the prefix *u-* encodes agreement with a second person singular subject and the prefix *ni-* with a first person singular object. In (6.1b), the prefix *ni-* encodes agreement with a first person singular subject and the prefix *wa-* with a third person plural object. Note that unless emphasized, personal pronouns are usually omitted because the information is recoverable from the agreement prefixes; hence, there is no subject or object pronouns in these sentences.

---

[2] African prenasalized stops are often written with apostrophes in Latin script transcription although this may sometimes indicate syllabic nasals instead.

(6.1) a.   u-   ta-   ni-   busu
            2SG.SBJ- FUT-   1SG.OBJ- see
            'You (singular) will kiss me.'

      b.   ni-   li-   wa-   busu
            1SG.SBJ- PST-   3PL.OBJ- kiss
            'I kissed them.'

There is also a tense prefix in each of these examples – the prefix *ta-* in
(6.1a) and the prefix *li-* in (6.1b) – which encode the future tense and the past
tense, respectively. Other tense prefixes in Swahili include *na-* for the so-called
definite tense (which typically translates into English as the present progressive),
a- for gnomic tense (expressing indefinite time), *me-* for perfect tense and *hu-*
for habitual tense.[3] Negation too is expressed in Swahili through a prefix *h-*and a
change of the past tense prefix *li-* into the negative past tense prefix *ku-*, as shown
in the examples below (from Childs 2003: 104).

(6.2) a.   Juma a-li-m-pikia   Ahmed ugali.
            Juma 3SG.SBJ-PST-3SG.OBJ-cook Ahmed porridge
            'Juma cooked Ahmed some porridge.'

      b.   Juma h-a-ku-m-pikia   Ahmed ugali.
            Juma NEG3SG.SBJ-PST.NEG-3SG.OBJ-cook Ahmed porridge
            'Juma did not cook Ahmed some porridge.'

It is not unusual to find some doubly marked negation in languages of the world,
both in Africa and elsewhere. For example, in Zande (an Adamawa-Ubangi language spoken by 730,000 people in Democratic Republic of the Congo) negation
is marked by a sentence-final *té* and a verbal suffix *-ngà(à)*, as in the following
example from Boyd (1995: 188):

(6.3)   ānī ā-bātī-ngāà   yò   té
         we TMA-shelter-NEG there NEG
         'We will not manage to shelter ourselves over there.'

Similarly, in Moroccan Spoken Arabic negation is expressed by the two-part
marker *ma-...-ʃi* which surrounds the entire verbal composite including direct
and indirect object pronouns:

(6.4) a.   kteb   'he wrote'
            ma-kteb-ʃi   'he didn't write'
            ma-kteb-hom-li-ʃi   'he didn't write them to me'

      b.   ka-y-kteb   'he writes'
            ma-ka-y-kteb-ʃi   'he doesn't write'
            ma-ka-y-kteb-hom-li-ʃi 'he doesn't write them to me'

Note that the *ma-* part of negation comes from the Classical Arabic negative
marker *ma*, while *-ʃi* is a development of Classical Arabic *ʃayʔ* 'thing'. Thus,

---

[3] The prefix *hu-* does not co-occur with subject agreement prefixes.

the development of the negation marker *ma-. . . -ʃi* in Moroccan Spoken Arabic is similar to the development of the French negation marker *ne . . . pas*: *ne* comes from Latin *non* 'not' and *pas* comes from Latin *passus* 'step'.[4] In Moroccan Arabic, negative pronouns such as *walu* 'nothing' or *hta wahed* 'nobody' could be added to the sentence, in which case the suffix *-ʃi* would be omitted; similarly, in French *rien* 'nothing', *personne* 'nobody' or *jamais* 'never' can be used instead of *pas* 'not'.

But let's now return to the morphology of Niger-Congo languages, the most distinguishing and "exotic" feature of which is NOUN CLASSES. Noun classes are similar to gender in familiar Indo-European languages, but unlike gender systems, which typically have two genders (e.g. in French and Swedish) or three genders (e.g. in Russian and German), noun class systems range anywhere from 4 to over a dozen classes. Smaller noun class systems with 4–5 classes are found in Northeast Caucasian languages of Dagestan and in Australian aboriginal languages (see Sections 4.2 and 9.2, 9.3, respectively). But Bantu languages are known for especially rich systems of noun classes: for example, Luganda (over 4 million speakers in Uganda) has 17 noun classes, Sesotho (6 million speakers in South Africa and Lesotho) has 18 noun classes and Shona (11 million speakers in Zimbabwe, Botswana and Zambia) has 20 noun classes. But the most noun classes are found in Fula, in some dialects of which linguists count up to 26 noun classes!

But let us illustrate how noun classes work with Swahili, which has 12 noun classes.[5] Each noun in Swahili appears with a prefix which indicates its noun class. For example, nouns belonging to class 7 in Swahili appears with the prefix *ki-*; in the plural these nouns (now considered class 8) have the prefix *vi-*. Thus, the singular 'knife' is *ki-su* and the plural 'knives' is *vi-su*. This sort of prefix alternation applies to loanwords as well: for instance, the singular of 'book' in Swahili is *ki-tabu*. It is a loanword from Arabic (see Section 5.2) but reinterpreted as prefix *ki-* plus stem *tabu* instead of the Arabic root √K-T-B plus vowel template that gives the meaning 'book'. The plural of *kitabu* in Swahili is – you guessed it – *vitabu*.

As in familiar Indo-European languages, adjectives, demonstratives, numerals and verbs must agree with the noun in noun class. In some noun classes the agreeing words appear with the same prefix as the noun. Here and below numbers in the gloss indicate the noun class prefix.

[4] Originally, *pas* would have been used to emphasize negation with motion verbs, as in 'I didn't walk a step', and then was generalized to other verbs.

[5] Noun classes are usually numbered, with odd-numbered classes being singular and even-numbered classes being plural. For the sake of convenience in comparative work, related forms are given the same label in different languages. But as a result of this numbering convention, particular languages may have gaps. For example, Swahili has no classes 12, 13 or 14 but has a class 15. Hence, some sources say that Swahili has 15 noun classes, not taking into account the missing classes.

(6.5)   ki-kapu   ki-kubwa   ki-moja   ki-lianguka.
          7-basket 7-large   7-one   7-fell
          'One large basket fell.'

However, for other noun classes the agreeing words may have different prefixes, as with noun class 1 in Swahili, which has the prefix *m-* for nouns and numerals, but prefix *a-* for verbs. Note also that some noun classes may have the same sounding (i.e. homophonous) prefixes; for example, (singular) noun classes 1 and 3 in Swahili have the prefix *m-*, as in (6.6a, b), and differ in the verbal prefixes (*a-* vs. *u-*) only. Finally, a certain noun class may have a zero-morpheme marking it, as with noun class 5 (it is marked by the prefix *li-* on the verb; see (6.6c)).

(6.6) a.   m-toto   m-moja   a-meanguka.
             1-child 1-one   1-fell
             'One child fell.'

      b.   m-ti   m-moja   u-meanguka.
             3-tree 3-one   3-fell
             'This one tree fell.'

      c.   Ø-chungwa   Ø-moja   li-meanguka.
             5-orange   5-one   5-fell
             'One orange fell.'

The plural is not marked by a unique morpheme for all nouns; instead each class for singular nouns corresponds to a different class for plural forms. For instance, as mentioned above, singular nouns of class 7 correspond to plural nouns of class 8 (with prefixes *ki-* and *vi-*, respectively). In a similar vein, singular nouns of classes 1 and 3 (recall that these nouns have the same prefix *m-*) correspond to plural nouns of classes 2 and 4, with prefixes *wa-* and *mi-*, respectively.

(6.7) a.   classes 1/2:
             m-tu 'person' *wa-tu* 'persons'

      b.   classes 3/4:
             m-ti 'tree' *mi-ti* 'trees'

Note that two different classes for singular may correspond to the same class in the plural; for instance, singular classes 9 and 11 both correspond to the plural class 10 in Swahili and a number of other Bantu languages. The different noun classes in Swahili are summarized in Table 6.1.[6]

---

[6] There are some exceptions to this system where a noun from a particular singular class has a plural form from an unexpected plural class. For example, the word *rafiki* 'friend' belongs to class 9, but its plural form *marafiki* 'friends' is of class 6, even if most nouns of class 9 have the plural of class 10. It is because of such exceptions that noun classes are often referred to by combining their singular and plural forms; e.g. *rafiki* would be classified as "9/6", indicating that it takes class 9 in the singular and class 6 in the plural.

Table 6.1. *Noun classes in Swahili.*

Class	Semantics of nouns in the class	Singular prefix	Example	Plural prefix	Example	Verbal agreement (SG/PL)
1/2	persons	m-	*mtu* 'person'	wa-	*watu* 'persons'	a-/wa-
3/4	plants, (some) body parts	m-	*mti* 'tree'	mi-	*miti* 'trees'	u-/i-
5/6	fruit, uncountables, everyday objects, augmentatives, etc.	Ø- or ji-	*tunda* 'fruit'	ma-	*matunda* 'fruits'	li-/ya-
7/8	man-made objects, (some) body parts, languages, diminutives, etc.	ki-	*kisu* 'knife'	vi-	*visu* 'knives'	ki-/vi-
9/10	abstract and concrete things, animals, natural elements, etc.	Ø- or n-	*nguo* 'cloth'	Ø or n-	*nguo* 'cloth'	i-/zi-
11/10	[no clear semantics]	u- or w-	*uso* 'face'	Ø or n-	*nyuso* 'faces'	u-/zi-
15	abstract concepts, nouns derived from verbs	u-	*utoto* 'childhood'			

Like Indo-European gender systems, Bantu noun class systems are loosely based on semantic concepts which vary from language to language: there may be separate classes for people, animals, long flexible objects (such sticks, ropes, hair and certain fruit), man-made objects, liquids, etc. For example, in Swahili augmentative nouns (i.e. those denoting large objects) belong to class 5/6 (e.g. *Ø-joka* 'giant snake'); diminutive nouns (i.e. those denoting small/cute objects) belong to class 7/8 (e.g. *ki-toto* 'baby', *ki-joka* 'tiny snake'). The class 7/8 is also where one finds non-prototypical human beings. People with disabilities belong to the class 7/8: *ki-pofu* 'blind person', *ki-ziwi* 'deaf person' and *ki-wete* 'lame person', as well as *ki-twana* 'slave' (Childs 2003: 103).

However, the association between meaning and noun class is fairly loose: not all nouns in a given noun class will have the meaning associated with other nouns in the class. For instance, not all nouns in class 7/8 are diminutives (see (6.5) above); nouns denoting man-made objects typically belong to this class as well. Curiously perhaps, names of languages too belong to class 7 – is it because languages are "man-made" or because they are "cute", I wonder? In the case of such language names as *ki-Swahili* 'Swahili' (from the Arabic word *sawahil* 'coasts'), *Kirundi* (literally, 'the language of Rundi'), *Kinyarwanda* (literally, 'the language of Rwanda') – the English tradition is to write most of them with

Ki, but not in the case of *Swahili* and a few others, which do not have *ki-* as part of their English names.

Interestingly, the same stem can appear with prefixes for different noun classes and the meaning of the noun changes correspondingly. Thus, the stem *-ti* meaning 'tree, wood' may appear with the prefix *m-* for class 3 (for plants), in which case it means 'a (living) tree', or with the prefix *ki-* for class 7 (for man-made objects), in which case it means 'a (wooden) chair'. Similarly, the stem *-toto* may appear with the prefix *m-* for class 1 (for persons) meaning 'child', with the prefix *ki-* for class 7 (for diminutives) meaning 'baby' or with the prefix *u-* for class 14 (for abstract concepts) meaning 'childhood'.

Furthermore, different languages may distribute nouns into classes in different ways. For example, Lunda (a Bantu language, spoken by 628,000 people in Zambia and Angola) assigns all animates to gender 1/2, while a closely related language Luvale (also a Bantu language in Zambia and Angola, spoken by 632,000 people) has only a few non-human animates in this gender (see Corbett 1991: 98). One such non-human animate that is assigned to class 1/2 in Luvale is *muumbe* 'jackal'; it has been suggested that jackal is treated in this way because a personified jackal often appears in folk tales.

Overall, the meanings of noun classes appear to be deeply grounded in the cultural practices and mythology of the people: "only with that knowledge can one understand how cows, fire and the sun all belong to the same noun class" (Childs 2003: 103). This is not unlike the noun class systems of Australian languages such as Dyirbal, discussed in more detail in Section 9.4.

Amazingly, alongside Bantu and Fulani-Wolof languages with those incredibly rich and complex systems of noun classes we find other Niger-Congo languages that not only lack noun class systems but have isolating morphology more typical of the languages of eastern Asia (see Chapter 7 for details). This is true of Éwé and Akan (both Kwa languages), Kpelle (a Mande language) and Yoruba (which is classified alternatively as Kwa or as Benue-Congo). Speakers of Kwa languages inhabit the coast of Gulf of Guinea from Ghana to Nigeria, while speakers of Mande languages live in Guinea, Mali and neighboring countries.

Consider, for example, Yoruba: there is no noun classes or genders; the only remainder of the Proto-Niger-Congo noun class system is the distinction between human and non-human nouns, and this distinction is only apparent in the interrogatives, where human nouns are replaced by *tani* 'who?' and non-human nouns by *kini* 'what?'. In the verbal domain, tense and aspect are marked in Yoruba not by verbal prefixes, as in Swahili, but by preverbal particles such as *yio* for the future tense (e.g. *Emi yio wè* 'I will wash') and *ti* for past tense (e.g. *O ti lo* 'He has gone'). Negation is likewise expressed by a preverbal particle *kò*. Location and direction of movement are expressed through prepositions, such as *ní* 'on, at, in' and *sí* 'onto, towards'.

Another peculiar feature of many Niger-Congo languages, including Yoruba and Èdó, is the so-called SERIAL VERB CONSTRUCTIONS where a series of verbs – with no conjunctions! – performs a function comparable to what in English would be accomplished by either a single verb (as in (6.8a) below), a verb and a preposition (as in (6.8b)), several conjoined verb phrases (as in (6.9a, b)) or even by a resultative construction (as in (6.9c)). The closest approximation of a serial verb construction in English is sequences in which the verbs *come* and *go* are used to express aspectual notions, as in ***Come talk*** *to me* or *Whenever I have* ***time, I go watch*** *a movie*. Serial verb constructions in Niger-Congo languages may have similar aspectual meanings, or can have a number of other meanings, such as a sequential meaning as in (6.8a) and (6.9a, b), or a resultative meaning, as in (6.8b) and (6.9c).[7]

(6.8)   Yoruba

    a.   o **mu** iwe **wa**.
        he took book came
        'He brought the book.'

    b.   fémi **tì** akin **subú**.
        Femi push Akin fall
        'Femi pushed Akin down.'

Note that the two verbs in a serial verb construction share not only the same subject, but also the same tense marker, as in the following example from Èdó. In some cases, the two verbs even share a direct object, such as *èwé* 'goat' in (6.9b).

(6.9)   Èdó

    a.   Òzó ghá **gbè** èwé **khièn** ùhùnmwùn érèn.
        Ozo FUT hit goat sell   head   its
        'Ozo will kill the goat and sell its head.'

    b.   Òzó ghá **gbè** èwé **khièn**.
        Ozo FUT hit goat sell
        'Ozo will kill the goat and sell it.'

    c.   Òzó ghá **gbè** èwé **wù**.
        Ozo FUT hit goat die
        'Ozo will strike the goat dead.'

6.3   Khoisan languages

      The third language family found in sub-Saharan Africa is the Khoisan family. With the exception of two languages – Hadza and Sandawe – whose speakers live in Tanzania, the rest of the Khoisan languages are limited to the Kalahari desert in the southwestern part of the African continent. One finds Khoisan languages in Botswana, South Africa, Namibia and Angola, spoken alongside Bantu languages. There are some 30 languages in the Khoisan family, but the family's internal classification is contested and some scholars do not even agree that all languages classified as Khoisan are indeed related. Overall, about 100,000 people speak a Khoisan language. Some of the Khoisan languages are

---

[7] Yoruba example in (6.8a) is from Foley and Olson (1982); example in (6.8b) is from Lord (1974: 197–201). Èdó examples in (6.9) are from Baker and Stewart (1999).

robust: Nama has 250,000 speakers in Namibia, Botswana and South Africa; Ju|'hoan has 33,600 speakers in Namibia and Botswana; and Vasekela Bushman has 61,300 speakers in the West Caprivi area of Namibia. But the majority of Khoisan languages are either endangered (e.g. Xiri with 87 speakers and N|u with 12 speakers) or extinct (e.g. Kwadi, Korana, Seroa, |Xam and ||Xegwi). Khoisan speakers are typically quite distinct from the Bantu and other Africans both in their physical appearance (they have lighter, yellowish skin and narrow, slanted eyes and tend to be very short in stature) and in their culture (they are among the few remaining hunter-gatherers).

The reason for the limited distribution of Khoisan speakers is the Bantu expansion. Starting around 3,000–2,500 BCE Bantu groups started spreading within West Africa, and from about 1,500–1,000 BCE they migrated over several millennia from their homeland in what is today's Cameroon and Nigeria in the eastwardly and southwardly directions, displacing and assimilating Khoisan-speaking groups. Bantu speakers developed new techniques for agriculture and metalworking, which allowed them to colonize new areas with widely varying ecologies in greater densities than hunting and foraging permitted. But their true trump card was their ability to adopt and adapt: for instance, they adopted livestock husbandry from other peoples they encountered.

Between the thirteenth and fifteenth centuries CE, the relatively powerful Bantu-speaking states on a scale larger than local chiefdoms began to emerge in the Great Lakes region, in the savannah south of the Central African rainforest, and on the Zambezi river where the Monomatapa kings built the famous Great Zimbabwe complex. Such processes of state-formation occurred with increasing frequency from the sixteenth century onward. These states were supported by the increased trade among African communities and with European, Swahili and Arab traders on the coasts, and in turn the Bantu states promoted the expansion of Bantu languages and their adoption by non-Bantu groups. Even the pigmies of Equatorial Africa, so different from other inhabitants of the continent in their physical appearance and in their lifestyle, did not maintain their original language(s), but switched to Bantu languages.

Two Khoisan languages – Hadza and Sandawe – require a special mention. Unlike the other Khoisan languages, these are spoken in Tanzania. Hadza has about 800 speakers and Sandawe is more robust with about 40,000 speakers. So Hadza and Sandawe present an interesting puzzle to linguists, as well as population geneticists. In theory, two explanations are possible for the geographic discontinuity between Hadza and Sandawe and other Khoisan speakers. First, it is possible that Hadza and Sandawe speakers are originally Bantu, but switched to Khoisan languages. An alternative explanation is that the small pockets of Hadza and Sandawe are remainders of the earlier Khoisan population in East Africa, now surrounded by Bantu speakers as a result of Bantu expansion. Earlier genetic studies seemed to support the first theory since the Hadza were shown to be genetically closer to the Pygmies of Central Africa and Sandawe – somewhat closer to the Bantu than to Khoisan speakers. Curiously, according to these studies

Table 6.2. *Symbols for click sounds in Khoisan.*

Bilabial	Dental	Alveolar	Palatal	Lateral
⊙	|	!	ǂ	‖

the Sandawe are not genetically related to the Hadza, despite their proximity and the similarity between their languages.

However, this theory leaves it unclear why these two groups – Hadza and Sandawe – would switch to a Khoisan language if the closest Khoisan speakers are thousands of miles to the south. At present, more scholars are leaning towards the alternative theory according to which Hadza and Sandawe are originally Khoisan and maintained their language but their genes have changed over the centuries. How could this have happened? Hadza and Sandawe populations are relatively small, and there has been a great deal of intermarriage with Bantu groups, which resulted in washing out their peculiar Khoisan genetic pool. However, being hunter-gatherers, Hadza and Sandawe were separated from Bantu farmers by socio-economic factors, so they managed to preserve their language but not to prevent genetic exchange. Moreover, a recent study (Henn *et al.* 2011) found a genetic link between the Hadza and Sandawe and Khoisan speakers of Southern Africa, which is to be expected if Hadza and Sandawe are indeed remnants of the previously more widely spread Khoisan population.

Khoisan languages have large and rich inventories of sounds, especially of consonants. But the sounds for which they are particularly famous are the so-called CLICK SOUNDS. These sounds have been touted as "exotic" in the popular press, so few people realize that we are not as unfamiliar with them as it might seem. For example, we make the dental click *tsk-tsk* (alternatively written as *tut-tut*) as a sign of disapproval or pity, the lateral click *tchick!* – to spur on a horse and the alveolar click *clip-clop!* – to imitate a horse trotting. And not to forget the bilabial click which we do not really consider a sound at all, but rather a gesture for an air-kiss (except that for the bilabial click the lips are closed flat as for /p/ or /m/ rather than rounded as for /w/).

Technically, clicks are consonants pronounced with two closures (points of contact) in the mouth, one forward and one at the back. The pocket of air enclosed between the two points of contact is rarefied (i.e. the air pressure is decreased) by a sucking action of the tongue. The forward closure is then released, so that the air rushes into the mouth. This results in what may be the loudest consonants in the language. Clicks are classified according to the position of the forward closure as bilabial (at the lips), dental (at the upper teeth), alveolar (at the alveolar ridge), palatal (at the hard palate) and lateral (at one side of the tongue). The different types of clicks are transcribed by special IPA symbols, given in Table 6.2. Some of these are found in the names of several of the Khoisan languages, such as |Xam, !Xóõ, ǂHua and ‖Gana.

Khoisan languages vary as to which of these click sounds they have: for example, Sesotho has only the alveolar click, while Sandawe and Hadza have dental, alveolar and lateral clicks, but no bilabial or palatal clicks. Bilabial clicks are found in ǂHõã, N|u, |Xam and !Xóõ, while palatal clicks are found in the same four languages, as well as in Korana, Nama and !Kung.

Clicks can also be voiced or voiceless, oral or nasal in articulation, aspirated or unaspirated. Such "accompaniments" can combine with each of the places of articulation in Table 6.2; for example, the dental click may be: voiceless (the plain IPA symbol [|] is used), voiced (IPA: [g|]), nasalized (IPA: [ŋ|]), aspirated (IPA: [|ʰ]), glottalized (IPA: [|ʔ]) and breathy-voiced (IPA: [|̤]). When one considers that some of "accompaniments" can be combined, it is clear that an inventory can easily swell. Unsurprisingly, some languages have up to 30 different click sounds. This is true, for instance, of the Ju|'hoan language which has 30 clicks among its 90 or so sounds. !Xũ has only 3 plain (unaccompanied) clicks – it lacks the bilabial and dental clicks – but 44 accompanied ones, including the "breathy voiced lateral affricated click" (Maddieson 1984: 421–422).

Partially because of the clicks, many of the Khoisan languages have very large sound inventories, and !Xũ – with its 47 clicks – is the absolute champion in this respect: according to Snyman (1970), it has 141 different sounds in its inventory! This is in contrast with other sub-Saharan languages, such as Mura (a Chadic language of Cameroon and Nigeria) which is reported to have only 11 sounds![8]

Note also that several of the Bantu languages – Yeyi, Xhosa, Zulu, among others – have click sounds as well. However, only dental, alveolar and lateral clicks are found in Bantu languages. Bantu scholars traditionally use c, q and x to transcribe them.

Grammatically, Khoisan languages generally have isolating morphology (see Chapter 7 for a more detailed discussion of this type of morphology) and use word order to indicate grammatical relations; the most typical word order is SVO. The only exception to this generalization are the two Khoisan languages of Tanzania – Hadza and Sandawe – which have large numbers of inflectional suffixes.

6.4   Focus on: Official languages, trade languages and creole languages in sub-Saharan Africa

In this section we will take a wider look at the complex mosaic that is the linguistic situation in sub-Saharan Africa. Unlike in Europe and (parts of) Asia, where nation states were established based at least in part on language and ethnicity, in Africa there seems to be little correlation between states and

---

[8] Other languages with tiny sound inventories include Rotokas (Papuan) and Hawaiian (Austronesian); see Chapters 8 and 9. For comparison, English and Zulu both have around 40 sounds, a high but not unusual number.

languages, with many countries being highly diverse. For instance, the *Ethnologue* lists 538 languages for Nigeria alone and even more conservative estimates give at least 250 languages in that country. This has made language policy in many sub-Saharan countries a vital issue. The current trend is towards multilingualism; for instance, all African languages are considered official languages of the African Union (AU). However, although many mid-sized languages are used on the radio, in newspapers, and in primary-school education, and some of the larger ones are considered national languages, only a few are official at the national level.

In general, the map of official national languages in sub-Saharan Africa replicates pretty closely the map of colonial divisions. Three European languages are particularly common as official national languages in Africa: French, English and Portuguese. They typically remain official languages in those countries that used to be colonies of France, Belgium, the United Kingdom and Portugal.[9] Only in a small country in tropical Africa is Spanish used as an official language. This country is Equatorial Guinea with the capital Malabo on the northern coast of Bioko Island (formerly Fernando Pó). Earlier on, Germany too had colonies in Africa but after Germany's defeat in World War I, they were divided between the victors: the United Kingdom, France and Belgium. Hence, no country in Africa today has German as its official or co-official language.

French is still the official language of many of the former French and Belgian colonies: Mali, Niger, Senegal, Guinea, Cote d'Ivoire, Togo, Benin, Gabon, Congo and the Democratic Republic of Congo (former Zaire). It is also a co-official language in Chad, the Central African Republic, Rwanda, Burundi and Madagascar. Portuguese serves as the official language in the former Portuguese colonies of Angola, Mozambique and the tiny west African country of Guinea-Bissau. The rest of the countries in Tropical Africa use English as the official or co-official language: Nigeria, Ghana, Liberia and Sierra Leone in West Africa; and Botswana, Zambia and Namibia in the south. English is also a co-official language in the stretch of countries that run from south to north through the east of the continent, including South Africa, Lesotho, Swaziland, Malawi, Tanzania, Kenya, Rwanda, Uganda, Sudan and Eritrea. Note that Cameroon has both English and French as its co-official languages.

At this point, it is interesting to note the difference in the linguistic situations of former French-speaking and English-speaking colonies. The French typically imposed their colonial language on the locals: it was taught in all primary schools from first grade up. But the British set up schools where local languages were the medium of instruction through primary school; only people who continued into secondary education learned English. As a result, in the former British colonies local tongues developed into full-fledged languages to be used in various domains:

---

[9] Recall that Belgium itself has two official languages: Dutch (Flemish) and French, but it is the French language that was the official language of Belgium during its colonial days, so it is French that became the official language of the former Belgian colonies, such as the Democratic Republic of Congo and Rwanda.

newspapers are published in local languages and some of them – such as Swahili – even have their own literature. In the former French colonies, the situation is very different: not only is it hard to find newspapers or books in the local languages, but many of them do not even have writing at all.

One of the reasons why so many African countries kept a former colonial language as the official language to be used in government, education and the media is because of linguistic diversity: with so many local languages, choosing one or a few of them to serve the official functions would inevitably discriminate against the others. And selecting the former colonial language, which is perceived as "nobody's own language" allows these countries to avoid some of the ethnic and linguistic quagmires.

Besides the former colonial languages of English, French, Portuguese and Spanish, only a few indigenous African languages are official at the national level in sub-Saharan Africa. These are: Swahili in Tanzania, Kenya, Uganda, Burundi and Rwanda; Chichewa in Malawi; Kinyarwanda in Rwanda and the closely related Kirundi in Burundi; Sango in the Central African Republic; Swazi in Swaziland and South Africa; Shona in Zimbabwe; Afrikaans, Ndebele, Xhosa, Zulu, Pedi, Sotho, Tswana, Swazi, Venda and Tsonga in South Africa, the only multilingual country with widespread official status for its indigenous languages, in addition to English.[10]

Alongside official languages, one also finds the so-called trade languages in many parts of sub-Saharan Africa. In fact, such trade languages are an age-old cultural and linguistic phenomenon in the African linguistic landscape: innovations spread along trade routes and languages of peoples dominant in trade developed into languages of wider communication (also known as *linguae francae*).[11] Particularly important in this respect are Arabic (North Africa and the Horn of Africa), Hausa (eastern West Africa), Jula (western West Africa), Fulfulde (West Africa, mainly across the Sahel), Lingala (Congo) and especially Swahili (East Africa), a Bantu language whose second-language speakers outnumber native speakers 16 to 1.[12]

The complex linguistic mosaic in sub-Saharan Africa together with the establishment of colonial borders by European powers following the Berlin Conference in 1884–85 resulted in the phenomenon of "cross-border languages": many indigenous African languages are spoken in more than one country. Some African politicians see this phenomenon as a factor that can promote African unity, but

---

[10] Two other Indo-European languages are widely spoken in South Africa: Hindi and Urdu (890,000 and 170,000 speakers, respectively). Interestingly, Hindi and Urdu speakers have a special niche in the South African economy: many Hindi and Urdu speakers are in the textile business.

[11] The term *lingua franca* (literally, 'the language of the Franks') originally referred to a medieval pidgin spoken between European traders and later the crusaders, on the one hand, and the people of the eastern Mediterranean region (e.g. Arabs, Turks), on the other hand. Pidgins are discussed in more detail in Section 12.1.

[12] Hausa and Arabic are Afro-Asiatic languages. See Sections 5.2 and 11.1.

it also inevitably leads to a process of gradual divergence of language on the two sides of the border, especially when the official languages are different.

While we shall postpone a detailed discussion of creole languages to Section 12.2, it is important to mention here that a substantial proportion of the world's creole languages are found in Africa, in large part due to its multi-lingualism and its colonial past. Some creoles are based on European languages. For example, Krio in Sierra Leone, Cameroon Pidgin and Nigerian Pidgin in the respective countries, are based on English. Kabuverdianu in Cape Verde and Upper Guinea Crioulo in Guinea-Bissau and Senegal are based on Portuguese. Seselwa Creole French in the Seychelles and Morisyen in Mauritius are based on French. But other African creoles are based on Arabic, another important trade language. These include Juba Arabic in the southern Sudan and Nubi in parts of Uganda and Kenya. Yet other creoles are based on local languages, such as Sango, the main language of the Central African Republic, which is based on Ngbandi (a language in the Adamawa-Ubangi grouping within the Atlantic-Congo branch of the Niger-Congo language family, spoken by 250,000 in the Democratic Republic of the Congo).

7 Languages of eastern Asia

In the last section of Chapter 5 we looked at two languages, Maltese and Uzbek, that have some rather uncharacteristic features due to contact with neighboring languages. In this chapter we focus on languages of eastern Asia, a region including China and Southeast Asia and defined in historical terms as the area influenced by Classical China, and we will see that contact among languages again leads to some sharing of grammatical features, creating an impression of a family relationship and descent from a common ancestral language.[1] However, languages of eastern Asia belong to three major language families: Sino-Tibetan, Austro-Asiatic and Tai-Kadai, which will be the subject of the next three sections. In the past, Vietnamese and other languages of Southeast Asia were classified as members of the Sino-Tibetan family; however, their similarities to Chinese are currently credited to language contact by most linguists outside of China, though in the Chinese scholarly community, some of the Southeast Asian languages are still included in the Sino-Tibetan family.

There are also three languages in eastern Asia whose family relationships have not been determined and remain controversial: Japanese, Korean and Ainu. These languages will be considered in more detail in Chapter 11.

7.1   Sino-Tibetan languages

The Sino-Tibetan language family comprises 449 languages and is second only to the Indo-European language family in number of speakers. The two main branches of the Sino-Tibetan family – as suggested by the name – are Sinitic (or Chinese) languages and Tibeto-Burman languages. The Sinitic branch contains only 14 languages, but they are spoken by over a billion people. Mandarin Chinese alone has some 840 million speakers (92% of the population in China speaks Mandarin Chinese), while "smaller" Chinese languages have tens of millions speakers each: for example, Wu Chinese (also known as Shanghainese) has over 77 million speakers, Yue (also known as Cantonese) has

---

[1] In some cases we know the direction in which a given feature diffused; in others, a feature is simply present in the languages of the area, but it is impossible to tell which language it may have started in and which languages it has spread to.

Map 7.1. *Languages of eastern Asia.*

52 million speakers, Jinyu (spoken mainly in Shanxi Province) has 44 million speakers and Min Nan Chinese (also known as Taiwanese) has 25,700,000 speakers in China (plus 15,000,000 in Taiwan, 2,660,000 in Malaysia, 1,170,000 in Singapore, 1,080,000 in Thailand and significant communities in Brunei, Indonesia, the Philippines and elsewhere).[2] Naturally, these languages are not uniform and have many dialects. For instance, Mandarin Chinese has many dialects organized into four dialect groups: Northern dialects (spoken in Hebei, Henan, Shandong, Northern Anhui, northeastern provinces and parts of Inner Mongolia), North-western dialects (spoken in Shanxi, Gansu, Qinghai, Ningxia and parts of Inner Mongolia), Southwestern dialects (spoken in Sichuan, Yunnan, Guizhou, north-west Guangxi, Hubei and northwest Hunan) and Eastern or Jiang-Huai dialects (spoken in central Anhui and Jiangsu north of the Yangtze River). Similarly, Wu Chinese has a number of dialects grouped into Northern and Southern dialects; the former have been influenced more by the neighboring Mandarin dialects, especially in the vocabulary. Generally speaking, a higher degree of dialect differentiation is found in the more densely populated coastal areas in comparison

---

[2] Most of the Chinese immigrants who came to the United States in 1800s come from Cantonese-speaking areas. Cantonese is also an important language for the Chinese entertainment industry, whose center is in Hong Kong, where Cantonese is spoken.

to the interior of China, where there is still much mutual intelligibility among the different linguistic varieties.

Despite not being mutually intelligible, the various Chinese languages are often considered to be the same language by the speakers because of the unifying effect of the writing system. Thus, written language is understood throughout China by educated, literate speakers across different languages. This is because the Chinese use a logographic system of writing which does not represent the pronunciation of words in the same way as alphabetic systems do (such as the Roman alphabet used for English, French or Croatian). In fact, a Chinese character will typically have very different sound value from language to language but will have the same meaning across the various Chinese languages.

The Tibeto-Burman languages are much smaller by the number of speakers. Some of the largest include Burmese (32,000,000 speakers in Myanmar plus 300,000 in Bangladesh), Khams Tibetan (1,490,000 speakers in China), Meitei (1,370,000 speakers in India plus 15,000 in Bangladesh and 6,000 in Myanmar), Central Tibetan (1,070,000 speakers in China plus 189,000 in India, 5,280 in Nepal and 4,800 in Bhutan) and Amdo Tibetan (810,000 speakers in China). But many Tibeto-Burman languages count less than a 1,000 speakers: for example, Lunanakha and Seke are spoken by 700 speakers each (in Bhutan and in Nepal, respectively), while Jad and Brokkat are spoken by 300 speakers each (in India and in Bhutan, respectively).

There are also some significant linguistic differences between Sinitic and Tibeto-Burman languages, so that some scholars, such as Christopher Beckwith (1996) and Roy Andrew Miller, argued that these two families are not related at all. They point to what they consider an absence of regular sound correspondences, an absence of reconstructable shared morphology, and evidence that much shared lexical material has been borrowed from Chinese into Tibeto-Burman. In opposition to this view, scholars in favor of the Sino-Tibetan hypothesis, such as W. South Coblin, Graham Thurgood and James Matisoff, have argued that there are regular correspondences in sounds, as well as in grammar. One of the main reasons why it is so difficult to apply the comparative method that we are familiar with from the previous chapters to the Sino-Tibetan languages is the morphological paucity in many of these languages, including modern Chinese and Tibetan.

This brings us to consider one of the most characteristic features of Sino-Tibetan languages – their ISOLATING MORPHOLOGY. In an extreme isolating language, words are composed of a single morpheme, in contrast to agglutinative or fusional languages, where words are composed on multiple morphemes. To illustrate, consider the following sentences from Mandarin Chinese (7.1) and Burmese (7.2):[3]

---

[3] POSS indicates a particle encoding possessor, CL indicates a classifier (see explanation in the text below) and FUT indicates a future tense particle. Superscripted numbers indicate tones on the preceding vowels (see in the text below). In general, there are several systems of symbols for

(7.1)   mi²ngti¹an wo³ de   pe²ngyou hui⁴ we⁴i wo³ zuo⁴ yi² ge
         tomorrow   I   POSS friend   will for   I   make one CLF

         she¹ngri da⁴n'ga²o
         birthday cake
         'Tomorrow, my friends will make a birthday cake for me.'

(7.2)   mane'hpyan kyano ye.   thangechin: mwei:nei. kei'moun. ta   ban:
         tomorrow   me   POSS friend   birthday   cake   one CLF

         hpou' pei: myi
         bake   give FUT
         'Tomorrow, my friends will make a birthday cake for me.'

In these examples, the first person singular possessor ('mine') is expressed by two separate words: the personal pronoun (*wŏ* in Mandarin and *kyano* in Burmese) and a possessive particle (*de* in Mandarin and *ye.* in Burmese). Likewise, plurality and singularity are not expressed morphologically; instead, they can (but do not have to) be expressed through the so-called CLASSIFIER CONSTRUCTIONS, where a noun phrases consists of a noun, a classifier (in these examples, *ge* in Mandarin and *ban:* in Burmese) and a numeral (in these examples, 'one': *yí* in Mandarin and *ta* in Burmese). These classifier constructions are somewhat similar to such English constructions as *three heads of garlic* and *three heads of cattle*, but whereas in English such constructions are used in counting what we think of as a mass term (e.g. *garlic* and *cattle*), in Chinese classifier constructions are used with nouns which we would consider countable (e.g. 'cake' in examples 7.1 and 7.2 above). The order of the three elements (noun, classifier and numeral) differs from language to language: in Mandarin, a numeral is followed by a classifier which is followed by a noun, whereas in Burmese a noun is followed by a numeral which is followed by a classifier. The classifiers themselves also vary within each language depending on the noun they appear with: for example, in Mandarin the classifier *ge* (see (7.1) above) can appear with almost any noun, while other classifiers such as *zhi¹* in (7.3a), *be³n* in (7.3b) and *we⁴i* in (7.3c) are more specialized.

(7.3) a. ji³   zhi¹ gou³
          several CLF dog
          'several dogs'

      b. yi¹   be³n shu¹
          one   CLF   book
          'one book'

representing tones: they can be represented by superscripted numbers, by a 2- or 3-digit number or by accent marks over the vowels. For example, the same high level tone associated with /a/ (as in the Mandarin word for 'mother' (see the main text below) can be represented as a¹, a 55 or ā. For more details, see below in the main text.

    c.   sa^{1}n we^{4}i ke^{4}re^{2}n
           three CLF guest
           'three guests'

Similarly, in the verbal domain the tense is not expressed morphologically (e.g. by a suffix or a prefix), but by a separate word such as a tense particle (e.g. *myi* in Burmese) or by an adverb such as 'tomorrow' or auxiliary-like verbs such as *qu^4* 'go':

(7.4)   Mi^{2}ngtia^{3}n wo^3 qu^4 ka^{4}n dia^{4}nyi^{3}ng.
           tomorrow I   go look movie
           'I will see a movie tomorrow.'

The only exception to this generalization in Mandarin is certain aspectual morphemes which are suffixes on verbs, such as the perfective suffix *-le* and the durative suffix *-zhe*.

(7.5) a.   wo^3 chi^1-le sa^{1}n-wa^{3}n fa^{4}n
          I   eat-PFV three-bowls rice
          'I ate three bowls of rice.'
     b.   ta^1 ma^{4}i-zhe ta^1-de   che^{1}zi
          s/he sell-DUR s/he-POSS car
          'S/he is selling his/her car.'

Furthermore, grammatical relations such as subject and object are not expressed morphologically either; that is, there is no case marking in Mandarin or Burmese and no agreement in the verb to indicate "who did what to whom". Instead, grammatical relations are expressed through word order: Subject-Verb-Object (SVO) in Mandarin and Subject-Object-Verb (SOV) in Burmese.

You may be wondering at this point about the superscripted numbers in the Mandarin Chinese examples above. These numbers encode tones of the preceding vowels, which brings us to another characteristic property of (some) Sino-Tibetan languages (especially in the Sinitic branch) – their TONAL SYSTEMS. These languages use pitch to distinguish lexical or grammatical meaning. Consider English: it uses pitch only as intonation, for instance, for emphasis, to convey surprise or irony, or to distinguish a question from a declarative sentence. Moreover, in non-tonal languages like English pitch/intonation is a property of utterances and not of words.

In contrast, tonal languages such as Chinese languages use pitch to distinguish words. For example, in Mandarin most syllables carry their own tone, and many words are differentiated solely by tone. The often-cited example of this is the Mandarin syllable *ma*, which pronounced with one of the four different pitch patterns has four different meanings: pronounced with the high level tone *ma^1* it means 'mother', *ma^2* with the high rising tone means 'hemp', *ma^3* with the low falling tone – 'horse' and *ma^4* with the high falling tone – 'to scold' (see Table 7.1). Other Chinese languages have even richer tone systems. For example, Cantonese has six tones, so for instance, the syllable *si* can be pronounced six different ways, with six different meanings: 'poem' (high level tone), 'to try'

Table 7.1. *Tones in Mandarin.*

Name	Numerical representation	Example	Translation
high level	55	fu[1] or fū	'skin'
high rising	35	fu[2] or fú	'fortune'
low falling	213	fu[3] or fŭ	'axe'
high falling	41	fu[4] or fù	'woman'

Table 7.2. *Tones in Cantonese.*

Name	Numerical representation	Example	Translation
high level	55	si[1]	'poem'
mid level	33	si[2]	'to try'
low level	22	si[3]	'matter'
low falling	21	si[4]	'time'
low high	24	si[5]	'to cause'
low mid	23	si[6]	'city'

(mid level tone), 'matter' (low level tone), 'time' (low falling), 'to cause' (low high tone) and 'city' (low mid tone); see Table 7.2. In the grammar of Modern Chinese tone plays a minor role, but in older forms of Chinese tones did have morphological significance (and some Yue Chinese dialects still use tones for morphological purposes in a restricted way).

In 1930 the famous Chinese scholar Y. R. Chao devised the tone symbols representing the relative pitch of the corresponding vowels in terms of an imaginary five-point scale, one being the lowest point and five being the highest. For example, the high level tone in the Mandarin word for *mā* 'mother' (also in *pā* 'eight' and *sān* 'mountain') is a level, relatively high tone and is represented as 55. The second Mandarin tone, the high rising tone – found in *má* 'hemp', *ná* 'grasp' and *mén* 'door' – starts somewhat below the register of the first tone and rises in pitch to the level of the first tone, hence its numerical representation is 35. The third tone, the low falling tone – found in such words as *mǎ* 'horse', *pǐ* 'pen' and *wǒ* 'I' – is represented as 213. Finally, the fourth tone, the high falling tone – as in words *mà* 'scold', *pù* 'not', *wèn* 'ask' – is represented in Chao's system as 41. The Mandarin tonal system with additional examples is summarized in Table 7.1. Similarly, the six tones in Cantonese are listed in Table 7.2.

Numerous languages in eastern Asia are tonal, including all the Chinese languages (though some, such as Shanghainese, are only marginally tonal) and, as we will see below, Vietnamese (an Austro-Asiatic language; see Section 7.2) and Thai and Lao (both Tai-Kadai languages; see Section 7.3). Some eastern Asian languages, such as Burmese, Korean and Japanese have simpler tone systems, which are sometimes called 'register' or 'pitch accent' systems.

However, some languages in the region are not tonal at all, including Mongolian (a Mongolic language; see Section 11.2 below), Khmer (an Austro-Asiatic language; see Section 7.2) and Malay (an Austronesian language; see Chapter 8). Of the Tibetan languages, Central Tibetan (including the dialect of the capital Lhasa) and Amdo Tibetan are tonal, while Khams Tibetan and Ladakhi (spoken mostly in the Jammu and Kashmir province of India) are not. Thus, tonal systems appear to be an areal rather than a genealogical feature of languages.

One might ask how a tonal system may arise in language in the first place. Typically, tonal systems arise as an after effect of the loss or merger of consonants (such trace effects of disappeared sounds have been nicknamed Cheshirisation, after the lingering smile of the disappearing Cheshire cat in Lewis Carroll's *Alice in Wonderland*). As it turns out, in non-tonal languages the pronunciation of consonants affects the pitch of preceding and/or following vowels; when such consonants disappear as a result of regular sound change (recall our discussion of lenition from Chapter 2), the distinction in pitch may be preserved and used to distinguish meanings formerly distinguished by the consonants. And voilà – a tonal system is created! For example, in the development of Chinese languages final consonants, which affected the pitch of preceding vowels, weakened to /h/ and finally disappeared completely, but the difference in pitch – now a true difference in tone, carried on instead of the disappeared consonants. Moreover, the nature of initial consonants also affected which tone a given vowel carried: when the consonants lost their voicing distinction, vowels preceding a voiceless consonant acquired a higher tone, while those preceding a voiced consonant acquired a lower tone. The same changes affected many other languages of eastern Asia, such as Thai, Vietnamese and the Lhasa dialect of Tibetan, and at around the same time (AD 1,000–1,500). As far as tonal systems are concerned, we do not know (and may never know) whether a tonal system first arose in one language and diffused to others, or whether tonal systems arose independently in different languages of the region.

So far, we have considered the characteristic morphological and phonological properties – isolating morphology and tonal systems of Sino-Tibetan languages – but what about their syntax? Since we cannot consider the full range of syntactic properties of these languages in great detail, we will focus here on only one interesting property of (some) Sino-Tibetan languages – the so-called wh-in-situ phenomenon, which involves the way that questions are formed. But first consider how questions are formed in a more familiar language: English.

There are two types of questions: yes/no question (which can be answered by 'yes' or 'no') and content questions. Here, we are interested in the latter type of question, also known as wh-questions, because most question words in English start with wh-: *who, what, where, when, why,* etc. (hence, they are referred to as the wh-words).[4]

---

[4] In fact, wh-question may contain a wh-phrase consisting of more than just a wh-word; for instance, **Which textbook** *should we read for this class?* In what follows, we will ignore such more complex wh-questions.

In English, wh-questions are formed by placing the wh-word in the beginning of the sentence, regardless of which element is being questioned. This fronting of the wh-word is accompanied by the subject–auxiliary inversion that places the auxiliary (or the dummy verb *do*, if an auxiliary is not present) in the second position (in line with the general Germanic tendency for Verb-Second; see Chapter 1). This is illustrated below (the wh-word and the element that replaces it in the declarative are boldfaced):[5]

(7.6) a.   **Who** will you see?   (cf. You will see **Tom**.)
   b.   **What** did she buy?   (cf. She bought **the pizza**.)
   c.   **Where** can I park the car? (cf. I can park the car **in lot A**.)

The same strategy – fronting of the wh-word and subject-verb inversion – are employed in other languages, such as Spanish and Irish, except in these languages a lexical verb can invert as well.[6]

(7.7) a.   Spanish:
   Qué compró Juan?
   what bought Juan
   'What did Juan buy?'

   b.   Irish:
   Caidé chonnaic tú
   what   saw   you
   'What did you see?'
   (Dochartaigh 1992: 38)

Note also that subject–verb inversion need not accompany the fronting of the wh-word; for instance, in Russian (Slavic; Indo-European) the wh-word is placed sentence-initially, but the verb follows the subject, as it does in declaratives:[7]

---

[5] It is possible in English to place an interrogative phrase later in the sentence, but this word order is not normally used in neutral questions. It is used either in echo-questions, where the speaker is expressing surprise or incredulity at something that they have just heard, as in (ia), or by a teacher asking students questions, as in (ib):

(i) a.   You are leaving **when**?!?
   b.   Napoleon died **in what year**?

[6] Note that lexical verbs cannot undergo subject–verb inversion in Modern English but this was possible in earlier forms of English, as late as the sixteenth century. Witness the following (now ungrammatical) examples from Shakespeare's *The Merchant of Venice*:

(i) a.   What sum owes he?
   b.   Why sweat they under burdens?
   c.   What says the leaden casket?

[7] In other languages, such as Hebrew (Semitic; cf. Chapter 5), whether subject–verb inversion occurs depends on a number of factors, such as whether the subject is a noun phrase or a pronoun, as well as other semantic and phonetic factors.

(7.8)   **Čto** ty   kupil?
          what you bought
          'What did you buy?'

Let's now return to Sino-Tibetan languages. In these languages – and in others, as we shall see below – wh-words are not obligatorily fronted to the sentence-initial position. Instead, they occur in whatever position is natural for the corresponding phrase in the declarative (i.e. the answer to the question). For example, in the following question from Mandarin Chinese, the wh-word *she²nme* 'what' occurs not in the sentence-initial position but following the verb because Mandarin Chinese is an SVO language and *she²nme* 'what' functions as object. Hence, *she²nme* 'what' occurs in the normal position for objects, immediately following the verb.

(7.9)   Lisi ka⁴ndao **she²nme**?
          Lisi see   what
          'What did Lisi see?'

This phenomenon is called wh-in-situ (in Latin: 'wh- in place'). While it may seem odd and foreign to speakers of most European languages, it is not true that wh-in-situ is completely absent from these languages: for example, spoken French allows the wh-word not to be fronted, as in the following example:

(7.10)   Tu   vas **où**?
          you go   where
          'Where do you go?'

Whether a given language employs the fronting strategy (with or without an accompanying subject–verb inversion) can be construed as a linguistic parameter (see Section 3.4), which can be formulated as "Obligatorily front wh-words". In languages like English, Spanish and Russian, the value for this parameter is set as "yes", and in languages like Mandarin Chinese it is set as "no". As we shall see below, other languages of eastern Asia have the "no" value for the wh-fronting parameter too.

7.2   Austro-Asiatic languages

The Austro-Asiatic language family consists of 169 languages spoken from eastern India across to Vietnam and down to the Nicobar Islands and peninsular Malaysia, although in most of this region they are interspersed among other, more widely spoken languages. There are two main branches to this family: Western Austro-Asiatic (or Munda) and Eastern Austro-Asiatic (or Mon-Khmer). The Western Austro-Asiatic (or Munda) branch includes 22 languages spoken in small pockets in India and Bangladesh; most of these languages have small numbers of speakers, the two exceptions being Santali with nearly 7 million speakers and Mundari with approximately 1.5 million speakers. The Eastern Austro-Asiatic (or Mon-Khmer) branch consists of 147 languages spoken in Vietnam, Laos, Cambodia, Malaysia and the Nicobar Islands.[8] Of all the Austro-Asiatic languages, we have a detailed recorded history only for Vietnamese, Khmer and Mon. These are also the largest Austro-Asiatic languages by the number of speakers, spoken by 66 million, 12 million and 851,000, respectively. Thus, Vietnamese has several times more speakers than all the other Austro-Asiatic languages together. But one should not forget that in some ways it is quite different from the other members of the family, as discussed below. Of the Austro-Asiatic languages, only Khmer and Vietnamese have official status (in Cambodia and Vietnam, respectively), while the rest of the languages are spoken by minority groups. However, Mon was a historically important language as it played an important role in the development of Burmese and Thai culture. It is still spoken in the delta area to the east of Yankon (Rangoon).

Like Finno-Ugric languages, discussed in Section 3.1 above, Austro-Asiatic languages are spoken over non-contiguous chunks of territory, separated by areas where other languages are spoken. The explanation for this distribution resembles the explanation given for the non-contiguity of the Finnic branch of the Finno-Ugric family: speakers of Austro-Asiatic languages are native to Southeast Asia and the eastern part of the Indian subcontinent, but were later displaced by speakers of Indo-European, Tai-Kadai, Dravidian and Sino-Tibetan languages. As a result of the interactions of Austro-Asiatic speakers with speakers of these other languages, Austro-Asiatic languages developed certain similarities with these other, unrelated languages.

For example, it appears that in the distant past Vietnamese exhibited more characteristics common to other languages in the Austro-Asiatic family, such as the presence of inflectional (i.e. non-isolating) morphology and a richer set of consonant clusters, which have subsequently disappeared from the language. In their stead, Vietnamese developed isolating morphology, a classifier system and a tonal system, not unlike that of Chinese.[9] This is illustrated with the following example (from Comrie 1989: 43).

(7.11)   khi   tôi dên   nhà   ban   tôi, chúng tôi bát   dâu làm bài.
         when I   come house friend I   PL   I   begin do   lesson
         'When I came to my friend's house, we began to do lessons.'

As can be seen from this example, Vietnamese does not use prefixes and suffixes to express grammatical relations. For example, note that there is no morphological expression of possession and other grammatical relations, comparable to the English possessive *'s* and the Latin cases, or of grammatical number

---

[8] Some scholars are doubtful as to whether Mon-Khmer is a valid grouping.

[9] Even though both Chinese and Vietnamese have developed tonal systems, we cannot be sure whether these systems diffused from Chinese to Vietnamese or diffused from Vietnamese to Chinese, or developed independently.

Table 7.3. *Tones in Vietnamese.*

Name	Numerical representation	Example	Translation
low falling	21	mà	'but'
high rising	35	má	'cheek'
mid dipping-rising	212 or 313	mả	'tomb, grave'
high breaking-rising	35[a]	mã	'horse'
low falling constricted	32	mạ	'rice seedling'
mid level	33	ma	'ghost'

[a] This tone is high and rising so its contour is roughly the same as that of the high rising tone in 'cheek', but it is accompanied by the rasping voice quality occasioned by tense glottal stricture. In careful speech such syllables are sometimes interrupted completely by a glottal stop (or a rapid series of glottal stops).

(e.g. 'we' vs. 'I') or tense (e.g. on 'come' and 'begin'). Instead, these grammatical notions are expressed either through separate words (e.g. the plural particle *chúng*), word order (e.g. the possessor noun comes after the possessed, as in *nhà ban*, literally 'house friend') or context (cf. the temporal relationship between coming and beginning). Like many other isolating languages, Vietnamese has a fixed word order: in sentences it is Subject-Verb-Object (SVO) and as is typical of Verb-Object languages, the modifier comes after the modified (see Section 3.4 above).

Like Chinese, Vietnamese has a classifier system: a noun used in a definite noun phrase, with a numeral or with a focus marker *cái*, must appear with a classifier. As in other classifier languages, which classifier is chosen depends on the noun with which it is being used. For example, the classifier *con* is used with the noun *chó* 'dog' or *ngựa* 'horse' (and other nouns denoting animals and children), while the classifier *cây* is used for stick-like objects (plants, guns, canes, etc.).

Also like Chinese and unlike many other Austro-Asiatic languages (e.g. Khmer), Vietnamese has a tonal system. Specifically, there are six tones in (northern varieties of) Vietnamese, summarized in Table 7.3: low falling tone (marked by a grave accent) as in *mà* 'but', high rising tone (marked by an acute accent) as in *má* 'cheek' (also 'mother' in southern dialects), mid dipping-rising tone (marked by a hook) as in *mả* 'tomb, grave', high breaking-rising (marked by a tilde) as in *mã* 'horse' (a Sino-Vietnamese word, cf. the Mandarin for 'horse' above), low falling constricted tone (marked by a dot below) as in *mạ* 'rice seedling' and mid level tone (no mark) as in *ma* 'ghost'.

The final similarity between Vietnamese and Chinese to be considered here involves their strategy for forming wh-questions. As discussed in the previous section, Chinese forms wh-questions not by fronting a wh-word but by keeping it in situ. The same is true of Vietnamese. Note that Vietnamese wh-questions may also include a question particle, glossed as Q, but the use of this particle is optional.

(7.12) a. Tân mua **gi**   the?
           Tan buy   what   Q
           'What did Tan buy?'
     b.   Tân mua **gi**?
           Tan buy   what
           'What did Tan buy?'

These similarities between Chinese and Vietnamese are not altogether surprising: after all, Chinese came to predominate politically in Vietnam in the second century BCE and remained the governing power for nearly ten centuries. Since Chinese was for a long period the language of literature and government, as well as the primary written language in Vietnam, the Chinese writing system was imported and used in a modified form to write Vietnamese. Moreover, with the political dominance of the Chinese came a wave of Chinese lexical borrowings: Vietnamese has borrowed extensively from Cantonese, especially in the domain of abstract vocabulary, not unlike English borrowings from Latin and Greek. There are also many Sino-Vietnamese words which combine native Vietnamese roots with Chinese "imports". It is estimated that some 30–40% of Vietnamese vocabulary comes from Chinese.

Another wave of influence came to Vietnam with European colonization: for example, the Chinese system of writing was replaced with Romanized writing developed in the seventeenth century by Portuguese and other Europeans involved in proselytizing and trade in Vietnam (however, the Romanized script did not come to predominate until the beginning of the twentieth century, when education became widespread and a simpler writing system was found more expedient for teaching). When France invaded Vietnam in the late nineteenth century, French gradually replaced Chinese as the official language in education and government, and Vietnamese borrowed many French words, such as *đầm* 'dame' (from the French *madame*), *ga* 'train station' (from *gare*), *so' mi* 'shirt' (from *chemise*), *búp bê* 'doll' (from *poupée*) and *cà phê* 'café' (from *café*).

All in all, Vietnamese is rather atypical when it comes to Austro-Asiatic languages. This is particularly clear from a comparison with Munda languages, such as Mundari (spoken by 1.5 million speakers in Orissa and Jharkhand provinces of India) and Korku (spoken by 478,000 speakers in southern Madhya Pradesh province of India). Munda languages are spoken in small areas surrounded by Indo-European (more specifically, Indic) and Dravidian languages, which have greater social prestige. As a result, Munda languages have been greatly influenced by their neighboring languages and exhibit many linguistic characteristics that make them dissimilar from Vietnamese and other Mon Khmer languages to which they are related (see Donegan and Stampe 1983).

For instance, Munda languages are agglutinative rather than isolating, and very long sequences of suffixes may be found, especially in verbs. This is an influence of Dravidian languages. Nouns in Munda languages have two gender categories (animate and inanimate) and three numbers (singular, dual and plural).

Grammatical categories expressed by case marking in familiar Indo-European languages are signaled by word order, postpositions and pronominal affixes on verbs. The word order is typically Subject-Object-Verb (SOV), unlike in Vietnamese. Except for Korku, Munda languages do not have tonal systems.

However, these differences between Munda and Mon Khmer branches of the Austro-Asiatic family are not always attributable to influences of Dravidian and/or Indic languages. For example, the verb structure of the Munda languages (especially of North Munda languages, such as Mundari and Korku) is extremely synthetic, indeed significantly more so than what is found in either Dravidian or Indic languages. In this way, they share certain structural affinities with some of the Tibeto-Burman languages, with which they may have formed an earlier areal group, prior to the intrusion of Dravidian- and Indic-speaking populations.

7.3   Tai-Kadai languages

The Tai-Kadai language family (also known as Daic, Kadai, Kradai or Kra-Dai) includes 92 languages found in southern China and Southeast Asia: in Thailand, Vietnam, Laos and Myanmar. There are three major subfamilies of the Tai-Kadai family. The largest subfamily is the Kam-Tai branch (also known as Kam-Sui), which includes 76 languages; the other two branches are the Kadai subfamily, consisting of 14 languages spoken in Vietnam and China, and the Hlai subfamily, which includes only 2 languages (both spoken in China).

Probably the best known members of the Tai-Kadai family are Thai and Lao, closely related and to some degree mutually intelligible languages.[10] Both Thai and Lao are members of the Southwestern grouping within the Kam-Tai branch of the Tai-Kadai family. Thai is spoken as a first language by 20 million speakers and as a second language by 40 million speakers in Thailand, where it serves as the official language of the country, medium of education and of most mass communication. It is also spoken in the Midway Islands, Singapore, United Arab Emirates and the United States. The word *thai* means 'free' in the Thai language; yet, Thai people have not always been free from outside political influence and dominance: in fact, they became independent in the mid-thirteenth century, but prior to that they were dominated by the Mon and then later by the Khmer.

Lao is spoken by 3 million people in Laos, especially in the Mekong River Valley and Luang Prabang south to Cambodia border. There is a closely related linguistic variety – Isan – often referred to as Northeastern Thai; 15 million of

---

[10] Thai is also known as Siamese because of the earlier name for the country – Siam. In 1939, Siam's fascist-influenced government renamed the country "The Kingdom of Thailand" to help forge its different Tai-speaking peoples into a single nation. A concerted "Thaification" program followed, spreading Standard Thai (Siamese) through schools and government, discouraging the use of the local dialects, such as Isan in the northeast (see the main text below).

Table 7.4. *Tones in Thai.*

Name	Numerical representation	Example	Translation
low falling	21	nà:	(name)
high falling	51	nâ:	'face'
high rising	45	ná:	'aunt/uncle'
low falling-rising	213	nǎ:	'thick'
mid falling	32	na:	'paddy field'

Isan speakers (who are ethnically Lao) live on the Khorat Plateau of northeastern Thailand and comprise roughly a third of Thailand's population. If Isan speakers are considered as part of the Lao group, there is more Lao in Thailand than in Laos. Thus, Thailand and Laos is one of the many areas in the world where language, ethnicity and nationality do not match up.

It should be noted that while today only a few of the Tai-Kadai languages are spoken in southern China, Chinese historical records show that Tai-Kadai speakers used to live further north than they are found today, inhabiting a large area of China south of the Yangtze River. This theory is further confirmed by the fact that the diversity of the Tai-Kadai languages reaches its highest degree in southeastern China, especially in Hunan, suggesting that this is close to their historic homeland. The migration of Thai-Kadai speakers into the Indochina peninsula occurred already in historical times, around 2,000 years ago. Due to Han Chinese expansion, Mongol invasion pressures and a search for lands more suitable for wet-rice cultivation, the Tai peoples moved south towards India, down the Mekong River valley and as far south as the Malay Peninsula, moving into what was formerly Austro-Asiatic territory, inter-marrying with – and borrowing culture from – local Khmer (Cambodian) and Mon peoples. Given this history and the relatively high levels of intermarriage between the Thais and the Chinese, it should not come as a surprise to find strong Chinese influence on the Thai language. As is the case with Austro-Asiatic languages, Thai developed certain grammatical characteristics through diffusion from Chinese, among them isolating morphology and a classifier system. Also, like Chinese and Vietnamese, Thai is a tonal language, although once again we cannot be sure if this property of Thai diffused from Chinese/Vietnamese, or arose independently or under areal pressures.

Let's consider the tonal system in Thai more closely. There are five tones in Thai: low falling as in *nà:* (a name), high falling as in *nâ:* 'face', high rising as in *ná:* 'aunt/uncle', low falling-rising as in *nǎ:* 'thick' and mid falling as in *na:* 'paddy field'. The Thai tones and their numerical representations in Chao's system are summarized in Table 7.4.

Similarly, (standard) Lao has six tones: rising tone (e.g. ě) which can represented numerically as 24 or 214; high level tone (e.g. é) represented numerically as 44, high falling tone (e.g. ê) represented numerically as 53, mid level tone (e.g. ē) represented numerically as 33, low level tone (e.g. è) represented numerically as 11 and low falling tone (e.g. ẹ) represented numerically as 31. Other dialects of Lao have from 5 to 7 tones.

When it comes to morphology, Thai is an isolating language: its nouns are not marked for gender, number or case, nor are its verbs marked for person, number, tense, aspect or mood. These grammatical features are expressed instead by separate, free-standing words – particles – such as the plural number particle *phuak* in (7.13a) and the progressive aspect particle *kamlang . . . yuu* in (7.13b):[11]

(7.13) a.   **phuak** khaw
      PL   s/he
      'they'

    b.   Khaw **kamlang** rian   phasaa   thaai **yuu**
      S/he PROG   study language Thai at
      'She**'s** study**ing** the Thai language.'

Furthermore, Thai uses a free-standing particle *kaan* to form nouns out of verbs, for instance the noun for 'studying' out of the verb for 'study', as in the following example:

(7.14)   **Kaan** rian   phasaa   thaai sanuk maak
      NMLZ study language Thai fun   much
      'Study**ing** Thai is fun.'

Like other languages of Southeast Asia, Thai has an intricate system of nominal classifiers. Classifiers follow the numeral and precede the noun; different classifiers are used depending on the noun (e.g. *tua* for animals, *khone* for people, *jahn* for platefuls, *ahn* for things in general); there are separate classifiers for different classes of people, objects of different shapes and functions, clothes, foods, animals, etc.

In addition to the progressive aspect particle in (7.13b) above, we should note three other types of verbal particles in Thai: mood particles, questions particles and politeness particles. All of these occur at the end of the sentence, which otherwise typically has a Subject-Verb-Object (SVO) order (as expected from a Verb-Object language, adjectives follow the noun they modify; see Section 3.4). Mood particles in Thai express the attitude of the speaker towards the situation and thus play the same role as mood morphology in languages like Spanish or French (think about imperative, conditional, subjunctive mood). Tense is likewise not expressed morphologically; instead, temporal relationships are to be construed based on adverbials and the context. Question particles occur in yes/no questions and the choice of a specific particle depends on whether the speaker has

[11] Note that like Finno-Ugric languages (see Section 3.1) and Turkic languages (see Section 5.1) Thai does not distinguish masculine and feminine gender even in pronouns. Note also that tones are omitted from the following examples.

expectations as to what the answer may be.[12] Finally, politeness particles serve to express deference towards the addressee. Social norms in Thai require that a politeness marker be at the end of every sentence. Such markers differ according to the gender of the speaker: men will show deference by ending their questions and statements with *khrahp* to show respect and refinement, while women end their questions and statements with *khah*.

Lao and Isan have very similar isolating morphology, using free-standing particles instead of bound morphemes to express grammatical notions, such as number, tense, etc. Like Thai, Lao and Isan are SVO languages, but Lao and Isan use pronouns more frequently than Thai.

Finally, consider once again wh-questions. Like Chinese and Vietnamese, Thai employs the wh-in-situ strategy, as shown by the following example, where the wh-word questioning the object appears after the verb, in the typical object position:

(7.15)   sùda: hěn **ʔàray**?
           Suda see what
           'What did Suda see?'

7.4   Focus on: Isolating morphology and language change

In the preceding sections we characterized (some) Sino-Tibetan, Austro-Asiatic and Tai-Kadai languages as having isolating morphology. Recall that an ideal isolating language is one where every word is composed of a single morpheme and no bound morphemes exist at all. Thus, isolating morphology is contrasted with two other morphological types: agglutinative and fusional. An agglutinative language is one where a word typically consists of several morphemes that have clear boundaries and each morpheme expresses one type of grammatical meaning. In contrast, a fusional language is a language where a word likewise involves several morphemes, but some or all of them are fused together so that the boundaries between morphemes are not clear and one morpheme may express more than one grammatical feature (e.g. case and number, or tense and agreement).

While a distinction is made between these three basic morphological types – isolating, agglutinative and fusional – most of the world's languages do not clearly fit any one of the three types. For example, as discussed above in connection with (7.5), Mandarin Chinese – although largely isolating – has some bound morphemes, such as the perfective suffix *-le* and the durative suffix *-zhe*. These two morphemes, however, developed as suffixes in Modern Chinese; there were

---

[12] One example of a yes/no question particle in a more familiar language may be the French *est-ce que*: it is appended to the beginning of a declarative sentence and turns it into a yes-no question, as in *Paul peut venir* 'Paul can come' versus *Est-ce que Paul peut venir?* 'Can Paul come?'

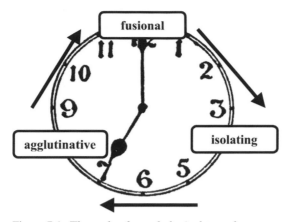

Figure 7.1. *The cycle of morphological type change.*

no (agglutinative) affixes in older forms of Chinese. Thus, in effect (Mandarin) Chinese is developing from a purely isolating language into an agglutinative one. And as it turns out, Chinese is not the only language to undergo this sort of change. In fact, historical linguists now postulate a cycle of change by which a fusional language can develop into one of the isolating type, an isolating language can become agglutinative and an agglutinative language may move towards a fusional profile. Moreover, a language at any stage of its development may be analyzed as occupying an intermediate position, which we can refer to by using the clock metaphor (Dixon 1994: 184), illustrated in Figure 7.1.

Numerous historical developments serve to illustrate the separate stages of this morphological type clock. For instance, while Proto-Indo-European is reconstructed to be a nearly purely fusional language, its descendant languages have all moved – albeit at different rates – towards a more isolating profile. One example of a language that has made much progress in this direction is English, which in the course of its development from Old English to Modern English has lost most of the inflectional bound morphology; another good example is French, which too lost most of its inflectional bound morphemes (both Modern English and Modern French can be characterized as 'three o'clock' languages). Other, more conservative Indo-European languages – such as Russian and Lithuanian – have preserved more of their bound morphology, remaining closer to one or two o'clock.

As has been already mentioned above, Chinese illustrates the isolating-to-agglutinative change. More precisely, Early Chinese is now thought to have been a nearly purely isolating language but with (still) some elements of fusion (at about three o'clock), while Classical Chinese was even closer to the isolating ideal (roughly at four o'clock). But the clock of morphological type change keeps ticking, moving Modern Chinese in the direction of an agglutinative language, towards five o'clock.

Another proto-language, Proto-Dravidian was on the isolating side of agglutinative (at about seven o'clock), while its descendants – modern Dravidian languages – have moved along to a more agglutinative type at nine o'clock. Proto-Australian, the ancestral language of Australian aboriginal languages (see Chapter 9) can be placed at about seven o'clock; modern languages from the Pama-Nyungan family have become more agglutinative, at eight or nine o'clock, while the non-Pama-Nyungan languages have moved even more radically, towards ten or eleven o'clock, having developed strong elements of fusional morphology. A similar degree of fusional morphology has been developed by many modern Finno-Ugric languages (also at ten or eleven o'clock), while their ancestral language, Proto-Finno-Ugric, probably was more purely agglutinative, at around nine o'clock.

One may ask how long it takes to complete the cycle and if there are any known examples of languages that have gone successively through all the stages. The estimates for the length of the cycle are difficult to provide: according to Dixon (1994: 185), it can take "under normal conditions of change, probably anything from two or three thousand years to fifty thousand and more". Given the length of the cycle and the fact that we have written records going back at the most five thousand years (and even that only for very few languages) and we can reliably reconstruct aspects of proto-languages going back about 6,000 to 8,000 years, it is unsurprising that there are no good examples of complete cycles based on a single language. The best example we have is of Egyptian (see Chapter 5), which has a long recorded history. According to Hodge (1970), Old Egyptian (about 3,000 BCE) had a complex verb structure which included reference to person; most of these affixes were lost by Late Egyptian (about 1,000 BCE), which used periphrastic constructions involving auxiliaries. By the time of Coptic (200 CE on) a new complex verb structure has developed, using quite different forms from those of Old Egyptian.[13]

Let's now consider what processes may change a language of one morphological type into another. The change from an isolating profile to an agglutinative one, as in the development of (Mandarin) Chinese, happens through the application of such processes as augmentation, which makes distinct words become grammaticalized as affixes. This is how the two aspectual suffixes of Mandarin Chinese developed. Another example of augmentation involves the fate of the Russian reflexive marker -sja: in Old Russian it was an independent word, whereas in Modern Russian it turned into a bound morpheme (linguists disagree on whether it is a clitic or an affix, but either way it is a bound morpheme). It is so thoroughly connected to the verb that some verbs cannot appear without it: for example, there are verbs *bojat'sja* 'to be afraid' and *smejat'sja* 'to laugh', but no *sja*-less version

---

[13] A much faster turnaround may be witnessed in the formation of pidgins and the subsequent pidgin-to-creole evolution (while pidgins are typically isolating, creoles tend to develop some agglutinative morphology). For a more detailed discussion of pidgins and creoles, see Chapter 12.

bojat' and *smejat'*. Yet another example of augmentation involves creation of case markers from postpositions, verbs or nouns (for examples and a detailed discussion, see Blake 2001: 161–175). This process happens because markers that start out as independent words appear frequently right next to certain kinds of words. For example, auxiliary verbs frequently appear right next to lexical verbs, and postpositions next to nouns. This frequent juxtaposition leads to independent words being reanalyzed as bound affixes.

The change from an agglutinative profile to a fusional one happens due to inevitable phonological changes, which preserve the same morphological elements but fuse their realizations: here a vowel is omitted, there two adjacent consonants are blended, and before you know it, the boundaries between morphemes are not as clear-cut anymore.

A further application of phonological changes that leads to withering of grammatical morphemes, in combination with morphological simplification, where, for example, inflectional affixes may be dropped (especially, if they consist of sounds likely to be withered, such as unstressed vowels or a single consonant), will inevitably result in a fusional language moving in the direction of an isolating one. This is what happened to Proto-Germanic case inflection, which was expressed through special suffixes. However, Proto-Germanic had word-initial stress (Modern English preserves this stress pattern in words of Germanic origin), which made the case markers unstressed and as a result more predisposed to being lost with time.

8   Languages of the South Sea Islands

In the previous chapter, we talked about languages of eastern Asia; but there is one family spoken in the far southeast of Asia and in Oceania that we have not touched on so far. This family – the Austronesian family – is the subject of this chapter. Although most geographic definitions of Oceania include Australia and Papua New Guinea but not Indonesia, in accordance with our principle of dividing the world into geo-linguistic rather than purely geographical zones, we will defer the discussion of languages spoken in Australia and Papua New Guinea till the next chapter, while languages of Indonesia will be discussed here. A more precise definition of the Austronesian realm is given in the following section.

The existence of the Austronesian family, although not the full extent of it, was first recognized as early as 1706 when Adriaan (Hadrian) Reland, a Dutch scholar, cartographer and philologist, published a work titled *Dissertatio de linguis insularum quarundam orientalum*, in which he noted similarities between Philippine languages, Indonesian and Malagasy, as well as Polynesian languages, such as Futuna, based on word lists collected as early as 1616 by Reland's compatriots, explorers Jacob Le Maire and Willem Schouten (on Dutch explorations in the Austronesian realm, see also Chapter 1). But the first researcher to extensively explore Austronesian languages using the comparative method was a German scholar Otto Dempwolff (1871–1938). In the 1920s and 1930s he was able to reconstruct Proto-Austronesian based on the many languages spoken on the islands of Southeast Asia and in the Pacific Ocean. Today, the Austronesian family is on a par with Bantu, Indo-European and Semitic language families as one of the best-established ancient language families.

8.1   The Austronesian realm

The Austronesian realm – the linguistic zone where languages of the Austronesian family are spoken – is the vast area that stretches from Taiwan in the north to New Zealand in the south and from Madagascar off the east coast of Africa in the west to Easter Island (or Rapa Nui, geopolitically part of Chile) in the east. Since most of this territory comprises islands, large and small, and only a few of the Austronesian languages are spoken in mainland Asia, the name of the language family is quite appropriate: it comes from Latin

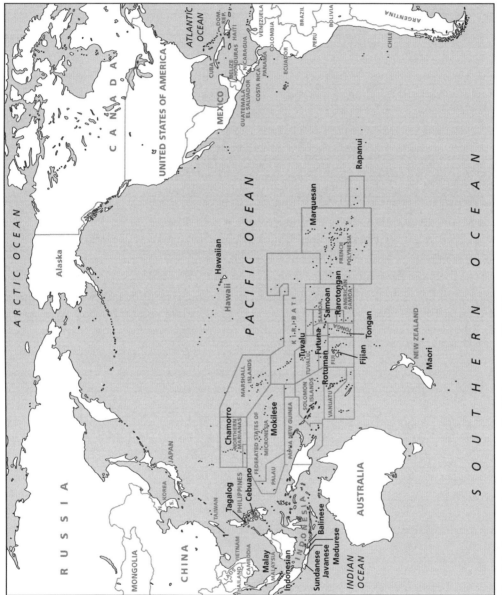

Map 8.1. *Austronesian languages. For Malagasy, see Map 6.3.*

auster 'south wind' and Greek *nêsos* 'island'. The island part of the Austronesian realm is conventionally divided into Indonesia, Micronesia, Melanesia and Polynesia, based on the writings of the French explorer Jules Dumont d'Urville from the 1830s. The etymology of these terms combines the already-familiar Greek *nêsos* 'island' with *indo-* (referring to India), *micro-* ('small'), *mela-* ('black'), and *poly-* ('many'). However, these terms are somewhat misleading: there are "many" islands in all four regions; "micro" islands (atolls) are also widespread in Melanesia and Polynesia; and a few Micronesian islands, such as Guam and Palau, are substantial. And whereas Micronesia and Polynesia were named after the supposed attributes of the islands themselves, the term Melanesia refers to the skin color of the indigenous inhabitants.

The Austronesian language family includes some 1,250 different languages spoken by approximately 180–250 million speakers. Many Austronesian languages have very few speakers, but the major ones are spoken by tens of millions (more on this below).

The Austronesian family is typically split into two major branches: Formosan and Malayo-Polynesian. The Formosan branch includes some 20 languages aboriginal to Taiwan (formerly called Formosa), such as Kavalan, Paiwan and Thao.[1] However, the degree of diversity among these languages is so great that some researchers treat the Formosan grouping as a number of distinct branches of Austronesian, on a par with the Malayo-Polynesian branch. It should also be pointed out that as a group Formosan languages have nearly been replaced by Chinese (see Chapter 7): while prior to the 1600s all of Taiwan was Austronesian-speaking, now Formosan languages are found mostly in the eastern, rugged part of the island. Sadly, most individual Formosan languages are endangered. For example, the two surviving languages in the Western Plains branch – Babuza and Thao – have only 10 speakers between them, and the third language in that branch – Papora-Hoanya – has recently become extinct. Another sad example of a Formosan language that has been displaced by Chinese is Kavalan. Only 24 speakers remain, mostly older adults, and they have been displaced from their original homeland to the northeast coast of Taiwan.

The Malayo-Polynesian branch comprises the other, non-Formosan Austronesian languages and is typically broken down into three subgroupings: Western Malayo-Polynesian, Central Malayo-Polynesian and Eastern Malayo-Polynesian. Of the three, the Western Malayo-Polynesian happens to be the most conservative, that is, most like Proto-Austronesian, and the Eastern Malayo-Polynesian is the least conservative, that is, the most distinct from Proto-Austronesian. For example, Eastern Malayo-Polynesian languages have lost word-final consonants and simplified consonant clusters, to the point of not having consonant clusters at all in some of the languages (see Table 8.1 below and the surrounding discussion).

The best-known Austronesian languages in the Western Malayo-Polynesian subgrouping include **Javanese**, which is spoken by nearly 85 million people in

---

[1] For more information on Thao, see Blust (2003).

Table 8.1. *Cognates in Western and Eastern Malayo-Polynesian.*

	Malay	Futuna
'two'	dua	lua
'eye'	mata	mata
'ear'	telinga	talinga
'stone'	batu	fatu
'fish'	ikan	ika
'louse'	kutu	kutu
'die'	mati	mate

Java as well as Malaysia and Singapore and has the longest written tradition and one of the major literatures among all Austronesian languages; **Sundanese** and **Madurese**, spoken respectively by 34 million and by 13.5 million speakers in Java and Bali; **Malay** and **Indonesian**, two languages closely related linguistically but distinguished geopolitically (both Malay and Indonesian are important trade languages in this region); **Balinese**, spoken by over 3 million people on the island of Bali; **Tagalog**, **Cebuano** and numerous other languages of the Philippines; and **Malagasy**, spoken on Madagascar off the east coast of Africa.

The Central Malayo-Polynesian subgrouping includes a number of smaller languages, spoken on the Maluku Islands (also known as the Moluccas, the Moluccan Islands or the Spice Islands) in Indonesia. Many of these languages are endangered.

Among the Eastern Malayo-Polynesian languages are such languages of the South Sea Islands as **Hawaiian** in the north Pacific, **Chamorro** on Guam and the Marianas Islands, **Maori** in New Zealand, **Fijian** in the group of islands comprising Fiji and **Rapanui** spoken by the approximately 2,000 inhabitants of Easter Island (Rapa Nui), which is one of the most isolated inhabited islands in the world.

8.2   The Austronesian prototype

Since the Austronesian languages are spoken over such a vast area comprising many islands and island archipelagos, it is perhaps rather surprising to find that the various Austronesian languages share many common grammatical features, as well as large chunks of their (basic) vocabulary. This common core can be considered "the Austronesian prototype".

Let us consider the **vocabulary** first. Table 8.1 presents some cognate terms from Malay (a member of the Western Malayo-Polynesian subgrouping) and Futuna (a Polynesian, Eastern Malayo-Polynesian language).

Table 8.2. *Numerals in Austronesian.*

Language	1	2	3	4	5	6	7	8	9
Samoan	tasi	lua	tolu	fa	lima	ono	fitu	valu	iva
Tuvalu	tasi	iua	tolu	fa	lima	ono	fitu	valu	iva
Rarotongan	tai	rua	toru	a	rima	ono	itu	varu	iva
Maori	tahi	rua	toru	wha	rima	ono	whitu	waru	iwa
Hawaiian	kahi	lua	kolu	ha	lima	ono	hiku	walu	iwa
Rapanui	tahi	rua	toru	ha	rima	ono	hitu	vau	iva
Tongan	taha	ua	tolu	fa	nima	ono	fitu	varu	hiva
Fijian	dua	rua	tolu	va	lima	ono	vitu	walu	civa
Rotuman	ta	rua	folu	hake	lima	ono	hifu	valu	siva
Cebuano	usa	duha	tulo	upat	lima	unum	pito	walo	siyam
Tagalog	isa	dalawa	tatlo	apat	lima	anim	pito	walo	siyam
Malay	satu	dua	tiga	empat	lima	enam	tujuh	lapan	sembilan
Malagasy	isa	roa	telo	efatra	dimy	enina	fito	valo	sivy
Thao[a]	tata	tusha	turu	pat	rima	–	pitu	–	–

[a] The two missing numerals in Thao are *makalhturuturu* 'six' and *makalhshpashpat* 'eight'. They are not cognate to the corresponding numerals from other Austronesian languages but formed by *makalh*-prefixation and reduplication of 'three' and 'four', respectively. The numeral for 'nine' – *tanacu* – is also not cognate with the corresponding Austronesian terms. For a further discussion of Thao numerals, see Blust (2003: 204).

As can be seen from Table 8.1, there is a remarkable similarity between the basic lexical stocks of the two languages. Some words, such as *lima* 'five', *mata* 'eye' and *kutu* 'louse', are exactly the same in the two languages, while others, such as the word for 'fish', exhibit a regular pattern of sound correspondence: namely, Futuna has lost the word-final consonants present in Malay.

The same pattern of striking resemblance and regular sound correspondences is obvious if – following the example of James Parsons (see Chapter 2) – we consider numerals 1 through 9 in various Austronesian languages (see Table 8.2).[2] An examination of the numerals from 1 to 9 highlights three important points. First, all these languages are clearly related. This is particularly obvious from the numerals for '5' and '6': 8 of the 14 languages have *lima* for '5', and 9 of the 14 languages have *ono* for '6'.

Second, we can observe several regular patterns of sound correspondences between the languages: for example, the /l/ in Samoan, Tuvalu, Hawaiian, Fijian, Rotuman and Cebuano corresponds to /r/ in Rarotongan, Maori, Rapanui and

[2] A much bigger list of cognate Austronesian numerals may be found at the Austronesian Basic Vocabulary Database online (http://language.psy.auckland.ac.nz/austronesian/word.php?c=Numbers).

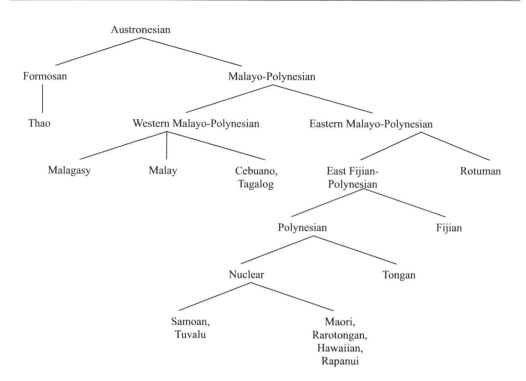

Figure 8.1. *The Malayo-Polynesian branch of the Austronesian language family (simplified).*

Thao (cf. the numerals for '3' and '5' in these languages). It is true of many languages around the world and especially of the Austronesian languages discussed here that they do not use both /l/ and /r/ to distinguish meaning (as does, for example, English: *lime – rhyme*). Such languages either have just one of the two LIQUID CONSONANTS, that is, either /l/ or /r/. For example, in Mandarin Chinese only /l/ is found and in Japanese only /r/. Similarly to Mandarin Chinese, Tuvalu, Tongan and Hawaiian have only /l/; similarly to Japanese, Rarotongan, Maori, Rapanui have only /r/.

Another regular pattern of sound correspondence involves /v/ in Samoan, Tuvalu, Rarotongan, Rapanui, Tongan and Malagasy and /w/ in the corresponding positions in Maori and Hawaiian (cf. the numerals for '8' and '9' in these languages).

The third and final point illustrated by Table 8.2 is that various Austronesian languages are close to differing degrees. For example, Thao is the least closely related. Conversely, Samoan and Tuvalu are closer to each other than to any other of the languages, and so are Maori, Rarotongan, Hawaiian and Rapanui. Similarly, Cebuano and Tagalog are close to each other but are more distantly related to the other Austronesian languages. The relative relatedness of these languages is schematized in Figure 8.1.

Table 8.3. *Some Polynesian cognates.*

	'hand'	'skin'	'bone'	'woman'	'to spit'
Samoan	lima	–	ivi	fafine	anu
Hawaiian	lima	'ili	iwi	wahine	–
Tahitian	rima	'iri	ivi	vahine	tutuha
Maori	ringa(ringa)	kiri	iwi	wahine	tuha
Rapanui	rima	kiri	ivi	bahine	aanu

The close connection and some regular sound correspondences among Polynesian languages is further illustrated by the cognates in Table 8.3 (from Greenhill *et al.* 2008: 276). This is found in many languages around the world as well; compare, for example, the Russian *pjat'* 'five' and *pjad'* 'measure of length between the spread thumb and forefinger', or the Arabic *khamsa* 'five' and 'a palm-shaped amulet'. In the case of the word 'to spit', Table 8.3 illustrates two pairs of cognates: *anu/aanu* in Samoan and Rapanui and *tutuha/tuha* in Tahitian and Maori.

But the Austronesian languages not only share their basic vocabulary, but also have similarly structured sound systems and share many grammatical properties. First, let's consider the **sound systems**. Most Austronesian languages have relatively simple sound systems, with fairly small sound inventories. This is especially true in far-flung Polynesian languages like Maori and Rapanui (with 10 consonant phonemes each) and Hawaiian (8 consonant phonemes only).[3] To compensate for the lack of distinction in the quality of sounds, many Austronesian languages use length to make additional meaningful distinctions. Such length distinctions can be drawn for both vowels and consonants. For instance, in Malay *siku* means 'elbow' and *s:iku* means 'hand tool', while *makɛ* means 'to eat' and *m:akɛ* means 'to be eaten' (quite a difference, right?).

Not only do Austronesian languages have small inventories of sounds to work with, there are also pretty strict rules about which sounds can come next to which sounds – such rules are called PHONOTACTIC RULES. Such rules particularly concern the possible sequences of consonants and vowels that are possible in the language: most Austronesian languages, including Hawaiian, Maori and Tongan, disallow consonant clusters and syllables ending in a consonant. Thus, only syllables consisting of a (short or long) vowel or a consonant followed by a vowel are permitted (consider, for example, such Hawaiian place names as *Honolulu*, *Oahu*, *Molokai*, etc.). These restrictions on possible consonant–vowel sequences also affect loanwords in these languages: for instance, consonants are typically deleted or vowels inserted in Hawaiian loanwords of both English and Chinese

---

[3] When it comes to having a small sound inventory, Polynesian languages compete with some Papuan languages (see Chapter 9).

origin, as in *pipi* 'beef', *kaalaa* 'dollar', *pele* 'bell', *Kalikimaka* 'Christmas' and *konohii* 'Chinese New Year' (from Cantonese *kung hee* 'congratulations').

To turn to grammatical properties that constitute the Austronesian prototype, one of the most characteristic properties of these languages is their extensive use of **infixation** and **reduplication** to mark such grammatical categories as number (on nouns) and tense (on verbs). First, let's consider INFIXATION, that is, use of morphemes that – unlike prefixes or suffixes – attach not to the beginning or the end of the stem, but rather are inserted into the stem. The following example illustrates the use of the infix *-um-* in Tagalog (this morpheme marks the so-called Actor Topic, which is similar to the active voice in English; topic-marking in Tagalog is discussed in more detail below). This morpheme is inserted after the first consonant of the stem (before reading further, what do you expect the past tense form of the verb *takbuh* 'run' to be?).[4]

(8.1)   sulat 'write'   **sum**ulat 'wrote'
         hanap 'seek'   h**um**anap 'sought'
         lapit 'approach'   l**um**apit 'approached'
         lakad 'walk'   l**um**akad 'walked'

In contrast to prefixes, suffixes and infixes, REDUPLICATION involves not attaching the same sounding morpheme to different stems, but repeating part of the stem or the whole stem. For example, reduplication is used in Tagalog to mark future tense of verbs: the first consonant–vowel sequence (syllable) is repeated. Since only a part of the stem is repeated, this is known as partial reduplication.

(8.2)   sulat 'write'   **su**sulat 'will write'
         hanap 'seek'   **ha**hanap 'will seek'
         lapit 'approach'   **la**lapit 'will approach'
         lakad 'walk'   **la**lakad 'will walk'

But the whole stem can be repeated as well, as is done in Indonesian to form words meaning 'all sorts of X', as in *oraN* 'man' – *oraN **oraN*** 'all sorts of men' and *anak* 'child' – *anak **anak*** 'all sorts of children'. This is called full reduplication. Full reduplication only is found in such languages as Rapanui and Fijian, while both full and partial reduplication are found in many Austronesian languages including Balinese, Chamorro, Hawaiian, Madurese, Malagasy, Maori, Marquesan, Mokilese, Sundanese, Thao and others.

Another interesting property that is part of the Austronesian prototype is the distinction between **INCLUSIVE AND EXCLUSIVE** first person pronouns. In English, where such distinction is not made, when one says *we* it is not clear whether the hearer is included: for example, if I say *We're going to a party tomorrow*, it is not clear whether you, the hearer are going with me or whether I am going with some other people. In contrast, speakers of many Austronesian languages such as Tagalog, Indonesian, Fijian, Rapanui, Hawaiian, Chamorro, Maori, Paiwan and Malagasy must specify whether the hearer is included in the

---

[4] **Answer:** *tumakbuh*.

first person plural 'we' or not. For example, if a Tagalog speaker wishes the hearer to come to the party, s/he will use the pronoun *táyo* 'we' and if the speaker is going only with some other people, s/he will say *kamí* 'we' instead; similarly, a Thao speaker would use *ita* 'we' in the first situation and *yamin* 'we' in the second situation (Blust 2003: 207).

Furthermore, many Austronesian languages, including Indonesian, Sundanese, Paiwan, Thao, Chamorro, Fijian, Samoan, Rapanui, Maori and Malagasy, do not distinguish **genders** even in third person singular; in other words, there are no separate pronouns for 'he', 'she' and 'it' – if I were writing in one of these languages, it would make the last sentence of the previous paragraph less clumsy!

In addition, many (although not all) Austronesian languages feature **verb-initial word order**. Among the non-verb-initial languages are several languages spoken in Indonesia and Melanesia which have the Subject-Verb-Object (SVO) order and Austronesian languages spoken in coastal areas of Papua New Guinea which have Subject-Object-Verb (SOV) order (probably as a result of contact with Papuan languages; see Chapter 9). Motu, an Austronesian language of the Port Moresby area, exemplifies this (Capell 1976a):

(8.3)   tau ese au-na imea bogarai-na-i vada e hado
         man ERG tree-the garden middle-its-at PFV 3SG plant
         'The man planted a tree in the middle of the garden.'

As can be seen from this example, in Motu the verb appears sentence-finally, with all nominals preceding it. Spatial relations are marked by postpositions, such as *bogarai* 'middle' to which a locative suffix *i* 'at' is attached. In all these features Motu resembles Papuan languages more than Austronesian ones, even though it belongs to the latter family. This illustrates the point that Austronesian languages spoken in proximity to Papuan languages borrowed structural features from the latter.

Verb-initial Austronesian languages come in two kinds: they either have the Verb-Subject-Object (VSO) order (e.g. Chamorro, Niuean and especially Polynesian languages such as Hawaiian and Tongan) or the Verb-Object-Subject (VOS) order (e.g. Formosan languages on Taiwan, the languages of the Philippines and adjacent parts of Borneo and Sulawesi, as well as Malagasy). The following examples illustrate these two verb-initial orders; note that in VSO languages like Tongan, other sentence elements such as adverbs or indirect objects (highlighted in boldface) come at the end of the sentence, after the object, while in VOS languages like Malagasy, such elements come also after the object but before the sentence-final subject (the sentence-initial verb is italicized).

(8.4)   VSO:
    a.   Tongan
         Na'e manatu'i 'e he tamasi'i 'a e faiva kotoa **'aneafi**.
         PST remember ERG DET boy ABS DET movie all yesterday
         'Yesterday the boy remembered all the movies.'

b.   Chamorro
Ha-bisita   si Dolores si Juan.
TENSE.3SG-visit Dolores   Juan
'Dolores visited Juan.'
                    (Chung 1990: 565)

(8.5)   VOS:
a.   Malagasy
N-i-vidy   ny fiara **ho an-dRasoa** iRabe.
PST-AT-buy DET car for OBL-Rasoa Rabe
'Rabe bought a car for Rasoa.'

b.   Seediq
M-n-ekan   bunga   ka   Pawan.
AT-PST-eat sweet.potato NOM Pawan
'Pawan ate sweet potatoes.'
                    (Holmer 2005: 177)

The final property that may be considered a part of the Austronesian prototype is the so-called **Philippine-style topic marking**. It is found not in all Austronesian languages but in the Philippine languages (such as Tagalog), in Malagasy and in the Formosan languages. This is a grammatical device that serves the function of tracking who did what to whom as well as highlighting the "special argument" of the sentence (explained in more detail immediately below). Thus, it is similar, on the one hand, to case and agreement systems (discussed in Chapters 2, 3 and 4) and, on the other hand, to the active–passive voice distinction in languages like English. But, as we shall see below, there are some crucial differences between all of those grammatical devices. So before we plunge into a description of the Philippine-style topic marking system, let's once again consider case and agreement as well as the active–passive voice in more familiar languages.

First, recall that case and agreement systems serve to track who is doing what to whom. For example, in a Russian sentence in (8.6) we understand that the boy kissed the girl rather than the other way around.[5] Two grammatical devices allow us to figure this out: (1) the noun phrases which refer to the event participants, *mal'chik* 'boy' and *devochku* 'girl', are marked for nominative and accusative case, respectively, indicating that *mal'chik* 'boy' is the grammatical subject and *devochku* 'girl' is the grammatical object, and (2) the verb *poceloval* 'kissed' is marked for agreement with masculine singular subject (so since *devochku* 'girl' is feminine, it cannot be the subject). Ergative case systems, such as the ones found in Basque (see Chapter 3) and Northeast and South Caucasian languages (see Chapter 4) serve a similar purpose.

(8.6)   **Mal'chik**   poceloval   **devochku**
boy(M)-NOM kissed.M.SG girl(F)-ACC
'The/a boy kissed a/the girl.'

---

[5] Russian noun phrases are not marked for definiteness; hence the English translation is indeterminate as to whether it is "a boy" or "the boy" who kissed either "a girl" or "the girl".

The active–passive voice interacts with the case/agreement system to indicate how event participants are expressed in the sentence. In the active voice, the grammatical subject of the sentence corresponds to the "doer", the one who performs some action such as kissing in the above examples (the technical term is the AGENT); in contrast, the grammatical object of the sentence corresponds to the participant to whom the action is applied, in this case, the one who gets kissed (the technical term for this role is THEME or PATIENT).

In the passive sentence in (8.7), the two noun phrases switch their grammatical functions, although their roles in the event are still the same: it is still the boy who kisses the girl. Note also that the form of the verb changes as well. So if we compare the active sentence in (8.6) with the passive counterpart in (8.7), three things are immediately apparent: (1) the object *devochku* 'girl' becomes the subject and its morphological case changes from accusative to nominative, (2) the subject *mal'chik* 'boy' becomes an oblique, which is marked in Russian with instrumental case instead of the nominative, and in English with the preposition *by*, and (3) the form of the verb is changed: it now has passive morphology (e.g. suffix *-n* in Russian; auxiliary *be* and passive participle of the verb in English) and agrees with the new subject. Hence, it is feminine singular in (8.7).

(8.7)   **Devochka**   pocelovana   **mal'chikom.**
          girl(F)-NOM   kissed.PASS.F.SG   boy(M)-INS
          'The/a girl is kissed by a/the boy.'

Now let's turn our attention to the Philippine-style topic marking, which we will illustrate with Malagasy here. In every sentence, the verb bears an affix signaling the semantic role of one of the event participants. The event participant whose role is thus signaled by the verb is expressed by the most grammatically prominent noun phrase in the sentence; in other words, it has a special set of morphological and syntactic properties.[6] Let's look at how this works one sentence at a time. First, look at the Actor-topic sentence in (8.8). Two things are important here. First, the verb (italicized the examples here) is marked with the Actor-topic morphology (glossed as AT).[7] Second, the Actor (i.e. the event participant whose role is signaled by the topic morphology on the verb) appears at the end of the sentence (it is highlighted in boldface here). There is no case marking of any sort in Malagasy.

(8.8)   *Manasa*   ny lamba   amin'ny savony   **ny zazavavy.**
          AT.wash   the clothes with the soap   the girl
          'The girl washes the clothes with the soap.'

---

[6] Unfortunately, there has been a great deal of terminological confusion in the literature surrounding the Philippine-style topic marking. This "special argument" has been variably referred to as "subject", "topic", "trigger", "pivot" and "external argument". Given that all of these terms have been used for something else as well, it is hard to choose the best, most appropriate and non-confusing term. Here, I will use the term "topic" for the sake of consistency.

[7] Because the actual morphology is rather complicated, we will not try to identify the specific AT morpheme.

Now let's look at the Theme-topic sentence in (8.9). Note two crucial changes that are apparent here. First, the verb form is changed: it is now marked with Theme-topic morphology (glossed as TT), thus signaling the role of a different participant. And second, the new participant whose role is signaled by the verb (i.e. the Theme *ny lamba* 'the clothes') is now sentence-final. The Actor *ny zazavavy* 'the girl' appears adjacent to the verb. Note also that although the Theme-topic sentence in (8.9) is translated into English as passive, it is not a passive form in Malagasy. There is a separate way to form a passive sentence in Malagasy, which we will not consider here.

(8.9)   *Sasan'*   ny zazavavy amin'ny savony   **ny lamba**.
        TT.wash the girl   with   the soap the clothes
        'The clothes are washed with the soap by the girl.'

But the possibilities do not end here. Unlike with the active–passive voice in English or Russian, Malagasy allows yet another way to express the same situation: with a Circumstantial-topic. In this case, the verb form is changed yet again – it is now marked with Circumstantial-topic morphology (glossed as CT), thus signaling that the role of the "special participant" is something other than the Agent or the Theme. In this case, this "neither Agent nor Theme" participant is the instrument by which the Agent applies the action to the Theme. In this specific example, the Circumstantial participant is the instrument or means by which the girl (the Actor) washed the clothes (the Theme). Also, note that it is the "circumstantial participant" (i.e. "neither Agent nor Theme") *ny savony* 'the soap' that occurs at the end of the sentence. When a "circumstantial participant" is chosen to be the "special participant", it loses the preposition *amin'ny* 'with'.

(8.10)   *Anasan'* ny zazavavy ny lamba **ny savony**.
        CT.wash the girl   the clothes the soap
        'The soap was washed (with) the clothes by the girl.'

To recap, the "special participant" whose role is signaled by the topic morphology on the verb must appear sentence-finally. But this "special participant" is treated as special by the Malagasy grammar in other ways as well. For instance, one can question only the "special participant" whose role is signaled by the verb's topic morphology. In other words, if one wants to question the Agent who performed the action, one must use the Agent-topic structure in (8.11a); if one wants to question the Theme to which the action is applied, one must use the Theme-topic structure in (8.11b); and if one wants to question the "circumstantial participant" such as the instrument, one must use the Circumstantial-topic structure in (8.11c). In these examples, *no* is the COMPLEMENTIZER, namely the word that turns a declarative sentence into a question. As in English, the question word *iza* 'who' or *inona* 'what' must appear at the beginning of the question.

(8.11) a.   Iza   no   *mividy*   ny vary ho an'ny ankizy?
            who COMP AT.buy the rice for the   children
            'Who bought the rice for the children?'

      b.   Inona no   *vidin'*   ny lehilahy ho an'ny ankizy?
            what   COMP TT.buy the man   for the   children
            'What was bought for the children by the man?'

      c.   Iza   no   *ividianan'* ny lehilahy ny vary?
            who COMP CT.bought the man   the rice
            'Who was bought rice (for) by the man?'

And if this seems too complicated to you, let me tell you about Tagalog, which
is a prime example of a language with the Philippine-style topic marking. Unlike
Malagasy, Tagalog distinguishes not three but eight types of topic: in addition
to the already familiar Agent- and Theme-topic, Tagalog also has Location-,
Beneficiary-, Instrument-, Reason-, Direction- and Reciprocal-topic structures,
all with the corresponding topic morphology on the verb. And to make things
even more complicated – or fascinating, depending on how you look at it! – in
Tagalog a noun phrase has a different form depending on whether it expresses the
"special participant" in the sentence. For example, the noun phrase expressing an
Agent will have a different form depending on whether one uses Agent-topic or
some other type of topic.

Recall that this type of topic marking is found only in the more conservative
Austronesian languages from the Formosan and Western Malayo-Polynesian
branches of the family. But what about Polynesian languages that seem to be
more distinct from the other Austronesian languages and thus also from the
reconstructed Proto-Austronesian language? The question of whether speakers
of Polynesian languages are related to other Austronesians is the subject of the
following section.

8.3   The Polynesian controversy

In the year 1778 his third voyage took Captain James Cook thousands
of miles north from the Society Islands to an archipelago so remote that even
the old Polynesians on Tahiti knew nothing about it. Imagine his surprise when
the natives of Hawaii came paddling out in their canoes and greeted him in a
tongue familiar from his explorations of scores of islands across the breadth
of the Pacific, from the lush New Zealand to the lonely wastes of Easter Island.
Marveling at the similarity of Polynesian languages, he wrote in his journal: "How
shall we account for this Nation spreading it self so far over this Vast ocean?"
That question has perplexed many inquiring minds for centuries. Indeed, who
were these amazing seafarers? Where did they come from? And how could a
Neolithic people with simple canoes and not much in the way of navigation gear

manage to find, let alone colonize, hundreds of far-flung, tiny islands scattered across an ocean that spans nearly a third of the globe?[8]

Recall from the previous section that although Polynesian languages such as Hawaiian, Rapanui, Maori and Tongan share many of the properties in the Austronesian prototype, they do not have the Philippine-style topic marking. There are also other differences between Polynesian languages and those of other Austronesian peoples in Micronesia, Melanesia and Indonesia; there are cultural differences as well. More generally, even though all Polynesian languages are closely related and can be convincingly shown to have descended from a common ancestor, it is not a priori clear where that ancestral language was spoken. Because Polynesia is situated halfway between Asia and the Americas, two possibilities for the Polynesian homeland become immediately apparent: they must have come from (a) Southeast Asia or (b) South America. And while by now this controversy is all but settled, here we will examine it as an illustrative example of how linguistics can contribute to our understanding of various peoples' prehistoric past.

While many historians, archeologists, ethnographers and linguists would place the Polynesian homeland in Southeast Asia, a controversy was stirred by a Norwegian ethnographer and explorer Thor Heyerdahl (1914–2002) who put forward the Kon-Tiki hypothesis. According to Heyerdahl, it was the Neolithic people from Peru who colonized the then-uninhabited Polynesian islands as far north as Hawaii, as far south as New Zealand, as far east as Easter Island, and as far west as Samoa and Tonga around 500 CE. Thor Heyerdahl's evidence in favor of this hypothesis came from a number of different sources. First, there was ethnographic evidence based on the Incan legend about "white men" from Lake Titikaka migrating to the Pacific coast and then . . . disappearing into the sea! Second, archeologists have long pondered the similarity of the enormous stone statues and step pyramids of Polynesia with those in Peru. Third, there was some botanical evidence of plants that "migrated" from South America to Polynesia over the huge expanse of the ocean – but how? After all, plants do not fly or swim. Yet, the strongest card in Thor Heyerdahl's deck of evidence was – or so he thought! – the fact that it is just so easy to sail from Peru to Polynesia by using major westward currents and winds of the South Pacific.[9]

To support his hypothesis, Thor Heyerdahl mounted a scientific experiment: if the Neolithic inhabitants of Peru could sail to the Polynesian islands, so could he and his team. To show how this could be done, Thor Heyerdahl and his men (and they were all men) built a raft from balsa logs cut in Equador and on April 28, 1947, sailed from Callao (Peru) along the major oceanic currents and winds.

[8] The invention of the double outrigger canoe is currently dated at 6,000 years ago (or approximately 4,000 BCE).

[9] Because of the Coriolis effect, the major winds and currents in the northern hemisphere spin clockwise (think, for example, about the Gulf Stream) and in the southern hemisphere – counterclockwise. Similarly, when you unplug a bathtub, water spins in one direction or the other, depending on whether you are north or south of the equator.

On August 7 of the same year, they made landfall at the Raroia Reef in Eastern Polynesia. Thor Heyerdahl then went on to argue that sailing to Polynesia in the opposite direction (i.e. coming from Southeast Asia and going in the west-to-east direction) would be far more complicated, if not impossible, since one would have to fight major westward currents and winds. So could the future Polynesians sail against the winds and currents? For a while, this seemed an impossible proposition, throwing doubt on all the previously collected archeological and ethnographic evidence in support of the Southeast Asian homeland hypothesis. A major re-thinking of the Polynesian sailing and navigation techniques, supported by additional sailing experiments, was necessary.

While it has long been clear that Polynesians had unsurpassed navigational abilities (see "Pioneers of the Pacific" box), certain limitations were placed on them by the kind of sea craft that they used.[10] Although nobody has ever found one of their canoes whole or any rigging, even later Polynesian outrigger canoes would not allow their users to sail too close to the direction facing the wind (or as sailors call it, "close haul"). Probably, the best they could do was to sail at $60°$ to the wind. But that would lengthen the distance they would have to travel by as much as three times – yet an outrigger simply cannot accommodate enough supplies for a trip of that length! And we know that they did manage to bring along everything they would need to build new lives: their families and livestock, taro seedlings and stone tools – but how?

The easiest direction for a Polynesian canoe to take was at about $90°$ to the wind, which taking into account the westward winds would mean going north or south. Hence, once the Polynesians settled in what is now French Polynesia, it was no big problem for them to sail north to Hawaii or south to New Zealand. But how could they get from the Indonesian archipelago and the jungle-clad volcanoes of Papua New Guinea to Polynesia, Thor Heyerdahl's argument went? After all, neither sailing into the wind nor zigzagging at about $60°$ angle could get them there!

So the supporters of the Southeast Asian homeland theory had to think outside the box. The solution came from the colleagues in the climatology departments who discovered that the counterclockwise direction of winds and currents in the South Pacific is just the prevailing direction. But from time to time, El Niño – the same climate disruption that still affects the Pacific Ocean today – would reverse the regular east-to-west flow of the trade winds for weeks at a time, allowing the Austronesian mariners to sail from one archipelago to the next – if they were lucky enough to find small specks of land in the vast expanse of the ocean, of course! Recent discoveries in climate studies provided support for this El Niño theory: data obtained from slow-growing corals around the Pacific and from lake-bed sediments in the Andes of South America points to two series of unusually

---

[10] For more information on canoes and seafaring of early Oceanic peoples, see Pawley and Pawley (1998).

frequent El Niños coinciding with the timing of the two waves of Austronesian expansion, as proposed by archeologists.

These discoveries had the effect of turning the tables on Thor Heyerdahl's strongest argument: in effect, it is **too easy** to sail from Peru to Polynesia, while a possible return trip, in case no land was discovered, would be nearly impossible – just as Thor Heyerdahl argued sailing from Southeast Asia to Polynesia would be. But if the settlers of the Polynesian islands came in the eastward direction, sailing during short periods of favorable winds and currents caused by El Niño, they could always catch a ride home on the trade winds simply by turning their sails around. Well, there were many other troubles on the way, but at least it was not the wind. Thus, by watching wind and current patterns, by developing navigational abilities and just by sheer luck and perseverance, generations of Polynesian seafarers were able to spread through the vast triangle formed by Hawaii, New Zealand and Rapa Nui (Easter Island). And even more recently it turned out that Thor Heyerdahl was right after all about there being contact between Polynesians and South Americans, only that contact was made in the opposite direction. It was the Polynesians who reached the shores of South America, it would seem 75 years before Columbus, at which time they introduced chickens to South America and took back sweet potatoes to Polynesia.

Pioneers of the Pacific

The Pacific adventure began long before the Austronesian people reached Polynesia, since the end of the Solomon island chain was then the edge of the world. The nearest landfall, the Santa Cruz Islands, is almost 230 miles away, and for more than half of this way the Austronesian sailors would have been out of sight of land, with empty horizons all around them. And yet that passage, which they completed around 1200 BCE, was just the warm-up. Reaching Fiji, as they did a century or so later, meant crossing more than 500 miles of oceanic expanse. But these brave seafarers pushed on, sailing out beyond Melanesia and western Polynesia and into the central Pacific, where distances are reckoned in thousands of miles, and tiny specks of land are few and far between.

And consider this: when Magellan's fleet armed with top-notch navigation gear of the day crossed the Pacific in 1520–21 CE, they went nearly four months without setting foot on land, missing the Society Islands, the Tuamotus, the Marquesas and several other archipelagoes. Many of Magellan's sailors died of thirst, malnutrition, scurvy and other diseases before the fleet reached the Philippines. Yet, the early Polynesians found nearly every piece of land there was to find, although it took them centuries to do so. So what gave them the courage to launch out on such a risky voyage, pressing on day after day, and how did they find tiny motes of land in the great blue void of the Pacific?

The early generations of Austronesian mariners who worked their way through the archipelagoes of the western Pacific making short crossings to islands within sight of each other must have developed some amazing navigation skills that were passed down from generation to generation by oral tradition.

In order to locate directions at various times of day year-round, Polynesian navigators had to memorize such important facts as the position and motion of specific stars, and where they would rise and set on the horizon. They needed to be aware of the directions of swells on the ocean, and how the crew would feel their motion. And they kept track of weather patterns.

While out there in the 65-million-square-mile expanse of the Pacific, Austronesian seafarers would look for various – often rather subtle – clues to follow to land. Turtles, coconut shells and twigs carried out to sea by the tides would indicate proximity to land. Wave patterns would be disturbed by distant, invisible atolls. An afternoon formation of clouds on the horizon would point toward an island in the distance, not visible over the horizon. Volcanic eruptions, especially common in Melanesia, would send plumes of smoke billowing into the stratosphere and rain ash for hundreds of miles around. It appears that Polynesians were even able to taste the ocean water and tell by the most slight changes in the water salinity that land was nearby.

But it is the birds who were especially helpful to the ancient Polynesian navigators. Smaller birds in the sky indicated the proximity of land. The migratory paths of larger birds "connected the dots" between various island archipelagoes, so that mariners just had to follow those flyways. And remember the story of Noah's Ark and the dove? One theory is that Polynesians would have taken a frigate bird (*Fregata*) with them: these birds refuse to land on the water as their feathers will become waterlogged making it impossible for them to fly, so when the voyagers thought they were close to land, they would release the bird, which would either fly towards land or else return to the canoe.

Amazing techniques, don't you think? No wonder that these way-finding techniques along with outrigger canoe construction methods were kept as guild secrets and that skilled navigators had a very high status in Polynesian society: in times of famine or other difficulties these skilled navigators would be indispensable for trading for aid or evacuating people to neighboring islands.

But what about linguistic evidence: does it favor the Southeast Asian homeland hypothesis or Thor Heyerdahl's Kon-Tiki theory? The answer is: the former. Recall from our discussion of the Proto-Indo-European homeland controversy in Chapter 2 that there are two linguistic strategies for determining where a given linguistic group originated from: finding the area of highest diversity and identifying their physical environment through a reconstruction of the basic vocabulary. As far as the question of language diversity is concerned, recall from our earlier discussion that the greatest degree of diversity among the Austronesian languages is found in the Formosan branch (see Section 8.1); in the words of Bernard Comrie (2001: 28):

> the internal diversity among the . . . Formosan languages . . . is greater than that in all the rest of Austronesian put together, so there is a major genetic split within Austronesian between Formosan and the rest.

Hence, the Austronesian homeland must be looked for in Taiwan. The reconstruction of the Proto-Austronesian vocabulary also points to Taiwan or neighboring coastal south China: Proto-Austronesian had words for rice, sugar cane, water buffalo and other cattle, plows, axes and canoes – and archeological evidence for such things being in use was found in Neolithic sites in Taiwan and coastal south China. Furthermore, Proto-Malayo-Polynesian (i.e. the common ancestral language of all Austronesian languages except the Formosan ones) – but not Proto-Austronesian – had words for taro, breadfruit, yam, banana, sago and coconut, which places Proto-Malayo-Polynesian in the Philippines or elsewhere on lands bordering the Sulawesi sea (for more on the plant vocabulary in Austronesian and especially Eastern Malayo-Polynesian languages, see Ross *et al.* 1998). Note that these words in Proto-Austronesian and Proto-Malayo-Polynesian were reconstructed on the basis of various descendent languages including the Polynesian ones, meaning that Polynesians – or at least their language – came from Southeast Asia, not Peru.[11]

Two other points can be made by linguists in support of the Southeast Asian homeland hypothesis: first, Polynesian languages exhibit no connection whatsoever to languages of South America. Second, their close connection to the western outlier within the Austronesian family – Malagasy – could not be explained under Thor Heyerdahl's Kon-Tiki theory. And indeed, Polynesian languages exhibit a surprising similarity to Malagasy: for example, compare Malagasy numerals with their counterparts in the farthest-flung Polynesian languages such as Hawaiian, Maori and Rapanui (see Table 8.2 above). What can explain the Malagasy *roa* 'two' (actually pronounced [rua]) vs. the Maori *rua* 'two'; or the Malagasy *fito* 'seven' vs. the Rapanui *hitu* 'seven'; or the Malagasy *valo* 'eight' vs. the Hawaiian *walu* 'eight'? In the next section, we will consider Malagasy and its connection to the Austronesian language family a bit more closely.

8.4   Focus on: The mystery of Malagasy

Having examined Bantu languages in Chapter 6 and Austronesian languages in the preceding sections of this chapter, we are now in the position to take a closer look at Malagasy. Recall that it is spoken on Madagascar, the world's fourth-largest island approximately 285 miles (460 km) off the east coast of Africa. If one considers the physical appearance of Madagascar's inhabitants, it quickly becomes apparent that there are two distinct ethnic groups on the island: unlike the Betsimiaraka tribe, the people in the Merina and Betsileo tribes look decidedly non-African. Recent DNA studies, such as Hurles *et al.* (2005), confirm that Madagascar's inhabitants derive from two distinct stocks: one African and the other non-African. More specifically, the non-African genetic signatures

---

[11] In fairness to Thor Heyerdahl, it must be noted that the possibility of some admixture of settlers from South America cannot be excluded altogether, but Peru could not have been **the** homeland of the Polynesian peoples.

correspond to those found in Indonesia, Borneo and Taiwan. Thus, leaving aside the coastal tribes of Madagascar, which are mostly of African origin, among the Malagasy-speaking population of the Plateau roughly one third of the Y-chromosomes tested showed an East African marker and one third showed one of the two markers for Borneo. The remaining one third displayed other markers traceable to Africa, the Austronesian realm or Europe. So, if Madagascar's inhabitants are of a mixed African and Austronesian origin genetically, what about their language, Malagasy? Should it be considered a mixed Austronesian-Bantu language too?

As discussed in Section 8.2 above, Malagasy exhibits many features of the Austronesian prototype: about 90% of its basic vocabulary is of Austronesian origin, it exhibits a verb-initial (VOS) word order and it relies on the Philippine-style topic marking morphology to encode grammatical relations. Yet, there are also substantial Bantu-influenced elements in Malagasy. For example, Malagasy vocabulary contains many words of Bantu origin, especially in the domain of animal names and terms for domesticated plants: *ondry* 'sheep', *ampondra* 'donkey', *amboa* 'dog', *omby* 'cow', *osy* 'goat', *akangga* 'guinea fowl', *mamba* 'crocodile', *papango* 'kite', *tongolo* 'onion', *ampemby* 'sorghum', *akondro* 'banana' and others. Malagasy has even borrowed the Bantu word for 'eye' – *maso* in Malagasy – in place of the Austronesian-derived **matɛ* (cf. *mata* 'eye' in Futuna and Malay; Table 8.1 above). According to Adelaar (2009b: 726), this is to avoid the homophony that would arise between the words for 'eye' and 'dead'. Malagasy has also borrowed separate Bantu-derived morphemes, such as the Bantu noun class prefix *ki-* (see Chapter 6), which in Malagasy typically forms nouns with a diminutive meaning (e.g. *ki-lalao* 'toy' from *lalao* 'to play'). In the sound system, the influence of Bantu languages can be seen in the presence of prenasalized consonants.

Even in the domain of grammar, where the Austronesian roots of Malagasy are most clear, some scholars see a possible influence of Bantu languages. For example, Adelaar (2009b: 740) suggests that

> *a possible Bantu influence is the development of the circumstantial voice, which can raise all sorts of non-core arguments to subject position. A semantically similar construction raising non-core arguments to object position by means of an applicative exists in Bantu languages.*

To be clear, the actual morphosyntactic phenomenon of raising non-core (that is, non-Agent, non-Theme) arguments to the subject – or "special argument" – position (which in Malagasy, as you would recall from our discussion in Section 8.2 above, is associated with the sentence-final position and the possibility of being questioned) is Austronesian. But it is treating non-core arguments as a group and applying the Philippine-style topic marking to them that may be an example of Bantu influence. The relevant construction, found in many Bantu languages, is the so-called APPLICATIVE CONSTRUCTION, where a non-core argument with one of the range of meanings, including beneficiary, recipient, goal, location and reason, to mention a few, may appear in the syntactic object position when a special applicative morpheme is attached to the verb. The following examples are from Chingoni, a Bantu language spoken by 170,000 people in Southern Tanzania and 53,000 people in Mozambique. In all of the examples in (8.12), the verb has a special applicative morpheme -il/-el attached to it. In (8.12a) the applied object va-jukulu 'children' is a beneficiary, that is, the participant who benefits from the action. In (8.12b) the applied object va-jukulu 'children' is a goal, that is, the participant who receives something. In (8.12c) the applied object chi-pula 'knife' is an instrument; in (8.12d) it is ma-tevele 'peanuts', an ingredient; and in (8.12e) it is ku-m-fuleni 'river', a location marked with the locative prefix ku- before the nominal prefix m-.[12] (Numbers in the glosses here refer to noun classes; see Chapter 6; FV is the final vowel, which need not concern us here.)

(8.12) a. Kuku   a-ku-va-geg-el-a   va-jukulu   ma-gela.
           1-grandpa 1SBJ-PRS-2OBJ-carry-APPL-FV 2-grandchild 6-hoe
           'Grandpa is carrying hoes for the grandchildren.'

     b.   Kuku   a-ku-va-pelek-el-a   va-jukulu   v-aki chi-viga.
           1-grandpa 1SBJ-PRS-2OBJ-send-APPL-FV 2-grandchild 2-his 7-pot
           'Grandpa is taking the pot to his grandchildren.'

     c.   Mi-jokwani v-i-dumul-il-a   chi-pula.
           4-sugar.cane 2 SBJ-PRS-cut-APPL-FV   7-knife
           'They use the knife to cut the sugar cane with.'

     d.   Li-kolo   v-i-telek-el-a   ma-tevele.
           6-vegetable 2 SBJ-PRS-cook-APPL-FV   6-peanut
           'They cooked the vegetables with peanuts.'

     e.   v-i-telek-el-a   ku-m-fuleni.
           2 SBJ-PRS-cook-APPL-FV   17–3-river
           'They are cooking at the river.'

Yet, despite Bantu influences, the bulk of the basic vocabulary and deep grammatical patterns in Malagasy are from Austronesian, which means that Malagasy is an Austronesian language. Note also that while genetically a certain group may be characterized as being, for example, "60% Austronesian and 40% African", in linguistics a language is never characterized in such proportionate terms, for example as "60% Austronesian and 40% Bantu". Thus, contact with and influences of other languages may make a given language significantly different from its relatives, but they do not change the fact that the language descended from a particular ancestral tongue. In the case of Malagasy, that ancestral tongue is an Austronesian language (which one is discussed in more detail below). Similarly, as discussed in Section 5.3, Uzbek is a Turkic language despite its contact with and the influences of Iranian languages, and Maltese is a Semitic language despite its contact with and the influences of Romance languages. Likewise, English is a Germanic language even though a large proportion of its vocabulary derives

---

[12] These examples are from Ngonyani and Githinji (2006: 34–35).

Table 8.4. *Some cognates in Malagasy and Ma'anyan.*

	Malagasy	Ma'anyan
'bone'	táolana	taʔulaʔ
'liver'	áty	atey
'hair'	vólo	wulu
'tongue'	léla	lelaʔ
'person'	ólona	ulun
'woman'	vávy	wavey
'rope'	tády	tadi
'feather'	vólo	wulu
'fruit'	vóa	wuaʔ
'stone'	váto	watu
'moon'	vólana	wulan
'rain'	orana	uran
'one'	ísa	isaʔ
'two'	róa	rueh
'three'	télo	telo
'four'	éfatra	epat

from Romance languages, and French is a Romance language despite the strong Germanic influences.

To return to Malagasy, which Austronesian language may have been its ancestor? Based on careful linguistics detective work, Otto Christian Dahl – a Norwegian missionary-turned-linguist who served in Madagascar from 1929 to 1959 – came up with the hypothesis that Malagasy comes from Ma'anyan, an Austronesian language of the Barito grouping, spoken by 150,000 people in the southern Barito Valley of Kalimantan, Indonesian Borneo. Some cognates between Malagasy and Ma'anyan are illustrated in Table 8.4.

Note, however, that although Malagasy shares many cognates in the basic vocabulary with the Barito languages, it has an entirely different syntax. As Alexander Adelaar (2009a: 150) describes it:

> the morphosyntactic structure of Malagasy is more conservative than SE Barito languages. This type of structure is referred to as "Philippine" . . . In it, several parts of the sentence can become subject, such as actor, undergoer, recipient, location, or instrument, with an affix on the verb indicating which part of the sentence is the subject . . . But Maanyan has evolved toward a West Indonesian (Malay-type) morphosyntactic structure. This structure basically allows only the actor and undergoer of the verb to become subject (in a way not unlike the active versus passive option in European languages).

This strongly suggests that, contra to Dahl's proposal, Malagasy did not descend directly from any known Barito language, but that both Malagasy and modern Barito languages descend from a common ancestor. If the common ancestral language was indeed grammatically more similar to Malagasy than to modern Barito languages, a question arises as to why the modern Barito languages have changed, while Malagasy has not. Adelaar (2009a: 150) explains it in terms of a "longstanding and sustained influence of Malay" on Barito languages.

Curiously, today the Barito languages, which are the closest relatives of Malagasy, are spoken in landlocked areas by people with no knowledge of maritime skills. So although the linguistic similarity to Malagasy is unquestioned, this relationship begs the question of how these people undertook a voyage that would make them the first permanent settlers of an uninhabited island far across the Indian Ocean. Moreover, if Malagasy speakers originally came from Borneo, when might they have made that voyage? And was it one voyage or many?

When it comes to dating the Malagasy migration from Borneo to Madagascar, Otto Dahl was again the first one to propose an answer. He noted that Malagasy has only a few loanwords from Sanskrit and based on this observation he postulated that the emigration from Kalimantan took place at the beginning of Indian influence there, rather than later, when one would expect to find a stronger influence of Sanskrit on Malagasy. Since some early Sanskrit inscriptions dating to 400 CE turned up in eastern Kalimantan, he reasoned that the Malagasy emigration must have been about that time (Dahl 1991: 12). While later dates have been argued for by other scholars, the general consensus appears to be that the Malagasy migration must have happened somewhat later than Dahl originally proposed, around 700 CE. This date is further bolstered by an archeological finding in Diego Suarez at the northern tip of Madagascar, carbon-dated to *ca.* 700 CE (Randrianja and Ellis 2009: 20).

As for whether Austronesian ancestors of present-day Madagascar inhabitants came in one migration or many, there is more speculation regarding this question than solid answers. According to Brown (1979: 13),

> *the present-day distribution of the Indonesian/Polynesian outrigger canoe in the Indian Ocean, and notably in Ceylon, the Maldives, the East African coast and, significantly, the west coast of Madagascar, is strong support for the northern route.*

By "northern route" he means a gradual migration, perhaps generations long, from Indonesia to Madagascar. In contrast, Adelaar (2009a: 164) endorses the idea that emigration was first to East Africa (nicely explaining the presence of Africans in the settlement population). However, Adelaar (2009a: 158) cannot refrain from citing anecdotes about a WWII survivor of a ship sinking in the Sunda Strait of Indonesia drifting safely to Madagascar. Peter Tyson (2001: 216) too argues for the all-in-one-voyage hypothesis:

> *Did a single oceangoing outrigger canoe from Indonesia, perhaps trading along the Indian coast, get blown in a storm to Madagascar? We know this is possible.*

> *In 1930, a boat of fishermen from the Laccadive Islands off India's southwest*
> *coast drifted all the way to Madagascar, coming ashore safely as Cape Est,*
> *on the northeast coast south of Antalaha.*

However, genetic studies suggest that Malagasy migrants came in more than one wave. According to the study by Hurles *et al.* (2005), the Malagasy population exhibits ten different haplogroup types, whereas, for example, the population of the Cook Islands in the South Pacific exhibits only two. The implication of these findings is that a small number of settlers arrived to the Cook Islands relatively recently, where they were not subject to much intermixing with later-settling populations. In contrast, Madagascar either had a more diverse pioneer population, or achieved its relative diversity through multiple independent settlements, probably over a period of many years or even centuries. Overall, much more work in archeology, anthropology and genetics is needed before the mystery of how people got from Indonesia to Madagascar can be solved, but linguistics is indispensable in answering the question of from where exactly (and to some extent also when) Austronesian migrants came to Madagascar.

9   Aboriginal languages of Australia and Papua New Guinea

With the exception of Austronesian languages, discussed in Chapter 8, languages spoken in Australia and Papua New Guinea are relatively poorly studied, nor are the genetic relationships among them clear either. Although some sources refer to these languages as constituting Australian and Papuan language families, these groupings are best understood as geographical terms rather than as valid linguistic classifications since convincing proof for these groupings is yet to be presented.

Attempts have been made – most notably by Joseph Greenberg – to relate Papuan languages to languages outside Papua New Guinea. For instance, Greenberg (1971) proposed that all Papuan languages, as well as Andamanese and the now extinct Tasmanian languages constitute a macro language family which he named "Indo-Pacific", but other linguists accept the more cautious theory that while some of the languages of Papua New Guinea are related to each other, not all of them are.[1]

Another such geographical rather than truly linguistic classification is the division of Australian languages into Pama-Nyungan and non-Pama-Nyungan languages. The former is a bona fide language family: these languages descend from a common ancestor – you guessed it – Proto-Pama-Nyungan! Yet, the proposed non-Pama-Nyungan language family lumps a number of language groupings whose relationship to each other (as well as to Pama-Nyungan languages) is not well understood. Therefore, I think it is wise to be conservative and assume the smallest (but best-proven) language families, of which there are up to 60 in Papua New Guinea and up to 20 in Australia. Many additional languages are to be considered isolates, since their genetic affiliation with any established language groupings has not been conclusively proven.

Furthermore, the question whether Papuan and Australian languages are related remains open. Until recently, no plausible link has been found, in part because researchers looked in the wrong place: the south coast of New Guinea, immediately above the Torres Strait and the Arafura Sea. It is a logical place to look, for sure, as it is the area closest to Australia, but unfortunately, no languages spoken there today show any evidence of a link to Australian languages. More recent studies suggest that a possible link between Papuan and Australian languages

---

[1] Based on information that has recently come to light, some linguists now believe that the extinct Tasmanian language was related to languages of Australia, not Papua New Guinea.

may be found in an unexpected location: in the highlands of New Guinea (see Foley 1986: 271–275).

One of the reasons the classification of languages in Australia and Papua New Guinea is so difficult is the sheer number of languages involved. There are about 270 languages in Australia and over 800 languages spoken in Papua New Guinea (see the "Language diversity and density" box below). Many of these languages are not well documented and little to nothing is known about the earlier stages in their development. To make matters even worse, many of these languages are severely endangered and several have become extinct in recent times (and many more will probably become extinct in the near future). Another factor that complicates language classification in Australia and Papua New Guinea is the widespread borrowing and diffusion from one language to another. Since we do not know in principle which features of language can be diffused and which cannot, it is difficult to establish which patterns of similarity across these languages are due to diffusion and which ones indicate common descent (Florey 1988: 154).

Language diversity and density

Papua New Guinea has what is probably the highest language density on the planet, with some 1,000 languages in a land area of some 900,000 km^2 (or nearly 350,000 square miles) – this is one language every 900 km^2! And in some areas the density is even greater than that, with as much as one language per 200 km^2. This language density is unparalleled elsewhere. But why such a plethora of languages in Papua New Guinea, of all places?

Three major factors have been postulated for the extreme linguistic diversity in Papua New Guinea. First of all, Papuans have inhabited this area for some 40,000 years, which allows ample time for the natural processes of language change and diversification. Consider Foley's (1986: 8–9) model: if we assume the initial situation with a single community speaking a single language and a language splitting into two every 1,000 years – both conservative assumptions, according to Foley – "this alone would result in 10^{12} languages in 40,000 years", and this is not taking into account language contact, language mixing and language extinction.

The second major cause for linguistic diversity in Papua New Guinea, as elsewhere, is the topography. For example, mountains have long been correlated with a higher degree of language diversity and density; therefore, other areas of high language density include Nepal and the Caucasus (see Chapter 4). Other topographic features that pose genuine barriers to social interaction and therefore favor linguistic diversity are islands, rugged coastline, swampland and tropical forests – and Papua New Guinea has it all! Most of its territory is "steep, forest-covered mountains with precipitous drops, swirling rivers, dense, nearly impenetrable rainforests and endless tracts of swampland" (Foley 1986: 9).

But it is not just time and physical geography that determine the degree of language density. There is also a correlation between the social structure, cultural attitudes and language diversity. For example, the existence of a large national state typically correlates with a smaller number of dialects/languages, while a tribal system supports the existence of many smaller languages. We can find traces of this correlation even in Europe: for example, in France, which was unified under one monarchy relatively early, few local dialects (or even separate languages, such as Corsican or Occitan) survive, while in Italy and Germany, which were unified relatively recently, many local dialects thrive to this day.

In Papua New Guinea language is often perceived as a badge of a community's unique identity, as that which defines each tribe in relation to the others, so that tribal system together with cultural attitudes towards language promote linguistic diversification.

So it is, after all, unsurprising that there are so many distinct languages in Papua New Guinea. It has got it all: difficult terrain, tribal societies and lots of time to accumulate differences in speech.

9.1   Languages of Papua New Guinea

As mentioned above, many languages of Papua New Guinea and the general linguistic situation in the region are extremely understudied. In fact, Papua New Guinea is one of the rare regions – the Amazonian jungle is probably the only other such place on Earth – where a new, hitherto unknown language may still be discovered. Even languages that have been discovered are typically not thoroughly documented, even in their current state, not to mention the earlier stages in their development. This also makes classifying languages of the region into language families very difficult, so that the precise relationships between many of the languages in Papua New Guinea have not been conclusively demonstrated. Furthermore, to date no connection has been confirmed between Papuan languages and any languages outside the region. The only exception to this generalization are Austronesian languages, spoken mostly along the coast of Papua New Guinea and on islands (many of these languages are endangered; see Chapter 8).

Putting aside the Austronesian languages, other languages in Papua New Guinea are often referred to as Papuan languages, but as mentioned above this term should be understood as a geographical rather than a linguistic term: it does not refer to a bona fide language family in the sense that they all descend from a common ancestor.[2] In other words, Papuan languages are those that occupy a certain territory, basically those areas of New Guinea and adjacent islands that are not claimed by Austronesian languages. This territory stretches from Alor and

---

[2] Some people prefer to use the term 'non-Austronesian' instead of 'Papuan', as it highlights the purely negative definition of these languages as those languages of the region that are not Austronesian.

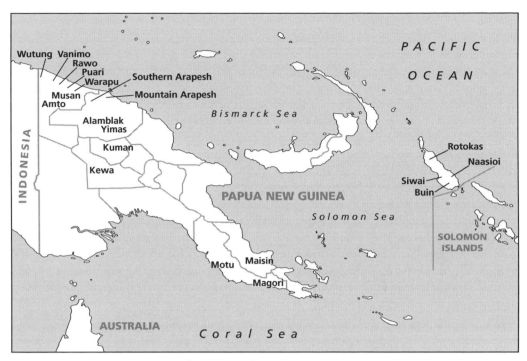

Map 9.1. *Languages of Papua New Guinea.*

Pantar, two small islands west of Timor in eastern Indonesia to the New Georgia archipelago in the western Solomon Islands.[3]

Although Papuan languages are not all related, certain groupings (numbering up to 60, each with its own common ancestral language) within Papuan languages have been established. These established families include: the controversial **Trans-New-Guinea family**, which includes some 470 languages and has a complex (and so far poorly understood) internal structure, with many branches and sub-branches; the **Sko family**, which includes such languages as Wutung (900 speakers, according to the *Ethnologue*), Vanimo (2,670 speakers), Rawo (640 speakers), Puari (35 speakers) and Warapu (300 speakers) spoken on the north coast of New Guinea in the West Sepik Province; the **Left May family**, including six languages none of which is spoken by more than 500 speakers; the **Amto-Musan family**, consisting of two languages – Amto and Musan/Siawi – spoken by 230 and 75 speakers, respectively, in the West Sepik Province; the **Torricelli family**, including 56 languages such as Southern Arapesh and Mountain Arapesh (also known as Bukiyup), each spoken by over 10,000 speakers in the East Sepik Province; the **South Bougainville** family, spoken in the southern third of Bougainville Island and consisting of such closely related languages as Naasioi

[3] There is some debate as to the genetic affiliation of the languages of the Reef and Santa Cruz islands, which lie between the Solomon Islands and Vanuatu.

(20,000 speakers), Buin (also known as Terei, 26,500 speakers) and Siwai (6,600 speakers); and numerous other families.

Given the sheer number of Papuan languages and their classification into numerous language families, we would expect them to be typologically quite different. And yet there are a number of so-called areal traits that are common to most Papuan languages.

Let us consider their sound systems first. Papuan languages are characterized by relatively small sound inventories: according to Foley (1986: 9), the Rotokas language (spoken by 4,320 speakers in the north of the Bougainville Island) contest with Hawaiian (an Austronesian language; see Chapter 8) and Mura (a Chadic language; see Chapter 6) the title of the language with the smallest sound inventory. According to Firchow and Firchow (1969), Rotokas has only 6 consonants and 5 vowels. Most Papuan languages distinguish only three places of articulation in consonants (labial, dental/alveolar and VELAR; though some of the Papuan languages also distinguish PALATAL consonants) and have 5 vowels: /i, e, a, o, u/. Like Mandarin Chinese, Japanese, Hawaiian and Rarotongan (see Chapter 8), most Papuan languages use only one liquid consonant, either /l/ or /r/.

According to Foley (1986, 1992), Papuan languages tend to have agglutinative morphology and use mostly suffixes (prefixes being extremely rare). Another characteristic common to many Papuan languages is complex verbal systems, which distinguish between dependent and independent verbs. The latter have a full range of inflectional possibilities, including subject agreement, tense, mood, etc.; they occur sentence-finally. In contrast, dependent verbs "occur before the independent verb, and are generally reduced in their inflectional possibilities" (Foley 1986: 11). Inflectional categories in Papuan languages include subject agreement (which is nearly universal) and object agreement (which is very common); examples of subject and object agreement are given in (9.3) below. In some Papuan languages, agreement with indirect objects is found as well. Tense and mood are indicated by verbal suffixes that follow the agglutinative pattern. Verbal suffixes would also be used to indicate number, which is rarely indicated on the nouns themselves. Finally, verbal morphology may be used to indicate how likely a certain event is to happen, as in the following examples from Yimas (a Ramu-Lower Sepik language spoken by 300 in the East Sepik Province); examples from Foley (1986: 161):

(9.1) a. tawra   kakanan ana-wa-n
          money   without POTENT.3SG-go-PRS
          'Without money, it is possible, but unlikely, that he will go.'

      b. tawra   kantikin ka-n-wa-n
          money   with   LIKELY-3SG-go-PRS
          'With money, he is likely to go.'

Gender and noun class systems vary from language to language. Some languages feature a simple two-gender system with the masculine–feminine distinction made in the third person singular, as in Alamblak (a Sepik language spoken by 1,530 people in the East Sepik Province). Other languages, such as Yimas, have a full-blown noun class system with a dozen classes. In this language, there are four semantically based classes: "one for male humans, another for female humans, a third for higher animals like pigs, dogs, cassowaries and crocodiles, and the fourth for plants and plant products with an important function in the culture" (Foley 1986: 86). The other eight noun classes in Yimas are phonologically determined.

Papuan languages tend to be ergative and use case suffixes to express spatial relations (instead of pre- or postpositions), as illustrated by the following sentence from Kewa (a Trans-New Guinea language spoken by some 45,000 people in the Southern Highlands Province); example from Foley (1986: 93):

(9.2)   áá-mé   mena   maapú-para tá-a
            man-ERG pig.ABS garden-LOC hit-3SG.PST
            'The man hit the pig in the garden.'

As can also be seen from the example above, Kewa – and Papuan languages more generally – have SOV as their prevalent basic word order, although as Foley admits, "the order of nominals is often quite free, [so] it seems more judicious to claim them simply as verb-final" (p. 10). In these languages the order does not determine which is the subject and which is the object; it is solely a function of the morphology, as illustrated with the following Yimas sentences (from Foley 1986: 167–168):

(9.3) a.   payum narmaŋ   na-mpu-tay
          man.PL woman.SG 3SG.OBJ-3PL.SBJ-see
          'The men saw the woman.'

     b.   payum narmaŋ   pu-n-tay
          man.PL woman.SG 3PL.OBJ-3SG.SBJ-see
          'The woman saw the men.'

In these examples, who saw whom is expressed not through word order (or case marking on the nouns themselves) but through agreement morphology on the verb: in the first sentence, the prefix *na-* indicates third person singular object and the prefix *mpu-* third person plural subject; in the second sentence the prefix *pu-* indicates third person plural object and the prefix *n-* third person singular subject.

In accordance with the typological generalizations discussed in Section 3.4, Papuan languages, which tend to be verb-final, have postpositions (rather than prepositions) and modifiers such as adjectives precede the nouns they modify.

Because of the proximity of Austronesian languages, there has been some contact and borrowing between Austronesian and non-Austronesian languages of Papua New Guinea. For instance, languages in the Torricelli family present an exception to the generalization that Papuan languages are verb-final. Instead, Torricelli languages have the SVO word order, as do Austronesian languages spoken in coastal areas adjacent to where the Torricelli languages are to be found. In some cases, linguistic diffusion has been so intense that a language becomes difficult to classify as either Austronesian or Papuan. Two famous cases of this are Magori of the south coast and Maisin of the Oro Province. After a very careful comparative study, Magori has been classified as an Austronesian language, but many of its speakers are also fluent in Magi, a Papuan language common in this area. This extensive bilingualism must be what resulted in massive "Papuanization" of Magori. The classification of Maisin proves to be even more elusive: the *Ethnologue* classifies it as an Austronesian language, but Capell (1976b) classified it as a Papuan language, which would exemplify the opposite process of "Austronesianization".

In-law language and other taboos

In our society, we use polite forms of speech when talking to certain people, such as people who are older than us, have a higher social status or occupy a specific position, such as a judge in court. But by and large, regardless of who we are addressing, we use the same words, same grammatical rules, etc.

But in many areas of the world, including most notably Papua New Guinea and Australia, certain social situations call for a distinct form of language, sometimes referred to as the "mother-in-law language" because some groups use such special forms of language to address their mothers-in-law or other affinal (i.e. related through marriage) relatives. Typically, such special forms of language involve some form of taboo for words homophonous (that is, same-sounding) or close in form to the names of one's in-laws. For example, the Yimas (a group of about 300 in the East Sepik Province) have a total prohibition against uttering the name of one's father-in-law or mother-in-law. The Kewa (a group of about 45,000 speakers of Kewa in the Southern Highlands Province) give a new name to a man upon marriage to be used by his wife's brothers: his original name cannot be said in their presence.

In many groups, situations requiring the use of a distinct form of language go beyond talking to one's in-laws. For example, on hunting expeditions many groups use special words to denote the animals being hunted, the rationale being that otherwise the animal might overhear the hunters' plans and conceal themselves or attack the hunters instead. These sorts of taboo words are found among the Yumas, the Buin (also known as Terei, a group of about 25,000 in the Southern Bougainville Province), the Kuman (a group of 115,000 in the Simbu Province) and other groups.

Although such replacement of taboo words referring to hunted animals may seem foreign to us today, a similar phenomenon occurred in many familiar Indo-European languages. For example, the original Proto-Indo-European root *rtkos* 'bear', reconstructed on the basis of Sanskrit *rksa*, Avestan *arša*, Greek αρκτος, Latin *ursus* and Welsh *arth*, has been replaced in Slavic languages by a compound *medued* meaning 'honey-eater' (hence, the Russian *medved'* 'bear' and the surname *Medvedev*). Similarly, in Germanic languages the words for 'bear' (e.g. English *bear*, Norwegian *bjørn*) are derived from 'brown'. Likewise, the Proto-Indo-European root *wlkʷ-* 'wolf' (see Table 2.7 in Chapter 2) has been replaced in English, although it is still *volk* 'wolf' in Russian and *vilkas* in Lithuanian.

Another traditional activity in Papuan societies that calls for special language is the annual gathering of pandanus nuts in the highland areas of Papua New Guinea. The pandanus trees grow in the deep forest in areas inhabited, according to Papuans' beliefs, by nature spirits and wild animals dangerous to man. In these areas – and only there – people such as the Kewa would use familiar words of their language, but with an entirely different (or at least extended) meaning. For example, while gathering pandanus nuts, the Kewa would use *yadira* which normally means 'nose stick' to mean 'nose', 'eye', 'seed', 'face' or 'head' – none of which are possible meanings of *yadira* in standard Kewa. Similarly, *palaa*, which means 'thigh' or 'branch' in standard Kewa, means 'tree' or 'fire' in the pandanus form of the language (both of these meanings are expressed by *repena* in standard Kewa). Other words used only in the pandanus form of Kewa are coined as compounds of standard language words: for example, *kadusupa* from *kadu* 'nose' plus *su* 'ground' and *pa* 'make' refers to all creatures that crawl along the ground, like snakes, lizards and certain insects.

But the specialized language goes beyond replacement of taboo words and creation of novel words whose use is restricted to the specific situations. There are some changes – typically simplifications – of grammar as well: for instance, while standard Kewa has two verb stems for 'give', one used when the recipient is third person and the other when the recipient is first or second person, the pandanus form of the language uses the same stem regardless of the person of the recipient – but surprisingly that stem is the reduplicated form of the stem for 'say'!

9.2   Languages of Australia

As mentioned in the introduction to this chapter, Australian languages do not seem to be related to Papuan or Austronesian languages. Indeed, there is little or no similarity in their vocabularies, sound systems or grammars. On the basis of phonological typology, it has been proposed that (some) Australian languages may be related to Dravidian languages of South India: both groups of languages make a rather rare three-way contrast between dental, alveolar and retroflex consonants (see Section 3.3). However, little else unifies these two groups of languages; furthermore, since Dravidian speakers are known to have come from further north on the Indian subcontinent and Australian aborigines to inhabit Australia for tens of thousands of years, it is hard to see how those two groups might have descended from the same ancestral group.

There are about 270 languages in Australia but many of them are on the verge of being extinct. Based on lexicostatistical methods and typological similarities, the tentative classification adopted by the *Ethnologue* groups Australian aboriginal languages into 16 separate families, 15 of which are located in Arnhem Land and the northern part of Western Australia. These families include: Laragiya (2 languages), Tiwian (1 language), Bunaban (2 languages), Daly (19 languages), Limilngan-Wulna (2 languages), Djeragan (3 languages),

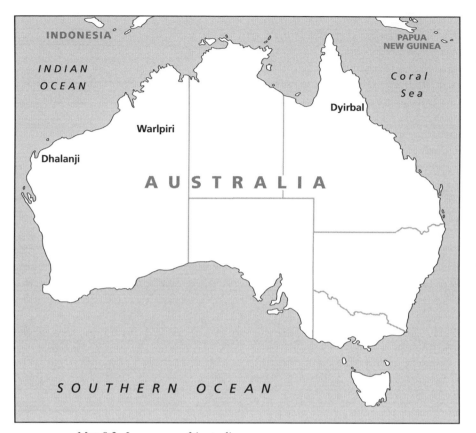

Map 9.2. *Languages of Australia.*

Nyulnyulan (8 languages), Wororan (7 languages), Djamindjungan (2 languages), West Barkly (3 languages), Yiwaidjan (4 languages), Giimbiyu (4 languages), Umbugarla-Ngumbur (20 languages), Gunwingguan (13 languages) and Garawan (1 language).

In the rest of Australia, only one family of aboriginal languages is found: the Pama-Nyungan family. It consists of 177 languages and covers the largest territory in Australia, especially in the north and east of the continent. Interestingly, one can find very long dialect continua here (recall from Chapter 1 that a dialect continuum is a chain of dialects such that the neighboring dialects are very similar and mutually intelligible, but the dialects at the ends of the chain are very different and not mutually intelligible). In Australia such dialect continua stretch for thousands of miles.

The sound systems of Pama-Nyungan languages are very similar: most of these languages lack (or nearly lack) fricatives and affricates, and stop consonants do not exhibit the voicing distinction. Vowel inventories are likewise typically small, consisting of the three basic vowels: /i/, /a/ and /u/.

From the typological point of view, these languages are agglutinative (like many Finno-Ugric and Turkic languages; see Sections 3.1. and 5.1, respectively); typically these languages have suffixes and almost no prefixes. Like many Bantu languages (see Chapter 6), Pama-Nyungan languages have noun classes, but typically fewer than in Bantu languages, on average only four or five. There are also complex demonstrative systems in Pama-Nyungan languages.

In terms of case marking, most Pama-Nyungan languages are ergative (like Basque and many languages in the Caucasus; see Sections 3.2 and Chapter 4) and many of them feature some form of split ergativity, that is, they are ergative in some domains and nominative–accusative in others. For example, Dyirbal has ergative case system for nouns, but nominative–accusative case system for first and second person pronouns (third person pronouns are even more complicated). In contrast, in Dhalanji the cut is made between first person pronouns, which follow the nominative–accusative pattern, and everything else, including second and third person pronouns and common nouns, which follow the ergative pattern. Another factor that may create an ergative split is animacy: for example, according to Dixon (1993) in Nyawaygi nominative–accusative case marking is used with animate pronouns and sporadically with animate nouns, but ergative case marking is used elsewhere. Similarly to Georgian (see Section 4.3), Warlpiri has an ergative case system, even for first and second person pronouns, but nominative–accusative agreement.[4] As we will see in Section 9.3, ergative alignment – that is, treating subjects of intransitives the same as objects rather than subjects of transitives – can extend beyond morphological case and agreement system and apply to syntactic phenomena such as word order, coordination, interpretation of unpronounced subjects in different types of constructions and relative clause formation. But before that, let us consider the syntax of Pama-Nyungan languages a little more closely.

First of all, Pama-Nyungan languages typically have SOV word order, if a basic word order can be established at all. Perhaps surprisingly (see Section 3.4), adjectives follow rather than precede nouns that they modify. But even more importantly, many Pama-Nyungan languages have a relatively free word order, so much so that adjectives need not be adjacent to the nouns they modify, but can appear elsewhere in the sentence. This is known as non-configurationality. In such non-configurational languages, "subjects and objects cannot be identified by word order and . . . constituency tests" (Baker 2001b: 409). The constituency

---

[4] Dhalanji is a nearly extinct Pama-Nyungan language, spoken by 20 people in Western Australia, Exmouth Gulf head inland to Ashburton River. Dyirbal is one of the best studied Pama-Nyungan languages, which too is nearly extinct, but was thoroughly described by Richard M. W. Dixon, who published an exemplary grammatical description of the language in the 1970s. Dyirbal is discussed in more detail in the following section. Nyawaygi – now extinct – was a close relative of Dyirbal and was spoken in an area adjacent to it to the south. Walpiri is yet another Pama-Nyungan language, spoken by over 2,500 people in Northern Territory, Yuendumu, Ali Curung Willowra, Alice Springs, Katherine, Darwin and Lajamanu. It too received much attention in the linguistic literature, especially because of its non-configurational syntax (see the main text below).

tests that Baker refers to include replacing the VERB PHRASE – the unit formed by the verb and its object – by the proform *do/did so* in English. Note that the subject and the verb do not form a similar unit and cannot be replaced by *do/did so*:[5]

(9.4) a.   Mary [ate the pizza] and Sue **did so** (too).

     b.   *[Mary ate] the pizza and **did so** the cookie (too).

Another phenomenon that shows that the verb and the object form a unit (i.e. a constituent), but the verb and the subject do not, is the verb phrase fronting: the verb and the object can be fronted together as a unit, but the verb and the subject cannot:

(9.5) a.   Mary said she would [eat the pizza], and [eat the pizza] I guess she did.

     b.   *Mary said she would [eat the pizza], and [Mary ate] I guess – did it.

Classical illustration of non-configurationality comes from the Pama-Nyungan language Warlpiri, which was studied extensively by Kenneth Hale. As he showed, "in Warlpiri any word order of the subject, verb and object is possible, as long as the auxiliary that bears tense and agreement is in the second position" in the sentence (Baker 2001b: 409). Examples below are from Simpson (1983: 140–141).

(9.6) a.   S-Aux-V-O
        Kurdu-ngku kaju nyanyi ngaju.
        child-ERG   AUX see   I.ABS

     b.   S-Aux-O-V
        Kurdu-ngku kaju ngaju nyanyi.
        child-ERG   AUX I.ABS see

     c.   V-Aux-S-O
        Nyanyi kaju kurdu-ngku ngaju.
        see   AUX child-ERG I.ABS

     d.   O-Aux-V-S
        Ngaju kaju nyanyi kurdu-ngku.
        I.ABS AUX see   child-ERG

     all: 'The child sees me.'

Importantly, more than one word can appear before the auxiliary, as long as those words form a noun phrase or some other sort of constituent. But the verb and its object cannot appear together in front of the auxiliary, so they do not form a constituent in this sense:

(9.7)   *Ngaju nyanyi kaju kurdu-ngku.
        I.ABS   see   AUX child-ERG
        intended: 'The child sees me.'

---

[5] In accordance with the accepted linguistic notation, the ungrammaticality of the resulting sentence is marked by an asterisk. *Too* may or may not be added to the sentence without any change in its grammaticality status, which is indicated by the parentheses.

Furthermore, even though as shown in (9.8) either the subject or the object (or both) may be omitted, in which case the "missing" elements are interpreted as third person pronouns, there is no proform in Warlpiri analogous to the English *do so* that would replace the verb and its object as a unit (examples below are from Hale 1983: 7).

(9.8) a.   Ngarrka-ngku ka pantirni.
        man-ERG   aux spear
        'The man is spearing it.'

     b.   Wawirri   ka pantirni.
        kangaroo.ABS aux spear
        'He/she is spearing the kangaroo.'

     c.   Pantirni ka.
        spear   AUX
        'He/she is spearing it.'

Another salient feature of a non-configurational language such as Warlpiri is that elements of a noun phrase, such as a noun and an adjective or a demonstrative that modifies it, need not appear in adjacent positions:[6]

(9.9) a.   Kurdu-jarra-ngku kapala maliki   wajilipinyi wita-jarra-rlu.
        child-DU-ERG   aux   dog   chase   small-DU-ERG
        'Two small children are chasing the dog.'

     b.   Wawirri kapirna pantirni yalmpu.
        kangaroo AUX   spear   that
        'I will spear that kangaroo.'

It may appear from the description above that a non-configurational language, such as Warlpiri, which has a rather free word order and allows various sentential elements to be omitted, is a grammar-less free-for-all. Some might even relate the putative linguistic primitive nature of Australian languages to the lack of material sophistication in the culture of the people who speak these languages. But as we will see from the following section, this view that relates technologically primitive groups with linguistically primitive languages is a long way from the truth.

9.3   Focus on: Is Dyirbal a primitive language?

Dyirbal is one of the best-described lesser known languages, thanks to the work of Richard M. W. Dixon, who published a detailed description of the language in 1972. A member of the Pama-Nyungan language family, Dyirbal is spoken in Northeast Queensland. It once had a steady population of about

---

[6] Note that the notion 'two' is expressed in (9.9) not by a separate word, as it is in English, but by a dual marker *jarra*. The example in (9.9a) is from Simpson (1991: 257) and the example in (9.9b) is from Hale (1983: 6).

3,000 people, but the number of speakers dwindled down to 40–50 in 1983. At present, there are estimated to be only a handful of speakers left (according to the *Ethnologue*), so it is a severely threatened language on the verge of extinction. According to Dixon, there were six dialects of the language, but three of them are extinct now.

The traditional Dyirbal people made their living off of the rainforest. During the dry season they moved around frequently, while during the rainy season they kept semi-permanent residences. They held strong beliefs in mythology and – through oral tradition – passed down stories about the creation of their homeland; interestingly, many of these stories were later verified with scientific evidence. Dyirbal tribes frequently fought each other and there have been reports of cannibalism. According to Dixon (1972: 28):

> *anyone who has persistently broken the social code may be killed by some of the senior men of the tribe, his flesh eaten and his blood offered to younger men to drink. No particular ritual seems to be attached to human killing but it is always done deliberately, after considerable discussion of the crime of the wrong-doer; there is no evidence that anyone was killed just for the sake of being eaten.*

If one ever expects to find a primitive language, Dyirbal seems to be as good a candidate as any. But their language is far from being the grammar-less lingo one would expect on the assumption that technologically unsophisticated peoples (by our standards, of course) would have linguistically primitive languages. In fact, no such thing as a language without grammar (or a group without a language possessing complex grammar) exists. And the Dyirbal language is certainly far from being grammar-less. Quite the opposite is true: it has a very interesting and complex system of grammatical rules. Here, we will examine only two of the grammatical phenomena that make Dyirbal particularly interesting: its system of noun classes and the split ergative system of case marking and syntax.

First, consider **noun classes** in Dyirbal (the notion of noun classes is first introduced in Chapter 6). As in many other Pama-Nyungan languages, there are four noun classes in Dyirbal. There is nothing in the phonological shape of the noun to indicate its class, but a noun is typically accompanied by a demonstrative-like "noun marker" which agrees with it in case. At first glance, the membership of Dyirbal nouns in the four classes, summarized in Table 9.1, appears arbitrary and random.

However, Dixon (1972: 306–311) shows that the membership in the four classes has a semantic basis after all. According to him, class I is associated with animateness and (human) masculinity, class II with (human) femininity, water, fire and fighting (go figure what those four concepts have in common!), class III with edible vegetables and fruit and class IV is the residue class dealing with everything else. There is an additional complication, however: a noun that would normally be classified as belonging to a particular noun class by virtue of its general semantic features may actually be assigned to another noun class

Table 9.1. *Noun classes in Dyirbal.*

Class I	men, kangaroos, possums, mats, most snakes, most fishes, some birds, most insects, moon, storms, rainbow, boomerangs, some spears, money, etc.
Class II	women, bandicoots (a kind of marsupial), dog, platypus, echidna, some snakes, some fishes, most birds, firefly, scorpion, crickets, grasshoppers, fire, water, sun and stars, shields, some spears, some trees, etc.
Class III	all trees with edible fruit
Class IV	parts of the body, meat, bees, honey, wind, yam-sticks, some spears, most trees, grass, mud, sand, stones, noises, language, etc.

because of a myth or belief that associates that particular noun with a particular property that marks another noun class. This complexity in the assignment of Dyirbal nouns to noun classes inspired the title of George Lakoff's book *Women, Fire and Dangerous Things. What Categories Reveal about the Mind.*

Let us now examine Dyirbal's **ergativity** (see Section 3.2). In terms of its morphosyntax, Dyirbal is in some respects a typical Pama-Nyungan language but it also differs from many other Pama-Nyungan languages in other respects. Like many other languages of the region, Dyirbal is a split ergative language, but it also takes ergativity beyond case marking and agreement, as we will see below.

Recall from Section 3.2 and Chapter 4 that in a language with ergative case marking, subjects of intransitives have the same form as objects (rather than subjects) of transitives, while subjects of transitives have a different form called ergative case. This is true of Dyirbal, where subjects of intransitives and objects of transitives (e.g. *ŋuma* 'father' in (9.10a) and (9.10b)) have the unmarked absolutive form and subjects of transitives (e.g. *yabu-ŋgu* 'mother' in (9.10b)) are marked with the ergative case marker *-ŋgu*. Note that in Dyirbal the verb comes at the end of the sentence, while the order of the noun phrases is typically defined in terms of case rather than grammatical function. More specifically, an absolute noun phrase precedes an ergative one.

(9.10) a. ŋuma   banaga-nyu.
            father.ABS return-NFUT
            'Father returned.'

       b. ŋuma   yabu-**ŋgu**   bura-n.
            father.ABS mother-ERG see-NFUT
            'Mother saw father.'

However, as mentioned above, Dyirbal is a **split ergative** language, the split being between first and second person pronouns, on the one hand, and lexical nouns and third person pronouns, on the other hand. While nouns (and third person pronouns) align in the ergative way, as shown in (9.10), first and second person pronouns align in the nominative–accusative way: subjects of intransitives pattern with subjects of transitives in that both are unmarked, and objects of transitives have a distinct, accusative marker -na:

(9.11) a. nyurra   banaga-nyu.
           you.PL.NOM return-NFUT
           'You returned.'

      b.   nyurra   ŋana-**na** bura-n.
           you.PL.NOM we-ACC see-NFUT
           'You saw us.'

The ergative alignment of nouns and the nominative–accusative alignment of pronouns can be mixed in the same sentence. If the subject is a pronoun and the object a lexical noun, both will appear unmarked, as in (9.12a). Conversely, if the subject is a lexical noun and the object a pronoun, both will have case markers, the ergative -ŋgu and the accusative -na, respectively, as in (9.12b).

(9.12) a. ŋana   jaja   ŋamba-n.
           we.all.NOM child.ABS hear-NFUT
           'We heard the child.'

      b.   ŋana-**na** jaja-**ŋgu** ŋamba-n.
           we.all.ACC child-ERG hear-NFUT
           'The child heard us.'

However, despite the nominative–accusative case marking on pronouns, there is evidence that Dyirbal pronouns, like Dyirbal nouns, follow an underlying ergative pattern. But to understand this, we need to consider the ways in which Dyirbal extends the ergative alignment beyond morphological case marking. There are several syntactic phenomena that can be used to illustrate the ergative alignment in syntax, including the interpretation of unpronounced arguments, relative clause formation, etc. Here, we will consider just one such phenomenon, called coordination or "topic chaining".

In English, if two conjoined sentences share a subject, the subject of the second conjunct may be omitted, as in (9.13a). In such cases, the omitted argument is understood as a subject of its conjunct and as referring to the same individual as the subject of the first conjunct (in this case, *mother*). Crucially, the omitted subject of the second conjunct cannot be interpreted as referring to the object of the first conjunct. To express that, a pronoun must be used, as in (9.13b).

(9.13) a. Mother saw father and **mother** left. = Mother saw father and left.
      b.   Mother saw father and **father** left. = Mother saw father and **he** left.

In Dyirbal coordination works in a different way: in the Dyirbal equivalent of the English sentence *Mother saw father and mother left* the second instance of *mother* cannot be omitted. If the second conjunct lacks a noun phrase, the missing phrase is interpreted as referring not to the subject, but to the object of the first conjunct (there is no word for 'and' in Dyirbal, so for ease of presentation, each conjunct is bracketed).

(9.14)   [ŋuma   yabu-ŋgu   bura-n]   [banaga-nyu].
         father.ABS mother-ERG see-NFUT return-NFUT
         'Mother saw father and **he** returned.'

The same is true in coordinated sentences with pronominal arguments instead of lexical nouns. Despite the nominative–accusative case marking on pronouns, the missing argument in the second conjunct is still interpreted as referring to the (accusative) object rather than the (nominative) subject of the first conjunct.

(9.15)   [ŋada   ŋinu-na   balga-n]   [baniɲu].
         I.NOM   you-ACC   hit-NFUT   came.here
         'I hit you and **you** came here.'

Another manifestation of ergative syntax in Dyirbal is the so-called **antipassive** construction: as we will see immediately below, in several ways it is the mirror image of the more familiar passive voice in languages like English. So let us start by considering the English active–passive contrast again. Recall from our discussion of the Philippine-style topic marking in Chapter 8 that the (English) active-passive switch is characterized by three changes: (1) special verbal morphology is added, (2) the (accusative) object of the active, which denotes the Theme/Patient, becomes the (nominative) subject in the passive and (3) the (nominative) subject of the active, which denotes the Agent, is demoted. The latter change can manifest itself in several ways. For example, the Agent may be omitted altogether as in *The taxes have been raised again*. If the Agent remains, it changes its position (i.e. it is no longer sentence-initial) and must appear in a prepositional phrase (e.g. *by*-phrase in English), as in *This book was written by Leo Tolstoy*. Recall from Chapter 8 that in other languages, such as Russian, the demoted Agent appears in an oblique case, such as instrumental in Russian.

In the Dyirbal antipassive construction, three similar changes occur: (1) special verbal morphology is added, (2) the ergative subject of transitive, which denotes the Agent, becomes the absolutive subject in the antipassive and (3) the absolutive object of transitive, which denotes the Theme/Patient, is demoted. Like the English passive, Dyirbal antipassive is an intransitive construction. All this is illustrated in (9.16) below. In the active transitive sentence in (9.16a), the subject/Agent *ŋuma* 'father' appears with the ergative case marker -*ŋgu*, while the object/Theme *yabu* 'mother' appears in the unmarked absolutive case. In the antipassive sentence in (9.16b), a special antipassive morpheme *ŋa* appears on the verb. Moreover, the agent *ŋuma* 'father' becomes the absolutive subject. The Theme *yabu* 'mother' is demoted: it can be omitted altogether (which is indicated by parentheses in (9.16b)), or it must appear sentence-finally and with a dative case marker -*gu*.

(9.16) a.   yabu   ŋuma-ŋgu bura-n.
            mother.ABS father-ERG see-NFUT
            'Father saw mother.'

   b.   ŋuma   bural-ŋa-nyu   (yabu-gu).
        father.ABS see-ANTIP-NFUT mother-DAT
        'Father saw someone/mother.'

Consider the parallels between the English passive and the Dyirbal antipassive. First, the change in verbal morphology is obvious. Second, the argument that has the marked case (accusative or ergative) becomes the subject of passive or antipassive; it also acquires the unmarked (nominative or absolutive) case in the process. Third, the unmarked (nominative or absolutive) argument is demoted in the sense that it becomes optional (i.e. it can be omitted), it occurs in an unusual place (i.e. it is no longer sentence-initial) and it appears in an oblique form (i.e. an oblique case or with a preposition).

I will conclude this brief sketch of Dyirbal with a short note on the so-called 'mother-in-law' form of the language. As discussed in the "In-laws and other taboos" box above, many languages of Papua New Guinea and Australia have special forms of language to be used in certain socially defined situations, such as talking to/about one's affinal (in-law) relatives. Dyirbal is no exception to this. Like Papuan languages Yimas and Kewa, Dyirbal used to have two variants that were used depending on whom the speaker was addressing: the Guwal variation was used in everyday speech, but the special Dyalnuy, or "mother-in-law", variety was used when the speaker was within earshot of certain taboo relatives, such as parents-in-law of the opposite sex, children-in-law of the opposite sex, and any father's sister's children or mother's brother's children.[7] The Dyalnuy variant was used until the 1930s, when speakers gradually began to use Guwal for all speech (Dixon 1972: 36). While the sound system and the grammar were pretty much the same in Guwal and Dyalnuy, the Dyalnuy variant had a completely different vocabulary – not a single word of it would be the same as in the Guwal variant – and the Dyalnuy vocabulary would be about a quarter of size of the Guwal vocabulary. This meant that a single word in the mother-in-law language would have multiple meanings. To make things even more complicated, often a word in the Dyalnuy variant of one dialect of Dyirbal was found in the Guwal variant of another dialect and vice versa (Dixon 1972: 32–33).

---

[7] With a parent-in-law of the same sex the Dyalnuy variant could but didn't have to be used.

10　Native languages of the Americas

Like the Caucasus (see Chapter 4), sub-Saharan Africa (see Chapter 6) and Papua New Guinea (see Chapter 9), the Americas are a veritable mosaic of languages. Not only are there many Native American languages, but they are also astonishingly diverse and different from each other. There are several reasons to be surprised at such a high degree of linguistic diversity. First, people have inhabited the Americas for a relatively short period of time. While anatomically modern humans are supposed to have come to, say, Papua New Guinea about 60,000 to 40,000 years ago, the first wave of migrants from Asia into the Americas could not have come before 30,000 years ago and it most likely happened even later, around 15,000 years ago. In fact, the Americas were the last continental landmass to be inhabited by humans. So Native Americans just did not have as much time to develop diverse languages as the inhabitants of Papua New Guinea or the Caucasus, not to mention sub-Saharan Africa, where modern humans developed in the first place.

Another curiosity about Native American languages is how little contact and mutual influence there has been among them. This is particularly interesting in light of the fact that they lived next to each other for centuries and share many cultural attributes; but even the tongues of the geographically and culturally closest tribes can be utterly different. Compare this to Eurasia, where the territory occupied by a single language family may stretch for thousands of miles and where even unrelated languages of neighboring peoples show a great deal of similarity because of language contact, borrowing and diffusion. What could be the explanation for such a mosaic-like picture?

The answer becomes apparent when we compare the spread of other technological and cultural innovations (such as agriculture, metallurgy, etc.) in Eurasia and the Americas. Both language families and technological/cultural innovations spread over large territories in Eurasia, but not in the Americas. The explanation probably lies in the geography of the two continental landmasses. As discussed in detail by Jared M. Diamond in his *Guns, Germs, and Steel: The Fates of Human Societies*, the most important difference between Eurasia and the Americas is in the axis along which the continent stretches: Eurasia is stretched east to west, in parallel to the climatic zones, which allows animals and plants – and with them people – to spread over greater distances. That means that Eurasians were bound to travel, communicate with each other and spread their cultural and linguistic innovations. In contrast, the Americas are stretched north to south, which means that travel over significant distances must inevitably cross climatic zones, and with them cultural boundaries. This resulted in a much more fragmented picture, where many groups live side by side but do not mix. And there were other cultural, and as we shall see later, linguistic factors preventing borrowing from one language to the next.

Because of the high degree of linguistic diversity in the Americas, there is little consensus as to how these languages are to be classified. Hence, in the next three sections we will take a closer look at the languages spoken in North America, Meso-America and South America. As we shall see, each of these regions presents its own unique and complex linguistic mosaic.

10.1   Languages of North America

To get a glimpse of the diversity of Native American languages in North America, let's call for Henry W. Longfellow's help. In 1855 he published *The Song of Hiawatha*, an epic poem loosely based on legends and ethnography of the Ojibwa and other Native American peoples. In the first chapter of the poem, Gitche Manito, the Master of Life, tired of human quarrelling, lights the Peace-Pipe and calls "the tribes of men together". And "the nations" come to him for a council. Here is how Longfellow describes the scene:

> *Down the rivers, o'er the prairies,*
> *Came the warriors of the nations,*
> *Came the Delawares and Mohawks,*
> *Came the Choctaws and Camanches,*
> *Came the Shoshonies and Blackfeet,*
> *Came the Pawnees and Omahas,*
> *Came the Mandans and Dacotahs,*
> *Came the Hurons and Ojibways,*
> *All the warriors drawn together*
> *By the signal of the Peace-Pipe,*
> *To the Mountains of the Prairie,*
> *To the great Red Pipe-stone Quarry*

In this short passage Longfellow mentions 12 Native American tribes – a drop in the ocean of linguistic diversity of North America, for sure. Still, it is a good place to start our discussion of Native North American languages and the peoples who speak them.

Delaware, **Blackfoot** and **Ojibway** (or Ojibwa) are all Algonquian languages. Recall that we first came across this family in Chapter 1 where I described the encounter between the Virginia Company settlers and the Powhatans. The now-extinct Powhatan was a close relative of these three languages mentioned by Longfellow. Because of their location on the Atlantic seaboard, speakers of Algonquian languages were the first "American Indians" encountered by the European settlers, and it is from these languages that English borrowed such

Map 10.1. *Languages of North America. For Tarahumara and Huichol, see
Map 10.2. 1: Huron, Delaware, Onondaga, Cayuga, Seneca. 2: Keres, Southern
Tiwa. 3: Caddo, Cherokee, Chickasaw, Comanche, Omaha, Pawnee, Wichita.
4: Menominee, Oneida, Winnebago.*

words describing Native Americans' culture as *wigwam*, *moccasin*, *totem* and
many others, and extended them to apply to cultural realities of other Native
American tribes, who naturally used different words for these objects. Beyond
the northern half of the Atlantic seaboard, Algonquian languages are found in
Illinois, Indiana, Michigan, Missouri, Iowa, Minnesota, North and South Dako-
tas, Montana and northern Wyoming, as well as in large swaths of eastern and
central Canada. This is a relatively large family, including over 40 languages
such as Ottawa, Cree and Montagnais in Canada and Shawnee, Menominee and
Illinois (also known as Miami) in the United States. The now-extinct Mohican
was a member of this family too (have you read *The Last of the Mohicans* by
James Fenimore Cooper?). Unfortunately, many of the Algonquian languages

will probably follow Mohican's fate: for example, Delaware has less than 100 speakers, and the population of Blackfoot, while over 4,000 now, is gradually decreasing. Of the three Algonquian languages mentioned by Longfellow, only Ojibwa is going strong, with the number of speakers in the tens of thousands.

Linguistically, one of the most interesting features of Algonquian languages is their polysynthetic morphology, a phenomenon explicated below in connection with Mohawk. Furthermore, Algonquian languages are among those that make a distinction between inclusive and exclusive pronouns, which we discussed in connection with Austronesian languages in Chapter 8.

Two other languages in Longfellow's list – **Mohawk** and **Huron** – belong to the Iroquois family, found in the Great Lakes area. Also in this family are such languages as Onondaga, Oneida, Cayuga, Seneka and Cherokee. Like speakers of Algonquian languages, speakers of Iroquois languages live in a geographically discontinuous area, as a result of their less than peaceful encounter with European settlers. And like so many of other Native American languages, most Iroquois languages are endangered or on the verge of extinction: for example, Oneida is reported to have only 250 speakers, Seneca – 175 speakers, Onondaga – 90 speakers, Cayuga – 60 speakers and Huron – only 24 speakers. The only two robust Iroquoian languages are Mohawk with nearly 4,000 speakers and Cherokee with over 16,000 speakers. It is for Cherokee that Sequoyah, who saw documents written in English but was not literate in that language, invented his SYLLABARY, that is, a writing system in which each symbol stands for a syllable rather than a single sound.

Let's take a closer look at Mohawk. Like many other languages in North America, such as the Algonquian languages mentioned above and Eskimo-Aleut languages discussed below, Mohawk is known for its POLYSYNTHETIC MOR-PHOLOGY (see Baker 2001a). What it means is that words typically contain many affixes (both prefixes and suffixes) that encode various grammatical concepts: tense, aspect, mood, agreement, etc. When it comes to agreement, verbs in polysynthetic languages exhibit MULTIPLE ARGUMENT AGREEMENT, that is, agreement not only with the subject but also with the object and even with the indirect object if one is present. Consider the following sentences: as shown in (10.1a), the verb must appear with a prefix *shako-* which encodes agreement simultaneously with a third person subject and a third person object. If the verb appears with the prefix *ra-* which encodes just the agreement with a third person subject, the resulting transitive sentence is ungrammatical, as shown in (10.1b). Of course, the prefix *ra-* will be useful for intransitive sentences, with only a subject and no object.

(10.1) a.   Sak shako-nuhwe's   ne owira'a.
             Sak 3.SBJ>3.OBJ-loves the child
             'Sak loves the child.'

       b.   *Sak ra-nuhwe's ne owira'a.
             Sak 3.SBJ-loves the child
             intended: 'Sak loves the child.'

Another aspect of the polysynthetic morphology is the so-called NOUN INCORPORATION, where the noun root becomes part of the verb. In (10.2a) the object *ne ka-nákt-a'* 'a/the bed' is an independent noun phrase and as such it receives the necessary morphology: the particle *ne*, the prefix *ka-* and the suffix *-a'* (the exact nature of these morphemes is immaterial here). The verb too has a number of affixes attached to it, as one would expect in a polysynthetic language: the prefix *wa'-* is a factual morpheme marking aorist (i.e. past completed) tense, the prefix *k-* marks agreement with a first person singular subject (since the information about the person and number of the subject can be recovered from the verb, an independent pronoun in the subject position is not necessary) and the suffix *-'* for punctual aspect (i.e. denoting an event of short duration that happened only once). In contrast, in (10.2b) the object is "incorporated" into the verb. It is no longer a separate noun phrase, and therefore it does not have the same morphology as the object in (10.2a). Instead, the object is part of the verb, which is now the only word in this sentence.[1]

(10.2) a. Wa'-k-hnínu-'   ne   **ka-nákt-a'**.
            FACT-1SG.SBJ-buy-PUNC PART PREFIX-bed-SUFFIX
            'I bought the/a bed.'

        b. Wa'-ke-**nakta**-hnínu-'.
            FACT-1SG.SBJ-bed-buy-PUNC
            'I bought the/a bed.'

Importantly, noun incorporation and multiple argument agreement go hand in hand. In sentences with noun incorporation, the incorporated object is no longer an argument to agree with; hence, in (10.3a) the verb appears with the prefix *ra-* which, as mentioned above, encodes agreement solely with a third person singular subject and does not encode object agreement at all. And as shown in (10.3b), noun incorporation is incompatible with object agreement.

(10.3) a. Sak ra-   wir'a- nuhwe's.
            Sak 3.SBJ- child- loves
            'Sak loves a child.'

        b. *Sak shako-   wir'a- nuhwe's.
            Sak 3.SBJ>3.OBJ- child- loves
            intended: 'Sak loves a child.'

According to the Parametric theory of language, introduced in Section 3.4, both noun incorporation and multiple argument agreement are overt instantiations of the same parameter, which is why both phenomena occur in the same set of languages. Baker (2001a) formulates this parameter as follows: languages differ as

---

[1] The closest thing that English has to noun incorporation is compounds where the object is incorporated at the same time as a suffix such as *-er* or *-ing* is added. That is why a *truck-driver* does not *truck-drive* and when you go *grocery shopping*, you do not go *to grocery shop*. To the extent that such compounds exist without the additional suffix, they are later backformations: e.g. *to baby-sit* was formed from *baby-sitter* and not vice versa.

to whether a verb must include some expression for each event participant (subject, object, indirect object), either via agreement affixes for all participants or via incorporated nouns. Obviously, English – which has neither object agreement nor noun incorporation on the sentential level – is not a polysynthetic language. In fact, morphologically English used to be a fusional language, like Spanish or Russian, but is now changing in the direction of the isolating model (see Section 7.4). But polysynthetic languages are found in many parts of the world and include such North American languages as Wichita (a Caddoan language in west-central Oklahoma; see below), Southern Tiwa (a Kiowa Tanoan spoken in New Mexico), Nahuatl (a Uto-Aztecan language in Central Mexico; see below). Outside North America, polysynthetic languages are found in South America (e.g. Mapudungun, an Araucanian language in Central Chile; see Section 10.3), Northeastern Siberia (e.g. Chukot and Koryak, two Chukotko-Kamchatkan languages in Chukotka and Kamchatka peninsulas of the Russian Far East), India (e.g. Sora, a Munda language; see Section 7.2) and Australia (e.g. Nunggubuyu, a Gunwingguan language; see Section 9.2).

Let's now return to Longfellow's list of Native American tribes. **Choctaw** is a member of the Muskogean language family, spoken along the coast of the Gulf of Mexico. Other languages in this family include Alabama, Muskogee and Chickasaw. Today, Choctaw is spoken only by 11,400 of the 120,400 ethnic Choctaw. More importantly, the number of Choctaw speakers is gradually decreasing, as most children prefer English, and Choctaw is now limited mostly to older adults. Still, Choctaw fares better than many other related languages: for example, Muskogee currently has around 4,300 speakers, Chickasaw about 1,000 speakers and Alabama is seriously endangered with just 100 speakers.

Comanche and **Shoshone** are both members of the Uto-Aztecan language family, a relatively large language family (by North American standards anyway) with over 60 languages, spoken in southern United States and Mexico.[2] Other languages in this family are Ute (1,980 speakers in southwest Colorado, southwest Utah, north Arizona and south Nevada), Hopi (5,260 speakers in Northeast Arizona and neighboring areas of New Mexico and Utah), Luiseño (35 speakers in Southern California), Nahuatl (over 1.7 million speakers in Mexico), Tohono O'odham (9,600 speakers in south-central Arizona), Tarahumara (55,000 speakers in Southwest Chihuahua in Mexico) and Huichol (20,000 speakers in Northeast Nayarit and northwest Jalisco, Mexico). Unlike those other Uto-Aztecan languages, especially those spoken in Mexico, Shoshoni and especially Comanche are endangered: Shoshoni is quite vigorous in several families and has altogether around 3,000 speakers, but Comanche has only 200 speakers and its population is decreasing.

Next on Longfellow's list are **Omaha**, **Mandan** and **Dakota** – all languages from the Sioux family, which is found in parts of the Midwest and central parts of

---

[2] The geographical discontinuity of the area where Uto-Aztecan languages are spoken is a result of large-scale long-distance migration prior to the arrival of the Europeans.

the United States. Omaha is spoken in eastern Nebraska by about 60 people and Mandan is spoken on Fort Berthold Reservation in North Dakota by just a handful of speakers. Languages in the Dakota grouping (including Assiniboin, Dakota and Lakota) are spoken by over 24,000 people in Northern Nebraska, southern Minnesota, North and South Dakota, northeastern Montana and in Canada. But despite the relatively significant numbers, the fate of these languages hangs in the balance as the number of speakers is decreasing and many younger people prefer English or do not speak a Dakota language at all.

Linguistically, Sioux languages tend to have SOV word order and all of them also feature the so-called ACTIVE SYSTEM of agreement. Recall from our earlier discussions that in nominative–accusative languages subjects of intransitives are marked with the same case or trigger the same kind of agreement as subjects of transitives, while in ergative languages subjects of intransitives are marked with the same case or trigger the same kind of agreement as objects of transitives. Note that in both types of languages, subjects of intransitives are marked uniformly, regardless of their semantic role. In an active case marking system, subjects of intransitives which denote an Agent are marked with the same case as subjects of transitives, while subjects of intransitives which denote a Theme/Patient are marked with the same case as objects of transitives. This is how the case system works, for example in Manipuri, a Tibeto-Burman language spoken in northeastern India. In an active agreement system, such as the one found with first and second person agreement in Lakota, subjects of intransitives which denote an Agent trigger the same agreement on the verb as subjects of transitives, while subjects of intransitives which denote a Theme/Patient trigger the same agreement as objects of transitives. Specifically, the subject of 'arrive' in (10.4a), which denotes an Agent, triggers a different agreement on the verb from that triggered by the subject of 'be bad' in (10.4b). In the latter case, the first person singular subject is expressed by the agreement prefix *ma-*, which also encodes agreement with the first person singular object of a transitive verb 'kill' in (10.4c).

(10.4) a.   **wa-i'**.
             1SG.A-arrive
             'I arrived.'

        b.   ma-si'ca.
             1SG.P-bad
             'I am bad.'

        c.   ma-ya- kte.
             1SG.P-2SG.A-kill
             'You kill me.'

Finally, let's look at **Pawnee**, which is one of the Caddoan languages. Originally, languages in this family were spoken in a larger area covering central United States from Dakota to Northern Louisiana and Texas but now it is a small family both in the number of languages (only 4 surviving languages) and in the number of speakers. Pawnee itself has only 20 speakers in north-central Oklahoma; other languages in the family are Caddo (25 speakers in Caddo County in western Oklahoma), Wichita (less than 5 speakers in west-central Oklahoma) and Arikara (20 speakers on Fort Berthold Reservation in North Dakota). Some scholars (e.g. Chafe 1973) believe that Caddoan languages are related to Sioux and Iroquoian languages, but others such as Campbell and Mithun (1979) feel that the evidence presented for this relation is not compelling.

To recap, the twelve languages mentioned by Longfellow belong to six different language families! As a mental experiment, imagine the Master of Life lighting his Peace-Pipe somewhere in Europe, Asia or Africa – can you name twelve languages from one of these regions that belong to six distinct language families (not branches or other lower-order groupings)? To get together, such diverse peoples of Europe, Asia or Africa would have to cross enormous distances and would probably have little knowledge of each other, at least prior to the age of mass media and the internet. But according to the Hiawatha legend, Gitche Manito called these tribes to get together to stop the constant fighting among themselves, which means that these groups must have known each other. And of course, these twelve tribes mentioned by Longfellow are far from being an exhaustive list: in describing the language families to which they belong, I named nearly thirty additional languages. So we could complicate our mental experiment and attempt to name forty languages of Europe, Asia or Africa. By now, if you have read the preceding chapters thoroughly, you should be able to name this many languages from each of the regions (try testing yourself!), but finding languages from as many as six distinct language families will still be difficult – there just isn't that much linguistic variation in those Old World regions!

But in fact there are even more language families in North America, whose languages did not make it into Longfellow's poem. Not mentioned there are families found along the Pacific coast, where one finds even more diversity than in the central and eastern parts of the continent. For example, 78 languages belonging to 18 separate language families are said to be indigenous to California alone.[3] It is on the Pacific coast that one encounters such families as Athabaskan, Salishan, Wakashan and Penutian. Nor have I yet mentioned the Eskimo-Aleut languages spoken in the far north of Canada and in the northern and western coastal Alaska. Finally, there is also a number of isolate languages in North America, such as Keres (11,000 speakers) and Zuni (10,000 speakers). So let's briefly review those families not mentioned in Longfellow's poem, starting with the Athabaskan languages.

Probably the best-known Athabaskan language is **Navajo**. It is the most robust of all Native North American languages, spoken by 178,000 speakers in

---

[3] This distribution of diversity is unsurprising if we assume that North America was settled through the Bering Straits, which makes the Pacific Coast to be the first area settled by Native Americans. Recall from our earlier discussions that the longer a given region has been inhabited by a certain linguistic group, the more diverse the languages become.

New Mexico and Arizona. It may also be the only indigenous North American language the number of native speakers of which is actually increasing rather than rapidly diminishing. Moreover, several newspapers and periodicals are published in this language.

Other Athabaskan languages are spoken in Central Alaska and in Canada, and the Athabaskan language family is probably a branch of a larger macro family called Na-Dené, which includes such other languages as Tlingit, Haida and Eyak.[4] Tlingit is spoken by 1,500 speakers along the western coast of Canada and southern Alaska; Eyak – now extinct – was spoken at the mouth of the Copper River in Alaska; and Haida is spoken by 55 people on Queen Charlotte Islands (Canada), as well as on the south tip of Alaska panhandle (USA). Overall, the Na-Dené family includes 47 languages spoken by approximately 200,000 people, but all of these languages, with the exception of Navajo, are seriously endangered or on the verge of extinction.

Linguistically, Na-Dené languages tend to have a relatively small number of vowels but compensate by using length and/or nasalization to encode meaning. Thus, vowels in these languages can be short or long, nasalized or non-nasalized. For example, Navajo uses only four basic vowels: a, e, i and o. However, each of these may occur either short or long, and either non-nasalized (oral) or nasalized. As a result, each of the basic four vowels has a four-way meaningful distinction between short oral, long oral, short nasalized and long nasalized vowel (e.g. the basic quality *a* gives us for phonemes in Navajo: /a/, /a:/, /ã/ and /ã:/), with the total of 16 vowel phonemes. The vowel inventory is further enriched by adding tones: for instance, Navajo has a high, low, rising and falling tones. In addition, many Na-Dené languages have rich consonant inventories which include glottalized ejectives (these sounds were discussed in connection with languages of the Caucasus in Chapter 4) and many complex LATERAL SOUNDS, that is, sounds pronounced with the air stream moving around the side of the tongue. Morphologically, Na-Dené languages are polysynthetic, that is, they are characterized by a very high number of morphemes per word. However, in contrast to many other polysynthetic languages, noun incorporation is practically absent from the Na-Dené languages.

Another group of languages found on the Pacific Coast is the Salishan language family, which is comprises 26 languages spoken in western Canada and neighboring areas of the USA. These languages include Halkomelem (200 speakers in southwestern British Columbia, Canada), Lillooet (200 speakers in southern British Columbia, Canada) and Spokane (50 speakers in northeastern Washingon). The Tillamook language of northwestern Oregon was a member of this family as well, but it became extinct in the 1970s. Linguistically, Salishan languages, especially Lillooet and Spokane, are known for their very rich consonant inventories, which include glottalized ejectives, uvular consonants, pharyngeal

---

[4] The term *Na-Dené* comes from Dené, the Navajo name for themselves.

consonants and voiceless laterals. From the morphological point of view, Salishan languages are polysynthetic.

Another language family in the area is the Wakashan language family, which is smaller than the language families discussed above, with just five languages, including Nootka (200 speakers), Kwakiutl (190 speakers) and Heiltsuk (300 speakers). These languages exhibit a number of similarities with their Salishan neighbors in sound systems and grammar, which led several scholars, most notably Edward Sapir, to consider them to be related (as well as possibly related to Algonquian languages, discussed above). However, there is no convincing evidence that Sapir was correct in this hypothesis.

The list of Penutian languages is longer than that of the Wakashan family, but many of the Penutian languages have recently become extinct (e.g. Takelma, Alsea and Siuslaw in Oregon). The surviving Penutian languages include Chinook (12 speakers in the Lower Columbia River area of Oregon and Washington), Yokuts (25 speakers in the San Joaquin Valley and on the slopes of the Sierra Nevada in California) and Nez Perce (200 speakers in North Idaho).[5] Note that Chinook was the basis of Chinook pidgin, which served as a trade language among different native groups living in northwestern United States and British Columbia, Canada (pidgins are discussed in more detail in Section 12.1).

One of the most interesting phenomena found in (some) Penutian languages is their use of the three-way case marking system. Recall from earlier chapters that nominative–accusative languages mark subjects of intransitives and subjects of transitives with the morphologically unmarked nominative case (whereas objects of transitives receive a special case called accusative), while ergative languages mark subjects of intransitives and objects of transitives with the morphologically unmarked absolutive case (whereas subjects of transitives receive a special case called ergative). In a THREE-WAY CASE MARKING SYSTEM, illustrated here with **Nez Perce**, all three elements – subjects of intransitives, subjects of transitives and objects of transitives – receive different cases. In a transitive sentence, the subject is ergative and the object is accusative, as in (10.5a). In an intransitive sentence, the subject is left unmarked morphologically, as in (10.5b). Note, by the way, that the word order in Nez Perce appears to be the cross-linguistically rare OVS.

(10.5) a.   Wewúkiye-ne pée-'wi-ye   háama-nm.
          elk-ACC   3.SBJ>3.OBJ-shoot-PFV man-ERG
          'The man shot an elk.'

---

[5] There is a great deal of controversy surrounding the Penutian language family. There are some rather questionable proposals that this family should include some languages of Mexico and even further south. And although there has been some progress linking up the "Penutian languages of California" and the "Penutian languages of the Plateau and Pacific Northwest", the overall grouping remains contentious.

b.   Hi-páayn-a   háama.
      3.SBJ-arrive-PFV   man
      'The man arrived.'

Finally, let's look at Eskimo-Aleut languages.[6] This family includes the various dialects of Aleut, Yupik, Inuktitut and Inupiatun. Altogether they are spoken by approximately 90,000 people in four countries: United States, Canada, Greenland and Russia. But the status of these languages in the four countries is quite different. In Greenland, Inuktitut is recognized as a co-official language (along with English) and is taught in schools (as a result, literacy rates there are quite high). Furthermore, Inuktitut is also used in electronic and print media in Greenland. In Canada, Inuktitut is also recognized as a co-official language of Nunavut Territory (along with English and French) and of the Northwest Territories (along with English, French, and several other indigenous languages). It also has legal recognition in Nunavik – a part of Quebec – where it is recognized in the Charter of the French Language as the official language of instruction for Inuit schools. It also has some recognition in Nunatsiavut – the Inuit area of Labrador. The Canadian Broadcasting Corporation has Inuktitut broadcasts and the language is also used in print media. The Inuit Circumpolar Conference has a commission dedicated to the preservation of Inuit and the development of a common writing system for the language. The situation is, regrettably, quite different in the United States, where Yupik is rarely taught in schools with the inevitable result of low literacy rates and language loss. And the situation is worse still in Russia, where Yupik is a dying language with a rapidly decreasing population (currently at about 1,000 speakers left).

According to the most recent thinking, the nomadic Inuit people were the last group of people to have crossed the Bering Straits. They originated in northeastern Siberia (hence, some scholars postulate a relation between Eskimo-Aleut languages and those in the Chukchi-Kamchatkan family of Eastern Siberia) and some time around 2,000 BCE began to migrate eastward across the Bering Straits to Alaska and then across northern Canada to Greeenland. This migration may have taken as long as 1,000 years. Today, most Inuit people have given up their nomadic lifestyle and live in settled communities.

Linguistically, Eskimo-Aleut languages are characterized by relatively small inventories of sounds: most languages in this family have three vowels /a/, /i/ and /u/ and use length distinction between short and long vowels to encode meaning. In some languages, such as Inupiaq, all stop consonants are voiceless, which means that Inupiaq has /p/, /t/ and /k/ but not /b/, /d/ and /g/. These languages all have a voiceless uvular stop /q/, as well as a voiced uvular fricative /ʁ/ and a voiceless uvular fricative /χ/.

---

[6] Another name for this family is *Inuit*. Speakers of these languages prefer the name *Inuit*, which means 'the people'. *Eskimo* is a derogatory word in Algonquian which means 'eater of raw flesh'. These languages are also referred to as Inupiaq in Alaska, Inuktitut in eastern Canada and Kalaallisut in Greenland.

Grammatically, all Eskimo-Aleut languages are polysynthetic (like Algo-nquian and Iroquoian languages; see above) and ergative. They use numerous affixes to encode grammatical functions, so that words can be very long and practically equivalent to whole sentences in less synthetic languages such as English (see the example from Central Yup'ik in (10.6) below; from Lyovin 1997: 356). And like other polysynthetic languages, Eskimo-Aleut languages have noun incorporation: for example, in (10.6) the object 'boat' has been incorporated into the verb making the sentence intransitive. As in other ergative languages, sub-jects of intransitives trigger absolute agreement affixes: here, the suffix -*quq* marks agreement with a third person singular absolute argument, in this case intransitive subject.

(10.6)   angya-li-ciq-sugnar-quq-llu
           boat-make-FUT-PROBABLE-3SG.ABS-also
           'Also, he will probably make a boat.'

10.2   Languages of Meso-America

Among the language families found in Meso-America, one family – the Uto-Aztecan family – has already been discussed in the previous section because some of its languages are spoken in the southwestern United States. Among those Uto-Aztecan languages spoken in Meso-America probably the best-known is Nahuatl, which descends from Classical Aztec, the main language of the Aztec Empire at the time of the Spanish conquest. The Aztecs were among the first Native Americans that the Europeans encountered, so it was from their language that the Spanish – and later other European languages – borrowed such words as *chocolate* and *tomato*. Unlike many of the languages in North America which are polysynthetic in their morphology, most northern Uto-Aztecan languages are agglutinative and use mostly suffixes. Yet, other Uto-Aztecan languages, such as Nahuatl, are polysynthetic.

There are several other language families found in Meso-America: Oto-Manguean, Mayan, Hokan (also in the southwestern United States), Mixe-Zoque and several other smaller families.

The **Oto-Manguean** family is composed of nearly 180 languages, including the many varieties of Mixtec, Otomi and Zapotec. These languages are spoken exclusively in Meso-America, for the most part in central Mexico. Most of the Oto-Manguean languages are tonal and have nasal vowels. Moreover, they are known for their verb-initial word orders.

The **Mayan** family includes nearly 70 languages, such as Tsotsil, Chontal and Yucatán Maya. These languages descend from the language of Ancient Mayas, who were the only Native American group to develop a writing system before the arrival of the Europeans. Their writing system, which has only recently been deciphered, originated as a logographic system, not unlike that used by

Map 10.2. *Languages of Meso-America.*

the Chinese. But eventually it developed into a syllabic system where individual symbols typically stood for consonant-vowel sequences (and consonant-vowel-consonant sequences had to be expressed by two symbols).

Grammatically, today's Mayan languages tend to be morphologically ergative. However, instead of using case marking to express grammatical relations such as subject and object, Mayan languages rely on verbal agreement. For instance, consider the following examples from Tzotzil (spoken in Chiapas, Mexico). The first verbal prefix expresses the aspect, and the following prefix or two prefixes express agreement with all the arguments. In transitive sentences like (10.7a, b), the prefix closest to the root expresses agreement with the ergative argument (that is, the subject of the transitive) and the prefix further away from the root expresses agreement with the absolutive argument (that is, the object of the transitive). Note that in an intransitive sentence (10.7c) agreement with the first person subject is expressed by the same prefix *i-* as is the agreement with the first person object in a transitive sentence (10.7b), while agreement with a first person subject of a transitive sentence (10.7a) is expressed by a different prefix *h-*. This is exactly the alignment that would be expected in an ergative language.

(10.7) a.　Ta-Ø-h-mah.
　　　　　　ASP-3.ABS-1.ERG-hit
　　　　　　'I am going to hit him.'

　　　b.　L-i-s-ma.
　　　　　　ASP-1.ABS-3.ERG-hit
　　　　　　'He hit me.'

　　　c.　Č-i-bat.
　　　　　　ASP-1.ABS-go.
　　　　　　'I am going.'

Compared to the Mayan language family, the **Hokan** family is much smaller, with only twenty-three languages, many of them severely endangered. Some scholars (e.g. Campbell and Mithun 1979: 42) take a more conservative view and question whether all the languages grouped under the heading of Hokan are indeed related. One interesting property of Hokan languages, such as Lowland/Oaxaca Chontal (spoken by 950 people in Southern Oaxaca, Mexico), is their use of various ejective consonants. Recall from our discussion of Caucasian languages in Chapter 4 that ejective consonants are voiceless consonants pronounced with a simultaneous closure of the glottis, the space between the vocal cords. Many of the world's languages have been reported to have ejective stops; that is, sounds that produced with an abruptly released closure somewhere in the mouth plus a simultaneous closure of the glottis. Languages that have such sounds include languages of the Caucasus, as well as those from Athabaskan, Salishan, Mayan, Afro-Asiatic, Nilo-Saharan, Khoisan, Chukotko-Kamchatkan and Austronesian families. What is peculiar about Lowland/Oaxaca Chontal is its use of ejective affricates; that is, sounds pronounced by creating an oral closure with an accompanying glottal closure, released into frication with continuing glottal closure. Lowland/Oaxaca Chontal has alveolar and palato-alveolar ejective affricates. Apart from Lowland/Oaxaca Chontal, ejective affricates are found in some Athabaskan and Mayan languages, but they are rarer cross-linguistically (and in that sense, "more exotic") than ejective stops.[7]

Finally, consider the **Mixe-Zoque** family, which has seventeen languages, mostly varieties of Mixe and Zoque spoken in Oaxaca, Chiapas and Veracruz states of Mexico. These languages are known for making a three-way distinction in vowel length. This can be illustrated with Coatlan Mixe, spoken by 5,000 people in east-central Oaxaca, Mexico. Unlike most languages that use length distinction in vowels to encode meaning (e.g. Japanese, Finnish), which distinguish

---

[7] An even more exotic type of ejective consonant is ejective fricative. Such sounds are found in a very small number of the world's languages, including Ubykh (a now extinct Northwest Caucasian language; see Chapter 4) and the related Kabardian; Tlingit (a Na-Dene language spoken in Southeast Alaska); Lakota (a Sioux language); and Necaxa Totonac (a Totonacan language of Northeast Puebla state, Mexico).

short and long vowels, Coatlan Mixe distinguishes short, long and extra-long vowels.[8] For example, *pet* with a short vowel means 'a climb', *pe·t* with a long vowel means 'a broom' and *pe:t* with an extra long vowel is a man's name. Recent experimental research has shown that a short vowel takes about 140 ms to pronounce, a long vowel – about 345 ms and an extra long vowel – about 480 ms.

10.3   Languages of South America

Approximately 11.2 million people in South America speak a language indigenous to the continent, and as elsewhere in the Americas these indigenous languages constitute a veritable mosaic of diversity. But unfortunately, the study of South American languages began in earnest only recently, so there is a great deal of dispute and disagreement about the proper classification of these languages. While Joseph Greenberg in his work in 1960s took a lumping approach grouping all South American languages into three macro families with very little evidence to support such a classification, others adopt a more conservative stance, accepting only those groupings for which the evidence is most convincing. For example, Čestimir Loukotka in his classification originally published in 1935 (see Lyovin 1997: 333) lists 113 groupings of South American languages. The *Ethnologue* takes an intermediate approach with 38 language families listed for South America (curiously, only 28 of them are mentioned in a more detailed classification in Lyovin 1997, based on Kaufman 1990). Even previously widely accepted genetic links, such as the one between Quechuan and Aymaran languages, have been questioned more recently, and the *Ethnologue* now lists them as two separate language families.

Given the shortage of information about these languages, it is not surprising that even the number of individual languages varies from source to source, with the *Ethnologue* listing including 465 languages (including 24 isolates) and other estimates going up to 1,000 languages. The greatest diversity of individual languages in South America is found in the Amazon and Orinoco Basins: there are many areas in this region that are difficult for western scholars to penetrate, so hitherto undocumented languages may still be found here.

Among the larger language families of South America we will mention four here. The first one is **Arawakan languages**, which are spoken from Central America to the Amazonian basin.[9] There are nearly sixty languages in this family, making it the largest single family in South America. This family represents

---

[8] Another language that makes a three-way distinction between short, long and extra-long vowels is Estonian (a Finno-Ugric language; see Section 3.1), although things are a bit more complicated with Estonian.

[9] Lyovin (1997: 336) following Kaufman (1990: 40) refers to this family as Maipúrean.

Map 10.3. *Languages of South America.*

Neo-Indian migrations after 200 CE. Many of languages in this family are by now extinct, for example Taino, which was once spoken in the Greater Antilles, but whose speakers have shifted to Spanish by now. Among the surviving Arawakan languages, I will mention Apurinã, which is spoken by some 4,000 people in the area of the Purus River (a tributary of the Amazon) in northwestern Brazil. This language is among the very few of the world's languages that have been reported to have the OSV word order, as in the following example:

(10.8)   anana   nota apa
           pineapple I   fetch
           'I fetch a pineapple.'

Later migrants to the Antilles and South America were speakers of **Carib languages**, a family of about 30 languages still spoken in Venezuela, Colombia, Suriname and Brazil. Several among Carib languages have been reported to have another rare word order: OVS. This is illustrated in (10.9) from Panare, spoken by approximately 3,500 people (of whom nearly all women are monolingual, but most men are bilingual in Spanish to varying degrees) in the Bolivar state of central Venezuela.

(10.9)   pi? kokampö unkï?
           child washes woman
           'A woman washes a child.'

Other Carib languages that have been reported to have the OVS as their basic word order are Hixkaryâna (600 speakers in northern Brazil), Pemon (also known as Arekuna; 6,000 speakers in Venezuela, Brazil and Guyana), Apalaí (450 speakers in northern Brazil next to the Suriname border) and Bacairí (950 speakers in central Brazil).[10]

The third language family is **Quechuan languages**, which includes forty-six different languages (again, according to the *Ethnologue*), all of them varieties of Quechua. This is the language that descends from the languages of the Inca Empire. Today, it consists of disparate varieties spoken by 8 million people in western South America, in the Andes and along the Pacific coast. It is a co-official language of Peru, where it is spoken by 27% of the population, and Bolivia, where it is spoken by 37% of the population (note that there are more Quechua speakers in Bolivia than those who speak Spanish). Additional speakers of Quechua live in Ecuador, where about 7% of the population speak a Quechua language. Finally, Quechua is also spoken by smaller numbers of speakers in Colombia, Argentina and Chile.

Grammatically, Quechua is a nominative–accusative language; spatial relations are expressed by a number of locative/directional cases (or possibly, postpositions), such as the locative -*pa* (e.g. *wasi-pa* 'at the house'), the illative (or

---

[10] In fact, two alternative basic word orders have been reported for Bacairí: the more rare OVS and the far more frequent cross-linguistically SOV.

directional) *-man* (e.g. *ñuqa-man* 'to me'), the ablative *-manta* (e.g. *wasi-manta* 'from the house') and the terminative *-kama* (e.g. *wasi-kama* 'up to the house'). In the first person plural, a distinction is made between the inclusive *ñuqa-nčik* 'we including you' and the exclusive *ñuqa-yku* 'we excluding you'. The verb in Quechua can encode person and number agreement with both subject and object (there is no grammatical gender in Quechua, except in Spanish loanwords, such as *amigu* 'male friend' vs. *amiga* 'female friend' or *loko* 'crazy.MASC' vs. *loka* 'crazy.FEM'), so that pronominal arguments are typically dropped. But when the subject and the object are both full noun phrases, the order is SOV:

(10.10)   wallpa-kuna saa-ta   miku-čka-n-ku.
             chicken-PL   corn-ACC eat-DUR-PRS-3PL.SBJ
             'The chickens are eating corn.'

The closest relative of Quechua appears to be Aymara, spoken by approximately 2 million people in Bolivia and Peru, as well as by smaller numbers in Chile and Argentina.[11]

The fourth significant language family of South America is **Tupi-Guaraní languages**, a family which includes 76 languages, spoken in the eastern part of the continent, stretching from Colombia and Venezuela through Bolivia and Brazil to Paraguay and Argentina. The center of this family is in the southern part of the Amazon Basin. The best-known among these languages is Guaraní, varieties of which are spoken in Brazil, Bolivia and Argentina; it is especially prominent in Paraguay, where it is spoken by 94% of the population, has the status of a second national language (alongside Spanish) and even the national currency has the same name: guaraní. In fact, Paraguay may be the most bilingual country in the world. According to official statistics, 94% of the population speak Guaraní and 94% of the population speak Spanish. Thus, very few people are monolingual in either Guaraní or Spanish. This high degree of bilingualism is rooted in the country's peculiar history as a Jesuit colony. It was common for the Jesuits to learn and promote the local language, as well as to teach Latin and Spanish. Unsurprisingly, it was the Jesuit missionaries who compiled grammars and dictionaries of Old or Classical Guaraní (of which modern Guaraní is a descendent), which used to be spoken during the colonial period (1604–1767) by approximately 300,000 speakers in Paraguay's Jesuit missions.

Another Tupi-Guaraní language worth mentioning is Kaapor (also known as Urubú) spoken by 800 people in northern Brazil. Like Apurinã mentioned above, Kaapor features the rare OSV word order (alongside a much more common SOV order). In general, the cross-linguistically unusual object-initial orders – OVS and OSV – seem to be an areal feature of languages in northern Brazil: in addition to the already mentioned languages from the Arawakan, Carib and Tupi-Guaraní families, several other languages from various families have been reported to have the OSV order, including Nadëb, a Maku language spoken by 300 speakers

---

[11] Evo Morales, the current president of Bolivia, is a speaker of Aymara.

along the Uneiuxi River, and Xavánte, a Macro-Ge language spoken by 10,000 speakers in Mato Grosso – both in northern Brazil.[12]

10.4   Focus on: The Pirahã controversy

While many indigenous languages of the Americas remain under-studied, one language in particular has caused a stormy debate. This language is Pirahã. It is spoken by an estimated 360 speakers in the Brazilian state Amazonas, along Maici and Autaces rivers. Their remote location means that most scholars have only indirect access to the Pirahã and are limited to reanalyzing the data collected by the few experts who lived with the Pirahã for some time and could study their language and culture directly. The most prominent linguist to study the Pirahã directly is Dan Everett, whose work sparked the Pirahã controversy.

What placed the Pirahã on the radar of experts and non-experts alike is Dan Everett's claim that the Pirahã language is unique among human languages. More specifically, Everett has made four claims about the unique features of Pirahã. First, he maintains that the Pirahã language does not allow embedding (or recursion more generally) and lacks some other (possibly, recursion-related) grammatical structures, such as numbers and quantification, 'relative tenses' and color terms. Second, Everett insists that the Pirahã have several peculiar cultural gaps as well, such as the lack of creation myths and fiction, the absence of any individual or collective memory of more than two generations past, the simplest kinship system yet documented and monolingualism maintained after more than 200 years of regular contact with Portuguese-speaking Brazilians. Third, Everett proposed that "Pirahã culture severely constrains Pirahã grammar" (Everett 2005: 622); in other words, he seeks to furnish a common explanation for both the grammatical and the cultural peculiarities of Pirahã. Finally, Everett (2005: 622) views the cultural explanation for the linguistic gaps as a challenge to foundational ideas in linguistics:

> *These constraints lead to the startling conclusion that Hockett's (1960) design features of human language, even more widely accepted among linguists that Chomsky's proposed universal grammar, must be revised. With respect to Chomsky's proposal, the conclusion is severe – some of the components of so-called core grammar are subject to cultural constraints, something that is predicted not to occur by the universal-grammar model.*

All four of these claims have been challenged by other researchers, most notably by Nevins, Pesetsky and Rodrigues (2009; henceforth, NP&R). Based

---

[12] The Maku family consists of 6 languages with approximately 2,650 speakers between them. Macro-Ge is a larger family, with 32 languages, eight of which are extinct and most of the others endangered. There are approximately 41,000 speakers of Macro-Ge languages.

on Everett's own data, NP&R argue that the "inexplicable gaps" of the Pirahã language are illusory, non-existent or not supported by adequate evidence. In addition, based on the work of the Brazilian anthropologist Marco Antônio Gonçalves (1993, 2001), NP&R argue that Everett's characterization of Pirahã culture as exceptional is not correct either; for instance, according to Gonçalves, Pirahã have creation myths and are not purely monolingual. Moreover, even assuming that Everett is correct in his characterization of the Pirahã language and culture as containing those unique gaps, NP&R show that the linguistic and the cultural gaps are not linked: the peculiar constructions found in Pirahã are also found in languages as varied as German, Chinese, Hebrew and Adyghe, whose speakers do not share the unusual properties ascribed by Everett to the Pirahã culture. Finally, NP&R assert that "even if such a connection [between language and culture] should exist, it poses no conceivable challenge to the proposition that some features of [Universal Grammar] are unique to language", thus requiring no revision of Hockett's or even Chomsky's model of language. Thus, NP&R's (2009: 360) conclusion is that Pirahã

> emerges from the literature as ... a fascinating language – but at the same time, it is just a language among other languages of the world, a claim that casts no aspersions on Pirahã.

In this brief overview, we will focus on the argument that Pirahã does not allow embedding; an interested reader is referred to NP&R's clear discussion of numerals and quantification and alleged linguistic gaps in Pirahã. Embedding is defined as "putting one [multiword] phrase inside another of the same type ... e.g. noun phrases in noun phrases, sentences in sentences, etc." (Everett 2005: 622). Thus, constructions involving embedding include among others recursive possession (noun phrase inside a noun phrase) and clausal objects (a clause inside a clause), which are bracketed in English examples below:

(10.11) a. Recursive possession: [*Mary's brother's*] *canoe has a hole.*

b. Clausal object: *John knows* [*how to make an arrow*].

As it turns out, Everett is right in that the Pirahã language does not have the constructions corresponding precisely to those in the English examples in (10.11). However, Pirahã has variations of these constructions that are found in many other (unrelated) languages.

To start with recursive possession, while a prenominal possessor is possible in Pirahã, a possessor noun phrase may not itself contain a possessor:

(10.12) a. xipoógi hoáoíi hi xaagá.
            Xipoogi shotgun 3 be
            'That is Xopoogi's shotgun.'
                (Everett 1986: 205)

b. *kó'oí hoagie kai   gáihií 'íga.
    Ko'oi son   daughter that   true
    'That is Ko'oi's son's daughter.'
                    (Everett 2005: 630)

However, the ban on possessor recursion is found not only in Pirahã, but also in such familiar languages as German:

(10.13) a. Hans-ens   Auto
            Hans-POSS   car
            'Hans' car'

    b. *Hans-ens Auto-s   Motor
        Hans-POSS car-POSS motor
        'Hans' car's motor'

It has been proposed that this prohibition against possessor recursion in German has to do not with the impossibility of embedding but with limitation of the genitive case; the same effect is found in other genitive environments in German, such as the direct objects of particular verbs and prepositions (see Krause 2000a, b). Crucially for our discussion of Pirahã, the fact that German appears to show the very same restriction suggests that "whatever syntactic switch turns off prenominal possessor recursion in German is also at work in Pirahã" (NP&R 2009: 368). Furthermore, it is pretty obvious that "the culture shared by most German speakers is more similar to that of most English speakers than either English-speaking or German-speaking cultures are to the culture of the Pirahã" (NP&R 2009: 368), so the explanation for the lack of recursive possession cannot be formulated in cultural terms.

The arguments based on clausal embedding is similar: the ways in which clausal objects are structured in Pirahã are similar to those found in other languages, which do not share the cultural peculiarities of Pirahã. For example, clausal objects in Pirahã must contain a special morpheme *-sai*, which is said to make the object clause more nominal (e.g. grammatical notions such as tense, aspect and agreement cannot be expressed by such nominalized clauses):

(10.14)   hi ob-áaxáí   [kahaí kai-**sai**]
            3 see/know-INTNS arrow make-NMLZ
            'He really knows how to make arrows.'
                    (Everett 1986: 263)

However, using nominalized constructions for clausal objects is not just a common trait among Amazonian languages, but it is found in many other languages including Quechua, Turkish, Inuktitut and Adyghe (a Northwest Caucasian language; see Chapter 4).

Moreover, Everett notes that in Pirahã clausal objects, as in (10.14), follow the verb while nominal objects precede the verb; for example, the nominal object *kahaí* 'arrow' precedes the (nominalized) verb *kai-sai* 'make', but the bracketed clausal object follows its verb *obáaxáí* 'really know'. However, this combination of OV order with nominal objects and VO order with clausal objects is also far from being rare cross-linguistically; a sampling of languages with this property includes German (illustrated below), Hindi and Wappo (an extinct Yukian language, once spoken in California). In the German examples below, the object is bracketed and the relevant verb is boldfaced.

(10.15) a.   OV (nominal object):
              Hans hat [die Kinder] **gesehen**.
              Hans has the children seen
              'Hans has seen the children.'

        b.   VO (clausal object):
              Hans **sagte** [dass er die Kinder gesehen hat].
              Hans said   that he the children seen   has
              'Hans said that he has seen the children.'

Upon an examination of various properties of Pirahã that Everett claims to be specially constrained by the speakers' culture, NP&R (2009: 359) conclude that

> *if speakers acquire the same types of languages whether their home is a German city, a village in the Caucasus, or the banks of the Maici River in Amazonas, Brazil, we have discovered just the kind of disassociation between language and culture that sheds light on the nature and structure of UG.*

And while this conclusion runs contrary to Everett's view of Pirahã as being surprising and unique among human languages, this result is extraordinary in its own way and "not at all mundane, in the end" (NP&R 2009: 359).

11 Macro families

In the previous ten chapters we have examined a number of well-established language families, such as Indo-European, Semitic, Turkic, Austronesian and others. A question that may be asked at this point is whether any of these language families are related to each other inside even bigger groupings. Such groupings are alternatively referred to as clades, phyla (singular: phylum) or macro language families. Here, I will use the latter term.

The question of such macro families has occupied many an inquisitive mind and hypotheses are plentiful. Various rather far-fetched theories, such as Amerindian, Nostratic, Eurasiatic and Proto-World, have received much attention not only in professional academic circles but in the popular press as well and have been featured in *Atlantic Monthly*, *Nature*, *Science*, *Scientific American*, *US News and World Report*, *The New York Times* and in BBC and PBS television documentaries. While some proposed long-distance relationships and macro families are quite well proven and as a result widely accepted among historical linguists, others are more controversial, and yet others are so far fetched that they are not accepted by linguists other than those who originally proposed them.

In this chapter, we will consider some of these macro family proposals, ranging from the widely accepted Afroasiatic macro language family to the more controversial Uralic (or even Ural-Yukaghir) and Altaic families concluding with the very controversial Nostratic and Eurasiatic hypotheses.

11.1   Afroasiatic languages

The Afroasiatic macro language family is the dominant grouping in most of north Africa and large parts of southwestern Asia.[1] There are 374 individual Afroasiatic languages. Although the geographical distributions of individual

---

[1] The term "Afroasiatic" (often written Afro-Asiatic) was coined by Maurice Delafosse in 1914, but did not come into general use until it was adopted by Joseph Greenberg in the 1950s. This term came to replace the earlier term "Hamito-Semitic", coined in reference to the descendants of the Biblical Ham and Shem, two of Noah's three sons (see our earlier discussion of James Parsons's work in Chapter 2). It was Joseph Greenberg who demonstrated that Hamitic is not a valid language family.

Afroasiatic languages have contracted and expanded, the distribution of the family as a whole goes back to antiquity. In fact, given the extremely deep divisions among the branches constituting the Afroasiatic macro language family, the parent language of this family – Proto-Afroasiatic – must be placed as far back as 12,000 years ago if not earlier (see Bomhard 1996: 7–8 and the references cited there).

The Afroasiatic macro language family consists of six smaller language families, the best-known among them the Semitic language family, discussed in Section 5.2. Recall that the Semitic family includes such languages as Arabic, Hebrew and Aramaic, as well as the now-extinct Akkadian and Phoenician. Let us now look more closely at the other five language families constituting the Afroasiatic macro language family: Egyptian, Berber, Chadic, Cushitic and Omotic.

The smallest language family within Afroasiatic is the Egyptian language family, consisting in fact of only one language, and an extinct one at that – Coptic. This language is a descendant of Ancient Egyptian, the language attested in various historical stages from the earliest writing in Egypt. The hieroglyphic writing system and its offshoots were used into the Common Era, but soon after Christianization hieroglyphs were replaced by a Greek-based script; it is this Greek-script-based variety that is known as Coptic. This language survived as a spoken tongue into the late Middle Ages (perhaps even as late as the sixteenth century CE), when it was finally replaced by Arabic. However, Coptic is still used as a liturgical language of the Coptic Church. The Egyptian language family is very important for a study of comparative Afroasiatic linguistics since its written records are among the oldest written records of any language and cover a period of 4,500 years from about 3,000 BCE to about 1500 CE.

Another family within Afroasiatic is that of the Berber languages, a family consisting of 25 individual languages spoken in a scattered pattern across north Africa from just east of the Egypt–Libya border. However, the majority of Berber speakers are nomadic tribesmen who live in the mountainous parts of Algeria and especially Morocco, and in the desert parts of Mali and Niger. Among the most widely spoken Berber languages are Kabyle (2.5 million speakers in Algeria), Tachelhit (3 million speakers in Morocco and Algeria), Tamazight (3 million speakers in Morocco and Algeria), Tashawit (1.4 million speakers in Algeria), Tarifit (1.5 million speakers in Morocco and Algeria) and Tamasheq (282,000 speakers in Mali and Niger). There has been a great deal of contact and diffusion between Berber languages and the neighboring Arabic varieties.

The Chadic family includes some 195 languages spoken in the sub-Saharan region west, south and east of the Lake Chad, in a belt centered on northern Nigeria and southern Niger. Most of the Chadic languages have few speakers, but there is one significant exception, namely Hausa, the dominant indigenous language of northern Nigeria and southern Niger, spoken by 18.5 million people and used as a trade language by many other speakers of neighboring Chadic and non-Chadic languages (trade languages are discussed in more detail in Section 6.4).

The fifth family within Afroasiatic – the Cushitic family – includes 45 languages spoken in the Horn of Africa: in Somalia, Djibouti, much of southern Ethiopia, and extending into Kenya and Tanzania to the east of Lake Victoria. The most widely spoken Cushitic languages are Somali (nearly 12 million speakers in Somalia, Ethiopia, Djibouti and Kenya), Sidamo (2.9 million speakers in Ethiopia), Oromo (17 million speakers of its three varieties in Ethiopia), Afar (approximately 1 million speakers in Ethiopia, Eritrea and Djibouti) and Bedawiyet (approximately 1 million speakers in Sudan and Eritrea). Whether the various branches of Cushitic actually form a language family is sometimes questioned, but their inclusion in the Afroasiatic macro family itself is fairly well established.

Finally, there is the Omotic language family, consisting of twenty-nine languages, spoken altogether by 1.5 million speakers along the Omo River in southeastern Ethiopia. The most widely spoken language in this family is Wolaytta, which has about 1.2 million speakers. The genetic link of Omotic languages to the rest of the Afroasiatic is the weakest; in fact, Greenberg (1963) and other scholars considered it a branch of Cushitic, while yet others have raised doubts about it being part of the Afroasiatic macro family at all (e.g. Theil 2006).

As mentioned in the introduction to this chapter, the Afroasiatic family as a whole is well established, despite some controversies that still exist as to the internal classifications within this macro family. The idea that Semitic and Berber languages may be related goes back to the ninth-century grammarian Judah ibn Quraysh of Tiaret in Algeria, a speaker of a Berber language familiar with Semitic through his study of Arabic, Hebrew and Aramaic. The Cushitic family (then known as "Ethiopic") was added to the mix by Theodor Benfey in 1844; the link to the Chadic language Hausa was suggested in the same year by T. N. Newman, but his proposal was not widely accepted for a long time. In fact, a "Hamitic" group – proposed by Friedrich Müller in 1876 – included only Egyptian, Berber and Cushitic, but not Chadic languages. The controversy continued with later proposals that linked some of the six families more closely to each other than to others. So today, while the disputes about the internal classification of the Afroasiatic macro family have not been settled, the overall validity of the Afroasiatic grouping is accepted by nearly all linguists.

If Afroasiatic is a bona fide language family; that is, a grouping of languages descending from a common ancestral language, we expect to find patterns of similarity both in the vocabulary (in the form of cognates) and in grammar. And indeed both types of similarities are found in Afroasiatic languages.

From the point of view of sound systems, Afroasiatic languages share a number of common features. For example, these languages distinguish not only voiced and voiceless consonants but also a third set of the so-called emphatic consonants, which can be realized as pharyngealized or velarized consonants (in many Semitic and Berber languages), as glottalized ejectives (in the Semitic languages of Ethiopia, as well as in South Arabian, Cushitic and Omotic languages),

Table 11.1. *Cognate consonantal roots in Afroasiatic.*

Root	Semitic (Hebrew)	Egyptian (Coptic)	Chadic (Hausa)	Cushitic (Proto-Cushitic)	Omotic (Dime)
*b-n- 'build'	bana 'he built'			*mĭn/*măn 'house'	bin- 'build, create'
*m-(w)-t 'die'	met 'he died'; mavet 'death'	mu 'die'	mutu 'die'		
*l-s 'tongue'	lašon 'tongue, language'	las 'tongue'	harshe 'tongue'		lits'- 'lick'
*s-m 'name'	šem 'name'	smi 'report, announce'	suna 'name'		
*d-m 'blood'	dam 'blood'			*dîm/*dâm 'red'	

or implosive (in the Chadic languages).[2] Many of these languages also have pharyngeal fricatives, which are otherwise rare cross-linguistically. While some languages in the Omotic, Chadic and Cushitic branches of Afroasiatic are tonal, languages in the Semitic, Berber and Egyptian branches are not.

Morphologically, Afroasiatic languages (with the exception of Chadic, Cushitic and Omotic languages) are known for their use of non-concatenative morphology (see Section 5.2) whereby roots consisting of consonantal sequences (most roots reconstructed for Proto-Afroasiatic are bi-consonantal) and vowels, as well as templates for combining vowels and consonants, are provided by grammatical morphology, which expresses lexical category (noun, verb, etc.), number, tense, aspect and so on. Some of these cognate roots and their cognates in five of the six Afroasiatic language families are listed in the Table 11.1.

To return to Afroasiatic morphology, these languages typically have a two-gender system in the singular, with the feminine gender marked by the suffix -*t*. Syntactically, most Afroasiatic languages, especially in the Semitic, Egyptian and Berber families have the basic VSO word order, although other word orders are found as well. For instance, Amharic (an Ethiopian Semitic language) and most languages in the Cushitic family are SOV. Languages in the Chadic family are mostly SVO (but VSO order is also found in some of them). Moreover, many modern Semitic languages – for example, Modern Hebrew and many colloquial varieties of Arabic – feature the SVO order as well.

To recap, numerous similarities in the vocabularies and grammars of Afroasiatic languages, some of which have been mentioned above, allow scholars to accept the unity of these languages as a macro language family. In the following sections, however, we will turn to more controversial macro families, such as Uralic and Altaic.

---

[2] Emphatic consonants are pretty much non-existent in Modern Hebrew.

11.2   Uralic languages

In Sections 3.1 and 3.4 we discussed Finno-Ugric languages such as Hungarian, Finnish, Estonian, Udmurt and others. It has been proposed that Finno-Ugric languages constitute a part of a larger family known as Uralic. In addition to the Finno-Ugric branch, this proposed Uralic macro family would also include Samoyedic languages. Samoyedic is a small language family, consisting of only six languages, all with small numbers of speakers, spoken along the northern fringe of Eurasia, roughly from the Kanin peninsula to the Taymyr peninsula. Among the Samoyedic languages are varieties of Enets (30 speakers altogether), Nenets (31,300 speakers), Selkup (1,640 speakers) and Nganasan (500 speakers). Nganasan is the northernmost language spoken in Siberia.

The proposal is that the diverse Finno-Ugric languages and the Samoyedic languages descend from a common ancestral tongue which must have been spoken over a continuous part of northeastern Europe and northwestern Asia. Later, speakers of Indo-European and Turkic languages displaced many of the original Uralic groups, so that various Uralic languages today are spoken in a geographically discontinuous area. In fact, there has been an extensive and prolonged contact between Uralic and Indo-European languages, which resulted in a great deal of lexical borrowing as well as diffusion of grammatical features. The ties are especially close between languages in the Finnic branch within Uralic and languages in the Balto-Slavic branch of Indo-European. For example, in both Russian and Finnish one finds an alternation in the case of the direct object in affirmative and negative sentences: in affirmative sentences, the object appears in the accusative case (as is expected in a nominative–accusative language), whereas in negative sentences the object appears in the partitive (Finnish) or genitive (Russian) case; this is shown in (11.1) and (11.2), respectively. Note that in Finnish this special partitive of negation is obligatory, whereas in (modern) Russian it is optional (the special negative verb *ei* in Finnish is discussed shortly below).

(11.1) a.   Hän luki   kirjan.
           s/he read.PST book.ACC
           'S/he read the book.'

      b.   Hän ei   lukenut kirjaa   / *kirjan.
           s/he not.3SG read   book.PRTV / *book.ACC
           'S/he didn't read the book.'

(11.2) a.   On čital   knigu.
           s/he read.PST book.ACC
           'S/he read a/the book.'

      b.   On ne čital   knigi   / knigu.
           s/he not read.PST book.GEN / book.ACC
           'S/he didn't read any/the book.'

Such similarities between Uralic and Indo-European languages have led some researchers to postulate a genetic link between the two families; however, even though a genetic relationship cannot be ruled out between Indo-European and Uralic, it cannot currently be proven either because we do not know which similarities are due to a genetic relationship and which to a diffusion of linguistic traits across language family boundaries. Recall also from the discussion in Section 3.1 that Russian speakers were in a prolonged contact with Finnic-speaking peoples such as Merya, Muroms and Meshchera, who were ultimately absorbed into the Russian-speaking population.

Typologically, Uralic languages range from agglutinative (e.g. Finnish) to synthetic/fusional (e.g. Estonian). According to Janhunen (1992: 208), Proto-Uralic was agglutinative, had SOV word order, two grammatical cases (accusative and genitive) and three local cases: dative, locative and ablative (see also Section 7.4). The verbal morphology in Uralic languages is usually fairly complex. The most striking feature is that Uralic languages have special negative verbs which one may translate as 'not to be, not to exist' and that are used as auxiliary verbs to negate other verbs. For example, in Finnish to say 'I don't know' one says *e-n tiedä*, where *e-n* is the negative verb in the first person singular present tense (cf. the negative verb in the first person plural *e-mme* or the negative verb in the third person singular *e-i*) and *tiedä* is a special negative form of the verb 'to know'. Another property common to Uralic languages is their use of vowel harmony (see Section 3.1).

While Uralic itself has not been conclusively proven to be a valid language family, attempts have been made to relate this putative macro family to other languages or language families. One such proposal relates Uralic languages to the Yukaghir family of languages which consists of just two languages: Tundra and Kolyma, spoken by 90 and 30 speakers, respectively, in the area of the Kolyma and Indigirka rivers in northeastern Russia. The link between Yukaghir and Uralic languages (sometimes referred to jointly as the Uralic-Yukaghir macro family) is quite tentative. Many linguists prefer treating Yukaghir languages as a separate language family (for example, the *Ethnologue*, which generally takes a splitter's approach, does so).

Other languages of Siberia whose relation to Uralic languages has not been successfully proven so far include Yeniseian languages, Nivkh and Ainu. All these languages are proving difficult to classify and some scholars unify them under the label of Paleo-Siberian languages. However, this label is as much a purely geographic term as a linguistic term.

The Yeniseian language family has only one living language, Ket, which is spoken along the Yenisei River in western Siberia, although other languages are known from historical records that became extinct between the eighteenth and the twentieth centuries. There have been attempts to relate Ket to Sino-Tibetan languages, but the evidence for this link is far from convincing.

Nivkh (also known as Gilyak) is a language isolate spoken at the mouth of the Amur River and on the Sakhalin Island in Russia's Far East. Though a written language was developed for Nivkh (primarily for its Amur dialect) in the 1930s, next to nothing has appeared in it. Like the languages of the Caucasus (see Chapter 4), Nivkh tolerates highly complex consonant clusters, whereas its vowel system is relatively simple. Morphologically, Nivkh is similar to Altaic languages (see next section). Among its most notable grammatical characteristics are a system of noun classifiers (see Chapter 7); a relatively simple case system with only a few cases (unlike in many other Uralic languages); a wide range of non-finite gerund forms; postpositions rather than prepositions and the SOV word order.

Finally, Ainu is now considered extinct (although there are around 15,000 ethnic Ainus, the language itself is spoken only as a second language by very few elderly people). Most recently, Ainu was spoken on Hokkaido Island in northern Japan; in earlier times, it was spoken on the northern half of Honshu Island, but the Ainus were gradually pushed northward by Japanese settlers. There is little similarity between Ainu and Japanese and such points of similarity can mostly be explained by borrowing and typological constraints. There have been attempts to relate Ainu not only to Uralic languages, but also to Altaic languages (see next section) and even to Indo-European languages. However, the evidence in support of such links has later been proven faulty, so most scholars prefer to treat Ainu as an isolate. The same applies to Ket and Nivkh. Although these so-called Paleo-Siberian languages share certain typological features (for example, they tend to be agglutinative to a certain degree and mostly exhibit SOV word order), there are also important differences among them. For instance, Ket is unlike the other Paleo-Siberian languages in that it uses tones to encode meaning (like some Sino-Tibetan languages and other languages of eastern Asia; see Chapter 7), has discontinuous root morphemes and infixes (not unlike Semitic languages; see Section 5.2) and few non-finite verb forms. Similarly, Nivkh is unlike other Paleo-Siberian languages in having a well-developed system of noun classifiers (see Chapter 7), while Chukchi and Koryak are unlike the others in being ergative and having vowel harmony.

Among other candidates for distant relatives of Uralic languages are Dravidian languages (see Section 3.4 for a detailed discussion of this idea) and even Eskimo-Aleut languages (Bergsland 1959). Finally, some scholars tried to link Uralic languages with the putative Altaic macro family (discussed in next section). However, very few linguists believe in the Ural-Altaic hypothesis these days.

11.3   Altaic languages

Altaic is a proposed genetic grouping that would include minimally the Turkic, Tungusic and Mongolic language families, and perhaps also Korean and Japanese. Each of these components is a well-established language family; for example, there is no doubt that all so-called Tungusic languages are all mutually related or that the various Mongolic languages are mutually related.

Korean and Japanese are typically treated as isolates. It is the relation between these groupings that is controversial and in general the idea of the Altaic language family lies perhaps at the dividing line that separates proponents of wide-ranging genetic groupings of languages from those that remain skeptical. It is important to remember that an alternative explanation for similarities across these languages is readily available: features are shared due to borrowing and areal diffusion. After all, these languages have been in continuous contact with each other over a long period of time, likely since prehistoric times. It is indisputable that these languages have borrowed from each other, so the real question is just how much can be accounted for by borrowing and how much is evidence of a possible common descent. This question is at the crux of this section.

But let's first consider the various families and the languages they contain within the supposed Altaic family. The Turkic languages are discussed in detail in Chapter 5, so here we will focus on Tungusic and Mongolic languages and will discuss Japanese and Korean below.

The Tungusic languages are spoken by very small groups scattered across the sparsely populated areas of central and eastern Siberia, including Sakhalin Island and adjacent parts of northeastern China and Mongolia. The one Tungusic language that is quite well known in history is Manchu, the language of the Manchu conquerors who established the Qing dynasty in China (1644–1911). Today, less than a hundred people still speak Manchu, while other ethnic Manchus have switched to Mandarin Chinese. Other Tungusic languages include Even (7,170 speakers in northeastern Siberia, scattered in the Yakut Autonomous Republic and Kamchatka Peninsula in the Russian Federation), Evenki (approximately 27,000 speakers spread thinly over large areas in Russia, China and Mongolia), Oroqen (1,200 speakers in Heilongjiang Province, China) and Nanai (3,890 speakers in the extreme far east of Russia, at the confluence of Amur and Ussuri rivers).

The Mongolic languages are spoken primarily in Mongolia and adjacent parts of Russia and China, although there are two Mongolic languages outside of this area. One of them – Mogholi (or Mogul) – was once the language of the Mogul Empire but is now spoken by only 200 elderly speakers in Afghanistan. In contrast, Kalmyk is spoken by a much larger group of about 154,000 speakers much further west, on the lower Volga in Russia. The most widely spoken and the only national Mongolic language is Khalkha-Mongolian, spoken in Mongolia and northern China by about 2.5 million speakers. Two other Mongolic languages – Buriat (spoken by 369,000 people to the south and east of Lake Baikal) and Kalmyk – have official status in the constituent republics of the Russian Federation: Buryatia and Kalmykia, respectively. The earliest Mongolian inscription is only five lines long and mentions the nephew of Genghis Khan, while the longest early literary work in Mongolian is *The Secret History of the Mongols*, an imperial chronicle written in Uighur script and thought to date from around 1240 CE. Few documents in Mongolian have survived from the period between the composition of that chronicle and the seventeenth century CE. Beginning in the seventeenth century, however, a rich Buddhist and historical literature begins to appear.

Table 11.2. *Proposed cognates in Altaic.*

	Turkic	Mongolic	Tungusic (Evenki, Manchu)
'me'	early Turkic ***män-***	written Mongolian ***min-***	***min-***
'you' (oblique)	early Turkic ***sän-***	written Mongolian ***chin-***	***sin-***
Accusative case	Turkish ***-i***	Mongolian ***-i***	–
Genitive case	Turkish ***-in***	Mongolian ***-in***	–
Plural	Turkish ***-lar***	Mongolian ***-nar***	–
'black'	Turkish ***kara***	Mongolian ***xar***	–
'blue'	Turkish ***gök***	Mongolian ***xöx***	–
'grey'	Turkish ***boz***	Mongolian ***bor***	–

So what is the evidence for the Altaic language family? Since Turkic, Mongolic and Tungusic are said to be the core of the Altaic macro family, I will now discuss these three groupings of languages. As with other language families the evidence of common descent would have to involve cognates from the basic vocabulary and recurring sound correspondences. Among the proposed Altaic cognates are first and second person pronouns, case and plural suffixes and some color terms. These are listed in Table 11.2.

Based on these sorts of similarities, scholars like Nicholas Poppe and Roy Andrew Miller have reconstructed the Proto-Altaic sound system, lexical and even morphological material. This proto-language would have been spoken sometime during the Neolithic period somewhere in northern Eurasia. Given how little is known about this possible proto-language, it is hard to be more precise about its homeland.

Furthermore, Turkic, Mongolic and Tungusic languages share certain grammatical features: vowel harmony (see Sections 3.1 and 5.1 for a detailed discussion), agglutinative morphology, Subject-Object-Verb (SOV) word order, postpositions rather than prepositions, auxiliary verbs following rather than preceding the lexical verb. However, recall from Section 3.4 that the last three features may well be part of a typological pattern controlled by the same linguistic parameter (the headedness parameter). Hence, this selection of features does not provide good evidence for common descent.

An additional reason to doubt the mutual relationship between Turkic, Mongolic and Tungusic languages comes from a comparison of similarities across modern languages and across earlier stages of these languages. Here is the logic of this argument: the further back into the past we go, the closer to the proto-language from which all of these languages have presumably sprung, the more similarities we should find. This is certainly true for Indo-European languages: there is more similarity between Latin and Sanskrit than between Italian and Hindi. But the same does not seem to work for Altaic languages: an examination of the earliest written records of Turkic and Mongolic languages, for example, reveals less rather than more similarities between them. In other words, we can observe convergence rather than divergence between Turkic and Mongolic languages – a pattern that is easily explainable by borrowing and diffusion rather than common descent.

Let's now turn to the possible "outlier" members of the proposed Altaic macro family: Korean and Japanese. Korean is a single language spoken by 42 million in South Korea, 20 million in North Korea, nearly 2 million in China, 670,000 in Japan and 149,000 in Russia. There are several dialects with varying degrees of mutual intelligibility; their boundaries typically correspond to provincial boundaries.

On the other hand, Japanese is, strictly speaking, not a single language but rather a family which includes not only Japanese proper (spoken by 121 million people in Japan) but also a number of smaller Ryukyuan languages, such as Okinawan (984,000 speakers) and Kunigama (5,000 speakers) spoken in Central Okinawa.[3] Although various Ryukyuan languages are not mutually intelligible with Japanese, there is no doubt that they are related. This family is sometimes called Japanese-Ryukyuan or Japonic.

Two questions to consider regarding Korean and Japonic languages are: (1) whether these languages are mutually related and (2) whether either or both of them are related to the proposed Altaic macro family. With regards to the first question, some evidence for a relationship between Korean and Japanese-Okinawan languages has been presented by Martin (1991a, b) and Frellesvig and Whitman (2008), among others. Still, there remains much skepticism in the scholarly community regarding this link.[4] In addition to the few proposed cognates, Japanese and Korean are typical SOV languages with agglutinative morphology and as such share a number of grammatical properties, illustrated in the examples below. For instance, location and direction are expressed by postpositions rather than prepositions (such as the Japanese *ni* 'at' and *e* 'to' and the Korean *-esə* 'from' and *-e* 'to', boldfaced in the examples below). The postposition phrase (italicized in the examples below) is placed before the verb (e.g. literally 'this hotel at stayed'). In addition, the relative clause (bracketed in the examples below) is placed before the noun it modifies (e.g. *sensei-wa* 'teacher' in the Japanese example and *kyosu-num-tŭl-i* 'professors' in the Korean example). Verbs exhibit agglutinative morphology with past tense and politeness expressed through independent suffixes. Yes/no questions are formed by adding a special interrogative morpheme, glossed as Q in the examples below: *ka* in Japanese and *k'a* in Korean. Both Japanese and Korean have nominative–accusative case marking systems and feature rich systems of honorifics and politeness markers,

---

[3] Many linguists consider these linguistic varieties dialects of Japanese rather than separate languages.

[4] The cultural and political tensions between Koreans and the Japanese may also be a factor clouding judgment when it comes to the question of whether the two languages are related.

such as *-mashi* in the Japanese example and *-num*, *-si* and *-pni* in the Korean example.

(11.3) a. Japanese:
      [Kinoo   *kono hoteru* **ni** toma-tta] sensei-ga   moo   *Tookyoo*
      yesterday this hotel   at stay-PST teacher-NOM already Tokyo

      e   kaeri-mashi-ta-ka?
      to return-HON-PST-Q
      'Has the teacher who stayed at this hotel yesterday returned to Tokyo already?'

    b. Korean:
      [*Mikuk-esə*   o-si-n]   kyosu-num-tŭl-i
      America-from come-HON-PST-REL professor-HON-PL-NOM

      Səul-e-to   ka-si-pni-k'a?
      Seoul-to-also go-HON-FORM-Q
      'Are the professors who came from America going to Seoul also?'

Although some cognates have been established between Japanese and Korean (note, for example, the similarity between the Japanese preposition *e* 'to' and its Korean counterpart *-e* 'to' and between the question markers in the two languages), true cognates are hard to find, suggesting that if a relationship between them exists, it is a distant one. In other words, if these languages are related at all, the split between them must have happened millennia ago, well before any written records. The influences of other languages, most notably Chinese, complicate matters even further.

When it comes to the question of the Altaic link for Japanese (and/or Korean), this idea has a long history: von Siebold was the first one to propose the Altaic connection for Japanese in 1832, nearly 200 years ago. But despite its long history and the extensive research on this subject, the Altaic hypothesis for the origins of Japanese and Korean remains controversial. Note first that some of the similarities between these two languages and other languages in the putative Altaic macro family can be explained away by general typological patterns. For example, Japanese and Korean share with Turkic, Mongolic and Tungusic languages a number of typological features already mentioned above in connection with the similarity between Japanese and Korean: the SOV word order, postpositions, relative clauses preceding the noun they modify, verb-final interrogative suffixes, agglutinative morphology, nominative–accusative case marking and lack of (in)definiteness marking. However, as we have seen in Section 3.4, such general typological similarities may not be enough to establish a genetic link between these languages. What is needed is a good set of cognates and a list of sound correspondences. Possible candidates for cognates between Altaic, Korean and Japanese include the items listed in Table 11.3.

Such cognates even allow the ascertainment of some sound correspondences. Given that sound change tends to follow the lenition pattern, we can hypothesize the change from [p] to [f] to [h] to zero-sound. As it turns out, Old Mongolian

Table 11.3. *Proposed cognates between Altaic, Korean and Japanese.*

	Modern Mongolian	Middle Mongolian	Tungusic (Manchu)	Korean	Japanese
'village, plain'	*ail*		*falga*	*pəl*	*hara*
'to blow'	*ulije-*	*hulie-*	*fulgije*	*pul-*	*huk-*
'to pray'	*iryge-*	*hiryge-*	*firu-*	*pil-*	
'season, year, spring'	*on*	*hon-*	*fon*	*pom*	*haru*

had [p] in such forms, while Middle Mongolian, illustrated in Table 11.3, had [h] and most modern Mongolian dialects have zero-sound. While some Tungusic languages such as Nanai retain the original [p], Manchu has [f]; other Tungusic languages have either [h] or the zero-sound. Korean may be fitted into this pattern as a language retaining the original [p], while Japanese would have undergone the change from [p] to [f] to [h]. Miller (1971), a strong defender of the Altaic affinity for Japanese and Korean, included a list of 58 sound correspondences between Japanese and Altaic and 36 correspondences between Korean and Altaic. Large lists of cognates have also been presented by Robbeets (2005): she thoroughly evaluated a large number of previously proposed Altaic cognates in Japanese and concluded that of the 2,055 gathered etymologies, "359 etymologies . . . show a perfect phonological fit for the initial consonant, the medial vowel and the medial consonant of the Japanese entry" (p. 378). Of these 359 strongest candidates for Altaic cognates, 45 words are among the 100 words in the list of the core vocabulary (presumably, the most conservative part of the lexicon) proposed in 1955 by Morris Swadesh and bearing his name. Among these 45 likely cognates are words for pronouns 'I' and 'you', numerals 'one' and 'two', adjectives like 'big', 'small', 'red', 'white' and 'new', body parts like 'blood', 'hand' and 'heart', other nouns like 'man', 'sun' and 'fire' and verbs like 'eat', 'sleep' and 'kill'.

However, many of these cognates have been questioned by other scholars, so that even some proponents of the Altaic macro family (composed of Turkic, Mongolic and Tungusic languages) do not accept evidence put forward in support of the Japanese–Korean–Altaic link. One of the main difficulties in establishing likely cognates is the tendency for consonant–vowel (CV) syllables: given this restriction on possible syllables and hence morphemes and words, and given a large enough vocabulary, it is not unlikely that some words will match even if there is no genetic relationship between two languages at all!

Because the Altaic connection for Japanese and/or Korean has not been conclusively proven, a door is open to alternative hypotheses and there is no shortage of these. Although here we cannot discuss all the ideas proposed in the literature, I will mention just one other proposal for the origin of the Japonic languages – the Austronesian hypothesis. According to this theory, Japanese traces its roots to one of the Austronesian languages (see Chapter 8): either Proto-Austronesian or one of its descendants.

One intriguing similarity between Japonic and Austronesian languages (especially those in the Oceanic branch of the family) is that both share the penchant for syllables consisting of a consonant followed by a vowel (see Chapter 8). Based on similarities of meaning and sound and a number of putative sound correspondences, several researchers have put together lists of possible (to them, all but proven) Japanese-Austronesian cognates. Such putative cognates include Japanese *hina* 'doll' and the Maori *hine* 'girl'; the Japanese *kaku* 'to write, to sketch' and the Hawaiian *kākau* 'to write, to tattoo'; the Japanese *nomu* 'to drink' and the Tagalog *inom* 'drink'. One of the most recent such lists can be found in Benedict (1990). If his list is compared to the Swadesh 100-word list of the core vocabulary, 45 of the 100 words on the Swadesh list are putative Austronesian cognates. Recall from above that Robbeets (2005) too found 45 cognates among the 100 words on the Swadesh list, but her list is of Altaic cognates. Based on these figures alone, there is a draw between the two hypotheses for the origins of the Japanese language: the Altaic or the Austronesian. However, the situation is more complicated that that: even though the Altaic and Austronesian hypothesis each claim 45 cognates from the Swadesh 100-word list, 21 of these cognates overlap! This list of overlapping cognates includes words for 'I', 'one', 'two', 'small', 'tree', 'skin', 'blood', 'bone', 'mouth', 'tooth', 'foot', 'hand', 'belly', 'eat', 'bite', 'sun', 'star', 'earth', 'fire', 'yellow', 'round'. Obviously, Robbeets and Benedict cannot both be right: a word cannot trace its origin to both Altaic and Austronesian simultaneously (unless we can show independently that those two families are closely related). This means that either Robbeets (2005) with her list of Altaic cognates or Benedict (1990) with his list of Austronesian cognates is wrong, or most likely both of them are partially wrong in claiming too many cognates for their favorite hypothesis.

While the exact lists of Altaic and Austronesian cognates are still disputed, it appears that both of these hypotheses have some merit. This led scholars like Ono (1970) to propose a mixed Austronesian-Altaic hypothesis for the origin of the Japanese language. Although non-linguistic evidence cannot provide a decisive proof for a linguistic theory, it is interesting to note that archeologists uncovered some traces of migrations of people into Japan both from the Asian mainland and from the south. The picture that emerges from this non-linguistic as well as the linguistic evidence discussed above involves two distinct peoples/cultures in the early Japanese history: the Jōmon culture and the Yayoi culture. The term *jōmon* refers to a straw-rope pattern, as the Jōmon people used straw-ropes to decorate their pottery. This group started out as nomads but gradually switched to a sedentary lifestyle. Rather unusually, the Jōmon remained hunter-gatherers; it is believed that the Japanese islands were so abundant in food, which, combined with the early knowledge of pottery allowed the Jōmon people to live relatively stationary lives without farming. However, around 400 BCE there seems to have been a great change which led the people to shift from hunting and gathering to farming, to adopt irrigated rice paddies as well as weaving, bronze tools and ironware; all this led to a dramatic increase in population. This new culture is known under the term Yayoi, but little is known about how these novel cultural and technological traits came to Japan: invasion, immigration or cultural transmission. While archeologists remain divided as to whether the Yayoi culture spread to Japan from the Korean peninsula (Ottosson and Ekholm 2007) or from Taiwan (Barnes 1999), linguists tend to associate the Jōmon people with Austronesian speakers and the advent of the Yayoi culture with Altaic-speaking groups.

However, as attractive as the mixed Austronesian-Altaic hypothesis appears to be in accounting for the two early Japanese cultures, it should be remembered that the linguistic evidence for this hypothesis is far from conclusive, and as a result this hypothesis has not received wide acceptance either among Japanese scholars or Austronesian scholars.

Still, there are even more controversial macro family proposals, most notably the Nostratic and Eurasiatic hypotheses, discussed in the next section.

11.4   The Nostratic and Eurasiatic hypotheses

So far we have seen that languages can be grouped into language families, whose proto-languages are either known directly (in the case of smaller families or branches of families, like Proto-North-Germanic, known as Old Norse, or Proto-Romance, known as Vulgar Latin) or reconstructed on the basis of descendant languages (e.g. Proto-Indo-European). In some cases these language families have been combined into larger groupings that I referred to as macro families: Afroasiatic, Uralic, Altaic. The assumption is that all languages in such macro families descend from a common ancestral language: Proto-Afroasiatic, Proto-Uralic, Proto-Altaic. The proto-languages of macro families are never known directly and must be reconstructed; most often such reconstruction is based not on modern languages or their older stages of which we have written records, but on smaller families' proto-languages, themselves reconstructed. For example, reconstructions of Proto-Afroasiatic are based not only on modern Afroasiatic languages, but on Proto-Semitic, Proto-Berber, Proto-Cushitic, etc. Of course, a reconstruction of a proto-language based on a reconstruction (rather than on actual descendant languages) introduces additional room for speculation and error, making the project more controversial. But this does not stop the more adventurous (or less conservative) linguists from trying. And the natural next step is hypothesizing about an even larger grouping of several known families and macro families – this is exactly what the Nostratic hypothesis is all about!

Originally proposed by Holger Pedersen in an article on Turkish phonology in 1903, the Nostratic hypothesis relates Indo-European languages to a number of other known families (see Figure 11.1). The term "Nostratic" derived from the Latin *nostrates* 'fellow countrymen'. According to Pedersen himself, Indo-European (which he refers to as "Indo-Germanic") was most clearly related to Finno-Ugric and Samoyed, and less clearly (or perhaps more distantly) to Turkish,

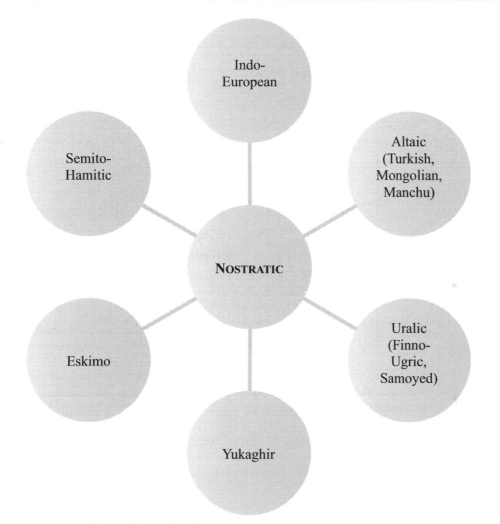

Figure 11.1. *Pedersen's Nostratic proposal.*

Mongolian, and Manchu; to Yukaghir; and to Eskimo (Pedersen 1931: 338). He also believed that "the Nostratic languages occupy not only a very large area in Europe and Asia but also extend to within Africa; for the Semitic-Hamitic languages are in my view without doubt Nostratic" (Pedersen 1903: 460–461).[5] In Pedersen's days, Basque was considered to be related to Semito-Hamitic languages, so presumably it too was a member of the proposed Nostratic family (as discussed in Section 3.2, Basque is no longer classified as related to Semitic or any other known language family, but rather as an isolate). To translate this into modern-day classification, we would say that Pedersen was positing a genetic

---

[5] The idea that Indo-European and Semitic languages are related was also argued for by Hermann Möller (1906).

relationship between Indo-European and the Uralic, Altaic, Yukaghir, Eskimo and Afro-Asiatic language families. Note also that Pedersen did not see this list of Nostratic languages as exhaustive, leaving room for adding more languages and language families:

> *The boundaries for the Nostratian [sic] world of languages cannot yet be determined, but the area is enormous, and includes such widely divergent races that one becomes almost dizzy at the thought... The question remains simply whether sufficient material can be collected to give this inclusion flesh and blood and a good clear outline.*   (Pederson 1931: 338)

In Pedersen's lifetime, the Nostratic hypothesis did not receive much attention, but after years of neglect it was resuscitated in the 1960s by two Soviet scholars, Vladislav M. Illyč-Svityč (1934–66), a specialist in Indo-European, Altaic and Kartvelian languages, and Aaron B. Dolgopolsky (b. 1930), an Indo-Europeanist and Hamito-Semitist.[6] They expanded the proposal to include additional language families (see Figure 11.2) and Illyč-Svityč prepared the first comparative dictionary of the hypothetical Proto-Nostratic language (the presumed common ancestral language of the Nostratic languages), which was published posthumously (see Illyč-Svityč [1971] 1984). Their work has been continued by Vladimir Dybo, Vitaly Shevoroshkin and to some extent Sergei Starostin (his Dené-Caucasian hypothesis is discussed below).

The kind of evidence in support of the Nostratic hypothesis is by the now familiar methodology of compiling potential cognates and identifying sound correspondences. For instance, consider Table 11.4, which presents some of the proposed cognates from the descendants of the Proto-Nostratic language, the proto-languages of the Nostratic constituent families (data from Bomhard 1996: 11–13).[7]

Based on this table, the following three sound correspondences of consonants in the initial position can be established. First, the Proto-Indo-European *b[ʰ]- corresponds to *b- in Proto-Kartvelian, Proto-Afroasiatic and Proto-Altaic, and to *p- in Proto-Uralic and Proto-Dravidian; the corresponding sound in (Proto-)Nostratic is reconstructed as *b-. The second correspondence involves the Proto-Indo-European *p[ʰ]-, which corresponds to *p[ʰ]- in Proto-Kartvelian and Proto-Afroasiatic, and to *p- in Proto-Uralic, Proto-Dravidian and Proto-Altaic; the corresponding sound in (Proto-)Nostratic is reconstructed as *p[ʰ]-. Third, the Proto-Indo-European *m- corresponds to *m- in Proto-Kartvelian, Proto-Afroasiatic, Proto-Uralic, Proto-Dravidian and Proto-Altaic; naturally, the corresponding sound in (Proto-)Nostratic is reconstructed as *m-.

While Soviet scholars worked on the Nostratic hypothesis, in the West a similar but not exactly the same proposal has been put forward by Joseph Greenberg and

---

[6] Aharon Dolgopolsky later moved to Israel, where he continued his work on Nostratic.

[7] PN = Proto-Nostratic; PIE = Proto-Indo-European; PK = Proto-Kartvelian; PAA = Proto-Afroasiatic; PU = Proto-Uralic; PD = Proto-Dravidian; PA = Proto-Altaic.

Table 11.4. *Proposed Nostratic cognates.*

Approximate meanings	PIE	PK	PAA	PU	PD	PA
'to bore, to pierce'	*b[ʰ]or-	–	*bar-	*pura	*pur-	*bur
'to cover, to enclose'		*bur-		–	*pōr	*büri-
'grain'	*b[ʰ]ars-	–	*bar-	–	*par-	–
'to fly, to flee'	* p[ʰ]er-	*p[ʰ]r-in-	*p[ʰ]ar-	–	*par-	–
'to bear, to bring forth'	*p[ʰ]er-	–	*p[ʰ]ar-	–	*per-	*pure
'to hurry, to quiver'	*p[ʰ]et[ʰ]-	*p[ʰ]et[ʰ]k[ʰ]-	*p[ʰ]at[ʰ]-	–	*pat-	–
'me'	*me-	*me-	*ma-	*me	–	–
interrogative pronoun	*me-	*me-n-	*ma-	*mi		*mi
'to twist, to turn'	*mer-		*mar-	*mur-		*muru-

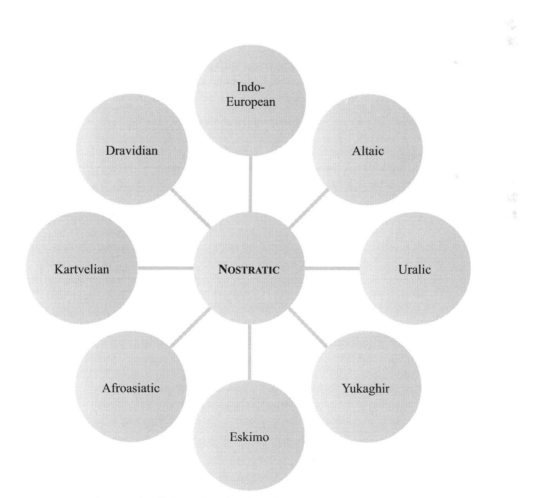

Figure 11.2. *Illyč-Svityč and Dolgopolsky's Nostratic proposal.*

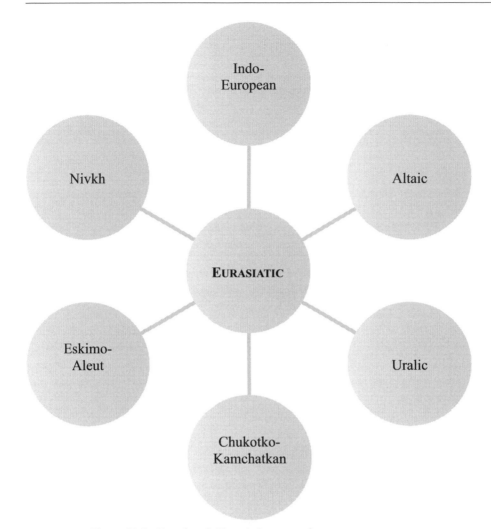

Figure 11.3. *Greenberg's Eurasiatic proposal.*

his colleagues (see Figure 11.3). They called their proposed macro family Eurasiatic and included not only Indo-European, Altaic, Uralic and Eskimo-Aleut but also Chukotko-Kamchatkan and (with reservations) Nivkh. Note that Afroasiatic, Dravidian and Kartvelian languages are not included under the Eurasiatic proposal. Greenberg did not reject outright a relationship of Afroasiatic, Kartvelian or Dravidian to the other Eurasiatic languages, but he considered it likely to be a much more distant relationship.[8]

---

[8] In some treatments, the proposed Eurasiatic macro family includes Korean, Japanese-Ryukyuan and Ainu. For a further discussion of these languages, see Sections 11.2 and 11.3 above.

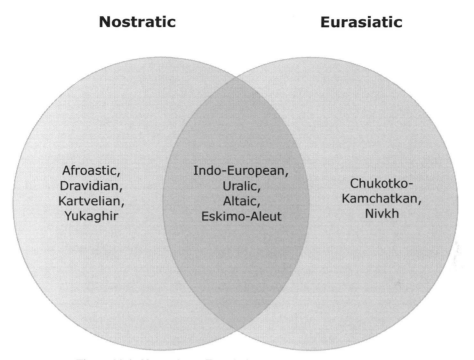

Nostratic   **Eurasiatic**

Afroastic,   Indo-European,
Dravidian,   Uralic,   Chukotko-
Kartvelian,   Altaic,   Kamchatkan,
Yukaghir   Eskimo-Aleut   Nivkh

Figure 11.4. *Nostratic vs. Eurasiatic.*

Thus, there is a certain overlap between the proposed Nostratic and Eurasiatic macro families, as shown in Figure 11.4.[9] Given the significant overlap between the Eurasiatic and Nostratic proposals and the unclear evidence regarding Chukotko-Kamchatkan languages and Nivkh, it has also been proposed that Eurasiatic is in fact a branch of Nostratic, as shown in Figure 11.5.[10]

In recent years, the work on Nostratic/Eurasiatic proposals continues: in 2008 an updated version of Dolgopolsky's *Nostratic Dictionary* has been published online and a comprehensive two-volume set *Reconstructing Proto-Nostratic* has been published by another dedicated Nostraticist, Allan Bomhard. The Nostratic hypothesis even received some attention in the popular press when *The New York Times* published an article on the topic in June 1995.

But while the overall reaction to the Nostratic idea can be described as "skeptical fascination" (Salmons and Joseph 1998: 1), scientific opinions are divided.

---

[9] Dolgopolsky (but not Illyč-Svityč) includes Chukchi-Kamchatkan under the heading of Nostratic.

[10] Some Nostraticists believe in a more complex structure of the family, with the first split being between Afroasiatic and the rest, the second split between Dravidian and the rest and the Kartvelian being the closest relative of the Eurasiatic languages. However, it has also been proposed that Indo-European is more closely related to Afroasiatic than to any other language groupings (Hodge 1998).

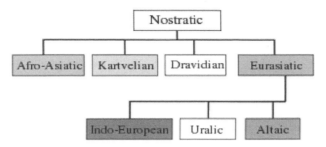

Figure 11.5. *Eurasiatic as a branch of Nostratic.*

Supporters (Vovin 1998, Ramer *et al.* 1998, Bomhard 1998, among others) contend that "Nostratic theory cannot be dismissed out of hand by a responsible historical linguist as something not being worthy of further discussion" (Vovin 1998: 257). Moreover, they argue that the assumption of Nostratic not only answers the age-old question of "what came before" but can also yield cogent solutions to language-particular problems in subgroups of Nostratic. Other scholars (Vine 1998, Campbell 1998, Ringe 1998, inter alia) voice criticisms; yet others, such as Merritt Ruhlen, propose similar but not identical classifications. But perhaps the majority of linguists remain agnostic on the subject, taking it to be an issue that can be neither proved nor disproved with the means available to historical/comparative linguistics: after all, a reconstruction based on a reconstruction based on a reconstruction gives a very shaky building indeed.

Thus, it is not the very idea of looking for distant relationships between languages that raises most eyebrows but the methodological issues: many linguists think that time depth constrains the utility and validity of the comparative method. In the words of Salmons and Joseph (1998: 4):

> As elsewhere in science, methodological flaws can undermine reliability and replicability of results. Just as acoustic phonetic investigations can be fatally compromised by background noise or sociolinguistic studies can be felled by problems in representativeness of sampling, so too can comparative linguistic houses be built on methodological sand.

The chief methodological problem, aptly formulated by one of the strongest defenders of the Nostratic proposal, Allan Bomhard (1996: 5), is:

> the problem is in knowing which languages to compare and in knowing what to compare since not all aspects of language are equally relevant to comparison. To be meaningful, comparison must strive to eliminate chance resemblances and to separate borrowings from native elements. This is often easier said than done.

This difficulty of separating borrowings from true cognates is exacerbated further when we know little to nothing about the interactions between different linguistic groups. While attempts have been made to figure out which lexical items are less likely to be subject to borrowing (including work done by Dol-gopolsky, one of the authors of the Nostratic hypothesis), such lists have drawn heavy criticisms from other linguists. And this is not the only problem with the comparative research into the Nostratic hypothesis.

Other critics of the Nostratic/Eurasiatic work point out that the data from indi-vidual well-established language families that is used in Nostratic comparisons contains many errors: for example, Campbell (1998) demonstrates this for the Uralic data. Another potential problem concerns the kind of comparison done to evaluate possible cognates: much of the Nostratic work consists of binary com-parisons which tend to lead to distortions (while in multi-language comparisons each language serves as a control on others). A further problem is raised by the focus on grammatical morphemes: some of these forms being compared are just two small to be compared reliably (the same is true to some extent of lexical forms being compared by Nostraticists as well).

In their defense, the proponents of the Nostratic hypothesis now employ com-plex statistical methods for lexical comparisons of multiple languages (see Oswalt 1998) and extend their work to conduct morphological and even syntactic com-parisons. And indeed it appears that the future of Nostratic linguistics lies in developing mathematical methods for sifting through vast amounts of data and figuring out what portions of those data are due to relatedness and which are due to borrowing or even to pure chance.

11.5   Other hypothesized macro language families

While Nostratic and Eurasiatic hypotheses focus on possible relations of Indo-European languages with other language families, similar macro propos-als have been made for other languages both in Eurasia (mostly in East Asia), Africa, Oceania and the Americas. These proposals range from the more modest to the more far-reaching. Here, we cannot discuss all such proposals but will focus on just a few.

Let's first look at the Sino-Caucasian hypothesis, proposed by a Russian scholar Sergei Starostin (1953–2005). According to Starostin, Northwest Cau-casian and Northeast Caucasian languages (see Sections 4.1 and 4.2) form a larger North Caucasian language family. Moreover, Sergei Starostin was instrumental in reconstructing its proto-language, Proto-North-Caucasian. Furthermore, Sergei Starostin was a firm believer in the Altaic language family and reconstructed its proto-language as well; he also dedicated much of his work to showing that Japanese is a member of the Altaic family (see Section 11.3 above). His other proto-language reconstructions include Proto-Tibeto-Burman and Proto-Yeniseian. This reconstruction work led him to argue for the Sino-Caucasian hypothesis, which posits that the Yeniseian languages and North Caucasian lan-guages form a macro family with Sino-Tibetan languages. The Sino-Caucasian

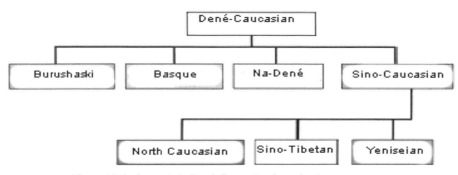

Figure 11.6. *Starostin's Dené-Caucasian hypothesis.*

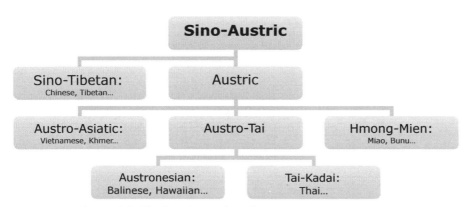

Figure 11.7. *The Sino-Austric hypothesis.*

hypothesis has been expanded to the Dené-Caucasian hypothesis, which adds the Na-Dené languages of North America, Burushaski (otherwise a perfect isolate) and perhaps even Basque (see Figure 11.6).[11]

But Starostin's Dené-Caucasian hypothesis is not the only proposal relating Sino-Tibetan languages to other language families. For example, Sagart (2005) suggested that Sino-Tibetan languages are related to the macro family called Austric. This proposed Austric macro family is an extension of the so-called Austro-Tai macro family, originally proposed by Paul Benedict in 1942 and expanded upon in his later work (Benedict 1975, 1990). The Austro-Tai macro family combines Austronesian languages (see Chapter 8) with Thai-Kadai languages (see Section 7.3). The expanded Austric proposal adds Austro-Asiatic languages (see Section 7.2) and Hmong-Mien languages (spoken in Vietnam, Laos and southern China). The Sino-Austric proposal is schematized in Figure 11.7.

---

[11] Other scholars attempted to extend the Dené-Caucasian macro family to include Sumerian, in addition to the languages in Figure 11.6 (Ruhlen 1994: 24–28).

It is important to note here that the evidence for the Dené-Caucasian and Sino-Austric hypotheses is extremely tentative, as several of the constituent families (North Caucasian, Austric and even Austro-Tai) have not been conclusively demonstrated. Moreover, some scholars even doubt the validity of the Sino-Tibetan family itself.

But perhaps the most far-reaching – and hence the most controversial and tentative – proposal is for the so-called Borean "mega-super-phylum" (Fleming 1987, 1991) which would combine Nostratic, Dené-Caucasian and Austric macro families. The name "Borean", based on Greek βορέας, means 'northern' and reflects the fact that this super family includes most language families native to the northern hemisphere, but is not thought to include language families native to the southern hemisphere. According to Fleming's original model, Borean includes ten different groups: Afrasian (Fleming's term for Afroasiatic), Kartvelian, Dravidian, a group comprising Sumerian, Elamitic and some other extinct languages of the ancient Near East, Joseph Greenberg's Eurasiatic (including Indo-European, Uralic, Altaic, etc.; see Section 11.4), Macro-Caucasian (proposed by John Bengston and including Caucasian languages, as well as Basque and Burushaski), Yeniseian, Sino-Tibetan, Na-Dené and Amerind. These groupings are included in Borean on an equal footing: Fleming rejects Nostratic, a proposed macro family which is broader than Eurasiatic, and withholds judgment on Dené-Caucasian. Furthermore, he sees Borean as associated with the appearance of the Upper Paleolithic in the Levant, Europe and western Eurasia from 50,000 to 45,000 years ago, and observes that it is primarily associated with human populations of Caucasoid and Northern Mongoloid physical appearance, the exceptions being southern India, southern China, southwestern Ethiopia, northern Nigeria and the Chad Republic.

The Borean hypothesis was further developed by Sergei Starostin – whom we have already encountered in connection with the Dené-Caucasian hypothesis – but he believed that Borean is composed of two groupings: one comprising the Dené-Caucasian and Austric macro families, and the other being Nostratic. Thus, his model includes most languages of Eurasia, as well as the Afroasiatic languages of North and East Africa, the Eskimo-Aleut languages and the Na-Dené languages of the New World. Furthermore, he estimated that the Borean proto-language was spoken during the Upper Paleolithic, approximately 16,000 years ago, much more recently than in Fleming's original model.

The Borean "mega-super-phylum", its constituent macro families and their degree of recognition are summarized in "The Borean proposal" box.

The Borean proposal

- Nostratic (speculative)
  - Afroasiatic (commonly recognized family)
  - Eurasiatic (speculative)
  - Indo-European (commonly recognized family)

- o Uralic (commonly recognized family)
- o Macro-Altaic (controversial)
- • Turkic (commonly recognized family)
- • Mongolic (commonly recognized family)
- • Tungusic (commonly recognized family)
- • Korean (language isolate)
- • Japonic (commonly recognized family)
  - o Kartvelian (commonly recognized family)
  - o Dravidian (commonly recognized family)
  - o Paleosiberian languages (geographic rather than phylogenetic unit)
  - o Nivkh (language isolate)
  - o Eskimo-Aleut languages (commonly recognized family)
  - o Yukaghir languages (commonly recognized family; sometimes grouped with Uralic)
  - o Chukotko-Kamchatkan languages (commonly recognized family)
- • Dené-Caucasian and Austric
  - o Dené-Caucasian (speculative)
  - o Na-Dené (commonly recognized family)
  - o Basque (language isolate)
  - o Sino-Caucasian (speculative)
- • Sino-Tibetan (commonly recognized family)
- • North Caucasian (speculative)
- • Northwest Caucasian
- • Northeast Caucasian
- • Yeniseian (commonly recognized family)
- • Burushaski (language isolate)
  - o Austric (speculative)
  - o Austro-Asiatic (commonly recognized family)
  - o Hmong-Mien (or Miao-Yao; commonly recognized family)
  - o Austro-Tai (speculative)
- • Austronesian (commonly recognized family)
- • Tai-Kadai (commonly recognized family)

While the Borean hypothesis is certainly the most speculative of all the different proposals for macro families, more modest proposals linking various other languages and language families are worth noting. These proposals concern languages in three parts of the world: Africa, Oceania and the Americas.

With respect to African languages, the one proposal that should be mentioned here is that of merging the Niger-Congo and Nilo-Saharan language families into a Niger-Saharan (or Kongo-Saharan) macro family (Gregersen 1972, Williamson 1989: 8–9, Bender 1997: 9). According to this proposal, Nilo-Saharan languages are seen as the older, earlier branch of the macro family, while Niger-Congo languages are most closely related to the Central Sudanic languages (currently classified as part of the Nilo-Saharan family). The evidence for this link between Niger-Congo and Nilo-Saharan languages is mostly morphological, such as the noun class prefix *ma-* for liquids or mass nouns in Nilo-Saharan which corresponds to ŋ- in Kordofanian (Blench 1995: 88). Other common features, such as the presence of labio-velars, have been argued to be areal features (Greenberg 1983).

In Oceania, it has been proposed that all Papuan languages plus the Andamanese and Tasmanian languages form a grouping called Indo-Pacific (Greenberg 1971). However, at this point it remains doubtful that all Papuan languages are mutually related, let alone related to any languages outside Papua New Guinea. For a further discussion of this issue as well as of a possible link between (some) Australian and (some) Papuan languages, see Chapter 9.

When it comes to languages of the Americas, a classification that all linguists can agree on is still to be developed. In particular, it remains to be seen whether lumping these languages into one Amerindian macro family (Greenberg 1987) or treating them as some twelve or so separate and unrelated language families is the right approach. One thing is clear though: Eskimo-Aleut and Na-Dené are not part of the Amerindian family. As discussed above, these languages have been grouped together with Nostratic and Dené-Caucasian languages, respectively.

Overall, there is a great deal of work still to be done when it comes to the classification of languages and establishing links between recognized language families, and this work will be shared by comparative linguists and mathematicians.

12 Pidgins, creoles and other mixed languages

So far, we have discussed how languages evolve from earlier forms through changes in pronunciation, vocabulary and grammar. As a result of this evolution, languages that share a common ancestor can be classified into groupings of various sizes, depending on how long ago that common ancestor was spoken. For example, Proto-West-Germanic, the common ancestor of West Germanic languages such as English, Dutch and German, was spoken more recently than Proto-Germanic, the common ancestor of those West Germanic languages, as well as North Germanic languages such as Icelandic, Norwegian, Swedish and Danish. In turn, Proto-Germanic was spoken more recently than Proto-Indo-European, the common ancestor of an even larger grouping, the Indo-European language family.

One important factor in the evolution of languages is language contact. As has been discussed in Section 5.3 and elsewhere throughout this book, language contact and the resulting lexical and grammatical borrowing may reshape the language to be quite different from its relatives. While all of the world's languages have at some time been influenced by some language or other, in this chapter we will discuss very specific types of languages that arise out of a particularly close contact between groups of people who do not speak each other's languages, but who for some reason or another simply must work out a means of communicating with each other. These languages are known as pidgins and creoles.

While pidgins and creoles are often discussed in one breath, there are important differences between them. Simply put, a pidgin is a simplified language with a limited lexicon and no BOUND MORPHEMES, while a creole is a pidgin that has become the native language of a community, and in the process undergone an expansion, whereby its structure has become as complex as that of any non-pidgin language. To what degree this expansion is related to universal properties of the human mind and to what degree it is due to the various native languages of the pidgin/creole users is, perhaps, the central question in the field of pidgin/creole studies.

After considering pidgins and creoles, we will focus in Section 12.3 on a number of mixed Jewish languages, such as Yiddish and Ladino. While the term "mixed languages" may imply hodgepodge, chaos and lack of grammatical norms, we will see that neither pidgins, creoles nor mixed Jewish languages are chaotic mixtures. Instead, like other languages that we have encountered throughout this book, these languages are beautiful systems of internalized rules and patterns.

12.1   Pidgins

When groups of people speaking different languages come into contact, they may not share a language in common and might need to create an "intermediary" language in a hurry. This intermediary language serves for communication between groups and is not a native language for anybody. Such a language is termed a PIDGIN.

Various situations may lead to a creation of a pidgin: wars and military occupation, mass migration, trade or plantations. Sometimes in a course of a war or military occupation, when large numbers of soldiers come into contact with other soldiers or civilians with whom they do not share a common language, they may create a pidgin, a makeshift means of communication. One example of such pidgin is **Bamboo English**, which was created during the occupation of Japan by American troops after World War II and used mostly by American GIs to communicate with Japanese bartenders, bar girls and so on. While the need for this pidgin and consequently the pidgin itself has faded in most of Japan, it is sometimes still used on Okinawa, where there is still a significant US military presence.

However, the presence of the military is not a necessary condition for a creation of a pidgin. It can also happen in the early stages of mass immigration/settlement, as was the case when large numbers of White (that is, anti-Bolshevik) Russians fled from Russia to Manchuria and other parts of northeastern China after the Russian Revolution of 1917. Thus, in the 1920s Russians constituted the third largest non-Chinese community in Shanghai after the Japanese and the British. This Russian community was tightly knit and settled mostly in the so-called French Concession around Avenue Joffre, lined with plane trees and jewelry stores, where many a Russian sold their family heirlooms to support their families (this street was even nicknamed "Little Russia" and "Nevsky Prospekt" after the main street in St. Petersburg). The Russians did not mix much with the Chinese. In fact, in Shanghai the Chinese themselves were not allowed to live in the international, urbanized core where the Europeans and the Japanese had settled. However, inevitably, the Russians came into contact with the Chinese, especially Chinese servants, which led to a creation of a **Russo-Chinese pidgin**. This pidgin was in use until the end of World War II, but like Bamboo English described above, the Russo-Chinese pidgin gradually faded as the financial status and the political importance of the anti-Bolshevik Russian community in China diminished throughout 1930s and 1940s. Many Russians later emigrated from

China to the United States and elsewhere; there is an especially large community of Russian-via-China immigrants in San Francisco.

Another pidgin that arose for communication between immigrant masters and local servants is **Butler English**, a pidgin spoken in India. It emerged when Indian servants had to find a way to communicate with their English-speaking masters. Currently, it is still spoken in hotels, clubs and households.

Another often-discussed type of situation that leads to a creation of a pidgin is plantations, where large numbers of workers speaking different languages are brought together. On plantations an intermediary language is needed both for the bosses to communicate with the laborers and for laborers to communicate among themselves. Such large-scale plantations during the era of the European colonial expansion produced a large number of pidgins, especially in the Caribbean region, where slaves were brought to from a large number of (mostly West) African ethnic and linguistic groups (recall from Chapter 6 that West Africa is one of the most linguistically diverse areas in the world). By now, most of these Caribbean plantation pidgins have grown into creoles, a development that is discussed in more detail in the next section.

Finally, trade may also lead to a creation of a pidgin. While each of the trading groups retains its own community language, one intermediary language is needed for brief periodic contacts between trading partners. In some instances, a language of one group, often the one that is most dominant in the region, is selected to be a trade language. Examples of such trade languages – Arabic, Hausa, Swahili and others – are discussed in Section 6.4. But in other cases, especially when the itinerant traders communicate with too many different linguistic groups, a special pidgin is likely to arise.

One example of a trade pidgin is **Chinook Jargon**. It used to be spoken in Alaska, the Pacific Northwest of the United States and in the adjacent regions of Canada. It was based on the Chinook language (of which only 12 speakers remain; see Section 10.1). European traders, who arrived to this area mostly from French Canada, found the pidgin quite useful for their purposes and enriched it with words from European languages, especially from French. As the various indigenous language of the Pacific Northwest became extinct and as more and more of their speakers learned European languages, the need for an intermediary language disappeared, and the Chinook Jargon disappeared with it.

Another example of a trade pidgin is **Russenorsk** (Broch and Jahr 1983, Jahr 1996, Kotsinas 1996). This was an intermediary language used by Russian merchants and Norwegian fishermen bartering fish, flour and grain along the Arctic coast of northern Norway (the counties Finnmark and Troms) for a period of approximately 150 years, from the end of the eighteenth century to the beginning of the twentieth. While the trade lasted, the contact was limited to a few summer months each year. Russians from the Murman coast and the White Sea coast came to Norwegian towns like Vardø, Vadsø, Hammerfest and Tromsø to purchase the surplus of fish (which it was difficult to sell in Norway during the summer months) and exchanged it for grain that the Norwegians lacked.[1] It has been claimed (Jahr 1996: 109) that

> *the Russian grain prevented starvation in northern Norway during the famine years in the beginning of the [nineteenth] century, and Norwegian expansion and activity in Finnmark during the nineteenth century would have been unthinkable without the Russian trade.*

But it is clear that the trade was quite profitable for both sides, so it developed despite being illegal in the beginning. However, gradually the social status of Russenorsk changed. While prior to 1850s "Russenorsk was commonly used by Norwegians, both fishermen and merchants, in dealing with the Russians" (Jahr 1996: 108), the pidgin was accepted as a language equal to other languages, thus enjoying a high status in society. As the Pomor trade developed from a barter to a cash-based trade and became more and more lucrative, "the [Norwegian] merchants learned more Russian by spending a year or two with colleagues in Russia and also by actively studying Russian in Archangel" (Jahr 1996: 108), so after 1850 Russenorsk was used mostly by lower class fishermen and its social status became devalued. As the need for Russenorsk declined, so did the number of people who spoke it. But the definitive end to the Russenorsk pidgin came in 1917 when the Russian Revolution and the resulting Bolshevik regime put an end to the Pomor trade that engendered it.

Russenorsk is unusual as a pidgin in that the two languages that came into contact to create it – Russian and Norwegian – were of similar social status. In a more typical situation, a pidgin is created on the basis of two (or more) languages with different social status: the SUPERSTRATUM LANGUAGE (i.e. the language of social prestige in the community) and the SUBSTRATUM LANGUAGE (i.e. the language of the group with a lower socio-economic status). The superstratum language typically provides most of the vocabulary for a pidgin (this is why it is also referred to as the "lexifier language"), while the substratum language "donates" some grammatical structures of a pidgin (while other grammatical structures are characteristic of the pidgin but not of either of the parent languages). For example, in the case of many of the plantation pidgins the European languages of the plantation owners and overseers were the superstratum languages and provided much of the pidgins' vocabularies, while the languages of the slaves or indentured laborers on the plantations were the substratum languages. In the case of Russenorsk, however, it is impossible to talk about superstratum and substratum languages.

However, in many other ways Russenorsk is a typical pidgin. As mentioned above, a pidgin is a simplified language which has a reduced vocabulary (usually about 800–1,000 words) and a limited range of grammatical structures. From the

---

[1] The White Sea coast is called *Pomor'e* in Russian and its inhabitants are known as the "Pomors", giving the trade its name – "the Pomor trade".

lexical point of view, Russenorsk has a limited vocabulary (its core vocabulary is estimated at 150–200 words) and exhibits a great deal of lexical variation. For example, 'tea' may be rendered alternatively as *te* (from Norwegian) or as *kjai* (cf. the Russian *čaj* 'tea'). Also, the negation word in Russenorsk likewise alternates between the Norwegian *ikke* and the Russian *njet*.

From the phonological point of view, a typical pidgin has a relatively small sound inventory with basic vowels, such as /a, e, i, o, u/, but not, for example, front rounded vowels. The consonant inventory is typically small to medium-sized; consonant clusters are not allowed and syllables ending in consonants are not allowed at all or severely limited. Pidgins do not have tones, even though many West African languages spoken by people who created and used, say, Caribbean pidgins have tones (see Chapter 6). In line with this pattern, Russenorsk phonology is based on the sounds and sound patterns of both Norwegian and Russian and sounds and consonant clusters not found in both languages are avoided or simplified.

One of the defining characteristics of a pidgin is the lack of bound morphemes, that is, affixes that cannot stand on their own. In other words, pidgins are the extreme case of isolating languages where each morpheme constitutes an independent word. For example, pidgins use separate words to indicate tense, aspect and agreement (if these notions are indicated at all). In accordance with this generalization, Russenorsk does not have bound verbal morphology to indicate tense, aspect or person. There is an all-purpose verbal marker *-om*, illustrated in (12.1), but it is not always used. (Here and below, Russenorsk words of Russian origin are marked by italics; words of Norwegian and other origins are in plain font.) Note that the marker *-om* can attach to verbs of both Norwegian and Russian origin.[2]

(12.1) a. *moja kop*-om   fiska
           I   buy-VERB fish-NOUN
           'I buy fish.'
                        (Jahr 1996: 115)

       b. *moja tvoja* på vater kasst-om.
           I   you   on water throw-VERB
           'I shall throw you in the water.'
                        (Jahr 1996: 116)

---

[2] Traditionally, sources on Russenorsk spell the all-purpose preposition *på* with å, indicating it as being of a Norwegian origin. However, its true origin is not clear, as both Norwegian and Russian have an all-purpose preposition that is pronounced [po] (e.g. the Russian term *Pomorje* for the White Sea coast comes from this preposition plus *more* 'sea'). It is possible that the preposition *po* was chosen as the all-purpose preposition in Russenorsk precisely because both Russian and Norwegian have it. In Russenorsk *på* can mark location, direction, origin, possession, indirect object and in some cases even direct objects; it has also been pointed out that *på* may occur before a verb, in which case it serves as the marker of future tense, aspect or even a polite imperative (see Kotsinas 1996 for a detailed discussion and examples).

Where context is not enough, tense may be marked by adverbs:

(12.2)   kanske marradag mera pris.
          maybe tomorrow more price
          'Maybe the price will be higher tomorrow/later.'
                              (Kotsinas 1996: 128)

Aspect is marked in Russenorsk via separate words, typically verbs placed in front of the main verb. For example, the ingressive aspect (that is, the starting point of an event) can be expressed by *kom*, as in (12.3); for more details, see Kotsinas (1996).

(12.3)   nokka lite *pjan* kom
          a   little drunk came
          'I got a bit drunk.'

Lexical verbs such as *stann-om* 'stay/stop', *ligge ne* 'lie down', *slip-om* 'sleep' and *spasir-om* 'walk around' may also lose their original meaning and be used as a locative copula in Russenorsk, as illustrated below:

(12.4) a. altsamma på salt ligge ne.
           everything on salt lie   down
           'Everything [the fish] is salted down.'
                              (Kotsinas 1996: 133)

       b. altsamma på salt slip-om.
           everything on salt sleep-VERB
           'Everything [the fish] is salted down.'
                              (Kotsinas 1996: 134)

This is another property characteristic of pidgins in general; as Naro (1978: 330) notes:

> *In nearly all pidgins, the usage of the verb 'to be' differs in some way from its use in the standard. It may be lost entirely or be replaced by, or be in free variation with, another verb or copula with a meaning like 'to remain', 'to stay', 'to sit', 'to be temporarily' etc.*

In the nominal domain, pidgins may indicate plurals of nouns and superlatives of adjectives with reduplication or not indicate it all, as is the case in Russenorsk, where nouns are not declined, and the suffix *-a* seems to have the general noun-marking function, in parallel with the verbal marker *-om* (for an example of this nominal marker, see (12.1a) above).[3] Pronouns are not declined either, with *moja* 'I/me/my' and *tvoja* 'you/your' – whose source is the Russian possessive pronouns – serving as subject, object and possessive forms.

---

[3] Curiously enough, *-a* served as a noun marker also in the Icelandic–Basque pidgin that was spoken in Iceland in the seventeenth century by Basque traders and Icelandic locals (Hualde 1984: 51). However, this may be a feature inherited from the Basque language, where the suffix *-a* is a definiteness marker and is part of the noun's citation form.

In the syntax, pidgins are again limited to simple clausal structures. Typically, pidgins avoid embedded clauses. In Russenorsk, subordination is attested only in a few instances, where it is achieved by means of a subordinating conjunction *kak* – from the Russian word 'how' – which also serves as an all-purpose question word in Russenorsk (coordination is achieved by means of coordinating conjunctions *ja* and *jes*):

(12.5)   *kak* ju   vil   skaffom ja   drikke te,   *davaj* på sjib *tvoja* ligge
          if   you will eat   and drink tea please on ship your lie

          ne   jes på slip-om.
          down and on sleep-VERB
          'If you want to eat and drink tea, please come on board your ship and lie down to sleep.'

                                                                    (Jahr 1996: 120)

In most cases, however, clauses are combined simply by juxtaposition:

(12.6) a.   Kristus grot vrei,   *tvoja ljug*-om.
            Christ very angry you   lie-VERB
            'Christ is very angry, because you lie.'
                              (Kotsinas 1996: 128)

      b.   *moja* ska si   ju: ju   grot   lyg-om.
            I   will tell you you much   lie-VERB
            'I tell you that you are a big liar.'
                              (Kotsinas 1996: 128)

While Russenorsk might be exceptional in allowing rare instances of embedding, it is a quite typical pidgin in featuring the basic SVO order; see (12.1a). However, if the sentence contains an adverb, the verb tends to come sentence-finally (see also (12.1b) above):

(12.7)   *moja tri*   vekkel stann-om.
          I   three weeks stand-VERB
          'I stayed three weeks.'
                         (Jahr 1996: 115)

While the basic SVO order may be ascribed to either of the "parent" languages – Norwegian or Russian – the verb-final order is marginal in Russian and impossible in Norwegian, and thus must be considered a rule of Russenorsk itself.

Another syntactic rule that cannot be attributed to either Norwegian or Russian concerns the position of the negation marker, which can alternatively be *ikke* (from Norwegian) or *njet* (from Russian). In Russenorsk, the negation word must come in the second position, following either the subject or a prepositional phrase:

(12.8) a.   *moja njet* lyg-om.
            I   not   lie-VERB
            'I don't lie.'
                (Jahr 1996: 116)

b.   [på den dag] ikke russefolk *robot*-om.
    on that day not Russians work-VERB
    'On that day, Russians do not work.'
                      (Jahr 1996: 116)

To summarize, Russenorsk exemplifies two important points that apply to pidgins in general: first, it relies on a limited range of simplified phonological, morphological and syntactic structures; and second, despite its superficial simplicity and chaotically mixed nature, Russenorsk has grammatical rules, some of which cannot be attributed to either of the parent languages. One may ask at this point where such grammatical rules come from if they do not come from either of the pidgin's parent languages. We will consider this question in the next section.

12.2 Creoles

Under the right conditions, which seem to arise particularly often in the plantation situation described in the previous section, pidgin speakers may intermarry and have children who are exposed mainly to the pidgin spoken by the parents. These children then acquire the pidgin as their native tongue. But in this process they change the pidgin itself, by injecting "grammatical complexity where none existed before, resulting in a brand-new, richly expressive language" (Pinker 1994: 33). A pidgin that acquires native speakers and becomes a community language is called a CREOLE.[4]

The process of creolization involves introducing not only more uniformity to the highly variable pidgin of the parents and other adults in the environment but also more complexity. In other words, children who create a creole out of a pidgin introduce new grammatical rules to the language. Where do these rules come from? What makes children introduce very similar rules regardless of which pidgin they turn into a creole? We will address these questions below after examining a few creoles and the kinds of grammatical rules and vocabulary items they involve.

The pidgin-to-creole cycle can be exemplified with Nigerian Pidgin English and Tok Pisin, both of which have some native speakers but are also used as a pidgin by other, non-native speakers.[5] For example, **Nigerian Pidgin English**

---

[4]   Technically, acquiring native speakers and becoming a community language need not be part of the same process. Indeed, there is a disagreement among scholars as to whether it is native speakers or use as a community language that turns a pidgin into a creole. Furthermore, this process is rather gradual and sometimes scholars talk about the "extended pidgin" stage in the pidgin-to-creole cycle.

[5]   The names of various pidgins and creoles can be quite confusing. For example, Nigerian Pidgin English is also known as Nigerian Creole English (which, given its large number of native speakers, might be a better name). Similarly, Tok Pisin is also known as Melanesian English, Neomelanesian, New Guinea Pidgin English, Pidgin or simply Pisin; none of its names reflect its creole nature.

is spoken by some 30 million speakers (this number includes both native and non-native speakers) in the southern parts of Nigeria. The *Ethnologue* classifies it as a "creole with native speakers, as well as used as a pidgin between Africans and Europeans, and Africans from different languages". **Tok Pisin**, which has an official status in Papua New Guinea, has 50,000–1,000,000 native speakers, mostly in mixed urban areas, in the northern parts of the country and in the Port Moresby area. However, it also serves as the language of administration and trade for another 4 million of non-native speakers.[6]

Among other important creole languages one should mention such English-based creoles as **Jamaican Creole** (known to its nearly 3 million speakers in Jamaica, as well as in Costa Rica and Panama, as "patois"); **Hawaiian Creole** (spoken by 600,000 in Hawaii); **Krio** (spoken by 473,000 speakers in Sierra Leone, mainly descendants of repatriated slaves from Jamaica); **Trinidadian Creole English** (spoken by 9,600 in Trinidad);[7] **Australian Kriol** (with 10,000 native speakers and up to 30,000 non-native speakers in western Australia); and the English-based but Dutch-influenced **Sranan** (spoken by 120,000 in Suriname). Among the French-based creoles the best known are **Haitian Creole French** (spoken by some 7 million people in Haiti, as well as in the Dominican Republic and Guadeloupe); **Louisiana Creole** (spoken 70,000 people in Louisiana, parts of East Texas and a small community in Sacramento, California); **Seselwa** or Seychellois Creole (with 72,700 speakers in the Seychelles); **Morisyen** or Mauritius Creole French (spoken by 800,000 people on the island of Mauritius); and **Réunion Creole French** (spoken by 555,000 people in Réunion). Iberian languages – Spanish and Portuguese – were the basis for many creoles, including **Papiamentu** (spoken by 179,000 people in Netherlands Antilles); **Crioulo** (spoken by 206,000 people in Guinea-Bissau and another 105,000 in Senegal); **Kabuverdianu** (spoken by 394,000 in Cape Verde Islands); **Chavacano** (spoken by 293,000 in the Philippines); and **Palenquero** (spoken by 500 people in Colombia, southeast of Cartagena). There are also some German-based creoles including **Rabaul Creole German** (or Unserdeutsch; spoken by about 100 people in Papua New Guinea).

Despite the fact that different creoles were based on different combinations of European and non-European languages, comparative studies show that creoles everywhere share a number of grammatical features in common. Interestingly, these features cannot be explained by such concepts as "simplification" or features of language that came into contact to produce the creoles in question or diffusion from one creole to another.

---

[6] Related contact languages Bislama and Pijin are spoken in Vanuatu and the Solomon Islands, respectively. While Bislama has only about 3,000 native speakers, it is used as a lingua franca by the majority of the 128,000 inhabitants of Vanuatu (where it has the status of the official language). Pijin – which is a creole and not a pidgin, despite its name – has about 1,300 native speakers and another 100,000 use it as a second language.

[7] Guadeloupe, Martinique, Saint-Lucia and Dominica have their own French-based creole, known as Lesser Antillean Creole French.

Among such shared creole features is unmarked inventories of sounds; and the use of auxiliary verbs (or particles) preceding the main verb to mark modal, aspectual and temporal distinctions. For example, the sound inventories of both Tok Pisin and Nigerian Pidgin English are unmarked in the sense that they include only "non-exotic" sounds. Tok Pisin has 17 consonants and 10 vowels (including the basic 5 vowels and 5 diphthongs), whereas Nigerian Pidgin English has 23 consonants and 7 vowels (including both low-mid vowels /ɛ/ and /ɔ/ and high-mid vowels /e/ and /o/). However, unlike pidgins, creoles develop more complex phonological elements, such as tones in Nigerian Pidgin English, and phonological rules that regulate their use.

Furthermore, creoles are known to rely on free-standing auxiliaries or particles to mark modal, aspectual and temporal distinctions. Recall that in pidgins, such as Russenorsk, lexical verbs may be called to serve as aspectual auxiliaries or copula (see (12.3), (12.4) and the surrounding discussion). The same verbs, however, can serve as lexical verbs as well. In creoles, certain lexical verbs undergo a process of GRAMMATICALIZATION: they lose their lexical status altogether and can be used only as auxiliaries or particles. Examples of such verbs that grammaticalized into auxiliaries/particles in Tok Pisin include: the future tense marker *bai* from 'by and by', the past tense marker *bin* from 'been', the immediate future marker *laik* from 'like' (note that this particle also has the meaning of 'wanting to do something'), the perfective marker *pinis* from 'finish' (this marker is often postverbal rather than preverbal), the habitual marker *sa* from 'save' (which first developed the meaning 'know' and then developed into the habitual marker) and the continuous marker *wok long* or *wok lo* from 'work long'.[8] (The transitive marker *-im* is discussed below.)

(12.9) a. em   bai   kam.
          he/she FUT come
          'He/she will come.'

      b. mi bin har-im   pairap blo   gan.
          I PST hear-TR   fire   belong gun
          'I heard the guns fire.'

                              (Smith 2002: 129)

---

[8] The particle *i* in these examples is usually called the predicate (or predicative) marker, but its proper analysis is unclear: it remains "one of the most troublesome items in the language" (Mundhenk 1990: 348). It typically appears between the subject and the predicate if the subject is a third person pronoun or a noun (but not if it is a first or second person pronoun), as shown in (i) and it probably derives from the resumptive pronoun (in boldface) in sentences like (ii).

(i) a.   mi kam   'I come'
    b.   yu kam   'You come'
    c.   em **i** kam   'He/she comes'
    d.   Tom **i** wok   'Tom works'
(ii)   The man, **he** talked to the woman.

c. em   i   laik   go long gaden.
    he/she PART is.about.to go to the garden
    'He/she is about to go to the garden.'

d. mi kuk-im pinis.
    I   cook-TR PFV
    'I have cooked it.'

e. Miplea sa   har-im ol gan i   pairap.
    we   HAB hear-TR PL gun PART fire
    'We (habitually) heard the guns firing.'

f. em wok lo tok...
    he CONT say
    'He was saying...'
       (Smith 2002: 133)

Similar particles for marking tense, aspect and mood are found in other creoles as well. For instance, in Nigerian Pidgin English we find a similar past
tense marker *bìn* from 'been', the future/irrealis marker *gò* from 'go', the perfec-
tive/completive marker *don* 'done' and other tense and aspect markers.

(12.10) a. A bìn layk nyam.
            I PST like yam
            'I like yams.'
            (Faraclas 1996: 197)

       b. A gò   chop nyam.
           I FUT eat yam
           'I will eat yams.'
           (Faraclas 1996: 198)

       c. A don kom.
           I PFV come
           'I have come.'
           (Faraclas 1996: 200)

Similarly, in Krio we find the past tense marker *bin* from 'been', the progressive
marker *de* and the perfective/completive marker *don* from 'done'.

(12.11) a. a bin rait
            I PST write
            'I wrote.'

       b. a de   rait
           I PROG write
           'I am writing.'

       c. a don rait
           I PFV write
           'I have written.'

Likewise, in Hawaiian Creole *go*, *stay* and *came* are used as grammatical
markers of tense and aspect:

(12.12)   One time when we go home inna night   dis ting **stay** fly   up.
           once when   we went home at night this thing PROG flying about
           'Once when we went home at night this thing was flying about.'

                                                                              (Pinker 1994: 35)

There are other properties of creoles that support the view that creoles are enhanced pidgins. First, as with many pidgins (although not all, as we have seen with the example of Russenorsk), creoles typically have parent languages of different social status: a superstratum language, which contributes most of the vocabulary, and a substratum language, which contributes some grammatical structures and a lesser part of the vocabulary. For example, English, which contributed the bulk of Tok Pisin's vocabulary, served as the substratum language, while Austronesian and Papuan languages (e.g. Malay Tolai), which contributed grammatical structures and some of the vocabulary, are the substratum languages.[9] Thus, in addition to the English-based vocabulary, Tok Pisin includes words from various Austronesian and Papuan languages, such as *lapun* 'old', *kumul* 'bird of paradise', *palai* 'lizard' from Tolai, and *binatang* 'insect', *lombo* 'chili', *sayur* 'vegetable leaf' from Malay. Finally, Tok Pisin includes some words of German origin (e.g. *gumi* 'rubber', *beten* 'pray', *raus* 'get out', *bros* 'chest'); the German influence is due to the fact that Germany was the colonial power in the northern part of New Guinea from 1884 till 1914.

Another characteristic of creoles such as Tok Pisin and Nigerian Pidgin English that reveals their pidgin past is the prevalence of the SVO word order (illustrated by the above examples), which is found also in most pidgins, independently of the word order patterns in their substratum and superstratum languages. For instance, in accordance with the generalization that grammatical structures typically come from the substratum languages, one would expect Tok Pisin to have the basic SOV order since most of the Papuan and Austronesian languages of Papua New Guinea have the SOV order (see Chapter 9). However, it has been suggested that the fact that SVO word order is typical of pidgin and creole languages has nothing to do with the characteristic patterns of either substratum or superstratum languages but is due to universal tendencies or ease of processing (Romaine 1988: 30). Unfortunately, there is no real way to prove (or disprove) this hypothesis since we know of no creole whose substrate and superstrate languages were both non-SVO. Therefore, the idea that SVO is a universally basic word order for some non-accidental reasons must remain a hypothesis (but see Kayne 1994).

Tok Pisin and Nigerian Pidgin English can also be used to illustrate two crucial differences between pidgins and creoles. First, unlike pidgins, creoles develop bound morphemes; that is, affixes that cannot stand on their own but must be attached to a noun, a verb or another type of root. One example of a bound morpheme in Tok Pisin that has already been illustrated in the examples above

---

[9] Tolai is also known as Kuanua. It is an Austronesian language (from the Western Oceanic subgrouping) spoken by 61,000 people in Papua New Guinea (specifically, on the Gazelle Peninsula in East New Britain Province). Malay is discussed in Chapter 8.

is the transitive suffix -*im*. Its etymology is from the English object pronoun *him*. But unlike the English source, which is an independent word, the Tok Pisin -*im* is a bound morpheme, meaning that it attaches to the verb and forms a single word with it. In some cases, its presence indicates a transitive use of an optionally transitive verb such as *rit* 'read' (see (12.13)) and in other cases its presence indicates a causative use of a verb like *boil* 'boil', as opposed to an inchoative/intransitive use (see (12.14)). Note that unlike most of the free morpheme particles, such as the tense, aspect and mood markers discussed above, bound morphemes such as the transitive marker -*im* follow rather than precede the verb.[10]

(12.13) a.   em   i   rit.
             he/she PART   read
             'He/she is reading.'

        b.   em   i   rit-im   buk.
             he/she PART   read-TR   book
             'He/she is reading a book.'

(12.14) a.   wara   i   boil pinis.
             water   PART   boil PFV
             'The water has boiled.'

        b.   Meri   i   boil-im   wara   pinis.
             woman   PART   boil-TR   water PFV
             'The woman has boiled the water.'

Another bound morpheme in Tok Pisin is the so-called adjectival suffix -*pela*, deriving from 'fellow', which is often reduced to -*pla* and occurs on numerals (e.g. *tripla* 'three'), demonstratives (e.g. *dispela* 'this'), adjectives (e.g. *grinpla* 'green', *naispla* 'nice') and non-singular pronouns (e.g. *yutupela* 'you two', *yutripela* 'you three' and *yupela* 'you all').[11]

Second, unlike pidgins, creoles develop more complex syntactic structures. For instance, creoles have subordinate structures introduced by complementizers that are practically never found in pidgins (for rare exceptions in Russenorsk, see the discussion surrounding (12.5) above). Tok Pisin has a number of complementizers (see Smith 2002: 158–161), the most frequent of which is *olsem* (from *all the same as*):

---

[10] Nigerian Pidgin English has an independent preverbal causative marker *mek* (from the English 'make'), as in the following example:

   (i)   im   gò   mek   mì   chop.
               he/she FUT   make   me   eat
               'He/she will make me eat.'

[11] Plurality can also be expressed in Tok Pisin by the suffix -*s* as in *bebis* 'babies'; reduplication as in *nil nil* 'spines' from the English *needle*; or the pluralizing particle *ol* from the English *all*, as in *ol man* 'men'.

(12.15)   mi no save **olsem** ol   i   wok-im dis-pela   haus.
           I   not know that   they PART work-TR this-SUFFIX house
           'I didn't know that they built this house.'

Similarly, in Nigerian Pidgin English subordinate clauses may be introduced
by the complementizer *se*:

(12.16)   a tink **se** dèm bay nyam.
           I think that they buy yam
           'I think that they bought yam.'

Furthermore, both Tok Pisin and Nigerian Pidgin English have relative clauses
(which are not found in pidgins), introduced by the markers *husat* (sometimes
shortened to *usat*) and *we*, respectively:

(12.17) a. ol   man **usat** bin   bagarap lo eksident.
            PL man REL PST injured in accident
            'all the people who were injured in the accident'
                                          (Smith 2002: 152)

        b. a si   dì   man **we** bìn chop.
            I saw ART man REL PST eat
            'I saw the man who ate.'
                            (Faraclas 1996: 36)

After reviewing the characteristic grammatical patterns found in various creoles, we are now in a position to address the questions posed earlier: for those
grammatical structures (or patterns, or rules) of creoles that cannot be derived
from either the substratum or the superstratum language, where do these structures come from? And what makes children who create creoles out of pidgins
introduce very similar rules regardless of which pidgin they turn into a creole?

One commonly accepted answer to these questions is known as the Bioprogram Hypothesis, formulated by Derek Bickerton (1983, 1984a, b). According
to this hypothesis, creoles based on different languages share characteristic features because the children who create them "fall back on the genetically preprogrammed default set of grammatical rules" (Lyovin 1997: 407). In other words,
all human children are genetically predisposed to learn a full-fledged human
language (Pinker 1994) and therefore when they are exposed to a very rudimentary and limited pidgin in their environment, they must fall on the UNIVERSAL
GRAMMAR to create a full-fledged language. Thus, creolization provides a particularly clear window on the innate grammatical machinery of the brain.

Interestingly, many of the features shared by creoles also appear as tendencies
which manifest themselves in the speech of all children as they learn their first
language whatever that language may be. Or, as Steven Pinker (1994: 35) puts it,
the basic grammar that children rely on in turning a pidgin into a creole:

> *also shows up . . . in the errors children make when acquiring more estab-*
> *lished and embellished languages, like some underlying design bleeding*
> *through a veneer of whitewash.*

It should be noted here that Bickerton's Bioprogram Hypothesis is not accepted by all scholars of creoles and some evidence adduced in its support remains controversial. Still, his basic idea received a stunning confirmation when the process of creolization by children could be observed in real time. This was the case with Idioma de Signos Nicaragüense (ISN), a sign language creole that was created by younger deaf children in Nicaraguan schools for the deaf, created when the Sandinista government took over in 1979. These children joined the school around the age of four and were exposed to a different form of a sign language – Lenguaje de Signos Nicaragüense (LSN) – an ad hoc sign language created on the playgrounds by an earlier generation of children who pooled the makeshift gestures that they used with their families at home. Thus, LSN is a pidgin, lacking a consistent and complex grammar of a full-fledged (sign) language, whereas ISN is a creole with many grammatical devices that were absent in LSN and can be used in jokes, poems, narratives and more. Most importantly, however, ISN is a collective product of many children communicating with each other, which supports the idea that humans are born preprogrammed to learn a full-fledged language from their environment or to create one if their environment lacks such a language.

12.3   Mixed Jewish languages

Among some of the best examples of mixed, or contact, languages are the so-called mixed Jewish languages: Yiddish, Ladino, Judeo-Italian, Judeo-Persian, Judeo-Arabic and others. This section is dedicated to an examination, however brief, of these languages.

We shall start with the best-known of the Jewish languages – Yiddish – which is classified as a Germanic language (see Chapter 2). However, it is a "language-in-contact" par excellence, as it arose through contact of Ashkenazic Jewry with German-speaking (and later, Slavic-speaking) groups.[12] The importance of Yiddish both for the Jewish people and for the study of languages cannot be underestimated, as prior to World War II the majority of the Jewish people (some say, as many as 11 million people) spoke Yiddish, whereas the territory occupied by Yiddish speakers in the Old World – from the German–French border in the west to as far as several degrees of longitude to the east of Smolensk – was second in size only to the Russian-speaking territory. Moreover, over this vast territorial expanse Jews coexisted with numerous other groups, whose languages affected Yiddish. Thus, studying the structure and development of Yiddish can shed new light on issues in historical, comparative and socio-linguistics.

---

[12] The word Ashkenazic derives from Ashkenaz, the name of one of Noah's grandsons, who, according to medieval rabbis, settled in Germany.

Yet, for a long time, Yiddish was looked down upon as a bastardized dialect of German or even a mere jargon, leading a Yiddish scholar Max Weinreich to quip that "a language is a dialect with an army and a navy" (neither of which Yiddish has ever had); see Chapter 1. This sentiment is echoed in Isaac Bashevis Singer's acceptance speech for the Nobel prize in literature in 1978, who described Yiddish as

> *a language of exile, without a land, without frontiers, not supported by any government; a language which possesses no words for weapons, ammunitions, military exercises, war tactics; a language that was despised by the gentiles and emancipated Jews.*

While Yiddish and German developed from the same source, Middle High German, Yiddish is not a dialect of German. While, unsurprisingly, there is a strong Hebrew/Aramaic influence on the vocabulary of Yiddish, the differences between Yiddish and German are not just lexical. For instance, in the sound system, Yiddish preserves a phonemic contrast between word-initial /s/ and /z/; witness such MINIMAL PAIRS as *sok* 'syrup, sap' (from Slavic) and *zok* 'sock' (from Germanic). This contrast is lost in German. Hence, German words never start with a [s]: before a vowel, word-initial *s* is pronounced as [z] and before a consonant as a [ʃ]: consider, for example, the word-initial [z] in *sagen* 'to say' and [ʃ] in *schlafen* 'to sleep' and *sterben* 'to die'. In morphology, Yiddish nouns can form plurals with the Hebrew-based suffix *-im*, which is not available in German. Furthermore, Yiddish uses *-s* plurals much more regularly than German.

In syntax, one example of a difference between German and Yiddish involves the Verb-Second phenomenon (or V2) (discussed in Chapter 1). In German, it is limited to main (or matrix) clauses; in embedded (or subordinate) clauses V2 is generally impossible. In Yiddish, V2 is found in embedded clauses, as well as in main clauses. As shown in the following examples, the finite/tensed verb in an embedded clause (in boldface) in German appears in the final position, whereas in Yiddish it appears in the second position, after the prepositional phrase *oyfn veg* 'on the way'.

(12.18) a. (Standard) German:
            Er sagt daβ die Kinder   diesen Film gesehen **haben**.
            he said that the children this   film   seen   have
            'He said that the children have seen this film.'

        b. Yiddish:
            . . . oyb oyfn   veg **vet** dos yingl zen a kats.
            whether on-the way will the boy   see a cat
            ' . . . whether on the way the boy will see a cat'
                                        (Santorini 1992)

Three historical developments brought about the formation of Yiddish as we know it today. The first one was the migration of Jews from northern France and northern Italy into the Rhine Valley.[13] These Jews spoke Judeo-Romance varieties (see discussion below) and bore a tradition of Hebrew and Aramaic writings, so when they adopted local varieties of medieval German in the towns where they settled, the resulting Jewish vernacular was different from that of the non-Jews. Exactly how different the Earliest Yiddish and Old German were we do not know since the earliest documentary evidence for Yiddish does not appear until later: the earliest dated text is a rhymed couplet inscribed in a Hebrew prayerbook dated in the city of Worms, Germany, 1272, while the earliest major document, the so-called Cambridge Yiddish Codex – a manuscript originally found in the Cairo Genizah (see the "Buried Treasures" box in Chapter 5) – bears the date 1382. But scholars estimate that between 15 and 20% of the Yiddish vocabulary comes directly from Hebrew.

The second historical development that affected the nature of Yiddish is the "internal Jewish migrations compelled as early as the eleventh century by the Crusaders (who disrupted the Jewish communities) and well advanced by the mid-fourteenth century, when persecutions associated with the Black Plague drove entire Jewish communities out of Germany" (Herzog 1978: 48). As a result of these internal migrations, Yiddish became a "melting pot" of German dialects. The roots of Yiddish are in the East Frankish and Bavarian varieties of German, as can be shown by such shared innovations as the formation of the diminutive plural in -lach (-lech, -lich), a contamination of -līn with the original collective suffix -ahi (Markey 1978: 61). Yet, Yiddish exhibits traits which were found in geographically distinct dialects of German.

The third and final historical development that created Modern Yiddish is the expansion of Jewish settlement into Slavic territories from the thirteenth century onward that resulted in the creation of a major Yiddish internal dialectal divide between Western Yiddish and Eastern Yiddish, corresponding roughly to the German–Slavic divide on the non-Jewish map. While Western Yiddish predominated in the earlier period, gradually the centers of population – and of rabbinical authority – shifted eastwards, and with that the importance of Eastern Yiddish grew. From 1750 on, Western Yiddish begins to fade under the pressure of Standard German and cultural assimilation. It survived into the twentieth century only in areas where the pressure from Standard German was minimal: in Alsace, Switzerland, Holland and western Hungary.

In the Slavic lands, Yiddish picked up not only lexical items from Slavic languages (Polish, Russian, Ukrainian, etc.) but also grammatical properties, such as the possibility of placing more than one question word at the beginning of a question. Thus, in English – and all other Germanic languages, including German – in a multiple question, only one question word can appear in the beginning of the sentence. All other question words must appear elsewhere in

---

[13] Historians disagree whether the earlier population of Jews who had settled in the Rhineland during the Roman times retreated together with the Romans in mid-fifth century under pressure from invaders from the East.

the sentence; more precisely, they are placed exactly where their answers would appear if the sentence were a declarative rather than a question. So one can say in English *Who bought what?* but not **Who what bought?* In such multiple wh-questions, one question word (*who*) appears sentence-initially, whereas the second (*what*) appears post-verbally, where the object would appear in a declarative sentence. In contrast, in Slavic languages, such as Russian or Polish, all question words must appear sentence-initially, as in the following Russian examples:

(12.19)　　Kto čto kupil?
　　　　　who what bought
　　　　　'Who bought what?'

Interestingly, multiple questions in Yiddish reveal both its Germanic roots and its contact with Slavic languages: one can either place only one question word sentence-initially (in which case the other question word must appear before the non-finite lexical verb, if there is one; see (12.20a)), or place all question words sentence-initially (see (12.20b)). The question in (12.20a) illustrates the Germanic pattern and the question in (12.20b) illustrates the Slavic-influenced pattern.

(12.20) a.　ver hot vos gekoyft?
　　　　　　who has what bought
　　　　　　'Who bought what?'
　　　　　　　　　(Diesing 2003: 53)

　　　　b.　ver vos hot gekoyft?
　　　　　　who what has bought
　　　　　　'Who bought what?'
　　　　　　　　　(Diesing 2003: 54)

The currently dominating Eastern Yiddish itself can be subdivided into three major dialectal areas: Central (or *Galitsyaner*) Yiddish in spoken in the area between the German-Polish frontier of 1939 and the Rivers Vistula and San; Northeastern (or *Litvak*) Yiddish in Lithuania, Belorussia, and northeastern Poland; and Southeastern (or Ukrainian) Yiddish in Ukraine, Eastern Galicia, Romania and southeastern Poland. For example, the three dialects of Eastern Yiddish differ with respect to the multiple questions discussed above: the possibility of placing more than one question word sentence-initially both in direct questions (as in (12.20b)) and in indirect (or embedded) question holds only in Southeastern Yiddish; in Central Yiddish placing more than one question word sentence-initially is possible only in indirect questions (see (12.21)), whereas in Northeastern Yiddish placing more than one question word sentence-initially is not possible at all.

(12.21)　　...farshteyn [ver mit vemen es shlogt zikh]
　　　　　to.understand who with whom he hits self
　　　　　... to understand who was fighting with whom'
　　　　　　　　　(Diesing 2003: 55)

As important as Yiddish is for the Jewish studies, one should not forget that Jews also lived outside the German- and Slavic-speaking areas: in the Romance-speaking lands, in Persia, in the Arab world – and everywhere they were in contact with local non-Jewish groups and created mixed languages. As mentioned above, Yiddish started when Jews migrated from northern France into the Rhineland, and these Jews spoke Judeo-Romance varieties. However, the term "Judeo-Romance" is an umbrella term for a number of distinct and mutually incomprehensible linguistic varieties; more specifically, the Jews of northern France spoke Judeo-French (also known as Zarphatic, from the Hebrew word *tsarfat* 'France'). The earliest texts that can be called Judeo-French are the glosses (i.e. translations of difficult words in a Hebrew text) of Menachem bar Helbo, which date from the eleventh century. The glosses of Rashi, also from the eleventh century, are more numerous and well known. These glosses are important not only for the study of contact languages and specifically of Judeo-French, but also for Romance philology in general: "very often his [Rashi's] use of a French word offers the oldest example known to exist" (Levy 1947: 7).

While Jews in northern France spoke Judeo-French, Jews in one particular part of what is now France spoke a different Judeo-Romance variety. The area in question is the historical region of Comtat-Venaissin, which is more or less coextensive with the modern department of Vaucluse in southern France. Before the French Revolution, the Comtat-Venaissin and the neighboring city of Avignon were papal territory, and therefore their Jewish residents did not have to leave when Jews were expelled from France in the fourteenth century and from Provence in the fifteenth century. These Jews spoke a variety referred to as either "Shuadit" (apparently, from the Hebrew word *yehudi* 'Jewish') or "Judeo-Provençal". However, this latter term is not very apt since the variety in question is quite distinct from that spoken in Provençal cities like Nice and Marseille; therefore, sometimes the term "Judeo-Comtadine" is used instead. Whatever the label, this language is now extinct, and the only remaining evidence of it is in a few inscriptions, Biblical glosses, translation of prayers and traditional songs.

While precious little is known about the linguistic properties of Judeo-Comtadine, two interesting phonological properties suggest that this variety itself is a result of a dialect mixture, with Jews moving into the Comtat-Venaissin both from the north and from the west of the area. On the one hand, in Judeo-Comtadine the Hebrew letters ת (tav), שׁ (sin) and ס (samekh) are all pronounced as [f]. Since the original Hebrew pronunciation of these letters is [t] and [s] (for the last two letters), scholars postulate an earlier stage of Judeo-Comtadine when these three letters were pronounced [θ], while later [θ] was replaced by a similar-sounding [f] (note that the [t]-to-[θ] change falls squarely under the umbrella of lenition and it is found in some Sephardic pronunciations; see below). The sound [θ] is found in Franco-Provençal dialects spoken to the north of the Comtat-Venaissin. On the other hand, Judeo-Comtadine also exhibits devoicing of [ʒ] in words like *juge* which are pronounced with [ʃ] instead. This devoicing process is reminiscent of the dialects to the west of the Comtat-Venaissin, where [ʒ] of Standard

French is pronounced as [ts] or [tʃ]. The hypothesis that Jews moved into the Comtat-Venaissin both from the north and from the west is further supported by the evidence from their family names such as Crémieux, which is the name of a town to the north, and Lunel and Bédarrides, which are the names of towns to the west.

The Jewish variety spoken in Italy is known as Judeo-Italian or "Italkian". It is difficult to tell how many speakers Judeo-Italian has, since it is hard to define a "speaker" in this case (as in many others, as we have seen throughout the book). The number of people who would occasionally use a Jewish word, construction or intonation is very large (Jochnowitz 1978: 67 estimates it at "a tenth of Italy's Jewish population of forty thousand"), but the number of people who consistently speak with a distinctly Jewish vocabulary, pronunciation and grammar – such as the use of the invariable definite plural article *li* and the lack of distinction between masculine and feminine nouns in the plural – is tiny.

There is a debate among scholars as to whether Judeo-Italian goes back as far as the twelfth or early thirteenth century, or whether it appeared only with the establishment of ghettos in the sixteenth century. Some scholars (e.g. Blondheim 1923, 1924) even trace it as far back as a Judeo-Latin dialect, which would have evolved parallel to Vulgar Latin. Moreover, there is a great deal of diversity among the varieties of Judeo-Italian spoken in different cities; for example, the Jewish speech of Turin may be closer to the non-Jewish Piedmontese dialect than it is to the Jewish speech in Rome. Hence, some linguists talk about separate varieties such as *giudeo-mantovano*, *giudeo-romanesco* and so on; in Ferrara the term *ghettaiolo* is used, while the Judeo-Italian variety spoken in Livorno (Leghorn) and Pisa is known as *bagito* (pronounced [baʒíto]). This later variety has been influenced not only by the local Livorno dialect, but also by Portuguese and Spanish. Sadly, only a few people who survived the Holocaust continued to speak *bagito* after World War II.

In addition to the already-mentioned loss of gender distinction in the plural of nouns and definite articles – with the resulting forms like *li donni* 'the ladies' instead of *le donne*, as in Standard Italian – Judeo-Italian also features many words of Hebrew-Aramaic origin. Moreover, Italian prefixes and suffixes are often attached to Hebrew roots: for example, *paxadoso* 'timid' and *impaxadito* 'frightened' from the Hebrew word *paxad* 'fear'. Recall from Chapter 5 that a reverse process is observed in Modern Hebrew and Maltese where English and Romance roots are "dressed up" by the Semitic "root-and-template" morphology. In Judeo-Italian there are also borrowings from other mixed Jewish languages: *orsái* from the Yiddish *yortsayt* 'anniversary of a death', *xalto* from the Judezmo (see below) *xaldéo* 'Ashkenazi' and many others. These borrowings from other Jewish languages are, of course, evidence of intra-Jewish migrations and contact.

As is often the case, together with words from other languages, Judeo-Italian has borrowed sounds that are not present in Standard Italian (or even in Italian dialects), such as the voiceless velar fricative [x] of *paxad* 'fear', *impaxadito* 'frightened' etc. (see above). In at least one Judeo-Italian word of Hebrew

origin – *šaxtare* 'to slaughter' (pronounced [ʃaxtáre]) – the voiceless velar fricative occurs before [t], with the resulting consonant cluster that is altogether foreign
to Italian.

While in some cases, such as the above-mentioned consonant cluster [xt],
Judeo-Italian has properties that are not found in non-Jewish Italian, in other
cases it exhibits a mixture of dialectal features found only in geographically
distinct dialects. Thus, as Yiddish is described above as a "melting pot" of
German dialects, Judeo-Italian is a "melting pot" of Italian dialects. For example,
the lack of masculine/feminine distinction in the plural (with forms like *li donni*
'the ladies' instead of *le donne*) is found in the dialects of the deep south of
Italy. The seven-vowel system of Judeo-Italian (i.e. /a/, /ɛ/, /e/, /i/, /ɔ/, /o/, /u/) is
also found in many non-Jewish dialects of central Italy and in Standard Italian.[14]
However, the combination of *li donni* and a seven-vowel system is not found in
any non-Jewish Italian dialect. This too is evidence of internal migrations and
contact among Jewish communities all over Italy.

So far, we have looked at a number of Judeo-Romance varieties, such as
Judeo-French, Judeo-Comtadine and Judeo-Italian, but probably the best-known
Judeo-Romance variety is Judeo-Spanish. It is known under various alternative
names: Dzhudezmo or Judezmo, Ladino and *hakitía* (the latter term is used
among Moroccan Jews).[15] In what follows, I will use the term Judeo-Spanish
to highlight that its earliest form goes back to Spain before the expulsion of the
Jews in 1492. Here is how Kiddle (1978: 75) describes these events:

> The Catholic Sovereigns of Spain, Ferdinand and Isabella, published a decree
> in 1492 ordering Spaniards of Jewish faith to leave Spain within three months.
> Those who converted to Christianity would be permitted to remain in the
> homeland. It is estimated that this harsh edict affected approximately 250,000
> Jews, who lived in 120 communities, principally in the south of Spain. Of
> these, 50,000 chose the alternative of conversion, but they were subjected to
> prolonged harassment because it was believed that they secretly practiced
> their original faith and that their Christianity was superficial. Perhaps 25,000
> Jews died of disease, starvation, and of emotional shock. The remaining
> 175,000 became refugees in foreign lands; and 125,000 accepted Sultan
> Bayazid II's invitation to settle in the extensive Ottoman Empire. These
> were the Eastern, or Balkanic, Sephardim, who settled in areas that today
> are parts of Greece, Turkey, Yugoslavia, and the islands of the Aegean and
> eastern Mediterranean Seas. Another 50,000 exiles went to North Africa
> or to Portugal, where they were given a temporary haven, and from there
> they went to Holland. These were the Western Sephardim, who were largely
> Portuguese-speaking, and who continued to use their language until the
> nineteenth century.

[14] The sounds /e/ and /ɛ/ and /o/ and /ɔ/ are truly different phonemes, as can be witnessed from the
minimal pairs such as /'peska/ 'fishing' and /'pɛska/ 'peach' (both spelled *pesca*) and /'botte/
'barrel' and /'bɔtte/ 'beatings' (both spelled *botte*).

[15] See Jochnowitz (1978: 65) for a discussion of the advantages and disadvantages of the different
labels given to this language.

With the decline of the Ottoman Empire and the rise of nationalism in the former Ottoman lands, Judeo-Spanish-speaking communities came under pressure and many emigrated to the New World starting at the time of the Turkish Revolution in 1908. In the Americas, Judeo-Spanish-speaking Jews were absorbed into the mainstream Spanish- and English-speaking communities and ceased to use their language.

The evidence that Judeo-Spanish goes back to the pre-1492 Spain derives from the common forms shared by the vernaculars of Jews in Turkey and Morocco despite there not being much post-exilic contact between these groups. Thus, forms like the diminutive suffix -ico and the expression el Dyo 'the God' instead of the Spanish Dios 'God' must have been brought by Jews both to Morocco and to the Ottoman lands from Spain when they left after the expulsion.

This example also highlights another important point: the distinctiveness of the mixed Jewish languages derives not only from the Hebrew/Aramaic elements, but also from the conservatism of Jewish languages (which, in the case of Judeo-Spanish, may have derived in part from the favorable attitude of Bayazid II towards the Sephardim and their resulting sense of cultural and linguistic superiority over their new non-Jewish neighbors in the Ottoman Empire). In the case of Judeo-Spanish el Dyo 'the God' vs. the Spanish Dios 'God', an older form dio from fifteenth-century Castilian Spanish has been preserved in the speech of the Jews but not of non-Jews (this makes Judeo-Spanish extremely valuable to historians of the Spanish language because "a Sephardic-speaker is almost like an informant from the Middle Ages", according to Kiddle 1978: 76). Among other conservative traits of Judeo-Spanish are lexical archaisms, such as mercar 'to buy' (cf. the Standard Spanish comprar), mancar 'to be lacking' (cf. the Standard Spanish faltar), inglutir 'to swallow' (cf. the Standard Spanish tragar) and many others. Judeo-Spanish also preserves the fifteenth and sixteenth century sounds such as [ʃ], [ʒ] and [dʒ] that later disappeared from Standard Spanish. For example, the [ʒ]-to-[x] change is illustrated by the comparison of [fiʒo], [hiʒo] and [iʒo] from various Judeo-Spanish dialects with the Standard Spanish hijo 'son', pronounced [ixo]. Similarly, in Standard Spanish the [ʃ] of deshar 'to leave' and the [dʒ] of gente 'people' developed into [x] but the original sounds are retained in Judeo-Spanish. Yet another example of grammatical conservatism of Judeo-Spanish is the preservation of the feminine gender for nouns in -or (e.g. calor 'heat', color 'color', favor 'favor', etc.): these nouns were feminine in the Middle Ages and are now commonly masculine in Standard Spanish.

This linguistic conservatism is most pronounced in the East (i.e. Turkey, the Balkans) and least pronounced in North Africa, which retained a greater contact with Spain. Note that there is nothing unusual about this situation: relative isolation from the home country typically leads to linguistic conservatism. Thus, American English retains some features of the sixteenth and seventeenth century British English (e.g. the pronunciation of bath as [bæːθ] rather than [bɑːθ]); Quebecois French is full of lexical archaisms; and the language of White Russian émigrés (see Section 12.1 above) is much closer to the nineteenth-century Russian than that of today's youth in Russia.

To go back to the *dio/Dios* example, the Modern Spanish form *Dios* owes its final *-s* to the influence of Church Latin *deus*. Naturally, the Spanish spoken by Jews was little affected by Church Latin compared to the Spanish spoken by Christians. In this sense, the common Hebrew elements in Jewish languages, especially when it comes to religion-related vocabulary, are not unique, but rather are very similar to the Byzantine Greek and Old Church Slavonic influences on languages of Orthodox countries (e.g. Russian), or the Latin influences on languages of Western Christian countries (including non-Romance languages like English and even non-Indo-European languages like Finnish and Hungarian).

What is unique about Hebrew influences on Jewish languages is that they extend beyond the religious vocabulary. Thus, Jewish languages even borrowed from Hebrew words with no religious significance. One example of such non-religious borrowing is the word *afilu* 'even, still', which is found in both Judeo-Spanish and Yiddish. Other examples include *ganav* 'thief' found in Yiddish, Judeo-Italian and Judeo-Spanish, and *galax* 'Christian priest' (from the Hebrew word for 'haircut', probably via meaning extension from 'tonsure' to 'the person with a tonsure'). While it cannot be proven conclusively when these words entered the various Jewish languages and whether they were borrowed independently by each Jewish language or borrowed from Hebrew just once and then diffused from one mixed Jewish language to another, the peculiarity of the meaning extension in the case of *galax* 'Christian priest' and the grammatical nature of *afilu* 'even, still' suggests that the borrowing happened once, probably into some Judeo-Romance variety, and then spread from one mixed Jewish language into another. This, again, speaks volumes of intra-Jewish migrations and contact.

Jews outside the Romance, German and Slavic lands also developed mixed Jewish languages which reflect both the Hebrew/Aramaic tradition and the peculiar history of the Jewish communities in these lands. Thus, Jews in the Persian-speaking area – including not only all of modern Iran, but also parts of Afghanistan, the Caucasus and Central Asia (especially Uzbekistan and Tajikistan) – developed a linguistic variety known as Judeo-Persian, whereas Jews in the Arab-speaking lands developed Judeo-Arabic. While we cannot examine these varieties here in great detail, they too highlight the points made above: (a) that mixed Jewish languages tend to be more conservative than their non-Jewish counterparts and (b) that mixed Jewish languages provide rich evidence for intra-Jewish migrations and contact. Therefore, a study of these languages is extremely valuable not only for a scholar of contact languages, but also for a scholar of the history of various languages that Jews came into contact with and for a scholar of Jewish history.

However, sadly, the assimilatory tendencies in the Americas; the tragic events of World War II, which decimated the Yiddish-speaking population of Europe; the persecution of Jews in the Soviet Union, both during the Stalin era and during the consecutive Communist years; the rise of nationalism in the Balkans, North Africa and the Middle East; and – ironically! – the creation of the State of Israel, which promoted Hebrew at the expense of other Jewish languages, all led to the weakening and even demise of many mixed Jewish languages, such as Yiddish, Judeo-Spanish, Judeo-Arabic and others.

In Israel, Judeo-Spanish and Judeo-Arabic were associated with Sephardim Jews who immigrated to Israel in the 1950s and were until recently the group with a lower socio-economic status. Yiddish, although associated with the socio-economically more prestigious group of Ashkenazic Jews, bore a stigma of the language of the ghettos, of "the sheep going to slaughter". Therefore, Israel's 300,000 Holocaust survivors refrained from speaking Yiddish in public and, until recently, only people in the Chassidic (ultra-Orthodox) world and the very elderly spoke Yiddish as their first language – or at all.

Today, the situation in Israel and worldwide is changing. More and more young Israelis are joining the revival of Yiddish, looking for their roots. Currently, four out of five Israeli universities have centers for Yiddish studies. However, as successful as these programs are, their achievements are a far cry from a true language revival because a language is considered living only if it has native speakers; that is, people who acquire it as babies from their parents. It is this intergenerational transmission that keeps a language alive. And it is this chain that was broken for Yiddish two generations ago.

Two morals can be drawn from this story of the demise and revival of Yiddish and other mixed Jewish languages: first, it is always easier to keep a language alive than to revive it from the dead, and second, attitudes very much matter to a language survival. And these morals can be applied to any language's life-and-death story around the globe.

Glossary

absolutive the case used to mark both the subject of an intransitive verb and the object of a transitive verb in an ergative–absolutive language.

active agreement system an agreement system where subjects of intransitives which denote an Agent trigger the same agreement markers as subjects of transitives, while subjects of intransitives which denote a Theme/Patient trigger the same agreement markers as objects of transitives.

adverb a part of speech that modifies any part of language other than a noun. Adverbs can modify verbs, adjectives, clauses and other adverbs.

affix a bound morpheme that attaches to the root (or stem) and modifies its meaning in some way or indicates person, number, tense, aspect or a similar grammatical meaning. Prefixes and suffixes are two common kinds of affixes.

affricate consonant a single consonant sound that consists of a stop followed by a fricative; for example, the first and last sounds of *church* and *judge*.

Agent the participant of a situation that carries out the action in this situation; for example, *John* in *John is eating an apple*.

agglutinative language a language whose words have several morphemes that attach to a root morpheme and each morpheme has only one distinct meaning.

alveolar consonant a consonant produced with a constriction or blockage between the tip of the tongue and the alveolar ridge; for example, the first sounds of *tip, sip, nip, lip*.

alveolar ridge the bone protrusion located just behind the upper teeth.

applicative construction a syntactic construction where a non-core argument with one of the range of meanings, including beneficiary, recipient, goal, location and reason, may appear in the syntactic object position when a special applicative morpheme is attached to the verb.

auxiliary a special kind of verb used to express concepts related to the truth of the sentence, such as tense, aspect, negation, question/statement, necessary/possible: *He **will** play. He **is** playing. He **doesn't** play*.

bound morpheme a morpheme that does not constitute an independent word, but must be combined with some other morpheme. All affixes and some roots are bound morphemes.

case a set of affixes or word forms that is used to distinguish the different roles of the participants in some event or state. Cases typically correspond to the subject, object, indirect object and the objects of various kinds of prepositions. In English, only pronouns have case forms: *he* vs. *him* vs. *his*.

classifier a word or morpheme used in some languages to classify the referent of a noun according to its meaning. In languages that have classifier systems, a classifier must be used in order for the noun to be used a count noun (e.g. with a numeral).

click sound a obstruent articulated with two closures in the mouth, one forward and one at the back. The pocket of air enclosed between is rarefied by a sucking action of the tongue and then the forward closure is released, producing a click sound.

complement a phrase that appears together with a verb, a preposition or a noun, completing its meaning: *He ate **the pizza**. He is under **the tree**. He is a scholar **of languages***.

complementizer a syntactic element that attaches a clause inside a bigger clause; for example, *that* in *John said **that** Bill liked the movie*.

consonant a sound produced with a closure or obstruction somewhere in the vocal tract.

copula the verb *to be* when it is used to link the subject and the predicate: *He **is** wise. The cat **is** on the mat*.

creole a language that developed from a pidgin by expanding its vocabulary and acquiring a more complex grammatical structure. Unlike pidgins, creoles have native speakers.

declension the inflection of nouns and other noun-like elements (pronouns, adjectives and articles) to indicate number, case and gender.

dental consonant a consonant produced with a constriction or blockage between the tip of the tongue and the upper teeth.

dialect continuum a phenomenon whereby a range of dialects is spoken across some geographical area, with the dialects of neighboring areas differing from each other only slightly, and the dialects from the opposite ends of the continuum being much less similar to each other and possibly not mutually intelligible at all.

diglossia a situation in which two dialects or languages are used by a single language community.

doubly articulated stop a stop consonant with two simultaneous primary places of articulation; for example, [kp].

ejective consonant a consonant pronounced with a simultaneous closure of the glottis.

ergative the case that marks the subject of a transitive verb in an ergative–absolutive language.

fricative consonant a consonant produced with the airflow channeled through a narrow opening in the vocal tract, producing turbulence; for example, the first sounds of *fill* and *sill*.

function words articles, conjunctions, auxiliaries, pronouns and some prepositions, which are used to specify grammatical information, like tense or case.

fusional (or synthetic) language a language in which morphemes have more than one meaning fused into a single affix.

gender a set of mutually exclusive kinds into which a language categorizes its nouns and pronouns. Typically, the genders of pronouns correspond to the sexes (*he* vs. *she*), and the genders of nouns are determined by their sounds (words ending in *a* are one gender, words ending in *o* are another gender, etc.) or are simply put into two or three arbitrary lists.

glottis the space between the two vocal cords.

grammaticalization a process by which nouns and verbs become grammatical markers, such as affixes, prepositions, etc.

grammatical object the constituent of the sentence that denotes an individual to which the action of the verb is applied; for example, in the sentence *John kicked **the ball**, the ball* is the object.

grammatical subject has certain special properties; for example, in English the grammatical subject controls the form of the tensed verb (in the present tense): *I play* vs. *He plays*. In some other languages, only the grammatical subject may control reflexives or only the grammatical subject may be questioned.

Great Vowel Shift a set of regular sound changes affecting the long vowels of English that took place in the fourteenth and fifteenth centuries. These changes account for many of the discrepancies between the pronunciation and the spelling of English words since the spelling was established before the pronunciation changes took place.

head the single word in a phrase that determines the meaning and properties of the whole phrase, such as a verb in a verb phrase, a noun in a noun phrase, a preposition in a prepositional phrase: ***eat** the tomatoes, the **president** of the club, **under** the chair*.

implosive a consonant sound that is pronounced by inhaling rather than exhaling the air.

infix an affix inserted inside a stem.

intransitive sentence a sentence that does not have a direct object: *He left. He lives in Paris*.

isogloss a geographical boundary of a certain linguistic feature, such as a pronunciation of a sound, a certain lexical choice or the use of some syntactic feature.

isolate an "orphan" language with no (living) relatives; such a language belongs to a language family of its own.

isolating language a language in which grammatical concepts like tense, number or grammatical relations ('who did what to whom?') are expressed primarily by word order and the use of free-standing words rather than by inflectional morphemes attached to words.

labial consonant a consonant produced by bringing together or closing the lips.

larynx the structure of muscle and cartilage at the upper end of the windpipe that contains the vocal cords.

lateral sounds a sound produced with the tip of the tongue touching the roof of the mouth, but with the air passing along one or both sides of the tongue.

lenition a change of a consonant considered "stronger" into one considered "weaker". Common examples include voicing; turning a stop into an affricate or a fricative; and other similar processes.

lingua franca a trade language; a language used as a means of communication among speakers of different languages.

liquid consonant a sound produced in such a way that the vocal tract is neither closed off nor constricted to a degree that produces friction; for example, the first sound of *liquid*.

loanword a word borrowed into a language from another language.

main verb the verb that is not an auxiliary: *He will **leave** tomorrow. We will have been **playing** chess.*

minimal pair a pair of words that differ only in one sound in the same position; for example, ***pit*** and ***bit***.

morphemes the smallest meaningful pieces into which words can be divided: *un-touch-abil-ity.*

morphology the component of grammar that builds words out of pieces (morphemes).

multiple argument agreement an agreement system where the verb must agree with more than one argument (including subject, object, indirect object).

nasal a sound produced with the velum lowered, enabling air flow through the nasal cavity; for example, the first sound of ***moon*** and ***noon***.

nominative case the case of the subject (in a certain type of) language: ***He** loves you.* (not: ****Him** loves you.*)

noun one of the major syntactic categories, comprising words that typically refer to a thing or person: *cat, apple, Mary, river, day.*

noun class a system of categorizing nouns in which a noun may belong to a given class because of characteristic features of its referent, such as sex, animacy, shape, etc.

noun incorporation a phenomenon by which a word (usually a verb) forms a kind of compound with its direct object or adverbial modifier, while retaining its original syntactic function.

noun phrase a phrase whose head is a noun or a pronoun.

palatal consonant a consonant produced with a constriction between the body of the tongue and the (hard) palate; for example, the first sounds of *you* and *university.*

patient *see* theme

personal pronoun a pronoun used as a substitute for proper or common nouns.

phoneme a sound of language that is used to discriminate meaning.

phonology the component of grammar that determines the sound pattern of a language, including its inventory of phonemes, how they may be combined to form natural-sounding words, how the phonemes must be adjusted depending on their neighbors, and on patterns of intonation, timing and stress.

phonotactic rules the patterns into which sounds of a given language can be arranged to form syllables, morphemes or words.

pidgin an ad hoc intermediary language used as a lingua franca. A pidgin typically has a very limited vocabulary and simplified grammatical structure.

place of articulation the part of the mouth, throat or larynx where the airflow meets the greatest degree of constriction in the production of a speech sound.

plosive consonant *see* stop consonant

polysynthetic language a language in which a word may be composed of a long string of prefixes, roots and suffixes.

postposition a preposition-like part of speech that follows (rather than precedes) its complement.

prenasalized consonant a phonetic sequence of a nasal and an obstruent (or a non-nasal sonorant) that behaves phonologically like a single consonant.

preposition one of the major syntactic categories, comprising words that typically refer to a spatial or temporal relationship: *in, on, at, near, by, under, after*.

proto-language a (typically reconstructed) language that is hypothesized to be the ancestor of some group of related languages.

reduplication the repetition of all or part of a word in order to modify its meaning in some way.

retroflex consonant a consonant produced by curling the tip of the tongue upward and backward; for example, the first sound of *retroflex* (for some speakers of English).

root the most basic morpheme in a word or family of related words, consisting of an irreducible, arbitrary sound–meaning pairing: *electricity, electrical, electric, electrify, electrician, electron*.

serial verb construction a syntactic phenomenon which strings two verbs together in a sequence in which neither verb is subordinated to the other.

stop consonant a consonant pronounced so that the airflow is completely blocked for a moment: *p, t, k, b, d, g*.

substratum language a language that influences an intrusive language that supplants it.

suffix an affix which is placed after the stem of a word.

superstratum language the counterpart to a substratum. When one language supplants another, it is termed the superstratum language (*see also* substratum language).

syllabary a system of writing based on syllables rather than individual speech sounds.

syntax the component of grammar that arranges words into phrases and sentences.

synthetic language *see* fusional language

theme the participant in a situation that undergoes the action described by the verb or whose state or location is changed in some way.

three-way case marking system a case marking system where subjects of intransitives, subjects of transitives and objects of transitives all receive different cases (i.e. absolutive, ergative and accusative, respectively).

tonal language a language in which variation in pitch makes a difference in the meaning of words.

transitive sentence a sentence containing a direct object: *John ate the pizza.*

universal grammar the basic design underlying the grammars of all human languages, consisting of principles and parameters that enable the child to deduce a grammar from the primary linguistic data.

uvular consonant a consonant articulated with the back of the tongue against or near the uvula, the flap of soft tissue hanging from the back edge of the soft palate (i.e. the back part of the roof of the mouth).

velar consonant a consonant articulated with the back of the tongue against the soft palate (i.e. the back part of the roof of the mouth, known also as the velum).

verb one of the major syntactic categories, comprising words that typically refer to an action or state: *break, run, love, appear.*

verb phrase a phrase whose head is a verb.

vocal cords the two muscular bands of tissue that stretch from front to back within the larynx. The vocal cords vibrate periodically to produce voiced sounds.

vowel harmony a long-distance assimilatory process by which vowels become more similar to each other in some way(s) across intervening consonants.

zero-marker a meaningful morpheme that has no sound associated with it.

References

Abaev, Vaso Ivanovich ([1958]1984) *Historical Etymological Dictionary of Ossetic*. 4 volumes. Leningrad: Izdatel'stvo Akademii nauk SSSR.

(1964) *A Grammatical Sketch of Ossetian*. Translated by Stephen P. Hill and edited by Herbert H. Paper. Bloomington: Indiana University.

Adelaar, Alexander (2009a) Towards an integrated theory about the Indonesian migrations to Madagascar. In: Pergrine, Peter N.; Ilia Peiros and Marcus Feldman (eds.) *Ancient Human Migrations. A Multidisciplinary Approach*. Salt Lake City, UT: University of Utah Press, pp. 149–172.

(2009b) Loanwords in Malagasy. In: Haspelmath, Martin and Uri Tadmor (eds.) *Loanwords in the World's Languages. A Comparative Handbook*. Berlin: Mouton de Gruyter, pp. 717–746.

Aksu-Koç, Ayhan (2000) Some aspects of the acquisition of evidentials in Turkish. In: Johanson, Lars and Bo Utas (eds.) *Evidentials: Turkic, Iranian and Neighboring Languages*. Berlin: Mouton de Gruyter, pp. 15–28.

Baker, Mark C. (2001a) *Atoms of Language. The Mind's Hidden Rules of Grammar*. New York: Basic Books.

(2001b) The natures of nonconfigurationality. In: Baltin, Mark and Chris Collins (eds.) *The Handbook of Contemporary Syntactic Theory*. Oxford: Blackwell, pp. 407–438.

Baker, Mark C. and Osamuyimen T. Stewart (1999) On double-headedness and the anatomy of the clause. Ms, Rutgers University.

Barnes, Gina L. (1999) *The Rise of Civilization in East Asia*. London: Thames and Hudson.

Beckwith, Christopher I. (1996) The morphological argument for the existence of Sino-Tibetan. *Pan-Asiatic Linguistics: Proceedings of the Fourth International Symposium on Languages and Linguistics, January 8–10, 1996*. Volume III. Bangkok: Mahidol University at Salaya, pp. 812–826.

Bender, Marvin Lionel (1983) Majang phonology and morphology. In: Marvin Lionel Bender (ed.) *Nilo-Saharan Language Studies*. East Lansing: Michigan State University, pp. 114–147.

(1997) *The Nilo-Saharan Languages: A Comparative Essay*. 2nd edition. Munich: Loncom Europa.

Benedict, Paul K. (1942) Thai, Kadai and Indonesian: a new alignment in south east Asia. *American Anthropologist* 44: 576–601.

(1975) *Austro-Thai: Language and Culture*. New Haven, CT: HRAF Press.

(1990) *Japanese/Austro-Tai*. Ann Arbor: Karoma Publishers.

Bergsland, Knut (1959) The Eskimo-Uralic hypothesis. *Journal de la Société Finno-ougrienne* 61: 1–29.

Bertorelle, Giorgio; Jaume Bertranpetit; Francesc Calafell; Ivane S. Nasidze and Guido Barbujani (1995) Do Basque- and Caucasian-speaking populations share non-Indoeuropean ancestors? *European Journal of Human Genetics* 3: 256–263.

Bickerton, Derek (1983) Creole languages. *Scientific American* 249(1): 116–122. Reprinted in: Clark, Virginia P. *et al.* (eds.) *Language: Introductory readings*. 4th edition. New York: St. Martin's Press, 1985, pp. 134–151.

 (1984a) The language bioprogram hypothesis. *The Behavioral and Brain Sciences* 7: 173–221.

 (1984b) The language bioprogram hypothesis and second language acquisition. In: Rutherford, W. E. (ed.) *Language Universals and Second Language Acquisition*. Amsterdam: John Benjamins, pp. 141–161.

Bielmeier, Roland (1977) *Historische Untersuchung zum Erb- und Lehnwortschatzanteil im ossetischen Grundwortschatz*. Frankfurt am Main: Peter Lang.

Blake, Barry J. (2001) *Case*. 2nd edition. Cambridge University Press.

Blench, Roger (1995) Is Niger-Congo simply a branch of Nilo-Saharan? In: Nicolaï, Robert and Franz Rottland (eds.) *Proceedings of the Fifth Nilo Sahran Linguistics Colloquium, Nice 1992*. Köln: Rüdiger Köppe, pp. 83–130.

Blondheim, David S. (1923) Éssai d'un vocabulaire comperatif des parlers Romans des juifs au moyen âge. *Romania* 49: 1–43, 344-388, 527–569.

 (1924) Les parlers Judéo-Romance et la Vetus latina. *Romania* 50: 541–590.

Blust, Robert (2003) *Thao Dictionary*. Taipei: Institute of Linguists (Preparatory Office). Academia Sinica.

Bomhard, Allan R. (1996) *Indo-European and the Nostratic Hypothesis*. Charleston, SC: Signum Publishing.

 (1998) Nostratic, Eurasiatic and Indo-European. In: Salmons, Joseph C. and Brian D. Joseph (eds.) *Nostratic. Sifting the Evidence*. Amsterdam: John Benjamins, pp. 17–49.

Bowern, Claire (2008) *Linguistic Fieldwork: A Practical Guide*. Basingstoke: Palgrave Macmillan.

Boyd, Raymond (1995) Le zande. In: Boyd, Raymond (ed.) *Le système verbal dans les langues oubangiennes*. Munich: Lincom Europa, pp. 165–197.

Broch, Ingvild and Ernst Håkon Jahr (1983) Does a pidgin necessarily give a low social status? The case of Russenorsk. *Nordlyd: Tromsø University Working Papers on Language and Linguistics* 7: 36–45.

Brown, Mervyn (1979) *Madagascar Rediscovered: A History from Early Times to Independence*. New Haven, CT: Archon Books.

Buder, Anja (1989) *Aspekto-temporale Kategorien im Jakutischen*. Wiesbaden: Harrassowitz Verlag.

Campbell, George L. (1991) *Compendium of the World's Languages*. Volume I: Abaza to Kurdish. London/New York: Routledge.

Campbell, Lyle (1998) Nostratic: a personal assessment. In: Salmons, Joseph C. and Brian D. Joseph (eds.) *Nostratic: Sifting the Evidence*. Current Issues in Linguistic Theory 142. Amsterdam: John Benjamins, pp. 107–152.

Campbell, Lyle and Marianne Mithun (1979) Introduction: North American Indian languages and principles of language change. In: Baldi, Philip (ed.) *Patterns of Change, Change of Patterns: Linguistic Change and Reconstruction Methodology*. New York: Mouton de Gruyter, pp. 15–30.

Capell, A. (1976a) Features of Austronesian languages in the New Guinea area in contrast with other Austronesian languages of Melanesia. *Pacific Linguistics* 39: 235–282.

(1976b) Austronesian and Papuan 'mixed' languages: general remarks. *Pacific Linguistics* 39: 527–579.

Carpelan, Christian and Asko Parpola (2001) Proto-Indo-European, Proto-Uralic and Proto-Aryan. In: Carpelan, Christian; Asko Parpola and Petteri Koskikallio (eds.) *The Earliest Contacts between Uralic and Indo-European: Linguistic and Archeological Considerations*. Papers presented at an International symposium held at the Tvärminne Research Station of the University of Helsinki, 8–10 January, 1999. Helsinki: Suomalais-Ugrilainen Seura.

Cavalli-Sforza, Luigi Luca (2000) *Genes, Peoples, and Languages*. New York: North Point Press.

Cavalli-Sforza, Luigi Luca and Francesco Cavalli-Sforza (1995) *Genes, Peoples, and Languages*. New York: Addison-Wesley.

Chafe, Wallace L. (1973) Siouan, Iroquoian and Caddoan. In: Sebeok, Thomas A. (ed.) *Current Trends in Linguistics*. Volume X (Linguistics in North America). The Hague: Mouton, pp. 1164–1209.

Charachidzé, G. (1981) *Grammaire de la langue avar (langue du Caucase Nord-Est)*. Paris: Jean Favard.

Childs, G. Tucker (2003) *An Introduction to African Languages*. Amsterdam: John Benjamins.

Chung, Sandra (1990) VPs and verb movement in Chamorro. *Natural Language and Linguistic Theory* 8: 559–620.

Clifton, John (2009) Do the Talysh and Tat languages have a future in Azerbaijan? *Work Papers of the Summer Institute of Linguistics*. Volume 50. University of North Dakota Session.

Clifton, John; Calvin Tiessen, Gabriela Deckinga, Laura Lucht (2005) *Sociolinguistic Situation of the Talysh in Azerbaijan*. SIL Electronic Survey Reports 2005.

Comas, David; Francesc Calafell; Nina Bendukidze; Lourdes Fañanás and Jaume Bertranpetit (2000) Georgian and Kurd mtDNA sequence analysis shows a lack of correlation between languages and female genetic lineages. *American Journal of Physical Anthropology* 112: 5–16.

Comrie, Bernard (1989) *Language Universals and Linguistic Typology*. 2nd edition. University of Chicago.

(1999) Spatial cases in Daghestanian languages. *Sprachtypologie und Universalienforschung* 52(2): 108–117.

Comrie, Bernard S. (2001) Language of the World. In: Mark Aronoff and Janie Rees-Miller (eds.) *The Handbook of Linguistics*. Oxford: Blackwell Publishing, pp. 19–42.

Corbett, Greville (1991) *Gender*. Cambridge University Press.

Creissels, Denis (2008) Spatial cases. In: Malchukov, Andrej and Andrew Spencer (eds.) *The Oxford Handbook of Case*. Oxford University Press, pp. 609–625.

Crowley, Terry (2007) *Field Linguistics: A Beginner's Guide*. Oxford University Press.

Csúcs, Sándor (1998) Udmurt. In: Abondolo, Daniel Mario (ed.) *The Uralic Languages*. London: Routledge, pp. 276–304.

Dahl, Otto Christian (1991) *Migration from Kalimantan to Madagascar*. Oslo: Aschehoug AS.

Diesing, Molly (2003) On the nature of multiple fronting in Yiddish. In: Boeckx, Cedric and Kleanthes Grohmann (eds.) *Multiple Wh-fronting*. Amsterdam: John Benjamins, pp. 51–76.

Dixon, Richard M. W. (1972) *The Dyirbal Language of North Queensland*. Cambridge University Press.

(1993) Suppress α. *Linguistics* 30: 999–1030.

(1994) *Ergativity*. Cambridge University Press.

Dochartaigh, Cathair Ò (1992) The Irish language. In: MacAulay, Donald (ed.) *The Celtic Languages*. Cambridge University Press, pp. 11–99.

Donegan, Patricia J. and David Stampe (1983) Rhythm and the holistic organization of language structure. In: Richardson, John F., Mitchell Marks and Amy Chukerman (eds.) *Papers from the Parasession on the Interplay of Phonology, Morphology, and Syntax*. Chicago Linguistic Society, pp. 337–353.

Dwyer, Arienne (2000) Direct and indirect experience in Salar. In: Johanson, Lars and Bo Utas (eds.) *Evidentials: Turkic, Iranian and Neighboring Languages*. Berlin: Mouton de Gruyter, pp. 45–59.

Eide, Kristin Melum (2009) Finiteness. The haves and the have-nots. In: Alexiadou, Artemis; Jorge Hankamer; Thomas McFadden; Justin Nuger and Florian Schäfer (eds.) *Advances in Comparative Germanic Syntax*. Amsterdam/Philadelphia: John Benjamins, pp. 357–390.

Engesaeth, Tarjei; Mahire Yakup and Arienne Dwyer (2009) *Greetings from the Teklimakan: A Handbook of Modern Uyghur*. Volume 1. Lawrence: University of Kansas Scholarworks.

Evans, Nicholas and Stephen C. Levinson (2010) Time for a sea-change in linguistics: response to comments on 'The Myth of Language Universals'. *Lingua* 120: 2733–2758.

Everett, Daniel L. (1986) Pirahã. In: Derbyshire, Desmond C. and Geoffrey K. Pullum (eds.) *Handbook of Amazonian Languages*. Volume I. Berlin: Mouton de Gruyter, pp. 200–326.

(2005) Cultural constraints on grammar and cognition in Pirahã: another look at the design features of human languages. *Current Anthropology* 46: 621–646.

Faraclas, Nicholas G. (1996) *Nigerian Pidgin*. London: Routledge.

Firchow, Irwin and Jacqueline Firchow (1969) An abbreviated phoneme inventory. *Anthropological linguistics* 11(9): 271–276.

Fleming, Harold Crane (1987) Proto-Gongan Consonant Phonemes: stage one. In: Mukarovsky, Hans G. (ed.) *Leo Reinisch. Werk und Erbe*. (Oesterreichische Akademie der Wissenschaften, Phil.-Hist. Klasse, Sitzungsberichte. 492.) Vienna: Oesterreichische Akademie der Wissenschaften, pp. 141–159.

(1991) A new taxonomic hypothesis: Borean or Boralean. *Mother Tongue* 14. Newsletter ASLIP.

Florey, Margaret J. (1988) A review of the classification of Australian languages. *Working Papers in Linguistics*. Department of Linguistics, University of Hawaii at Manoa. 20(2): 137–162.

Foley, William A. (1986) *The Papuan Languages of New Guinea*. Cambridge University Press.

(1992) New Guinea languages. In: Bright, William, *et al.* (eds.) *International Encyclopedia of Linguistics*. Volume III, pp. 86–91.

Foley, William A. and Mike Olson (1982) Clausehood and verb serialization. In: Nichols, Johanna and Anthony Woodbury (eds.) *Grammar Inside and Outside the Clause. Some Approaches to Theory from the Field*. Cambridge University Press, pp. 17–60.

Frellesvig, Bjarke and John Whitman (2008) The Japanese–Korean vowel correspondences. In: Endo Simon, M. and Peter Sells (eds.) *Japanese/Korean Linguistics*. Volume XIII. Stanford: CSLI Publications, pp. 15–28.

Gonçalves, Marco Antônio (1993) *O significado do nome: Cosmologia e nominação entre os Pirahã*. Rio de Janeiro: Sette Letras.

    (2001) *O mundo inacabado: Ação e criação em uma cosmologia amazônica: Etnografia Pirahã*. Rio de Janeiro: Editora da UFRJ.

Greenberg, Joseph H. (1963) *The Languages of Africa*. Bloomington: Indiana University Press.

    (1966) Some universals of grammar with particular reference to the order of meaningful elements. In: Greenberg, Joseph H. (ed.) *Universals of Language*. Cambridge, MA: MIT Press, pp.73–113.

    (1971) The Indo-Pacific Hypothesis. In: Sebeok, Thomas A. (ed.) *Current Trends in Linguistics*. Volume VIII: 1963–76. The Hague: Mouton.

    (1983) Some areal characteristics of African languages. In: Dihoff, Ivan (ed.) *Current Approaches to African Linguistics*. Dordrecht: Foris, pp. 3–21.

    (1987) *Language in the Americas*. Stanford University Press.

Greenhill, Simon J., Robert Blust and Russell D. Gray (2008) The Austronesian basic vocabulary database: from bioinformatics to lexomics. *Evolutionary Bioinformatics* 2008(4): 271–283.

Gregersen, Edgar A. (1972) Kongo-Saharan. *Journal of African Language and Linguistics* 4: 46–56.

Grjunberg, A. L. and L. Kh. Davidova (1982) Tatskij jazyk. In: Rastorgueva, V. S. (ed.) *Osnovy Iranskogo Jazykoznanija. Novoiranskie jazyki zapadnaja gruppa, prikaspijskije jazyki*. Volume III. Moscow: Academy of Sciences, USSR, pp. 231–286.

Hale, Kenneth (1983) Warlpiri and the grammar of nonconfigurational languages. *Natural Language and Linguistic Theory* 1: 5–49.

Haspelmath, Martin (1963) *A Grammar of Lezgian*. Berlin: Mouton de Gruyter.

Hebert, Raymond and Nicholas Poppe (1963) *Kirghiz Manual*. Indiana University Publications, Uralic and Altaic Series. Bloomington: Indiana University Press.

Henn, Brenna M., Christopher R. Gignoux, Matthew Jobin *et al.* (2011) Hunter-gatherer genomic diversity suggests a southern African origin for modern humans. *PNAS*. Available online at www.pnas.org/content/early/2011/03/01/1017511108. full.pdf+html.

Herzog, Marvin (1978) Yiddish. In: Paper, Herbert H. (ed.) *Jewish Languages. Theme and Variations. Proceedings of Regional Conferences of the Association for Jewish Studies Held at the University of Michigan and New York University in March–April 1975*. Cambridge, MA: Association for Jewish Studies, pp. 47–58.

Hewitt, B. G. (1979) *Abkhaz*. Amsterdam: North-Holland.

Hockett, Charles F. (1960) The origin of speech. *Scientific American* 203: 89–96.

Hodge, Carleton T. (1970) The linguistic cycle. *Language Sciences* 13: 1–7.

    (1998) The implications of Lislakh for Nostratic. In: Salmons, Joseph C. and Brian D. Joseph (eds.) *Nostratic. Sifting the Evidence*. Amsterdam: John Benjamins, pp. 237–256.

Hoffman, Joel M. (2004) *In the Beginning: A Short History of the Hebrew Language.* New York University Press.

Holmer, Athur (2005) Seediq. Antisymmetry and final particles in a Formosan VOS language. In: Carnie, Andrew; Heidi Harley and Sheila Ann Dooley (eds.) *Verb First. On the Syntax of Verb-Initial Languages.* Amsterdam: John Benjamins, pp. 175–202.

Hualde, José I. (1984) Icelandic–Basque pidgin. *Journal of Basque Studies in America* 5: 41–59.

Hualde, José I. and Jon Ortiz de Urbina (2003) *A Grammar of Basque.* Berlin: Mouton de Gruyter.

Hurles, Matthew E.; Bryan C. Sykes; Mark A. Jobling and Peter Forster (2005) The dual origin of the Malagasy in island Southeast Asia and East Africa: evidence from maternal and paternal lineages. *American Journal of Human Genetics* 76(5): 894–901.

Illyč-Svityč, Vladislav Markovich ([1971]1984) *Opyt sravnenija nostraticheskix jazykov.* 3 volumes. Moscow: Nauka.

Ivanov, Vyacheslav V. and Tamaz Gamkrelidze (1990) The early history of Indo-European languages. *Scientific American* 262(3): 110–116.

Jahr, Ernst Håkon (1996) On the pidgin status of Russenorsk. In: Jahr, Ernst Håkon and Ingvild Broch (eds.) *Language Contact in the Arctic. Northern Pidgins and Contact Languages.* Berlin: Mouton de Gruyter, pp. 107–122.

Janhunen, Juha (1992) Uralic languages. In: Bright, William *et al.* (eds.) *International Encyclopedia of Linguistics.* Volume IV. Oxford University Press, pp. 205–210.

Jochnowitz, George (1978) Judeo-Romance languages. In: Paper, Herbert H. (ed.) *Jewish Languages. Theme and Variations. Proceedings of Regional Conferences of the Association for Jewish Studies Held at the University of Michigan and New York University in March–April 1975.* Cambridge, MA: Association for Jewish Studies, pp. 65–74.

Kalaydjieva, Luba, Bharti Morar, Raphaelle Chaix and Hua Tang (2005) A newly discovered founder population: the Roma/Gypsies. *BioEssays* 27(10): 1084–1094.

Kaufman, Terry (1990) Language history in South America: what we know and how to know more. In: Payne, Doris L. (ed.) *Amazonian Linguistics: Studies in Lowland South American Languages.* Austin: University of Texas Press, pp. 13–73.

Kayne, Richard S. (1994) *The Antisymmetry of Syntax.* Cambridge, MA: MIT Press.

Kiddle, Lawrence B. (1978) Response. In: Paper, Herbert H. (ed.) *Jewish Languages. Theme and Variations. Proceedings of Regional Conferences of the Association for Jewish Studies Held at the University of Michigan and New York University in March–April 1975.* Cambridge, MA: Association for Jewish Studies, pp. 75–77.

Kıral, Filiz (2000) Reflections on *-miš* in Khalaj. In: Johanson, Lars and Bo Utas (eds.) *Evidentials: Turkic, Iranian and Neighboring Languages.* Berlin: Mouton de Gruyter, pp. 89–101.

Koivulehto, Jorma (1991) *Uralische Evidenz fur die Laryngaltheorie.* Vienna: Austrian Academy of Sciences.

Kotsinas, Ulla-Britt (1996) Aspect marking and grammaticalization in Rusenorsk compared with immigrant Swedish. In: Jahr, Ernst Håkon and Ingvild Broch (eds.)

Language Contact in the Arctic. Northern Pidgins and Contact Languages. Berlin: Mouton de Gruyter, pp. 123–154.

Krause, Cornelia (2000a) Anmerkungen zum pränominalen Genitiv im Deutschen. In: Bayer, Josef and Christine Roemer (eds.) *Von der Philologie zur Grammatiktheorie: Peter Suchsland zum 65. Geburstag.* Tübingen: Niemeyer, pp. 79–96.

   (2000b) On an (in-)visible property of inherent case. *North Eastern Linguistic Society* 30: 427–442.

Krishnamurti, Bhadriraju (2003) *The Dravidian Languages.* Cambridge University Press.

Levin, Beth (1983) Unaccusative verbs in Basque. *Proceedings of NELS* 13, pp. 129–144.

Levy, Raphael (1947) The background and significance of Judeo-French. *Modern Philology* 65: 7.

Lewis, Martin W. and Kären E. Wigen (1997) *The Myth of Continents: A Critique of Metageography.* Berkeley, CA: University of California Press.

Lord, Carol (1974) Causative constructions in Yoruba. *Studies in African Linguistics Supplement* 5: 195–204.

Lyovin, Anatole V. (1997) *An Introduction to the Languages of the World.* Oxford University Press.

Maddieson, Ian (1984) *Patterns of Sounds.* Cambridge University Press.

   (2008) Consonant-vowel ratio. In: Haspelmath, Martin; Matthew S. Dryer; David Gil and Bernard Comrie (eds.) *The World Atlas of Language Structures Online.* Munich: Max Planck Digital Library, Chapter 3. Available online at http://wals.info/feature/3.

Mallory, J. P. (1989) *In Search of the Indo-Europeans. Language, Archeology and Myth.* London: Thames and Hudson.

Markey, Thomas L. (1978) Response. In: Paper, Herbert H. (ed.) *Jewish Languages. Theme and Variations. Proceedings of Regional Conferences of the Association for Jewish Studies Held at the University of Michigan and New York University in March–April 1975.* Cambridge, MA: Association for Jewish Studies, pp. 59–63.

Martin, Samuel E. (1991a) Morphological clues to the relationships of Japanese and Korean. In: Baldi, Philip (ed.) *Patterns of Change, Change of Patterns: Linguistic Change and Reconstruction Methodology.* New York: Mouton de Gruyter, pp. 483–510.

   (1991b) Recent research on the relationships of Japanese and Korean. In: Lamb, Sydney M. and E. Douglas Mitchell (eds.) *Sprung from some Common Source.* Stanford University Press, pp. 269–292.

Matras, Yaron (2006) Romani. In: Brown, Keith (ed.) *Encyclopedia of Languages and Linguistics.* 2nd edition. Oxford: Elsevier.

Menz, Astrid (2000) Indirectivity in Gagauz. In: Johanson, Lars and Bo Utas (eds.) *Evidentials: Turkic, Iranian and Neighboring Languages.* Berlin: Mouton de Gruyter, pp. 103–114.

Miller, Roy Andrew (1971) *Japanese and Other Altaic Languages.* University of Chicago Press.

Miller, V. F. (1992) *Ossetian Essays.* Vladikavkaz, SOIGI.

Möller, Hermann (1906) *Semitisch und Indogermanisch.* Kopenhagen: H. Hagerup.

Morar, Bharti, David Gresham, Dora Angelicheva, *et al.* (2004) Mutation history of the roma/gypsies. *American Journal of Human Genetics* 75(4): 596–609.

Mundhenk, Norm (1990) Linguistic decisions in the 1987 Tok Pisin Bible. In: Verhaar, John W. M. (ed.) *Melanesian Pidgin and Tok Pisin*. Studies in Language Companion Series. Volume 20. Amsterdam: John Benjamins, pp. 345–373.

Naro, Anthony (1978) A study on the origins of pidginization. *Language* 54: 314–347.

Nasidze, Ivane S. and N. V. Salamatina (1996) Genetic characteristics of the Georgian population. *Genetic Geography* 10: 105–112.

Nasidze, Ivane S., Dominique Quinque, Isabelle Dupanloup, *et al.* (2004) Genetic evidence concerning the origins of South and North Ossetians. *Annals of Human Genetics* 68: 588–599.

Nevins, Andrew; David Pesetsky and Cilene Rodrigues (2009) Pirahã exceptionality: a reassessment. *Language* 85(2): 355–404.

Newman, Paul and Martha Ratliff (eds.) (2001) *Linguistic Fieldwork*. Cambridge University Press.

Ngonyani, Deo and Peter Githinji (2006) The asymmetric nature of Bantu applicative constructions. *Lingua* 116: 31–63.

Nichols, Johanna (1992) *Linguistic Diversity in Space and Time*. University of Chicago Press.

(1997) The epicenter of the Indo-European linguistic spread. In: Blench, Roger and Matthew Spriggs (ed.) *Archaeology and Language I: Theoretical and Methodological Orientations*. London: Routledge, pp. 122–148.

(1999) The Eurasian spread zone and the Indo-European dispersal. In: Blench, Roger and Matthew Spriggs (ed.) *Archaeology and Language II: Correlating Archaeological and Linguistic Hypotheses*. London: Routledge, pp. 220–266.

(2003) The Nakh-Daghestanian consonant correspondences. In: Tuite, Kevin and Dee Ann Holisky (eds.) *Current Trends in Caucasian, East European, and Inner Asian Linguistics: Papers in Honor of Howard I. Aronson*. Amsterdam: John Benjamins, pp. 207–251.

Ono, Susumu (1970) *The Origin of the Japanese Language*. Tokyo: Kokusai Bunka Shinkokai.

Oswalt, Robert L. (1998) A probabilistic evaluation of North Eurasiatic Nostratic. In: Salmons, Joseph C. and Brian D. Joseph (eds.) *Nostratic. Sifting the Evidence*. Amsterdam: John Benjamins, pp. 199–216.

Ottosson, I. and Ekholm, T. (2007) *Japans Historia*. Falun: Scandbook.

Pantcheva, Marina (2009) Directional expressions cross-linguistically: Nanosyntax and lexicalization. In: Svenonius, Peter, Gillian, Ramchand, Michal, Starke, and Taraldsen Knut Tarald (eds.) *Nordlyd* 36(1), special issue on Nanosyntax. Tromsø: CASTL, pp. 7–39. www.ub.uit.no/baser/nordlyd/.

Parsons, James (1767) *The Remains of Japhet, being Historical Enquiries into the Affinity and Origins of the European Languages*. London: printed for the author: Reprinted as a facsimile by Menston (Yorks.), Scolar P., 1968.

Pawley, Andrew and Medina Pawley (1998) Canoes and seafaring. In: Ross, Malcolm, Andrew Pawley and Meredith Osmond (eds.) *The Lexicon of Proto Oceanic. The Culture and Environment of Ancestral Oceanic Society*. Volume 1: Material Culture. Canberra: Pacific Linguistics, Research School of Pacific and Asian Studies. The Australian National University, pp. 173–209.

Payne, Thomas E. (1997) *Describing Morphosyntax: A Guide for Field Linguists*. Cambridge University Press.

Pedersen, Holger (1903) Türkische Lautgesetze. *Zeitschrift der Deutschen Mor-genländischen Gesellschaft* 57: 535–561.

(1931) *Linguistic Science in the Nineteenth Century: Methods and Results.* Translated from the Danish by John Webster Spargo. Cambridge, MA: Harvard University Press. (English translation of Pedersen 1924. Reprinted in 1959 as *The Discovery of Language: Linguistic Science in the Nineteenth Century*, Bloomington: Indiana University Press; paperback edition 1962).

Piazza, Alberto and Luigi Luca Cavalli-Sforza (2006) Diffusion of genes and languages in human evolution. *Proceedings of the 6th International Conference on the Evolution of Language*, pp. 255–266.

Pinker, Steven (1994) *The Language Instinct: How the Mind Creates Language.* New York: Harper Perennial.

Plungian, Vladimir Aleksandrovich (1996) *Pochemu jazyki takije raznye?* [Why are languages so different?]. Moscow: Russian Dictionaries.

Poppe, Nicholas (1964) *Bashkir Manual, Descriptive Grammar and Texts with a Bashkir-English Glossary.* Uralic and Altaic Series, volume 36. Indiana University Publications, Uralic and Altaic Series. Bloomington: Indiana University.

Ramer, Alexis Manaster; Peter A. Michalove, Karen S. Baertsch and Karen L. Adams (1998) Exploring the Nostratic hypothesis. In: Salmons, Joseph C. and Brian D. Joseph (eds.) *Nostratic. Sifting the Evidence.* Amsterdam: John Benjamins, pp. 61–84.

Randrianja, Solofo and Stephen Ellis (2009) *Madagascar. A Short History.* University of Chicago Press.

Rédei, Károly (1986) *Zu den Indogermanisch-Uralischen Sprachkontakten.* Vienna: Verlag der Österreichischen Akademie der Wissenschaften.

Renfrew, Colin (1987) *Archaeology and Language. The Puzzle of the Indo-European Origins.* London: Jonathan Cape.

Rijk, Rudolf P. G. de (2008) *Standard Basque. A Progressive Grammar.* Cambridge, MA: MIT Press.

Ringe, Don (1998) A probabilistic evaluation of Indo-Uralic. In: Salmons, Joseph C. and Brian D. Joseph (eds.) *Nostratic. Sifting the Evidence.* Amsterdam: John Benjamins, pp. 153–198.

Robbeets, Martine Irma (2005) *Is Japanese Related to Korean, Tungusic, Mongolic and Turkic?* Wiesbaden: Otto Harrassowitz.

Romaine, Suzanne (1988) *Pidgin and Creole Languages.* London: Longman.

Róna-Tas, András (2007) *Nutshell Chuvash.* www.lingfil.uu.se/afro/turkiskasprak/IP2007/NUTSHELLCHUVASH.pdf.

Ross, Malcolm; Andrew Pawley and Meredith Osmond (eds.) (1998) *The Lexicon of Proto Oceanic. The Culture and Environment of Ancestral Oceanic Society.* Volume 3: Plants. Canberra: Pacific Linguistics, Research School of Pacific and Asian Studies. The Australian National University, pp. 173–209.

Rüdiger, Johan Christian Christoph (1782) [reprinted in 1990]. Von der Sprache und Herkunft der Zigeuner aus Indien. In: *Neuester Zuwachs der teutschen, fremden und allgemeinen Sprachkunde in eigenen Aufsätzen.* 1. Stück. Leipzig. Hamburg: Buske, pp. 37–84.

Ruhlen, Merritt (1994) *On the Origin of Language: Studies in Linguistic Taxonomy.* Stanford University Press.

Sagart, Laurent (2005) Sino-Tibetan-Austronesian: an updated and improved argument. In: Sagart, Laurent; Roger Blench and Alicia Sanchez-Mazas (eds.) *The Peopling of East Asia: Putting Together Archaeology, Linguistics and Genetics*. London: Routledge Curzon, pp. 161–176.

Salmons, Joseph C. and Brian D. Joseph (1998) Introduction. In: Salmons, Joseph C. and Brian D. Joseph (eds.) *Nostratic. Sifting the Evidence*. Amsterdam: John Benjamins, pp. 1–12.

Saltarelli, Mario (1988) *Basque*. London: Croom Helm.

Santorini, Beatrice (1992) Variation and change in Yiddish subordinate clause word order. *Natural Language and Linguistic Theory* 10: 595–640.

Saussure, Ferdinand de (1916) *Cours de Linguistique Générale*. Edited by C. Bally and A. Sechehaye, with the collaboration of A. Riedlinger. Lausanne and Paris: Payot, translated into English by W. Baskin as *Course in General Linguistics*. Glasgow: Fontana/Collins, 1977.

Schulze, Wolfgang (2009) The Languages of the Caucasus. Ms. http://wolfgangschulze.in-devir.com/index.php?option=com_docman&task=doc_download&gid=63.

Shibatani, Masayoshi (1990) *The Languages of Japan*. Cambridge University Press.

Simpson, Jane (1983) Aspects of Warlpiri Morphology and Syntax. PhD dissertation, MIT.

(1991) *Warlpiri Morphosyntax: A Lexicalist Approach*. Dordrecht: Kluwer.

Smith, Geoff P. (2002) *Growing up with Tok Pisin. Contact, Creolization, and Change in Papua New Guinea's National Language*. London: Battlebridge Publications.

Snyman, J. W. (1970) *An Introduction to the !Xu (!Kung) Language*. Cape Town: Balkema.

Solodow, Joseph B. (2010) *Latin Alive. The Survival of Latin in English and the Romance Languages*. Cambridge University Press.

Theil, Rolf (2006) Is Omotic Afro-Asiatic? Paper presented at the David Dwyer Retirement Symposium. Michigan State University, East Lansing, October 2006.

Tompa, József (1968) *Ungarische Grammatik*. The Hague: Mouton.

Travis, Lisa deMena (1984) Parameters and Effects of Word Order Variation. PhD dissertation, MIT.

Trudgill, Peter (1999) Standard Eng: what it isn't? In: Bex, Tony and Richard J. Watts (eds.) *Standard English: The Widening Debate*. London/New York: Routledge.

Tyson, Peter (2001) *The Eighth Continent: Life, Death, and Discovery in the Lost World of Madagascar*. New York: Harper Perennial.

van der Hulst, Harry and Jeroen van de Weijer (1995) Vowel harmony. In: Goldsmith, John A. (ed.) *The Handbook of Phonological Theory*. Blackwell Handbooks in Linguistics. Blackwell Publishers, pp. 495–534.

Vaux, Bert; Justin Cooper and Emily Tucker (2007) *Linguistic Field Methods*. Eugene, OR: Wipf & Stock Publishers.

Vine, Brent (1998) Indo-European and Nostratic: some further comments. In: Salmons, Joseph C. and Brian D. Joseph (eds.) *Nostratic. Sifting the Evidence*. Amsterdam: John Benjamins, pp. 85–106.

von Siebold, Philipp Franz Balthazar (1832) Verhandeling over de afkomst der Japanners. In: *Verhandelingen des Bataviaasch Genootschaps* 13: 185–275.

Vovin, Alexander (1998) Nostratic and Altaic. In: Salmons, Joseph C. and Brian D. Joseph (eds.) *Nostratic. Sifting the Evidence*. Amsterdam: John Benjamins, pp. 257–270.

Wexler, Paul (1990) *The Schizoid Nature of Modern Hebrew: A Slavic Language in Search of a Semitic Past*. Wiesbaden: Otto Harrassowitz.

Williamson, Kay (1989) Niger-Congo overview. In: Bendor-Samuel, John (ed.) *The Niger-Congo Languages*. Lanham, MD: University Press of America, pp. 3–46.

Zuckermann, Gil'ad (forthcoming) *Mosaic or Mosaic? – The Genesis of the Israeli Language*. www.zuckermann.org/mosaic.html.

Index of languages

Index of terms